War Stories

War Stories

The Search for a Usable Past in the
Federal Republic of Germany

Robert G. Moeller

UNIVERSITY OF CALIFORNIA PRESS

Berkeley · *Los Angeles* · *London*

University of California Press
Berkeley and Los Angeles, California

University of California Press, Ltd.
London, England

First paperback printing 2003

Library of Congress Cataloging-in-Publication Data

Moeller, Robert G.
    War stories : the search for a usable past in the
  Federal Republic of Germany / Robert G. Moeller.
        p.   cm.
  Includes bibliographical references and index.
  ISBN 0-520-23910-5 (pbk : alk. paper)
      1. Political refugees—Germany (West)—
  History.   2. World War, 1939–1945—Forced
  repatriation.   3. Population transfer—German.
  4. Germans—Europe, Eastern—History—20th
  century.   I. Title.

  DD820.P72 G526   2001
  947'.000431—DC21   00-055964

Manufactured in the United States of America

11   10   09   08   07   06   05   04   03
10   9   8   7   6   5   4   3   2   1

The paper used in this publication meets the minimum
requirements of ANSI/NISO Z39.48-1992 (R 1997)
(*Permanence of Paper*). ∞

For Nora

Contents

Illustrations

Acknowledgments

Without the emotional and intellectual support of many friends and colleagues and the financial support of many institutions, I would not have written this book. A year's leave, financed by the National Endowment for the Humanities and the Woodrow Wilson Center for International Scholars, gave me time, leisure, and access to the extraordinary resources of the Library of Congress in the early stages of my research. Grants from the Committee on Research, the Global Peace and Conflict Studies Program, and the Humanities Center of the University of California, Irvine, funded research trips to Germany and mountains of Xeroxes. And the Center for German and European Studies of the University of California, Berkeley, provided money for a string of superb research assistants. I never cease to marvel at the fact that others will pay me to do work that I enjoy.

Parts of Chapter 4 first appeared in "'The Last Soldiers of the Great War' and Tales of Family Reunions in the Federal Republic of Germany," SIGNS 24 (Autumn 1998): 129–45. They reappear here with permission of the University of Chicago Press. The article is ©1998 by the University of Chicago Press. All rights reserved.

Since German unification, the Bundesarchiv in Koblenz has become an even better place to work; the charge of post–World War II German historians into the history of the German Democratic Republic—and archives in Berlin—means that the staff in Koblenz has even more time to meet the needs of those who continue to study the early history of that other former Germany. I am grateful to the staff in the reading room, particularly Werner Scharmann, who made sure I got the files I ordered and calmed my fears that Xerox copies would not make it to the United States. Particular thanks also go to the staffs of Bundesarchiv-Militärarchiv in Freiburg; the Bundesarchiv-Filmarchiv in Berlin; the Deutsches Filminstitut (formerly Deutsches Institut für Filmkunde) in Frankfurt, where Rüdiger Koschnitzki tolerated my interest in B movies from the 1950s; Peter Latta of the Stiftung deutsche Kinemathek in Berlin; the Politisches Archiv des Auswärtigen Amts in Bonn; the Verband der Heimkehrer, Kriegsgefangenen und Vermisstenangehörigen Deutschlands, e.V., in Bad Godesberg; Ingrid Klimmer of the Presse- und Informationsamt der Bundesregierung in Bonn; Heidrun Klein of the Bildarchiv preussischer Kulturbesitz; Paul Reichl and Stefanie Löster of Taurus Film, who generously provided me with copies of many West German movies from the 1950s; Hans-Joachim Westholt of the Haus der Geschichte der Bundesrepublik in Bonn; the Landesbildstelle Berlin; and, in this country, the National Archives in Washington, D.C. Thanks go also to Ellen Broidy, formerly the history librarian of the University of California, Irvine, who watched patiently as the library's holdings grew to include a number of *Heimatfilme,* and to the library's resourceful inter-library loan staff.

At the University of California, Irvine, I received excellent research assistance from Petyr Beck, Corinne Pernet, Felicia Lemus, Mia Lee, Philippe Weber, and Kai Herklotz. During my year in Washington, Rita Bashaw spent endless hours in the Library of Congress collecting materials, giving me time to read and write.

Early in the project, Alvia Golden and Carroll Smith-Rosenberg heard my stories and convinced me that they were worth telling. Many others have heard them since, and I tell them better because of their suggestions. Lily Gardner Feldman, Renate Bridenthal, Robert Weinberg, and Temma Kaplan labored through a very early draft of parts of the book. Volker Berghahn, David Crew, James Cronin, Mary Cronin, James Diehl, Geoff Eley, Gerald Feldman, Atina Grossmann, Elizabeth Heineman, Alf Lüdtke, Norman Naimark, Klaus Naumann, Molly Nolan, Eric Rentschler, Axel Schildt, Frank Stern, Ulrike Strasser, John Torpey, and Anne Walthall read various parts along the way. Michael Hughes generously made available to me a copy of his study of postwar debates over "equalizing the burdens" of the war before it was published. Constantin Goschler, author of a superb study of *Wiedergutmachung,* checked my knowledge of the reparations debates of the early 1950s, and John Connelly did the same for some of what I have to say about eastern Europe. Alice Fahs and Marilyn

Young both took time from their own work on history, memory, and war to comment extensively on my thoughts on those subjects. Jane Caplan offered encouraging responses to what became an article in the *American Historical Review,* and Michael Grossberg pushed me hard to write for readers who are not historians of modern Germany. Pertti Ahonen and Harold Marcuse not only read large parts of the manuscript, but they also made available to me copies of their own work. I have benefited enormously from my exchanges with Frank Biess and from his major comparative study of the reintegration of German POWs in East and West. Getting to know Omer Bartov has been one of the real pleasures that grew out of work on this project, and in many ways he has helped to make this a better book. Uta Poiger and Heide Fehrenbach have read every word, most more than once. They have taught me enormous amounts about West Germany in the 1950s, offered models of how to think about the intersection of politics and culture, provided constant companionship in virtual reality, and convinced me to stop when it was time to stop.

I remain an archival historian of modern Germany in part because I know that I can always find a weekend retreat with Heidrun Homburg and Josef Mooser. For two decades, they have been intellectual companions, friends, and incredibly generous hosts. Josef has also read much of the book and enriched it with his extraordinary knowledge of the 1950s and his unparalleled newspaper clippings file.

Sheila Levine saw the book through from beginning to end. I cannot imagine a better editor. Anne Canright helped me to express myself more clearly. And Jan Spauschus Johnson expertly guided the book through the production process.

Lynn Mally is my first and gentlest critic; she sees the worst and makes it better. She comforted me over the phone when I faced hapless hotel rooms at the end of long days in the archives; she gave me pep talks when I needed them; and she prevented me from taking myself too seriously. Nora Mally knows more about National Socialism, the Holocaust, bad German movies from the 1950s, and West German public memory than most American children her age. Her companionship, good humor, and love of musical theater helped me throughout the writing of this book. I dedicate it to her.

CHAPTER ONE

Listening to War Stories

In 1995, a half-century after the end of the Second World War, battles over the meaning of that event still raged. In the United States, veterans groups and the U.S. Senate roundly condemned the National Air and Space Museum's plan to use an exhibition on the *Enola Gay* mission to spur discussion of the broader implications of the bombing of Hiroshima and Nagasaki; their protest triggered an extended public dispute over the political uses of history and led ultimately to the museum's decision to cancel the originally planned exhibition.[1] In Japan, the fiftieth anniversary of defeat focused new attention on the question of Japanese war responsibility, war crimes, and the compensation of victims; it also allowed survivors of the atomic bombs dropped on Hiroshima and Nagasaki to offer their own perspective on the war's end.[2] And in Europe, from London to Moscow, from the beaches of Normandy to the gates of Auschwitz, public ceremonies allowed participants to relive old memories and retell a broad range of stories about the spring of 1945. Heads of state and historians discussed endlessly how best to commemorate May 8, and the debates made explicit the many ways in which history, politics, and national identity are intertwined.

Public controversy in Germany over the meaning of May 1945 was thus not exceptional, but in the nation whose history included National Socialism, reflection on the war's end involved particularly wrenching soul-searching. As the politics of commemoration in Germany vividly revealed, disputes over the meaning of the Second World War necessarily reflected how memories of the war had taken shape since 1945; old soldiers were not all dead, and neither were the war stories that had become part of public memory in the first postwar decade.

A high point in the extended public debate over how best to remember the destruction of the Third Reich came on 7 April 1995. In an advertisement in one of Germany's most important newspapers, the *Frankfurter Allgemeine Zeitung,* some three hundred prominent German citizens, among them politicians, journalists, and academics, called on the public to remember May 8 as a day of liberation and destruction. Quoting the first president of the Federal Republic, Theodor Heuss, the ad referred to the war's end as "the most tragic and questionable paradox for all of us." Although May 1945 brought an end to Nazi terror, it also, the ad explained, marked "the beginning of the terror of the expulsion and a new oppression in the East and the origin of the division of our country."[3] The ad exhorted readers to guard "against forgetting" (*gegen das Vergessen*) and made it clear that Germans should remember more than one past.

In the spring of 1995, it was easy to dismiss such a view as expressing the resentment of a neoconservative minority, one that was still able to mention May 8 as the "beginning of terror" without naming those for whom the destruction of the Third Reich meant terror's end. Other press reports emphasized the huge number of public ceremonies and museum exhibitions in which Germans not only alluded to Nazi crimes but also took care to remember the names and faces of the victims of the Third Reich.[4] However, a public opinion poll conducted by the weekly newsmagazine *Der Spiegel* indicated that many Germans shared the view that juxtaposing forms of terror and fates of victims effectively captured the "paradox" of 1945. When asked whether "the expulsion of the Germans from the east [was] just as great a crime against humanity as the Holocaust [was] against the Jews?" 36 percent of all respondents and 40 percent of those over sixty-five answered yes.[5]

The attempt to establish the equivalence of different "crimes against humanity" was not new; it conformed to established patterns of public memory in the Federal Republic. The pasts that circulated in the unified Germany of 1995 clearly echoed strains that could be heard everywhere in West Germany in the late 1940s and early 1950s.[6] In the newly created Federal Republic, many West Germans and a large majority of the West German parliament acknowledged that the National Socialist regime had persecuted millions of innocent victims, particularly Jews. But they paid even more attention to crimes committed against Germans

who were not Jews, crimes that, according to some contemporary accounts, were comparable to the crimes that some Germans had committed. The most important representatives of German victimhood were
the women, men, and children who had left or been driven out of eastern Europe by the Red Army at the war's end, and those in uniform for
whom captivity in the Soviet Union followed German surrender. Some
twelve million expellees survived the end of the war. In 1950, about two-
thirds of them resided in the Federal Republic; indeed, some 16 percent
of all West German citizens had hailed from parts of eastern Germany
ceded to postwar Poland or other areas in eastern Europe. In addition,
more than three million German soldiers spent some time in Soviet hands
following the war's end; of them, more than a million reportedly died
before their release.[7] Millions more who finished out the war in the west
had served on the eastern front and could identify with those forced to
remain in the Soviet Union against their will. Expellees and German
POWs in the Soviet Union were joined in public memory by their common experience of the "collapse" (*Zusammenbruch*) of the German Reich
on the eastern front, a front that moved steadily westward in late 1944
and early 1945.

In the east, the war was fought with extraordinary ferocity. Rates of
military and civilian casualties were extremely high, and as the war between the Wehrmacht and the Red Army continued, so too did the Nazis'
war against the Jews. No good social historical account of the end of the
war in the east brings all the participants in these events together as part
of one story.[8] Nor does this book attempt to do so. Rather, it explores
the ways in which a selective account of those events became part of West
German political consciousness in the 1950s. In particular, it looks at
how individual memories shaped a public memory that permitted West
Germans to acknowledge the war as part of their history and at the same
time to distance themselves from the National Socialist state—a state that
most Germans had supported and that bore complete responsibility for
the war in Europe.

By telling stories of the enormity of their losses, West Germans were
able to reject charges of "collective guilt," briefly leveled by the victors
immediately after the war, and claim status as heroic survivors. By focusing on the experiences of expellees and POWs in the Soviet Union,
they could talk about the end of the Third Reich without assuming
responsibility for its origins. In this abbreviated account of National
Socialism, all Germans were ultimately victims of a war that Hitler had
started but everyone lost. This focus contributed to an account of Na-

tional Socialism in which Nazi crimes were committed by a handful of fanatics who did not truly represent the German people. In the rhetoric of the 1950s, Jews and others had suffered extraordinary losses, but so too had Germans.

In the immediate postwar years, not all West Germans accepted this moral balance sheet. Writing in 1946, Eugen Kogon, the author of one of the earliest scholarly accounts of the Nazi policy of extermination,[9] who himself had spent seven years in Bergen-Belsen for his participation in the resistance to Hitler, raged against Germans who could see only the "remains turned to coal of their own women and children"; who could express emotion and sympathy for returning POWs but had no sensitivity for the survivors of concentration camps; who, when they acknowledged the enormity of Nazi crimes, went on to equate the "extermination of foreign peoples by the Germans" with the "deportation of twelve million Germans from the East"; and who failed to acknowledge the "blessing of defeat" as the possibility for a new beginning.[10]

In more modulated tones, the philosopher Karl Jaspers, also writing in 1946, stated that "virtually everyone has lost close relatives and friends, but how he lost them—in front-line combat, in bombings, in concentration camps or in the mass murders of the regime—results in greatly divergent inner attitudes." Jaspers insisted that "suffering differs in kind," and he was concerned that "most people have a sense only for their kind." "It is unjust," Jaspers lectured his readers, "to call all equally innocent. On the whole, the fact remains that we Germans—however much we may now have come into the greatest distress among the nations—also bear the greatest responsibility for the course of events until 1945. Therefore we, as individuals, should not be so quick to feel innocent, should not pity ourselves as victims of an evil fate, should not expect to be praised for suffering."[11] Communists—though a marginal presence in the West German political landscape—and German Jews who had survived in hiding or returned to Germany after the war were not inclined to equate the suffering of all the war's victims either.[12] However, these critical voices represented a distinct minority in the early postwar years. The past that dominated public discourse in the 1950s was that of German victims who were neither Communists nor Jews.

Expellees and POWs permitted West Germans to become legitimate participants in a moral competition over who had suffered most in the war. Indeed, tales of persecution carried into West Germany by POWs and those driven out of eastern Europe by the Red Army provided a way for West Germans, rejecting Jaspers's advice, to assert that they understood what others had suffered because they had suffered no less themselves. In the 1950s, such comparisons between Jewish and German victims defined one path along which West Germans approached the past. This book suggests some of the ways that the Jewish question and the German question were intertwined in the first decade after the war.[13]

The Cold War also frames the story told here. Anti-Communism in the 1950s drew in part on established modes of thought that had existed in Germany since the Russian Revolution and that the National Socialist regime honed to a fine edge, but the geopolitical conflict between East and West contributed as well, amplifying tales of Communist brutality. In that decade, descriptions of German suffering focused mainly on the losses inflicted by the Red Army, not on cities destroyed by American and British bombers; in a world divided between East and West, attacking the Soviet Union—past and present—was far easier than recounting the sins of former enemies who were now allies. Allied bombs were faceless. In popular memory, however, the face of the Red Army soldier was all too familiar; it often bore the signs of the racial stereotype of the "Mongol." This image had been disseminated by Nazi propaganda, and it survived German defeat and denazification to emerge in the political rhetoric of the Federal Republic. Tales of Communist crimes also shaped a history of the war in which the excesses of one form of totalitarian rule were matched by the excesses of another. By pointing a finger at the Russians, West Germans could insist that totalitarianism was a universal phenomenon of the twentieth century, the product of the crises of modern mass societies, not a uniquely German creation.

Remembering the end of the war in this manner was part of the process by which West Germans established legitimate political identities in the aftermath of National Socialism. The Basic Law (*Grundgesetz*), adopted in 1949 as the constitutional foundation for the Federal Republic of Germany, defined the institutions that would shape a democratic political system in those parts of Germany occupied in 1945 by the French, British, and Americans. However, the formal creation of the Federal Republic did not establish collective identities that could bind West Germans together socially and politically and so create an "imagined community," the phrase used by Benedict Anderson to describe the "deep horizontal comradeship" that can unify a nation. Anderson analyzes cases where an "imagined community" was largely shaped through an ideology of nationalism.[14] The problem for Germans after 1945 was not how to build a conception of the nation, but rather how to establish a collective identity that did not draw on a nationalist rhetoric contaminated by National

Socialism.[15] The revolution imposed from above by the victorious Allies provided no adequate framework; indeed, most Germans in the western zones of occupation deeply resented the Allied programs of democratic reeducation. In any case, these programs were largely abandoned by the late 1940s as the military powers that had crushed the Third Reich changed course, seeking now to accelerate the conversion of erstwhile enemies into Cold War allies. The division of Germany and the Federal Republic's forced march into an anti-Communist western alliance solidified geographic boundaries determined by the victors, but in the 1950s it was left to Germans, West and East, to create themselves.

An imagined community in the Federal Republic was shaped in part by stories of the "economic miracle" (*Wirtschaftswunder*), West Germany's rapid rise from devastation to prosperity. Currency reform in 1948 marked the end of the "war and postwar era" (*Kriegs- und Nachkriegszeit*), which had begun in 1943 with the German defeat at Stalingrad and intensified bombing of German cities and ended five years later when the money they carried in their wallets, the goods on offer in their shops, and the economic and political systems that structured their lives distinguished Germans in East and West.[16] In the next chapter of this tale of West Germany's emergence from the rubble, American loans and the Marshall Plan sparked European economic recovery, but, so the story goes, it was ultimately a uniquely German determination, hard work, and Economics Minister Ludwig Erhard's model of a "social market economy" that permitted the Federal Republic to bask so quickly in the warm glow of economic prosperity.

Shared values in the Federal Republic were not, however, based only on celebrations of present prosperity and predictions of uninterrupted economic growth. One of the most powerful integrative myths of the 1950s emphasized not German well-being but German suffering; it stressed that Germany was a nation of victims, an imagined community defined by the experience of loss and displacement during the Second World War. The stories of German victims, particularly expellees and POWs in Soviet hands, were central to shaping membership in the West German polity. Remembering what had been was of great significance for envisioning what was to come.

In the 1950s, when most West Germans spoke of victims, they were not referring to Germans who had suffered before May 1945 because of their race, religion, sexuality, or politics. The "war damaged" (*Kriegsbeschädigte*) included those who had experienced material losses, particularly from bombing, or who had lost their savings because of inflationary war financing. West Germans also readily acknowledged the suffering of the groups at the center of this study: expellees (*Vertriebene*) and prisoners of war (*Kriegsgefangene*). These German victims were members of the West German imagined community.[17] Victims of Germans were not. These mutually exclusive categories left in place some of the same barriers that had separated Germans who were part of the National Socialist *Volksgemeinschaft* from those who were excluded. When I repeat these categories, I do so to highlight the limitations of the rhetorical constructions of the 1950s, fully aware that those constructions did violence to the experience of German Jews and non-Jewish Germans who were victims not of falling bombs or Soviet aggression but of the Nazi state.

The suffering of all German victims was not the same. The experiences of POWs in the Soviet Union, for example, diverged from those of expellees in important respects. For one thing, the POW camp was a world without women, whereas in the westward "treks" of expellees women outnumbered men. In addition, for at least some of the students in the "barbed-wire university," as POWs called the camps, detainment ended only in the mid-1950s, while all but a few expellees completed the move from eastern Europe to West Germany by the late 1940s. Yet despite these differences, in certain respects the accounts of expellees and POWs were similar, for both groups directly confronted the onslaught of the Red Army and the Soviet defeat of Nazi Germany, and had their lives permanently changed in the process.

In the 1950s, the stories of expellees and POWs in the Soviet Union became the stories of all West Germans, and the fate of these groups came to represent the fate of postwar Germany. The Red Army's rape of German women as it moved westward in the spring of 1945 became the rape of the German nation, and the loss of homes and belongings in the east represented the eradication of a German *Heimat,* a sense of rootedness and belonging, that had existed for centuries in central Europe. The forced departure of expellees became a metaphor for the displacement of other Germans, driven from their homes by falling bombs. It also was a constant reminder of the division of the national *Heimat* between east and west. West Germans condemned the detention of German soldiers by the Soviets long after most prisoners had been released in the late 1940s, calling it ideologically charged arbitrary justice, based only on a desire for vengeance. A violation of international law, Soviet treatment of German POWs allowed West Germans to claim that the red variant of totalitarianism was just as capable of crimes against humanity in the early 1950s as the brown variant had been in the early

1940s. POWs, presumed innocent, were doing penance for all Germans. And self-congratulatory accounts of the successful social and economic integration of expellees and returning POWs into West German society were taken as evidence of the Federal Republic's ability to overcome and move beyond the ravages of war, as it created homes and a livelihood even for Germans who had lived elsewhere before 1945. The acknowledgment and commemoration of loss and suffering in the east fundamentally defined how West Germans moved beyond the defeat of May 1945, interpreting their past in a fashion that made them victims, not perpetrators, of the war's greatest injustices.

When Germans talked in the 1950s of the war in the east, they focused mainly on its end. Fifty years later, much of the story that was absent from their accounts is common knowledge to anyone who has studied the history of the Second World War in Europe. Because not all readers of this book will be familiar with this larger context, however, it is worth sketching in the outlines here.

The German attack on eastern Europe began on 1 September 1939, when the German army marched into Poland, initiating the war. The Germans wasted no time in undertaking the systematic murder of thousands of Polish civilians and the persecution and forced resettlement of Polish Jews. Parts of western Poland were annexed to the German Reich; the so-called Wartheland became the testing ground for "resettlement" policies that involved the murder or forced removal of Poles, who were judged not to carry any salvageable "racially valuable" Germanic traits, and their replacement with German "colonists." The same agency that controlled German resettlement regulated the "special treatment" of "racially inferior" groups. Between the Wartheland and the parts of eastern Poland conquered by the Red Army in accord with the Nazi-Soviet nonaggression pact of 1939 was the "General Government" (*Generalgouvernement*), an administrative area in which German officials ruled over the Polish population. Ethnic Germans, removed from the areas of eastern Poland occupied by the Soviets and resettled in the Wartheland, became participants in the Nazis' plan to extend eastward a racially homogenous Reich.[18] Before the invasion of Poland, Hitler made it clear that he sought the destruction of the Poles as a people; in his scheme, Germans, the "people with no space" (*Volk ohne Raum*), would find new territory to their east at the expense of Poles, and those Poles not murdered would become the menial labor force for an expanded Reich.[19]

The Führer's attitude toward Polish Jews was likewise explicit long before the German invasion of Poland. From the start, a racist ideology dictated strategy in the east. In the 1930s, nearly one Polish citizen in ten was a Jew, and the Jewish population in cities like Warsaw, Łódž, and Lwow exceeded 30 percent. Poland was thus not only a staging ground for German colonization, but it was also a site of the forcible resettlement of millions of Jews into ghettos. In these cities within cities, Jewish society, politics, and culture were cut off from the rest of the world. Among the most infamous ghettos was that in Łódž, transformed into Litzmannstadt in the expanded Reich. This city was also a central locale through which many ethnic Germans flowed, removed from Soviet-occupied Poland for resettlement in the Wartheland. Thus Łódž/ Litzmannstadt embodied the twin aspects of German racial policy. Most other ghettos, including the biggest, in Warsaw, the former capital, were in what had become the General Government. Characterized by appalling sanitary conditions, completely inadequate food supplies, and high death rates, the ghettos constituted a giant step in the German effort to eliminate Polish Jewry.[20]

Nazi hegemony in the east was achieved in part through direct control of vast amounts of territory. This policy was previewed in the Nazi takeover in the Sudetenland, part of Czechoslovakia, seized by Germany in 1938 with the sanction of Britain, France, and Italy, and in the creation of the Protectorate of Bohemia and Moravia in March 1939. Elsewhere, once the war began, huge parts of eastern Europe fell into the Nazi orbit with relatively little expenditure of military resources or human life. Alliances were formed with right-wing governments—the pattern in Hungary, Romania, and Slovakia, the client state carved out of what was left of Czechoslovakia and allowed nominal independence— and in Yugoslavia, the German military occupation of 1941 met with limited resistance and was even welcomed by some willing collaborators.[21] In those parts of eastern Europe where Germans ruled or real estate was directly annexed by the Reich, ethnic German minority populations assumed a privileged status virtually overnight. There and elsewhere, any opposition to the German presence did not initially translate into significant armed resistance. Until the summer of 1941, fighting in the east was limited to the blitzkrieg in Poland and the rapid military subjugation of Yugoslavia.

On 22 June 1941, however, the shooting war in the east returned to center stage as over three million German men in uniform, accompanied by another half million soldiers from countries allied with Germany, in-

vaded the Soviet Union. The invasion of Russia marked a dramatic in-
tensification of Hitler's drive for global hegemony and an escalation of
the racist war in the east. The Germans now not only pursued a tremendously expanded "war against the Jews" but also targeted virtually all
Soviets as racially inferior enemies. In the Soviet campaign, the Germans
erased the line between warfare and the racially motivated objective of
permanently removing the "Jewish Bolshevik" menace in the country
where, according to the Nazis, it was most firmly rooted. The combination of antisocialism and racism at the core of National Socialist ideology made every Jew a likely Communist, and all other Communists most
probably under the influence of the Jews. Clearing out occupied parts of
the Soviet Union was also crucial to the continued acquisition of German *Lebensraum* in the east. From the earliest days of the war against
the Soviet Union, the Schutzstaffel (SS), specially commissioned killing
squads (*Einsatzgruppen*), and some regular army troops participated in
the mass slaughter of Red Army commissars, Soviet POWs, Jews, and
countless other civilians.

For Hitler, the war in Russia was a "war of extermination." Echoing
the Führer's position, Field Marshal von Brauchitsch, commander-in-chief
of the army, told his commanders in March 1941 that the war against
the Soviet Union would be "a struggle between two different races."
German troops were authorized to act "with all necessary harshness."[22]
Unlike the war in the west, the war in the east was a "race war"
(*Rassenkampf*), designed to eliminate racially undesirable populations,
in particular Jews and Slavs, and open up new areas for settlement of
"superior" races.

Beginning in late 1942 and 1943, British and American fliers subjected
Germany to devastating waves of aerial bombing, leveling German cities
and forcing the evacuation of millions of civilians. By March 1945, British
and American troops had crossed the Rhine and pushed rapidly into Germany. But it was on the eastern front that Germany definitively lost the
war. The defeat at Stalingrad in February 1943 marked the moment when
German citizens fully realized that the war had gone sour; for them, this
decisive Soviet victory was permanently associated with massive casualties and the removal en masse of thousands of German soldiers to prisoner-of-war camps (Figs. 1 and 2).[23]

A year later, the Red Army was forcefully pushing the eastern front
out of Soviet territory into other parts of eastern Europe. In Romania,
a German ally, a coup displaced the collaborationist government, allowing the country to surrender before being fully conquered by Soviet

troops; and Hungary, also aligned with the Nazis, stayed in the war only because it was occupied by German troops in March 1944. The Germans, then, faced not only Red Army soldiers but also the resistance of subjugated eastern Europeans who sought to free themselves. An unsuccessful liberation attempt by democratic and Communist forces in Slovakia in late August 1944 was crushed in mid-October only after Slovak partisans had killed many Germans.[24] In Yugoslavia, an antifascist resistance movement led by Josip Broz Tito tied up Wehrmacht soldiers who might otherwise have been deployed elsewhere.

Passing through German-occupied Poland in late 1944, Red Army soldiers left in their wake a record of mass rapes and devastation as they pushed on toward Berlin.[25] In advance of this juggernaut, millions of Germans fled westward, abandoning their homes and belongings (Figs. 3–5). Here the standard account of the late twentieth century joins the story that West Germans did not hesitate to tell and retell fifty years earlier.[26] However, in recounting tales of loss and suffering, few West Germans pointed out that in January 1940 population transfers of a different sort, wagon trains of ethnic German peasants arriving in the Wartheland from eastern Poland, had marked an early step toward realizing Nazi dreams of a racial reordering of eastern Europe.[27] Five years later, the "treks" of Germans fleeing westward, which filled West German memories in the 1950s, symbolized the ignominious collapse of the Thousand Year Reich. Like the German colonists in the Wartheland, some Germans on the run had been resettled only recently, representatives of the attempt to "Aryanize" the east. But millions more fled or were driven from countries where they had constituted a minority presence for hundreds of years, long before the German army and Himmler tied them to a greater Reich.

By the time Germany accepted unconditional surrender on 8 May 1945, the number of combatants and the death toll on the eastern front exceeded those on all other fronts combined.[28] The war claimed the lives of at least 27 million Soviet citizens, one in seven of that nation's prewar population.[29] The number included over three million Soviet soldiers taken prisoner by the Germans; well over half of all Soviet POWs were the victims of starvation, maltreatment, and murder.[30] In addition, the staggering body count included some six million European Jews, shot, starved to death in the ghettos of eastern Europe, or murdered in concentration camps. The killing fields of Sobibor, Majdanek, Treblinka, and Belzec were in the General Government; Oswiecim (Auschwitz for the Germans) and Chelmno (Kulmhof) were in the part of Poland incorporated directly into the Reich and set aside for German colonization.

Germany's defeat had lasting consequences for the Germans of eastern and central Europe, and here again the standard account of the war
parallels what West Germans were eager to discuss in the 1950s. Meeting at Potsdam in July and August 1945, the victorious Allies sanctioned
the attempt by the Red Army, joined by partisans, to drive ethnic Germans from eastern Europe and from parts of the Reich that were ceded
to a reconfigured Poland, and they supported plans of postwar successor governments to remove any remaining Germans from Yugoslavia,
Czechoslovakia, Hungary, Romania, and Poland.

The war in the east that most West Germans remembered in the 1950s
was one of massive German loss and death. They chose not to dwell on
the war in which Germans in uniform murdered millions of people, including many, many civilians, and ethnic Germans displaced indigenous
populations from their homes and livelihoods in areas occupied by Germany. The devastating outcome of the war allowed West Germans to
remember selectively, to tell stories of a past in which they, not others,
were the war's most tragic victims.[31] Trauma and suffering are among
the most powerful forces capable of shaping "communities of memory."
In the 1950s, most West Germans created such communities by focusing on their own experiences, not on the trauma and suffering they had
caused for others.[32]

There are many ways to study how collective memories become rooted
in popular consciousness. Historians, seeking to illuminate what the
French sociologist Maurice Halbwachs called the "framework of collective memory,"[33] especially as it relates to war, have looked at the politics of public commemoration, including the memorials to those killed
in wartime.[34] They have studied how controversies over historic preservation and decisions to maintain, destroy, or restore parts of the built
environment reflect and structure different visions of the past.[35] Through
careful analyses of oral histories, they have shown how popular memories of war follow chronologies different from those laid out in scholarly
treatments by historians.[36] In the case of the Second World War, they
have explored how the Germans' "war against the Jews" was remembered and memorialized.[37] Read together, this scholarship reveals that
there are many ways to chart the memories of war, to locate what Iwona
Irwin-Zarecka calls the "'infrastructure' of collective memory," the "different spaces, objects, [and] 'texts'" where "memory work" takes place.[38]

In the 1950s, the memory work of establishing and preserving a set
of meanings of the end of the war on the eastern front took place in in-

terest group associations of expellees and POWs. It was carried out by teachers in public school classrooms, distinguished professors who headed institutes for the study of eastern Europe at major German universities, and the authors of critically celebrated novels, children's literature, and pulp fiction.[39] This book does not examine the entire range of structures that formed collective memories into lasting parts of the historical landscape in the 1950s. It focuses instead on a limited number of contexts where public memory was anchored—debates in the West German parliament, media representations, the work of prominent historians, and the cultural production of filmmakers—particularly important places where millions of West Germans could hear stories of their past.

In referring to public memory, I do not mean to suggest that an understanding of Germany's experience in the Second World War was strategically crafted by public officials in Bonn to create an acceptable past for the Federal Republic. Rather, memory work was carried out in a range of "infrastructures," which put into place a widely shared account of the war's end in the east. Some individual memories became part of this national narrative, accepted by most West Germans. For other memories, particularly those of German Jews and others persecuted by the Nazi state, the audience was extremely limited.

In the public memory of the 1950s, only a handful of Germans appeared as perpetrators, the overwhelming majority were victims, and no one was both: guilt and innocence were mutually exclusive categories. The dominant forms of public memory left little space for reflecting on the suffering Germans had caused others. Instead, it was the story of German suffering and the "loss of the German east" that filled the halls of parliament, thick volumes of "contemporary history," movie screens, and the pages of daily newspapers and mass-circulation illustrated magazines. At the levels of representation that this book explores, uncomplicated morality tales in which a few Nazis had brought suffering to everyone— Jews, Germans, other Europeans—and in which Germans had survived Communist brutality defined a usable past for the Federal Republic.

Social policy debates over compensation for victims of the war in the years 1949–53, the first electoral period of the West German parliament (Bundestag), were saturated with memories of the past. In the arena of public policy, different versions of the war's end were constantly being rehearsed. The conviction that expellees and POWs had every right to be compensated for their losses unified a political spectrum otherwise deeply divided between ruling Christian Democrats and opposition Socialists. The rhetoric of German victimization knew no left or right.

Compensating victims also involved acknowledging their losses as part of an official historical chronicle. Some of West Germany's most highly respected historians sought to make the "expulsion of the Germans from east-central Europe" into a chapter in West Germany's "contemporary history." A vast project funded by the federal government recorded in extraordinary detail the plight of Germans driven out of eastern Europe by the Red Army in late 1944 and on into 1945. Reviewers praised these "documents of horror" for their accurate descriptions of the "German tragedy," a tragedy that did not include the virtual obliteration of Jewish life and culture in the same part of the world.[40]

The popular press told a different set of stories. This book looks at how this medium framed the return of the last POWs from the Soviet Union in the fall of 1955, transforming private homecomings into a celebration of national unity. The returning soldiers' accounts of their experiences provided additional reminders of what Germans had suffered at Soviet hands, but the invocation of the past that they represented also allowed their stories to become commentaries on the development of West German society during the decade since the war's end.

Finally, memories of the war and the aftermath of defeat were depicted in movies, courtesy of the West German "dream factory" (*Traumfabrik*). On the silver screen, West Germans could view celebrations of the integration of expellees into a new *Heimat* in blockbusters like *Grün ist die Heide* (The heath is green) and dramatic tales of the noble survivors of Soviet POW camps like *Der Arzt von Stalingrad* (Doctor from Stalingrad).[41]

In different places—from public policy, to "contemporary history," to media accounts, to the movies—West Germans told different stories about the end of the war in the east. This book reviews these various representations of that past.

In examining the ways in which West Germans remembered the Second World War and National Socialism in the late 1940s and 1950s, this book takes issue with the widely held thesis that after the war the citizens of the Federal Republic largely avoided all memories of the years of Nazi rule. This position has a long and distinguished lineage. In 1959, a decade after the founding of the Federal Republic, the philosopher Theodor Adorno sternly excoriated Germans for their inability to "come to terms with the past." Reflecting on the process of remembering and forgetting, acknowledgment and denial, in the Federal Republic of the 1950s as West Germans sought to distance themselves from the Third Reich, he concluded: "The fact that fascism lives on, and that the much-cited work of reprocessing the past [*Aufarbeitung der Vergangenheit*] has not yet succeeded, and has instead degenerated into its distorted image—empty, cold, forgetting—is the result of the continued existence of the same objective conditions that brought fascism in the first place."[42]

For Adorno, what was missing in West Germany was a serious attempt to eradicate all traces of National Socialism and restructure the capitalist system that had given rise to fascism and that condemned most of the population to a "condition of political immaturity" in the 1950s no less than it had in the 1930s and 1940s. West Germans, in Adorno's view, had attempted to "master" the past—to put it behind them and lay it to rest—not "come to terms" with their accountability for the horrors of National Socialism.[43]

Writing in 1967, Alexander and Margarete Mitscherlich echoed Adorno's charge of a dangerous West German forgetfulness. They described the problems primarily in psycho-pathological terms, however, labeling the apparent unwillingness of West Germans to confront their responsibility for the National Socialist past as an "inability to mourn." Using Freudian categories to analyze the postwar German psyche, the Mitscherlichs argued that after 1945 Germans should have come to an understanding of their deep identification with Hitler and the "national community" (*Volksgemeinschaft*), thereby acknowledging their responsibility for crimes committed by the regime they had supported in overwhelming numbers. Leaving behind this difficult history was made possible by a massive self-investment in the "expansion and modernization of our industrial potential right down to the kitchen utensils."[44] In the psychic economy that the Mitscherlichs described, creating for the future was a way to avoid the past.

Variations on these themes have shaded many accounts of the Federal Republic's first decade. West Germans are depicted as repressing or denying their responsibility for the triumph of National Socialism and the horrors that the Nazi regime inflicted. The 1950s emerge as a decade of historical silence and willing forgetfulness before an explosion of critical self-examination beginning in the late 1960s.[45] In other accounts, the strategic silence that for Adorno and the Mitscherlichs was a vice becomes a necessity, if not a virtue. In 1983, at a conference to commemorate the fiftieth anniversary of the Nazi seizure of power, Hermann Lübbe argued that in the 1950s West Germans had of necessity maintained a "particular quiet" around memories of National Socialism. There was no easy way to judge and condemn a small group of leaders when the truth was that the majority of the German people had enthusiastically supported Hitler. According to Lübbe, however, keeping silent about the past was not the same as repressing it. A deliberate self-distancing from National Socialism was essential for moving beyond painful memories and creating a unified, democratic Federal Republic.[46] More recently, Jeffrey Herf has offered another version of this thesis. He argues that for the first chancellor of the Federal Republic, Konrad Adenauer, "Economic recovery and political legitimacy, not additional purges [of National Socialists], were the proper medicine. Democratic renewal went hand in hand with silence and the forgetting of a dark past. Too much memory would undermine a still fragile popular psyche."[47]

The story of German forgetting—whether pathological, therapeutic, or politically expedient—has had an extraordinary longevity. Only recently has a closer, critical look at the early history of the Federal Republic revealed that in the 1950s West Germans were neither disabled by their inability to mourn or their failure to demolish capitalism nor intentionally silent about National Socialism in order to get on with postwar reconstruction and democratic reeducation. Hardly "empty, cold, forgetting," as Adorno charged, West Germans remembered key parts of the first half of the 1940s with extraordinary passion and emotion. Many accounts of Germany's "most recent history" circulated in the fifties; remembering selectively was not the same as forgetting.

Although not in ways that satisfied Adorno or the Mitscherlichs, many West Germans acknowledged what Adenauer called the "saddest chapter" in their history and showed a willingness to make amends to Jewish survivors and the state of Israel.[48] Herf, in his massive study of how leading German intellectuals and politicians, East and West, viewed German responsibility for the Holocaust in the first decade after the war, demonstrates that even though West Germans were not inclined to prosecute criminals, their chancellor and the Social Democrats were nonetheless eager to find a basis for reconciliation with Israel.[49] Adenauer's pursuit of reparations for Israel and programs to provide compensation for some of those persecuted by the Nazi state defined a crucial public policy arena in which West Germans did account, at least in part, for the crimes of National Socialism.[50]

Path-breaking work by Norbert Frei has shown that when West Germans did discuss specific perpetrators—Nazis charged and sentenced by the Allies for particularly egregious offenses—they demanded that these felons with faces be granted amnesty.[51] In addition, Frei, Curt Garner, Ulrich Brochhagen, and James Diehl have detailed West German attempts to rehabilitate and reintegrate former Nazis through legislative measures that transformed them into the victims of misguided Allied denazification efforts premised on assumptions of "collective guilt" and the equation of membership in the Nazi party with responsibility for the excesses of the Nazi state.[52] In his study of the postwar business community, Jonathan Wiesen pursues some of the same themes, exploring how German entrepreneurs developed exculpatory tales of their forced participation in the National Socialist regime and crafted new identities as model citizens in a democratic capitalist order, thereby defining the present in a self-conscious response to the past.[53] And in his major study of the politics surrounding the "law for the equalization of burdens," passed in 1952, Michael Hughes offers an insightful account of how West Germans determined just compensation for those who counted themselves among the "war-damaged."[54]

Other war stories from the late 1940s and 1950s presented Germans not as innocent fellow travelers but as resisters of the regime, thus providing evidence of another, better Germany even within the depths of the Third Reich. West German discussions of the meaning and significance of resistance focused not on the opposition of Communists, a legacy claimed by those other Germans across the border in the East, but on the assassination attempt on Hitler of 20 July 1944, and on groups with no specific political affiliation like the White Rose. This version of the last years of the war provided proof that Germans had demonstrated their eagerness to liberate themselves from the Nazi yoke well before they were liberated by the Allies.[55]

In their early history, West Germans also discussed other legacies of the war. For millions of evacuees, driven from their homes by falling bombs, accounting for the past involved lobbying for victim status and demanding state assistance to gain new housing and a fresh start.[56] The high rate of military casualties occasioned not only remembrance and commemoration but also concern for the families left behind. War deaths meant that many families were deemed "incomplete" (*unvollständig*)—without adult males—and even when men returned, many marriages did not withstand the strains of long separation. There was a broad consensus that "more than any other societal institution, the family had fallen into the whirlpool created by the collapse" of Germany at the end of the war. Thus the family became "the central problem of the postwar era," in ways that were shaped by the experience of the war and its consequences.[57]

Concerns about youth, "endangered" by the instability and privation of the immediate postwar years and an inadequate supply of effective male role models, defined another important dimension of debates over the "crisis of the family" and the consequences of the war. As generational conflicts emerged by the mid-1950s, public concern about disaffected youth was colored by a past in which discontent had steered young people to the extremist solutions offered by National Socialism and Communism. In defining social policies intended to strengthen "normal" families and "protect" women and youth, West Germans displayed their awareness of Nazi attempts to subordinate families to the needs of the state. Those who advocated the creation of a "*Lebensraum*" for the family in a democratic West Germany self-consciously distanced themselves from memories of another German state that had sought a *Lebensraum* for healthy "Aryan" families in eastern Europe. The past loomed large in all discussions of these key social policy questions.[58]

Germans languishing in Soviet camps and the millions of expellees driven out of eastern Europe were other legacies of the war about which West Germans had much to say in the 1950s. This has been demonstrated in important recent works by Pertti Ahonen, who describes the continuing influence of expellee organizations on West German foreign policy,[59] and Frank Biess, who offers an insightful account of the social and political reintegration of returning POWs in East and West Germany.[60] It is something this book also sets out to do by analyzing how the experiences of these groups became part of West German public memory. Shifting the focus from what West Germans should have remembered or discussed—the critical mode of Adorno and the Mitscherlichs—to what they did remember reveals that a selective past, a past of German suffering, was in fact ubiquitous in the 1950s.

How East Germans commemorated the war is not the subject of this book, but it is worth covering the outlines of the official version of the war in that country, to indicate how assessments of the war's end diverged in the two Germanys. East Germans, like West Germans, confronted a task of crafting integrative founding myths and incorporating into a new nation a population that had enthusiastically supported National Socialism. However, an official ideology of "antifascism" defined their perspective on both the Nazi past and the contemporary Federal Republic, where, East Germans charged, one form of fascism had simply succeeded another.[61] If West Germany was the home of former fascists, East Germany was the home of those who had seen the light or had opposed Hitler from the start. Celebrating "victims of fascism" (*Opfer des Faschismus*) allowed for a different rhetoric of victimization in the East. It is hardly surprising that in the Germany occupied by Soviet forces and headed by many leaders who had sat out the war in exile in Moscow, the focus was not on Soviet barbarism and German suffering; instead, the officially recognized victims of fascism were those persecuted by the Nazis because of their religious views, their ethnicity, and, most important, their Communist politics.

In the German Democratic Republic, the war in the east was a war of liberation in which a triumphant Red Army destroyed not German homelands but German fascism; rather than clearing eastern Europe of Germans, it cleared the way for socialism. Soviets were saviors, not terrorists; they did not initiate, but ended, suffering. In the official categories of the German Democratic Republic, expellees were "resettlers" (*Umsiedler*); the 4.3 million who had "resettled" in the Soviet zone of occupation by 1949 were reminded that Hitler, not the Soviet Union, was to blame for their fate.

In the view of the East German state, German POWs in the Soviet Union were the beneficiaries of an antifascist education, and the most attentive students were immediately qualified for jobs building an antifascist Germany. At an official conference of POWs in Berlin in 1949, Germans provided testimony not of Communist tyranny but of their fair treatment by the Soviets and the many reasons "we are friends of the Soviet Union and will remain so." POWs detained in the Soviet Union after the late 1940s were not innocent victims of an arbitrary summary justice; rather, they were war criminals, rightly accused of extraordinarily vicious acts and justly sentenced for what they had done.[62] Although many private accounts doubtless diverged from these official public pronouncements, the East German state radically restricted the room in which competing memories of the war and its consequences could emerge. Just as Germans, East and West, pursued different paths of political and economic reconstruction after the war, so too did they construct different versions of the past.

Although the primary concern of this study is to illuminate how West Germans remembered key parts of the Second World War in the 1950s, it also offers a perspective on the politics of commemoration in the decades that followed.[63] In the 1960s and 1970s, West Germans reached a much more critical understanding of National Socialism. Memories of German victimization, dominant in the 1950s, were challenged by accounts in which Nazi crimes came to the fore. Still, as the events of the spring of 1995 made clear, this complication of public memory never meant the complete silencing or forgetting of another version of the past,

in which Germans suffered as much as Jews and others persecuted by
National Socialism. Analysis of how the destruction of National Socialism was understood, described, and commemorated in the early history
of the Federal Republic will illuminate how certain patterns for order-
ing the "paradox" of May 1945 emerged in the early history of the Federal Republic. Seen against the background of certain forms of public
memory in the 1950s, the themes of German victimization that surfaced
in the 1990s were not particularly novel; rather, they represented the
forceful return of what had never been completely repressed.

The fiftieth anniversary of the war's end made clear that in a unified
Germany there is no single means for locating National Socialism and
the Second World War in the continuum of modern German history. The
German search for a usable past is not at an end. It must include the continued study of National Socialism, European Jewry before the Holocaust, the "final solution," the Second World War, the collective experience of German loss and suffering that embraced millions of unique
stories, the emergence of the Cold War, and attempts to write a complex
history of the war's end, one in which all these strands appear. This book
adds to this agenda the need for a clearer understanding of how Germans transformed their pasts into public memory in the early history of
the Federal Republic.

CHAPTER TWO

Accounting for the Past

In his opening address to the newly elected West German parliament in September 1949, Chancellor Konrad Adenauer looked ahead to the future, but he did not avoid the past of National Socialism and the Second World War. He implicitly invoked one version of that past when he criticized nascent anti-Semitic tendencies in the Federal Republic, expressing profound disillusionment that "after all that has happened in our time, there should still be people in Germany who persecute or hate Jews because they are Jews."[1] However, the chancellor had even more to say about those Germans who, according to his account, were apparently persecuted simply because they were German. His allusions to the anti-Semitic crimes of Nazi Germany were made in the context of a far more detailed and explicit reckoning of non-Jewish victims of the war.

Leading Adenauer's roll call were "1.5 to 2 million German prisoners of war" whose whereabouts remained unknown. By the late 1940s, the western Allies had released all the German soldiers they had taken captive during the war; thus, POWs not accounted for were most likely in the Soviet Union. Nor should West Germans forget those Germans still held against their will by Communist governments in Poland, Czechoslovakia, and East Prussia, now under Soviet control. Also high on the chancellor's list were expellees, "whose deaths number in the millions."[2] When the victorious Allies had met at Potsdam four years earlier, they had promised that the transfer of Germans out of eastern Europe "should be effected in an orderly and humane manner."[3] However, those expellees who had survived the flight from the east bore scars that testified to the gap between these promises and Communist practice. Forcefully separated from their homes and possessions, they desperately needed immediate assistance to compensate them for their losses and integrate them into West German society (Fig. 6). The alternative, warned Adenauer, was that the Federal Republic would become the site of massive "political and economic unrest," triggered by this displaced group. He emphasized that social policies to relieve the dire circumstances of the victims of Communist oppression, now at home in the Federal Republic, depended on economic reconstruction and growth. Assisting these victims was an essential step toward a "distribution of burdens" of the war and the achievement of "social justice, the highest objective of our work" (Fig. 7).[4]

Competing memories of the Second World War pervaded public policy debates in the early history of the Federal Republic. In the first electoral session of the Bundestag (1949–53), West German politicians confronted the claims of both the victims of National Socialism and the victims of German defeat on the eastern front. Ghosts of these pasts, some Jewish, some German, often seemed to hover simultaneously in the halls of parliament, vying for recognition. Deeply divided over compensation payments for Jews and others persecuted by the Nazis, West Germans were ultimately led by a resolute chancellor to a reparations settlement with the state of Israel. When it came to addressing their own suffering, however, West Germans revealed no similar ambivalence. Acknowledgment of their losses unified West Germans; it became central to defining the Federal Republic as a nation of victims. A comparison of public policy debates over reparations for victims of Nazi persecution and measures to assist expellees and returning POWs reveals much about how West Germans viewed their responsibility for the atrocities of the Third Reich and how they measured their losses. In its early history, the West German parliament did not avoid the past; rather, it drew up balance sheets, calculated suffering, and, by accounting for the past, sought to put parts of that past to rest, while incorporating other parts into the foundations of the Federal Republic.

Nameless Victims, Faceless Criminals

In 1949, Adenauer knew that he faced a Bundestag deeply divided along political lines. He had come into office by the narrowest of margins, elected by the 139 votes of a coalition of the Christian Democratic Union

(CDU) and Christian Social Union (CSU) and dependent on support from members of the Free Democratic Party (FDP), heirs to the political liberalism of the Kaiserreich and Weimar. The union of *Christian* parties was a deliberate effort to overcome the deep political divide between Protestants and Catholics, a rift that dated to Bismarck's attempts in the 1870s to win favor with political liberals by attacking political Catholicism. The CDU/CSU was also unified in its opposition to political socialism, and it drew on many of the constituencies that had organized on the antisocialist right in the twenties.[5]

Opposing Adenauer's government at every turn was the tiny German Communist Party (KPD). By the late 1940s, Communism had been almost completely cordoned off behind the "iron curtain," with East Germany claiming to be the heir to the KPD of the 1920s, a claim that few West Germans cared to contest. The West German party, ultimately legally banned in 1956, could therefore easily be dismissed as the representative of precisely those forces of totalitarian repression that reigned supreme in the Soviet Union.[6]

Far more significant was the opposition of the Social Democratic Party (SPD), in control of the second largest parliamentary block, 131 votes. Presenting itself as the political voice of the working class and the heir to the German socialist heritage, the party was particularly critical of Adenauer's forced march toward integration into a western alliance headed by the United States. Wary of any geopolitical realignment that might put German unification in jeopardy, Social Democrats opposed the "chancellor of the Allies" and his government on many, many issues.[7]

Social Democrats also objected to Adenauer's assessment of German responsibility for the crimes of National Socialism. Kurt Schumacher, the leader of the party, expressed skepticism that Adenauer's government would ever adequately acknowledge the obligations of Germans to compensate those persecuted by the Nazi regime. In presenting his party's official response to Adenauer's September 1949 remarks, Schumacher harshly criticized the chancellor for saying so little about the "German forces of resistance and the victims of fascism." In particular, he called on Adenauer to make explicit the "horrible tragedy of the Jews in the Third Reich," the lasting dishonor to Germany's good name caused by the "extermination of six million Jews by Hitler's barbarism," and the "obligation of every German patriot to place the history of German and European Jews in the foreground and to offer help where it is necessary."[8] Behind Schumacher's rage was more than mere moral principle or the political vitriol of the opposition, for he himself was a victim of Nazi persecution. First arrested in July 1933, he had spent nearly a decade in Nazi concentration camps, including almost eight years in Dachau.[9] Although in the next four years the government of the Federal Republic showed no willingness to put the "history of German and European Jews in the foreground," before his death in August 1952 Schumacher would see the Christian Democratic chancellor politically commit himself to reconciliation with the state that was home to many of the survivors of Nazi attempts to eliminate all European Jews.[10]

In defining a basis for reconciliation with Israel, however, the chancellor demonstrated a keen understanding of West Germans' dislike of the models for atonement offered by the western Allies immediately following the war. Almost all citizens of the Federal Republic vehemently rejected the notion of responsibility, briefly advanced by the American and British forces of occupation, according to which all Germans shared a "collective guilt" for the crimes of National Socialism. To bring home this message, British and American forces of occupation confronted Germans with graphic representations of the evils committed by the National Socialist regime. By circulating photographic documentation, screening footage of the liberation of concentration camps, mandating visits to camps, sometimes by the entire population of a town, and forcing Germans into work details to bury the dead from the camps, the western Allies sought to compel Germans to face their responsibility, reminding them: "You are guilty of this."[11]

Other Allied policies underscored the point as well. The Nuremberg Tribunal's trials of leading Nazis generated massive amounts of paper, reams of evidence of German "crimes against humanity." In the American zone, all Germans over the age of eighteen were required to account for their past political activity as a means of measuring their support for National Socialism. And the Allies left little doubt that constructing a postwar German democracy would be possible only if Germany was rid once and for all of its military traditions. Demilitarization, denazification, and democratization were the "Three D's" of the western Allied occupation policy; a new beginning required that Germans admit their collective sins and break completely with the past.[12]

Most West Germans, however, saw in these programs little more than the Allies' own myopia. Germans claimed that they could not be collectively guilty for crimes of which they were ignorant. The Allied emphasis on German complicity implied possibilities for resistance that simply did not exist, and denied the realities of life in a terrorist state run by madmen.[13]

By the late 1940s, the western Allies were inclined to agree. Because of the growing tensions of the Cold War, they now abandoned the pursuit of a nation of potential war criminals, seeking instead to anchor rehabilitated West Germans in a western alliance. The postwar emphasis on "collective guilt" and denazification gave way rapidly to a more differentiated conception of accountability, in which the excesses of a handful of Nazis were acknowledged to be just that. True National Socialist believers had no place in a western military alliance, but the Allies were now willing to accept that most West Germans did not fall into that category.[14]

Even though West Germans were no longer deemed collectively guilty, the western Allies maintained that Germans remained collectively obligated to atone for the crimes of National Socialism. The United States in particular insisted on compensation for the victims of "racial, religious, or political" persecution by the Nazis. Acknowledging a past in which some Germans had been perpetrators of horrifying crimes was a prerequisite for the West German state to win recognition as a sovereign nation.

In September 1951, Adenauer sketched a way for West Germans to admit that crimes had taken place without pointing fingers at any specific criminals. In what is often cited as a turning point in postwar German-Jewish relations, Adenauer ceremoniously announced to the Bundestag that "the Federal Government and with it the great majority of the German people are aware of the immeasurable suffering that was brought upon the Jews in Germany and the occupied territories during the time of National Socialism. . . . Unspeakable crimes have been committed in the name of the German people, calling for moral and material indemnity." Adenauer's carefully formulated passive construction left open the question of culpability and differentiated between guilt and responsibility: criminals had no names. He was also quick to insist that "the overwhelming majority of the German people abominated the crimes committed against the Jews, and did not participate in them. . . . There were many among the German people who showed their readiness to help their fellow citizens at their own peril for religious reasons, because of a troubled conscience, out of shame at the disgrace of the German name." Nonetheless, if perpetrators remained unidentified and bystanders emerged as honorable opponents, Adenauer acknowledged that West Germans must squarely confront the claims of Jewish victims. "The Federal Government," he concluded, "is prepared, jointly with the representatives of Jewry and the state of Israel . . . to bring about a solution of the material indemnity problems, thus easing the way to the spiritual settlement of infinite suffering."[15] Once the West Germans had broken their silence, the Israelis followed suit, and direct negotiations over a reparations treaty began in earnest in March 1952.[16]

Adenauer's motives in aggressively pursuing a settlement with the Israelis are subject to more than one interpretation. There is much evidence that the chancellor wanted to convince the Allies that Germany was willing to acknowledge past crimes in order to gain full acceptance as an equal, autonomous partner in the postwar western alliance. In other accounts, and in his own recollections, Adenauer acted as he did on the basis of deeply held moral convictions, not as a response to Allied expectations and pressure. Ultimately, whatever the balance between ingenuous moralism and political realism, it is difficult to imagine that the Federal Republic would have pursued a postwar settlement with Israel without the chancellor's forceful intervention.[17]

Social Democrats, the group initially most skeptical of the chancellor's intentions on almost all issues, were alone in consistently supporting Adenauer's initiative. Few other West Germans applauded the overture to Israel. A survey conducted in the Federal Republic by the U.S. government in December 1951 revealed that more than one in five of those questioned unequivocally opposed any form of restitution; polls conducted by a West German survey institute corroborated these findings and indicated that only slightly more than one West German in ten unequivocally favored compensation for Jewish victims of National Socialist persecution.[18] Adenauer faced not only a hostile public but also the resolute resistance of some Christian Democrats, who claimed that compensation exceeded the German capacity to pay for the past and asserted that payments to victims, rather than atoning for misdeeds, would only fuel anti-Semitism among those who objected to preferential treatment for Jews.[19]

The Israelis and West Germans hammered out their agreement not in Germany or Israel, but on neutral territory—in England, France, Holland, and Luxembourg. Behind doors closed to the public, the representatives of the Federal Republic heard the demands for compensation for the millions of individual Jews who had suffered from Nazi persecution and for the new state of Israel, which had borne the costs of integrating millions of European Jewish émigrés in just a few years. The general public was also not privy to the rancor with which Adenauer's cabinet members fought over the size of West Germany's debt. Consistently opposing Israeli demands was Fritz Schäffer, the finance minister, who charged that the Israelis were demanding far too much; if Israel needed money, he proposed, it should seek foreign loans, not payments from Germany.[20] Also at odds with Adenauer was his justice minister, the Free Democrat Thomas Dehler, who maintained that Germany would long since have provided compensation to Jewish victims had not the Americans, following the plan of the "Jewish politician Morgenthau," hobbled German economic recovery after the war.[21]

Adenauer's success at overcoming the most serious sources of opposition did not put controversy to rest. In the final parliamentary debates over ratification of the treaty with Israel, he met with the steadfast intransigence of the German Party (DP), a relatively small political grouping on the extreme right wing; of the German Communists, at the other end of the spectrum; and of some members of the CDU and CSU, the bases of his own ruling coalition. The chancellor assured parliament that the treaty represented an essential move toward the "solemnly promised end of one of the saddest chapters in our history"; it was not a concession of "collective guilt," but an acknowledgment of the need to make amends for crimes committed in Germany's name.[22] This attempt to steer safely clear of any acknowledgment of complicity, however, did not still the criticism of the right-wing delegate Adolf von Thadden, who managed to reduce the number of European Jews before the war to "5.6 million" and the number killed by the Nazis to one million, and who wanted to respect at most the claims only of German Jews. Others, though ostensibly in favor of victim compensation, opposed a collective settlement and fretted that a German-Israeli reconciliation would alienate potential German allies among Arab League member states. The KPD was also in the opposition, maintaining that the only true beneficiaries of reparations in Israel would be capitalists and financiers.[23]

When the question was finally put to a vote in March 1953, 239 of the 360 members of the Bundestag supported the measure, a majority that included a unanimous SPD. Social Democrats, at odds with the Christian Democratic chancellor on many other issues in the early 1950s, now joined with him to ratify the treaty with Israel.[24] Eighty-six delegates registered their disapproval by abstaining, including Adenauer's finance minister Schäffer and many other members of the CDU/CSU coalition, and another thirty-five voted against ratification, among them all thirteen members of the KPD.[25] Still, a majority in the West German parliament was ready to support payments in twelve installments of 3.45 billion West German marks (DM) to Israel, with the understanding that of this sum, 450 million DM would go to the Conference on Jewish Material Claims against Germany (Claims Conference), which represented Jewish victims outside Israel.

The West German state also sought to move toward the "solemnly promised end of one of the saddest chapters" in its history by addressing the demands for compensation from others persecuted by the Nazis and still resident in the Federal Republic.[26] At the end of the war, the U.S. forces of occupation advanced measures to provide compensation (*Wiedergutmachung*) for the wrongs done to individual victims of "racial, religious, or political persecution." Once they had sanctioned the creation of the Federal Republic in 1949, the Allies pressured West Germans to define their own compensation scheme—and thus establish another measure of the Federal Republic's moral credibility. In the same year that it ratified the treaty with Israel, the West German parliament approved legislation that built on state initiatives, particularly in the American zone of occupation, and established a national framework for addressing the claims of these other victims of the Nazis.[27]

Debates over compensation schemes amply documented the clear limits most West Germans placed on "racial, religious, or political" persecution during the Third Reich. Legislation ultimately restricted legitimate victims to those who could document that their race or beliefs had caused their suffering and who lived in the Federal Republic at the end of 1952 or who had been deported by the Nazis or emigrated after 1945 but could prove residence within the 1937 borders of the German Reich. Citizens of other nations who had returned to their homes—for example, Poles and Soviets, who had made up most of the slave labor force in Germany during the war—were ineligible; their claims for compensation could be processed only via *national* demands for reparations.[28]

Many other victim groups were not forgotten in the 1950s; rather, West Germans heard, discussed, and rejected their claims to victim status. Thus, although National Socialism had tremendously broadened the criminal statute prohibiting homosexual relations between men, denouncing male homosexuals as a danger to the nation and the race, the courts in the 1950s uniformly denied claims that the intensified persecution of male homosexuals embodied "National Socialist ideas" (*nationalsozialistisches Gedankengut*) or Nazi "racial teachings" (*Rassenlehre*). Indeed, in considering appeals to suspend the tremendously expanded bases for criminal prosecution of male homosexuality introduced by the Nazis, the Federal Constitutional Court (Bundesverfassungsgericht) concluded that the revised law in no way violated the West German constitution or undermined the foundations of a democratic state.[29]

So-called asocials, a flexible designation easily stretched by the Nazis to include anyone who did not conform to the racial, political, sexual, and moral criteria of the Third Reich, also did not qualify for compensation. West German judges and policymakers retrospectively deemed their treatment—ranging from confinement in "protective custody" and imprisonment to sterilization—essential for the maintenance of social order, not the consequence of arbitrary discrimination and persecution.[30] Sinti and Roma ("gypsies") were similarly excluded because laws permitting their surveillance, restriction of movement, and incarceration were justified as measures for preserving public order.[31] "Aryans" sentenced for violating Nazi racial codes against sexual relations with "non-Aryans" did not qualify as victims, nor did those women punished for having sexual relations with foreign POWs, because their acts were not expressions of a "morally grounded view." Victims of forced sterilization had to prove that their treatment was motivated by racial, not legitimate medical or hygienic, considerations. Some who had resisted the regime and were persecuted on political grounds were recognized as victims, but Communists who had opposed the Nazis were not eligible if they were suspected of supporting another system of totalitarian rule in the present.[32]

For those acknowledged as victims of Nazi persecution, compensation was anything but automatic; a long review process to verify their claims and determine the extent of their disability followed.[33] Debates over the proper level of payments and the scope of persecution included absolutely no reflection on the process by which Jews and "asocial" groups had been the subject of legal discrimination and systematic exclusion from the larger society in Germany, under collaborationist governments, and in those areas occupied by Germans long before the "final solution" was put into place. There was also virtually no discussion of the one crime of National Socialism of which few Germans could have been ignorant: the involuntary importation from eastern Europe and the Soviet Union of workers, who were forced to labor for farmers and factory owners in Germany and in other areas of eastern Europe occupied by the Nazis.[34]

No reliable figures record how many people sought to claim legitimate victim status, but the parliamentary deliberations of the law to compensate victims suggest how few could expect to receive anything in the end. Hermann Brill, an SPD representative who had been active in the resistance and was sentenced to twelve years in Buchenwald in 1939, calculated that of 42,000 prisoners in the camp, 35,000 survived until liberation. Of these, 22,000 were Russians. Only 1,800 were Germans, and of these, only 700 were political prisoners. "The rest," Brill explained, "were asocials, homosexuals, those held in protective custody, professional criminals and so forth"—groups that the law did not cover. Constantin Goschler, in his analysis of this example, concludes: "There could be no more drastic formulation of the gap between the group of concentration camp prisoners and those entitled to compensation [under the law]."[35]

The readiness of most West Germans to acknowledge only narrow categories of crimes committed "in the name of the German people" reflected the tendency to collapse Nazi persecution into racialist anti-Semitism and National Socialist atrocities into incarceration, torture, and mass extermination of Jews. Most West Germans did not recognize the processes by which social marginalization had paved the way to mass extermination.[36] In the postwar world, victims of racism could make individual claims, but victims of national antagonisms could not. According to the logic that prevailed in the 1950s, the Nazis' treatment of some groups was not specifically National Socialist in origin or racialist in content; rather, it was dictated by the exigencies of war, concerns for public hygiene and health, the desire to keep the peace, and important moral principles. Indeed, West Germans defined racialism more narrowly than had the Nazis. In the casuistic thinking of the fifties, while Jews were persecuted because of their race, Poles were persecuted because of their nationality, not because the Nazis considered them to be racially inferior.[37]

Those victims who were ultimately entitled to make claims received virtually no opportunity to influence the definition of compensation schemes directly. The Union of Those Persecuted by National Socialism (Vereinigung der Verfolgten des Nazi-Regimes), an organization created in the late 1940s to represent all victim interests, was quickly shoved to the margins because it was dominated by Communists, and no other organization emerged to take its place.[38] Those forces lobbying most diligently for compensation of Jewish victims were often based not in Germany but in the United States, and Jewish organizations showed little interest in coordinating their efforts with other victim groups.

Even with a carefully restricted universe of potential claimants, the law encountered substantial criticism from many West German citizens and state officials, who argued that payments to "make good again" (*wiedergutmachen*) the losses of individual victims represented a violation of the principles of democracy by granting special privileges to specific victim groups. Opponents also maintained that many who had been sent to concentration camps were common criminals, not victims of an ideological regime. Anti-Semitism further fueled Schäffer's insistence on fiscal restraint, and within his ministry he charged that Jewish claims for reparations should be weighed against alleged tax evasion and suspect currency trading by Jews since the end of the war.[39] As with the reparations agreement with Israel, Adenauer's intervention and the support of Social Democrats were needed to create the majority capable of passing the compensation law to "make good again" the losses of at least some of the victims of National Socialism.

Despite significant opposition, the treaty with Israel, payments to the Claims Conference, and the establishment of an institutional framework to calculate compensation for other victims of "racial, religious or political" persecution were positive steps. In addition to acknowledging at least some responsibility for the crimes of National Socialism, they made the past part of the West German present in the years 1949–53. Debates over these initiatives, however, did little to illuminate the origins of National Socialism or to locate the Nazi state within the context of modern German history. Rather, they were aimed squarely at sealing off the past, prematurely closing a chapter that was defined as having started with mass extermination and ended in May 1945. Still, particularly in the first four years of its existence, the West German parliament and Adenauer, backed by the Social Democrats, sought to ensure that West Germans did not entirely forget, avoid, or repress Nazi crimes. However unsatisfactory and incomplete their attempts to confront that past, the federal government and a majority of the West German elected representatives did not deny the weighty legacy of Nazi terrorism or the attempt to exterminate all European Jews.

Legislative efforts to "make good again" past wrongs stood at a crucial juncture in the Federal Republic's early history, running parallel to negotiations with the western Allies over German integration into a European defense alliance. Not only did they tie Germans' "moral rearmament" to the military rearmament of the Federal Republic, but they also linked West Germany's settlement of its moral account with Israel and other victims of Nazi persecution with its pursuit of "equality" (*Gleichberechtigung*) in the international political arena, the final determination of German reparations obligations to the victor nations, and its credit standing in the international economy.[40] Ties with Israel thus strengthened ties with the western alliance. Establishing moral accountability made it possible for many West Germans to hope that the ledger could now be closed once and for all.

The Victim Next Door

In the final debate over the reparations treaty with Israel, a CDU spokesman, Eugen Gerstenmaier, decried the "outbreak of insanity" among those "who had power in Germany," an insanity that had resulted in the deaths of millions of Jews. Germans, he said, were liable for actions carried out by a fanatical regime that drove Jews into "ghettos and from there into exile or gas ovens." For these acts, all Germans had received just retribution, as "Germany, all of Germany, was transformed into a huge ghetto. For us Germans, less easily surmounted than the walls of an oriental ghetto were the walls of hate, scorn, and rejection that had already been built around us during the war and that still held us captive after the war." Reparations were the "documentation of a new spirit" in Germany; acknowledgment that many Jews had moved from a very different sort of ghetto to death camps was the way "to bring Germany out of the ghetto once and for all." Henceforth, Germans "no longer needed to be ashamed." Nazi crimes might have marked the "darkest chapter in German history," but that chapter was now at an end.[41]

Gerstenmaier's jarring analogy suggests the ways in which West Germans associated the fates of victimized Jews and victimized Germans in the early 1950s.[42] What linked Germans and Jews were not just real and metaphorical "ghettos" but physical atrocities as well. Germans had heard horrifying tales of German victimization and Soviet barbarism since the last years of the war. In the winter and spring of 1945, Goebbels's news broadcasts and newsreels featured the devastation, mass rape, and death that accompanied the Red Army's advance. The message was clear: Whoever did not fight to the finish would face a similar fate.[43] Memories of Communist atrocities did not fade once the shooting stopped; indeed, in the postwar years they made possible the explicit equation of the suffering of German victims—a group that included no Jews—and victims of Germans, a group that was almost exclusively Jewish.

Jews and Germans had experienced the same forms of persecution, stated Adenauer's minister of transportation, German Party member Hans-Christoph Seebohm, because "the methods that were used by the National Socialist leaders against the Jews and that we most vehemently condemn are on a par with the methods that were used against the German expellees."[44] Justice Minister Thomas Dehler likewise argued that because everything that had happened to Jews had happened to Germans—loss of political rights, life, and property—both sets of victims were entitled to compensation.[45] German expellees, a group estimated by some to number twenty million, became another category of victims, driven from their historic homelands because of their "ethnicity" (*Volkszugehörigkeit*). By means of such arguments, Jews were transformed into one group of victims among many.[46]

The SPD leader, Carlo Schmid, reminded the western Allies that they must bear responsibility for what they accepted at Yalta. There, in his view, they took the first step toward abandoning eastern Europe to the Soviets and a reign of terror that had transformed German POWs into "modern slaves," subjecting them and civilians hauled eastward to "inhumane treatment that deserves its own Nuremberg."[47] In debates over compensation for veterans returning from prisoner of war camps, Margarete Hütter, a staff member of the German Office for Peace (Deutsches Büro für Friedensfragen), grouped together the POW, "the representative of the sacrifice brought by all Germans," with the "victim of the concentration camp." These groups were the "most tragic figures of the politics of the Third Reich," both casualties of Hitler's Germany.[48]

West German politicians compared Jewish victims of National Socialism with victims of Communism in many other ways. On the agenda of the same session in which Bundestag delegates debated the final form of the treaty with Israel were initiatives to address the problems of those fleeing from the Soviet-occupied zone of Germany and those expelled from eastern Europe.[49] The ubiquitous term "millions" joined together victims of many sorts. "Six million disappeared" was the count not only of Jewish victims of Nazi terrorism but also of expellees—the victims of Communist terrorism—and contemporary estimates placed the number of POWs who had died in Soviet captivity at well over a million.[50] Claims by the head of the Ministry for Expellees, Refugees, and the War-Damaged that, in economic terms, expellees had suffered "a general and total execution" invoked other "final solutions."[51] POWs, "German men and also German women in foreign hands," noted the SPD representative Hans Merten, a minister who had served on the eastern front and was very active in all issues concerning POWs after 1945, were also victims of ethnic hatred and racial prejudice, held captive "under the most dishonorable conditions . . . [and] forced to labor for only one reason, . . . because they were German."[52]

Adenauer also linked compensation for German and Jewish survivors of forced population transfers in his initial public call for reconciliation with Israel. Whatever Israel received, the chancellor explained, would be limited by the "bitter necessity of caring for the innumerable war victims and the support of refugees and expellees" in Germany.[53] Attempts to meet Israeli claims also became the basis for German demands that "other powers in the world be prepared to fulfill their moral obligation to make good the wrongs [*sittliche Wiedergutmachungspflicht*] done to the Germans expelled from their homes."[54] What West Germans were ready to do for Israel, others should do for Germany.

However, if Jews, expellees, and German POWs were equal at the level of rhetoric, the victims of National Socialism remained ghosts lacking faces, families, names, identities, or a powerful political presence. Represented by others, they spoke for themselves only seldom. German victims, in contrast, lived, breathed, organized, demanded recognition, and delivered speeches from the floor of parliament. What Germans had inflicted on others remained abstract and remote; what Germans had suffered was described in vivid detail and granted a place of prominence in the public sphere.

Expellees and POWs detained by the Soviets were both powerful symbols of the outcome of the war in the east, but they carried their suffering into West Germany in different ways. In the immediate postwar period, the flood of some eight million expellees into the western zones of occupation caused enormous difficulties and often led to resentment and bitterness on the part of the local population. Germans barely able to meet their own needs as they emerged from the devastation and privation of the war were now expected to find room for the citizens of the Thousand Year Reich from eastern Europe and eastern Germany.[55] Expellees were no happier with their fate and noisily demanded that state governments move quickly to compensate them for their losses and facilitate their integration into West Germany.

Allied officials, concerned that expellee organizations might provide a locus for right-wing irredentist politics, forbade ethnic Germans from creating explicitly political bodies. By the late 1940s, however, a network of groups had emerged, some organized by occupation, some by place of origin, some for the defense of cultural interests, some affiliated with churches. Such ostensibly apolitical organizations proved fully capable of representing quite political interests.

With the official adoption in May 1949 of the Grundgesetz, the constitutional basis for the newly created Federal Republic of Germany, the "new citizens" moved quickly to form national pressure groups to represent their concerns. Regional organizations, *Landsmannschaften*, each with its own press organ and institutional structure, proliferated at a startlingly rapid rate, unifying in national coalitions and claiming between one and two million members by the early 1950s.[56] Expellees even won recognition at the level of Adenauer's cabinet in the form of a ministry assigned responsibility to look after their interests. Heading the Ministry of Expellees, Refugees, and the War-Damaged was Hans Lukaschek, a high-ranking official of the province of Upper Silesia in the 1920s who had been forced westward at the war's end and who in the 1950s had close ties to expellee interest group organizations.[57] Although Germans from eastern Europe and the parts of eastern Germany ceded to Poland differed dramatically in the dialects they spoke, their forms of cultural expression, and their political past, they eventually overcame those divisions and merged into national organizations that pledged to preserve the cultural heritage, history, and political interests of Germans from all parts of eastern Europe.

In the political arena, expellees participated in—and were wooed by—all major political parties, lobbying directly with the government in Bonn to make sure their "right to a home" (*Recht auf Heimat*) in eastern Europe remained on the Federal Republic's foreign policy agenda. In the meantime, expellee organizations and their political representatives called for the government at both the national and regional levels to do whatever was necessary to enable their constituents to start over in West Germany.[58]

For Germans from the former Reich—particularly Pomerania, East Prussia, and Silesia, who constituted the largest group of expellees in the Federal Republic—the demands included a return to the boundaries of 1937, nothing less than a revision of the postwar settlement that had ceded large chunks of territory to Poland.[59] Sudeten Germans, a group that had emerged as a forceful political presence in Czechoslovakia after 1918, remained a strong political presence in the Federal Republic, claiming a collective identity that encompassed the bulk of the nearly two million Germans driven out of Czechoslovakia after the war. Their demands included the international recognition of the Munich treaty of 1938 and the inclusion of part of postwar Czechoslovakia in postwar Germany.[60] Calls for German unification thus implied not just union of the four postwar zones of occupation but also major alterations of the postwar borders between Germany and eastern European nations (Fig. 8).

All major political parties and the overwhelming majority of West Germans supported expellees' demands for a revision of postwar boundary settlements, but these requests received little sympathy from the western Allies.[61] By the early 1950s, the British and Americans had long since made clear how little they liked Soviet influence in eastern Europe and how much they regretted the concessions made to Stalin at Yalta and Potsdam. However, they were also increasingly unwilling to challenge directly the Cold War status quo. The gap grew between American pronouncements that the final determination of Germany's borders was still open to question and American willingness to take action to revise the postwar settlement.[62] Because the Allies were also hardly ready to sanction a treaty negotiated by the Nazis, they granted the demands of Sudeten Germans no serious attention. As for meeting the material needs of expellees, this was the responsibility of the state that had started the war, not the states that had ended it, and by the early 1950s the U.S. High Commissioner John McCloy also noted that in an expanding economy, expellees represented an advantage, not a liability.[63] Although the western Allies were concerned lest expellees form a locus of radical politics in the Federal Republic,[64] it was up to the West German state to ensure that smoldering discontent did not burst into flames.

If the geopolitical demands of expellees won little support outside the Federal Republic, at home they became set pieces in a foreign policy repertoire that was crafted for domestic consumption and that underscored the anti-Communist consensus at the heart of West German politics. Because the western Allies stopped short of declaring Poland's postwar borders closed to negotiation, postponing a de jure settlement until the day Germany was once again unified, Bonn could still persevere, charging that Soviet, not Allied, intransigence was blocking the release of German territory from Polish control.[65]

Within the Federal Republic, politics also frequently combined with culture. Annual days to commemorate the lost *Heimat* and reunions sponsored by regional organizations brought together hundreds of thousands of eastern European Germans in traditional costumes, nostalgically invoking the past (Fig. 9). Such events also created a platform for broadcasting serious foreign policy pronouncements. Before an unequivocally partisan audience, the chancellor could insist that "one day Silesia will again be German," and an annual meeting of Sudeten Germans provided the ideal setting for another high-ranking federal official to recall a past in which the Sudetenland, that "organic link between East and West," had been washed away by an "Asiatic flood," the likes of which the "occident" had not experienced since Genghis Khan.[66] Against the background of debates over West German rearmament, expellee leaders in the early 1950s could insist that without a show of unity in demanding a revision of the Potsdam treaty, the western Allies could not expect wholehearted West German support for an anti-Communist western European defense alliance. Sudeten German interest group leaders ratcheted up the rhetorical volume another notch, claiming that if the United States accepted the postwar settlement, it would represent "the triumph of Morgenthau and Baruch": once again, the Jews would be to blame.[67] Although more respectable politicians did not indulge in such rhetorical flourishes, they also did nothing to defuse the context that made them possible. By participating in the annual meetings, government ministers and political leaders lent interest group organizations credibility and legitimacy, hoping that their reward would be the votes of expellees.[68]

Former POWs were also a vocal presence in the postwar political landscape. The League of Returning Veterans, POWs, and Relatives of Those Missing in Action, created in 1950 to coordinate activities of POW interest groups in the Federal Republic, by late 1951 claimed a membership of 160,00. Seeking just compensation for those whose return was delayed by a stay behind barbed wire, organized POWs also aggressively demanded the homecoming of comrades still in Soviet hands.[69]

The fate of POWs in the Soviet Union was one of the most important unresolved legacies of the war, and it defined a central theme in the politics of the Federal Republic in the early 1950s. Soviet unwillingness to release all remaining German soldiers became a particularly powerful symbol of Communist brutality. Returnees from the "Soviet-Russian paradise," explained Adenauer, could "proclaim loud and clear for everyone to hear what the Soviet Russian regime truly means,"[70] and he stated explicitly in early 1950 that the crimes of the Third Reich found a parallel in Soviet offenses against German POWs. On this point the Social Democrats again joined the chancellor, with the SPD's Carlo Schmid insisting that "despite everything, we Germans have a right to make accusations, and we demand that this right be fulfilled."[71]

Although the foreign ministers of France, Britain, the United States, and the Soviet Union had agreed in April 1947 that all German POWs would be home by the end of 1948, the Soviets ultimately did not fulfill this pledge or provide reliable information about how many prisoners remained in captivity. In May 1950, Soviet officials sent notification that only some 13,500 German soldiers were still in the Soviet Union, all charged with particularly heinous "war crimes" and justly sentenced to long terms.[72] Nearly another million German soldiers, claimed the Soviets, had already been released.

Lacking a full reckoning of the dead and missing in action, the West German state responded angrily that the numbers did not add up; still unaccounted for were over a million Germans who had gone to Russia and not returned (Fig. 10). Until there was reliable information about their whereabouts, the West German government announced, it had no reason to trust Soviet calculations or to abandon the idea that tens of thousands of German soldiers were alive, if not well, in Soviet camps. Protesting Soviet intransigence, Adenauer appealed to "world public opinion," charging that the Soviets were guilty of "crimes against humanity" (Fig. 11). At the same time, he called on Moscow to provide an open and honest record of the living and the dead, while rejecting Soviet claims that all those still detained were "war criminals," as opposed to prisoners of war.[73] Paul Löbe, speaking for the SPD, seconded these sentiments, appealing to all "democratic nations" to express their solidarity with the "freely elected representatives of the German people" by protesting the inhumane actions of the Soviets, "so that the hour of liberation will soon strike for the last prisoners of war of all nations."[74]

The West German obsession with estimating the numbers still held by the Soviets was understandable given the countless families whose relatives were known to have been taken captive or were missing in action at the end of the war.[75] The POWs still in the Soviet Union also touched the lives of many others who had participated in the war in the east and whose escape from Soviet capture or early release often reflected arbitrary decisions and luck. However, official concerns about those German soldiers still behind the iron curtain were not only for domestic consumption. Although the British and American governments responded with indifference to West German demands that they help ease the plight of expellees in the postwar Federal Republic, they showed no reluctance to champion the cause of POWs victimized by Communists, enthusiastically transforming German concerns into an international affair.[76] Demanding the release of those still held captive cost the Allies nothing; on the contrary, it provided them with one more opportunity to criticize Soviet barbarism.

Embracing the cause of West Germans who sought the release of all POWs from the last war also paralleled British and American pressures to ensure that chastened, rehabilitated Germans would once again take up arms if called on to fight the next.[77] In negotiations over West German rearmament in the early 1950s, the Bonn government had convinced the western Allies that acknowledging the untarnished honor of German soldiers who had fought Communists in the past was essential to ensuring the cooperation of the German soldiers who would fight Communists in the future.

In 1945, Dwight D. Eisenhower, the supreme Allied commander in Europe, publicly maintained that "the Wehrmacht, and especially the German officer corps, had been identical with Hitler and his exponents of the rule of force," perpetrators of the same crimes, subject to the same penalties.[78] Less than six years later, Eisenhower and the Allies had moved dramatically away from this global indictment; soldiers and Nazis could no longer be lumped together. In an official statement, hammered out by West German representatives and the U.S. High Commission, Eisenhower now averred that "there is a real difference between the regular German soldier and officer and Hitler and his criminal group. . . . The German soldier as such," Eisenhower assured West Germans, had not "lost his honor"; the "dishonorable and despicable acts" committed by a handful of individuals should not reflect on the overwhelming majority of Germans in uniform.[79] The same strategic inclination to forgive was also apparent in U.S. High Commissioner John McCloy's decision to pardon a number of Germans sentenced for war crimes, a move that embodied what historian Thomas Schwartz terms the U.S. policy of combining "moral compromises and political expediency" to integrate West Germany into the western alliance.[80]

For West Germans, POWs became not war criminals but victims of injustice and of a criminal Communist regime. Just as they had paved streets to rebuild a war-torn Soviet Union, they could also pave the way for the Federal Republic to enter the United Nations, where, with American and British sponsorship, West Germans charged the Soviets with lying and withholding information. In presenting the West German case to the United Nations, the American representative, Edith Sampson, called on that body to secure justice for Germans, comparing the plight of the POWs to "the problems of refugees . . . , the practice of genocide, . . . [and the task of] protecting and repatriating children." West Germans could align themselves with "free peoples everywhere" and call attention to violations of human rights, not of others by Nazis, but of German POWs and deported ethnic Germans by tyrannical Communists.[81] Both the U.S. State Department and the West German government clearly understood that by focusing on the mistreatment of German POWs by the Soviets, it would be possible to push the Federal Republic further westward. As an official of the U.S. High Commission in Bonn pointed out to Washington, international protest of Soviet treatment of German prisoners of war was capable of "further mobilizing anti-Soviet feeling among Germans, while giving them [a] real sense of participation with [the] West and in the processes of the UN."[82]

Based on a national registry of POWs conducted with the massive assistance of the German Red Cross and other charitable organizations

concerned with returning POWs, the West German state claimed that
there were more than 60,000 and as many as 100,000 German soldiers
still being held in the Soviet Union. These figures did not include the untold number of ethnic Germans—estimated to be as high as 750,000—
transported against their will to do forced labor in the Soviet Union at
the end of the war and never heard from again. Within the Foreign Office,
no one denied that these published figures were exaggerated; in the absence of accurate figures of wartime casualties, all those missing in action on the eastern front could be counted as potential Soviet prisoners.
By the spring of 1955, reliable information existed for only about 9,000
POWs who still corresponded with relatives in the Federal Republic, a
figure close to the numbers reported by the Soviets. However, government officials justified using the high-end estimate in public pronouncements by alleging that many POWs might be denied the opportunity to
write home.[83]

Within West Germany, the League of Returning Veterans and the federal government kept the POW story alive with constant public reminders
of the soldiers still in prison (Fig. 12). Daily newspapers regularly carried returnees' horrifying tales of "Russia, as I saw it," illustrated with
maps dotted with guard towers and barbed wire.[84] Prisoners released after 1950 also provided ample testimony that no remaining POW was a
"war criminal." Not German acts, but the sentences dished out by Stalin's
so-called justice were the real crimes that kept Germans in Soviet
camps.[85] Soon after Stalin's death in 1953 the Soviets released more than
12,000 POWs, in part to foster goodwill in the German Democratic Republic in the wake of social unrest that June.[86] The national reception
of those whose final destination was the Federal Republic created another forum in which POWs could loudly proclaim, "Everything in the
Soviet Union Is Lies and Deception."[87] When the returnees sent home
by the Soviets asked themselves, "What have we really done?" the question was rhetorical.[88]

The federally financed traveling exhibition "We Admonish," visited
by tens of thousands of West Germans in the spring of 1953, presented
the world of the German POW in Soviet captivity.[89] The poster advertising the exhibition displayed the shaved head of a POW behind barbed
wire (Fig. 13). Transferred to a ten-pfennig postage stamp released on
Mother's Day that same year, the image was a powerful indication of the
ways in which by the early 1950s these symbols were associated in West
German popular consciousness not with victims of Nazi concentration
camps (Fig. 14) but with German prisoners of war in the Soviet Union

(Fig. 15).[90] Similar depictions of innocent POWs victimized by a brutal Communist regime were the stuff of annual weeks of remembrance, occasions for public demonstrations, pledges of loyalty to those not yet home, community events to assemble care packages for detainees, and silent prayer (Figs. 16 and 17). As a symbol of solidarity, introduced by the West Berlin mayor, Ernst Reuter, West Germans displayed green candles, after the custom of fishermen who lit candles on the shore during storms, beacons signaling the way home for sailors in distress (Fig. 18).[91] In 1953, the highlight of the annual "week of remembrance" for POWs was a nationwide marathon in which young men clad in white gym suits ran from town to town bearing a torch that was used to light "flames of freedom," yet another reminder of those Germans who were still not free (Fig. 19).[92]

The POW of public commemoration ceremonies, newspapers, and the illustrated press was the common soldier, the "everyman," who had gone to Russia to do his duty and had been forsaken by Hitler and other fanatic Nazis, men with little comprehension of the real conditions of frontline warfare. POWs, who had sacrificed "the best years of their lives,"[93] were also celebrated for their contribution to the balancing of accounts at the end of the war. Symbolically for all Germans, these heroes were offering reparations to the Soviet Union. By the early 1950s, those calling for their release insisted that the POWs had long since squared accounts; the punishment no longer fit the crime. "In the name of the German people," Nazis had committed unspeakable acts; in the name of those same Germans, brave men in uniform had atoned, helping to rebuild Russia. Now it was up to all Germans to repay the debt, to permit POWs to "reconnect to a normal daily work routine" lest they "lose their humanity and sink into the mass."[94] As the SPD's Hans Merten put it, POWs and their families deserved compensation not only for what they had suffered but also for what they had accomplished, "acting for the entire German people."[95] POWs had earned the acknowledgment that, more than any other group, they had done penance for National Socialism's defeat in war. Explicitly equating the suffering of POWs and other victims, the League of Returning Veterans asked: "With what right does the state deny former prisoners of war the compensation . . . already provided to those persecuted by the Nazi regime?"[96]

The high visibility of POWs and expellees in the political limelight contrasted dramatically with the general tendency of the West German state to refer to victims of Nazi persecution in understated terms. Through public acts of commemoration and litanies of loss and suffering, expellees and POWs became "representatives of the entire German people,"[97] their concerns, in the words of Social Democratic representative Kurt Pohle, a veteran who had been detained in a U.S. camp after the war, "the concerns of the German people."[98] Victims of Germans represented a past that West Germans sought to leave behind; the past of expellees and POWs was one they were eager to embrace.

When parliamentarians crafted schemes to address the needs of "new citizens" and POWs returning from Soviet imprisonment, policymakers were reacting not to Allied pressure or the moral imperative presented by Jewish survivors who were now Israeli citizens; rather, they were seeking to acknowledge the just claims of their relatives, neighbors, friends, and constituents. They were also responding to their colleagues on the floor of the Bundestag. Debates over benefits and programs to reintegrate returning POWs into West German society provided a forum for a former prisoner to recount his shame at being treated "like the poorest of the poor," subject to the "public pity" of those who offered only cigarettes and scraps of bread, not dignified treatment and respect.[99] The soldier, now a member of parliament, who returned home soon after the war's end clad "only in an old soldier's coat" and then confronted the "lack of psychological understanding of the authorities," could address his colleagues and demand just compensation for the sacrifice he and his comrades had made for their country.[100] When the Bundestag discussed the experience of expellees, the minister for expellees himself could tell of starting a new life as he arrived from Upper Silesia with only his toothbrush and the few belongings his Soviet captors had allowed him to keep.[101]

By weaving their personal testimonies into the fabric of politics, explained Bernhard Reissmann, a Bundestag representative from Münster, expellees allowed those who had been spared the fate of the victim to put themselves "in the shoes of people who at the end of the war confronted the ruin of possessions that they had earned or that were theirs because of the diligence and frugality of generations; in the shoes of those who were forced to leave their homes with bags of rags and torn clothes and who arrived in a strange land, where virtually nothing is done to care for them; in the shoes of people who have lost all personal mementos, and who only under extraordinarily difficult circumstances have been able to get their bearings."[102] As they were represented—and represented themselves—expellees had survived to tell a tale that all Germans should take to heart. Their private stories profoundly shaped the agenda of public policy.

Legislative initiatives to compensate German victims allowed all political parties to acknowledge German loss and sacrifice. The face of the chief perpetrator of crimes against Germans remained the face of Germany's chief enemy in the Second World War; thus the Cold War facilitated continuities in anti-Communism from war to peace. A Social Democratic spokesman emphasized that restoring to expellees "a type of property that everyone should have, when their life has a purpose, a life of freedom and human dignity," was essential to prevent them from sinking into the "collective." Communism had robbed them of their livelihood; now West Germany must compensate them for that loss, lest disaffected expellees be driven into the arms of the Communists, weakening the "front of those who are prepared to defend what we know to be the most cherished and important values of our occidental culture."[103] Erich Mende, a Free Democratic member of parliament, argued that although West Germans had to "make good again" the wrongs done by a handful of Nazis, they were also obliged to "make good again" the wrongs done to millions of other Germans, "the victims of Bolshevism," that other form of twentieth-century totalitarian rule.[104]

The litany of German losses in eastern Europe also provided West Germans with a language for rejecting Allied moral balance sheets and the idea that what Germans had suffered was just retribution for the suffering Germans had caused. Allied unwillingness to assist with the material compensation of victims during the years of military occupation and the continued reluctance to assist with the costs of integrating expellees was attributed to the residual belief in German "collective guilt."[105] West German political leaders from all but the far left band of the political spectrum went even further, blaming the western Allies for their belated recognition of the dangers of Communism. Most notably, the British and Americans had acquiesced to Soviet demands—outlined at Teheran, specified at Yalta, finalized at Potsdam—that they occupy eastern Europe and expel Germans from their historic homelands. By accepting the mandatory removal of Germans from most areas seized by the Red Army, the Allies had responded to Nazi crimes with crimes of no less consequence and contributed greatly to an "expellee problem" of virtually "unmasterable gravity."[106] In general, the "lack of political instinct" on the part of the western Allies had created "mistrust toward the construction of a democratic German state." This left it up to Germans "to reap what the military governments had sown," while proving that they could govern themselves better than they had been governed by the forces of postwar Allied occupation.[107] Failure to meet the chal-

lenge, warned Adenauer's transportation minister, Hans Christoph Seebohm, was sure to create a "social atomic bomb" that Americans would
be unwilling to defuse.[108]

Discussion of public policy measures to aid expellees and returning
POWs created a forum in which the West German state could offer a far
more differentiated understanding of the nature of National Socialism
and a far more sympathetic view of the just demands of its citizens than
those put forward by the western Allies. "Coming to terms" with the
pasts of German war victims meant acknowledging that all Germans had
lost the war but few were truly responsible for its origin, and not all had
suffered its consequences equally. National Socialism had created countless victims, of whom many were Germans. Implicit in the tally sheet that
included fourteen million expellees, as many as two million killed by the
Soviets and Communist partisans, over a million POWs dead in the Soviet Union, and countless more still languishing in captivity, was the claim
that Germany's losses exceeded those of other victim groups. The language of millions was a powerful moral currency. Indeed, debates over
measures to meet the needs of expellees and returning POWs emphasized
how the suffering of these groups represented a collective penance that
allowed West Germans to close the moral ledger in the black. When Adenauer addressed parliament in October 1950 on the national day of commemoration and spoke of "those men, women, and children who have
not yet come home," he asked whether "ever before in history millions
of people had been sentenced with such chilling heartlessness to misery
and misfortune?" Although Adenauer sanctimoniously declared that it
would be up to history to judge, he seemed already to know what the
verdict would be.[109]

Meting Out Social Justice in a Nation of Victims

With extraordinary energy and thoroughness, the Bundestag took up
measures to meet the needs of German victims, particularly those expelled from eastern Europe or, as prisoners of war, prevented from returning home until well after the end of hostilities and disadvantaged
by their lengthy separation from work and family. Before 1949, measures to assist expellees and returning POWs were administered in each
of the zones of western Allied occupation by individual state governments, charitable organizations based in the churches, and the Red
Cross. The West German state's promise to provide a national response
to those "damaged by the war" was lodged in the Grundgesetz and was

realized by federal programs aimed at "equalizing the burdens" of the arbitrary consequences of war.[110]

A host of social welfare initiatives sought to mediate the differences between veterans who had returned immediately after the end of fighting and prisoners of war who were detained in the Soviet Union; between POWs in Soviet and western Allied hands; between POWs whose former homes were now "behind the iron curtain" and those who had lived in western Germany before the war; and between "new citizens" (*Neubürger*), driven from their homes in eastern Europe, and West Germans who had suffered no such dramatic displacement.[111] Federal funds went to education benefits, job training and placement programs, lump-sum cash payments, loans for starting up new businesses, and counseling programs to address professional and emotional needs.

The capstone of these efforts was the "law to equalize the burdens," passed in 1952. Combined with other measures to provide immediate assistance introduced in 1950, this law resulted in payments of nearly twenty-seven billion marks by 1957, 64 percent of which went to expellees.[112] Complementing these programs were unemployment payments, old-age pensions, and state investments in new housing for those who had arrived homeless in the Federal Republic. In the period 1952–56, other programs designed to provide former POWs with medical care, occupational training, and housing assistance amounted to over seven hundred million marks.[113] Although these amounts could not fully compensate individuals for losses of property or earnings, they did represent a massive transfer payment and a symbolic "reckoning for Hitler's war" that benefited German victims generally.[114]

Achieving some measure of social justice among those who had lost everything as opposed to those who had suffered little or nothing emerged as a key measure of the West German state's legitimacy.[115] The ability to integrate successfully its "new citizens" and heal the physical and mental wounds of those returning from postwar battles against Communist oppressors were the prerequisites to a domestic social contract between Germans and Germans, hammered out in Bonn, not Washington, Paris, Moscow, or London.

Despite the broad consensus favoring just compensation for returning POWs and victims of the expulsion, not all measures sailed effortlessly through the Bundestag. The recalcitrant finance minister Schäffer, tightly clutching the federal purse strings, warned against demands that exceeded the German government's ability to pay. To the Allies, Schäffer stressed that an impoverished Germany could make only a lim-

ited contribution to the European Defense Community, while to his domestic audience he constantly reiterated that the price tag for contain-
ing the Communist threat to the east in the present—a bill that included
rearmament and the costs of maintaining Allied troops on German
soil—placed severe limits on what could be spent on German victims
of Communism in the past.[116]

The German Communist Party did not share Schäffer's concerns, but
it did object that compensation was as likely to go to war criminals and
collaborators as comrades. The KPD also saw behind discussions of the
"war-damaged" little more than an attempt to reconstruct capitalism in
Germany and to fan the flames of anti-Communism. What most West
Germans saw as an expulsion it considered a population transfer and "resettlement," the fault not of Communists but of National Socialists; in
its view, the vast displacement of Germans from the east was essential to
ridding the European order of the fascist threat.[117]

Communists were all but alone in arguing that there was a relationship between Nazi aggression before 1945 and German misery after, and
in pointing out that the overwhelming majority of West Germans, not
just a handful of faceless criminals, had "cheered as long as the bells of
Hitler's victories had chimed in Germany."[118] However, the KPD was
dismissed as the agent of precisely the same terrorist system that had
driven Germans from their eastern homelands and still held German soldiers captive, the victims of "an insanity that destroyed our nation," then
"victims of bolshevism."[119] Although most Social Democrats, like their
colleagues in the CDU/CSU and FDP, stressed that "no catastrophe was
so profound as the catastrophe of the year 1945," they sometimes traced
the origins of German defeat back to 1933, when Hitler came to power
with broad popular support.[120] But such assessments aimed less at trig-
gering critical self-reflection than at delivering additional justification for
addressing the "just demands of the innocent millions who have fallen
into poverty and misery," victimized by both brands of twentieth-century totalitarian tyranny. Immediate action was essential to ensure that
postwar dissatisfaction not lead to the "massive poverty that had delivered such combustible material, such dynamite," in the late twenties and
early thirties.[121]

Political controversy arose not over whether German victims deserved
compensation, but over whether their needs had been met. The SPD vo-
ciferously criticized the ruling coalition for doing too little too late for all
German victims of the war and charged the CDU/CSU with budgeting
more for present-day defense than for the costs of the last war. A noisy

right wing was also critical of Adenauer's government, but in its case insistence on aggressively meeting the needs of German victims was linked to arguments against additional compensation for Jewish victims of Nazi persecution and demands that one class of victims not be elevated above another.[122]

Ultimately, neither POWs nor expellees received everything they wanted. Most programs were designed to assist them in making a fresh start, not to restore the social status that they had lost or, in the case of POWs, compensate them for the reparations they had delivered to the Soviets. The costs of Allied occupation and the unpredictability of an economy still in the throes of recovery placed serious constraints on the state's budget, as Schäffer repeatedly emphasized. Representatives of expellees and POWs were just as outspoken in their expressions of disappointment over the federal government's initiatives.

Discontent did not translate into massive political opposition to the central government, as had been the case in Weimar, nor did POWs or veterans move far to the right as they had in the 1920s.[123] In the late 1940s, it would not have been possible to predict this outcome, and many feared that displacement and loss could easily translate into discontent. By the early 1950s, just as the Allied High Commission surrendered its control over licensing new political parties to the Bonn regime, general dissatisfaction over the speed with which Adenauer's government was taking up the claims of the "war-damaged" did lead to the creation and official sanction of a national political party to represent the interests of those "driven from their homes and stripped of rights" (Block der Heimatvertriebenen und Entrechteten, or BHE). Its origins were in Schleswig-Holstein, one of the regions to which huge numbers of refugees had been channeled: in 1946, fully one-third of its population consisted of "new citizens." However, this national party never gained more than nominal representation in the parliament. Although its very existence forced all other parties to compete more vigorously for the votes of expellees, the BHE was ultimately unable to attract a constituency of its own and rapidly declined in significance.[124]

In part, the absence of political radicalism among expellees and returning veterans reflected the West German economy's ability to provide what the state alone could not. Although in the late 1940s currency reform had disastrous consequences for expellees and POWs, resulting in high unemployment and price increases that were not matched by increased public welfare allowances, by the early 1950s West Germany had entered a phase of rapid economic expansion.[125] Economists agreed with McCloy's optimistic assessment and argued that expellees and re-turning POWs were by no means a drag on the West German economy; rather, only because of these additional workers could the Federal Re-public realize its potential for growth. What had seemed like a tremen-dous liability in the late 1940s had become an enormous resource. Eco-nomic historians continue to debate the impact of the huge postwar population migration on the performance of the West German economy, but there is little doubt that the economic problems of those groups most forcefully displaced by the war diminished as the postwar economy ex-panded.[126] In this sense, Bonn confronted the problems of a lost war and integration of displaced groups under far more favorable circum-stances than had Weimar.

In addition, unlike Weimar, the Bonn government and the Bundestag consistently allowed those most prone to political disaffection an active role in defining solutions for their own problems and ensured that every-one achieved at least something of what they were after. Self-defined vic-tims participated in a process of consensus building for which the Weimar precedent offered a negative example; this process served a pow-erful integrative function and undermined the appeal of special-interest parties.[127] In the Bundestag, despite political divisions among the major parties over the best means to meet German victims' claims, all agreed on the desired end. The tremendous attention given to the needs of the "war-damaged" in the first four years of the Federal Republic's history lent credence to Adenauer's professed goal of seeking "social justice" for all injured by the war, even if the consequence was that no one group's demands were completely met.

The exhaustive public discussion of the needs and rights of expellees and POWs granted them a particularly important role in defining a post-war social contract based on the condemnation of all variants of au-thoritarian rule. The rhetorics of victimization that emerged in debates over compensation for these groups articulated a rejection of National Socialism and Hitler's war as forces that had victimized Germany.[128] They also expressed a clear critique of the Communist regimes that had pushed millions of Germans from their homelands, left others prisoners of war, and exercised a reign of terror even closer to home in the "East Zone," where "political terror and concentration camps [*Konzentrationslager*]" were the rule.[129] According to Linus Kather, a CDU representative who had lived in Königsberg until 1945 and who led one of West Germany's largest expellee interest group organizations, those driven from their homes by the Red Army contributed mightily to ensuring that "no land in Europe [was] so immune to communism as Germany,"[130] while former POWs were eyewitnesses to the brutality of life behind the iron curtain. Meeting the just demands of these groups was essential for the domestic social stability that would allow West Germany to serve as the first line of defense against potential Communist expansion westward.

Neither National Socialist nor Communist, the Federal Republic was also not American, British, or French; the West German government won acceptance for its initiatives to compensate expellees and returning POWs by stressing that these programs were singularly German, grounded in the best tradition of the German social welfare system and correcting the punitive policies imposed by the Allies in the years of postwar occupation. The state's sympathetic approach to the needs of the "war-damaged" and its commemoration of the past of German victimization indicated how the Federal Republic could at once acknowledge and distance itself from the National Socialist past. It also indicated the capacity of Adenauer's government to criticize the policies of the Allied forces of occupation even as the chancellor forcefully pushed West Germany into a western alliance.

Postwar debates over shared fates circumscribed a community of suffering and empathy among Germans, joined by the common project of distributing the costs of the war. Defining the just claims and rights to entitlement of some and the moral obligations of others was part of establishing the bases for social solidarity in West Germany.[131] The Bonn Republic, a nation of victims, succeeded the terrorist, belligerent, destructive, aberrant Germany of the Third Reich. In the realm of foreign policy, Adenauer's government sought to move a new Germany from pariah to sovereign state, able to act with "equal rights" in the international community. In the realm of domestic policy, meeting the needs of the expellees and POWs was a way for West Germans to move from a past as passive victims, the objects of "fate," to a present as agents, shapers of their own destiny.

All major political parties could agree on this mode for confronting the past, because it was ostensibly outside the arena of party-political wrangling.[132] It defined a terrain on which all but Communists could meet, where West Germans could agree on their moral obligations to one another stemming from their shared relationship to a common past. To be sure, this vision of the past was highly political. It transformed *Germans* into victims of the *Nazis'* war and attributed responsibility for the crimes of National Socialism to a handful of faceless individuals, not a thoroughly fascistic social order. And it seamlessly wove together the crimes of the Thousand Year Reich with the "postwar measures of certain victor nations" that, as SPD representative Kurt Pohle put it, had "amassed so much bodily, spiritual and material injustice that our generation alone, despite the greatest efforts, will not be able to make up for it."[133] The public discussions of the expellees and Soviet-held POWs outlined an agenda for social, economic, psychological, and political reconstruction in the early history of the Federal Republic; they also indicated which moral ledgers of the war's costs West Germans would leave open and which they would shut and set aside.

CHAPTER THREE

Driven into *Zeitgeschichte*

*Historians and the "Expulsion of the Germans
from East-Central Europe"*

In June 1952 a seamstress, Anna Schwartz, recorded her memories of
the end of the war in Danzig, the city that Hitler had incorporated into
the Reich when he invaded Poland in September 1939. Her testimony
appeared in print in 1953, part of a massive collection of eyewitness accounts entitled *Die Vertreibung der deutschen Bevölkerung aus den Gebieten östlich der Oder-Neisse* (The expulsion of the German population from the regions east of the Oder-Neisse).

This is what Schwartz recalled:

For Schwartz, German defeat came before the official surrender. In late
March 1945, the Russians marched into Danzig, setting the city on fire.
Falling bombs drove Schwartz and her neighbors into air raid shelters,
from which Russian voices, promising freedom and security, later beck-
oned them if they would surrender. Distrusting these assurances, Schwartz
unsuccessfully sought a place on one of the last boats leaving the port city
to cross the Baltic bound for northern Germany, though Russian fighter
bombers made this a perilous and uncertain escape route as well. Schwartz
compared her fate with that of German soldiers, holding out until the end
and facing imprisonment or death.

On March 27 Soviet soldiers entered the city. Seven years later,
Schwartz could still hear their cries for "watches, watches" ("*Urr, Urr*")
and smell the "stink of liquor, sweat, and dirty uniforms" as Red Army
troops, armed with machine guns, "liberated" Schwartz's jewelry and
other valuables. Other women also lost their honor, and Schwartz re-

membered the screams of women as they were "raped by Mongols."
Driven out of her basement shelter by a Russian officer, Schwartz could
see wounded men and horses, dive-bombing German aircraft, burning
houses, and countless Red Army soldiers—a landscape of devastation.

By evening, Schwartz found herself together with many other Germans
as a prisoner of the Red Army, under guard on a large farm. Here she
faced interrogation about her party loyalties and occupation. Marched
twenty-two kilometers daily to work on a farm outside Danzig, she returned to more nightly questioning. The sound of gunshots in the distance indicated that some Germans were receiving death sentences on
the spot. Schwartz speculated that local Poles had betrayed them.

Good Friday 1945 was a particularly vivid memory for Schwartz. She
could still picture the four hundred women with her in the cold stalls,
where humans had replaced livestock. Denied food or drink, the women
also had no protection from the chilly winds that raced through the broken windows of the barn. Mothers, separated from their children, cried.
The women joined in singing a number of familiar hymns, appealing to
a higher order to calm their fears and bring them hope, and Schwartz's
sister encouraged her to find solace in the thought that "we have not abandoned God, and neither will He abandon us." At that moment, Schwartz
noted, "These words gave me comfort and strength in the most difficult
times"—though as it turned out, those times were yet to come.

Involuntarily separated from her sister, Schwartz began what she called
a "passion procession" (*Leidensmarsch*), marching with some five hundred others to the city of Graudenz. Disheveled German women and men
passed a graveyard "where women with children, the aged, and sick stood
with their bundles between the graves, subjected to wind and weather in
a typically cool early April. . . . As I heard later, they had stood there for
days, forbidden from returning to their homes. In front of the houses,
their goods were strewn, and now and again we saw a crazed man or
woman running through the streets." For Schwartz, the 130–kilometer
march ended in a military prison. Here she was finally allowed to bathe,
but only in large common showers, where she was ogled and ridiculed
by her Russian guards.

Graudenz was a way station en route to forced labor in Siberia, a destination reached after an eighteen-day train ride in livestock cars into
which Schwartz was crammed together with others from West Prussia,
East Prussia, and Pomerania. Her new home was a camp surrounded by
a two-meter-high barbed wire fence with a watchtower at each corner.
Schwartz counted 639 other women and 1,760 men, with whom she was

assigned to a filthy barracks where the inmates slept on bare boards, "so close together that if one of us wanted to turn over, we had to wake those to the right and left." At first Schwartz did only light work in the camp, but after three weeks a medical examination, conducted in front of a team of Russian doctors who mocked her modesty and her skinny frame as they pinched her arms and legs, determined that Schwartz was capable of more. Now she worked daily on the construction of a rail line that was to connect two mines.

After six weeks of this hard labor, sustained only with thin, watery soup, Schwartz was suffering from "dystrophy," the medical term she used to describe her state of severe malnutrition. She was next sent to a nearby collective farm, where she and her co-workers lived in tents. When most of the German labor force moved back to the camp in November, Schwartz stayed on, one of seven women who spent the winter on the collective farm.

In the spring she returned to the camp to discover a new, harsher regimen that left inmates standing daily for endless roll calls. She estimated that meanwhile more than a thousand Germans had died in the camp. Assigned again to an agricultural work detail, Schwartz also practiced her trade, sewing for the Soviet officers, their wives, and girlfriends. Gradually provisioning improved, but inmates were constantly reminded that "who does not want to work does not have to eat." With so many of her compatriots dead, Schwartz was doubtless not convinced by walls adorned with Stalin's motto, "Hitlers come and go, but the German people and the German state will always remain." Yet despite the hardships, Schwartz described how her fellow inmates survived, as the camp spawned singing groups, a small orchestra, dances, and even humorous theatrical performances.

Three years of hard labor left Schwartz indifferent, moody, irritable, exhausted, and sullen. But news finally came of her imminent release and return home together with the sick, invalids, and all other women over thirty. In a train bedecked with pictures of Stalin and banners that announced, "Wonderful Stalin, We Thank You for Our Return Home," Schwartz and her cohorts became a moving advertisement that she would never endorse. The previous years had left her grateful to the Soviet leader for nothing. As her train rolled westward, she remembered passing traces of the war everywhere—German soldiers' graves, the ruins of downed German fighter planes, burned villages and forests, rusting tanks and heavy artillery abandoned in the wake of German retreat. Cities were in ruins, and what churches still stood seemed to have no purpose in this godless land. At most, they now served to store grain or house livestock. Where urban landscapes were restored in Minsk and Smolensk, Schwartz recognized the efforts of German prisoners of war, assigned to rebuild what the German army had destroyed.

On 25 July 1948, over three years after she had first confronted the Red Army, Schwartz arrived in Frankfurt an der Oder, at the border between Poland, still identified on West German maps of the early 1950s as part of the "eastern regions of the German Reich under Polish control,"[1] and the Soviet zone of occupation; but it was only when she crossed the border into the West "that we really felt ourselves to be free. We had not come home, but we had arrived in the Fatherland." The only living member of Schwartz's family, her sister, was there to greet her, and together with her she "began a new life." Schwartz closed her remembrance with the wish that "all German women will be spared my fate."[2]

Schwartz's story was remarkable but by no means unique. At the end of the war, the Red Army drove millions of Germans westward from their homes in eastern Europe, and thousands more were deported eastward to forced labor in the Soviet Union. Like Schwartz, they suffered incalculable losses, and many provided detailed accounts of what they had endured. Indeed, even as Schwartz dictated her story in 1952, it was possible to hear similar themes from the floor of parliament in the debates over how to "distribute the burdens" of the war. Tales as vivid as Schwartz's were also common fare in newspapers and illustrated magazines, a staple in the press of the interest groups that represented expellees in the Federal Republic, and readily available in memoirs, book-length first-person eyewitness accounts, and novels.[3]

Rape, the loss of loved ones, the separation of families, expropriation, humiliation, and physical, emotional, and psychological abuse—these were extraordinary experiences that became altogether too ordinary for many Germans, citizens of the eastern portions of the pre-1937 Reich and ethnic Germans long settled in eastern Europe, who were forcefully expelled from those regions in late 1944 and early 1945. In this chapter, I do not seek to reconstruct their experiences or to provide a social history of the expulsion.[4] Rather, I explore how West Germans remembered and recorded the meaning of those events in the late 1940s and early 1950s, incorporating them into their national political culture, their public memory, and their conceptions of contemporary history.

Schwartz's testimony is particularly interesting because it was included in an official West German "contemporary history," published with the imprimatur of some of the most eminent historians in the Federal Republic. Along with hundreds of other narratives of eastern European Germans, her "account from experience" (*Erlebnisbericht*) was part of a massive project that included five volumes, some with multiple parts, documenting all aspects of the expulsion of Germans from eastern Europe. These compilations of individual testimonies were complemented by three full-length diaries. Financed by Adenauer's Ministry for Expellees, Refugees, and the War-Damaged and promoted by the scholarly editors as an essential source for writing the history of the expulsion and consequences of the war in the east, the volumes recorded eyewitness accounts not only from regions that had become part of Poland but also from Czechoslovakia, Hungary, Romania, and Yugoslavia. Not content to leave the production of memory to the local pub, meetings of regional expellee interest groups, and the literary marketplace, the West German state, with the enthusiastic cooperation of some of the most accomplished and best-known historians in the Federal Republic, set out to record a chronicle of the expulsion that would combine coolly objective scholarly analysis with the emotional power of individual victims' voices. It sought to make the story part of German history, securing this past in the Federal Republic's present.

"A true representation of the reality of what happened"

In the 1950s, historians were not alone in their attempt to provide reliable, scholarly accounts of the expulsion. A flood of studies sought to provide objective assessments of the human costs of the end of the war in the east, the tensions generated by the massive population influx into a western Germany devastated by war, and the ultimate success of the Federal Republic at integrating these "new citizens." In much of this work, the expellee became not only the representative of a postwar Germany threatened by displacement and instability but also a characteristic figure of the modern age. The sociologist Elisabeth Pfeil transformed the expellee into the symbol of "humanity in the modern period, expropriated, not rooted, resigned to reliance on the help of the collectivity."[5] A German everyman, the expellee was both the representative and "the creation of an epic," who shared a common fate with all those forced from their homes "through bomb attacks, the process of political cleansing, [or] the collapse of the political and social forms of life that have prevailed up until now."[6] Bernhard Pfister, director of a major federally funded project to explore the regional integration of expellees, made explicit what Pfeil implied: "The expulsion of the Jews and the Germans" were comparable events. Both stemmed from "a spirit of national and racial hatred."[7]

In other accounts, it was precisely the merger of "new citizens" from the east with the indigenous western German population that led to the "beginning of a new nation." Eugen Lemberg, one of the most prolific students of expellees in the 1950s, concluded that the citizens of a new West Germany had, under the least favorable possible circumstances, joined together in "the creation of a new people [*Volk*]," combining two distinct pasts in a single future. Without denying the strains generated by the confrontation of eastern and western Germans, Lemberg emphasized that the new whole was bigger than the sum of its parts.[8] The story of the expellees thus became part of a West German celebration of overcoming postwar adversity; the "people without space" (*Volk ohne Raum*), who had aggressively expelled indigenous populations in the late 1930s and 1940s, seizing vast expanses of territory in eastern Europe for resettlement by proper "Aryans," had become a people with enough space to make a new home for eastern European Germans aggressively expelled by the Communists.

Social scientists addressed the present and analyzed the experience of expellees upon their arrival in the Federal Republic. The volumes that included the testimony of Anna Schwartz focused on the "expulsion from the east" that had forced Germans westward. Careful documentation would make the expulsion part of the "contemporary history" (*Zeitgeschichte*) of the Federal Republic, establishing that the loss of the "German east" was one of the central meanings of the war. Sociologists left little room for expellees to describe their own circumstances; for the most part, the expellee appeared in their studies as an abstract object of analysis. For the historians who published Schwartz's account, however, her first-person testimony was crucial; it was important that Schwartz be an active subject, allowed to record her own history in her own words.

By publishing Anna Schwartz's story, some of the editors of the *Documentation of the Expulsion of Germans from East-Central Europe* were reviewing a history that they themselves shared.[9] Theodor Schieder, recruited by the Ministry for Expellees, Refugees, and the War-Damaged to head the project, had come to Königsberg in East Prussia in 1934. A Nazi party member since 1937, he taught and lived in that city until he and his family fled the approaching Red Army in December 1944. Königsberg—Kaliningrad after 1945—was part of the Germany that "for now" was under Soviet control.[10]

Named to a professorship in Königsberg in 1942 and elected dean of the philosophical faculty a year later, Schieder was one of a conservative group of historians who harbored little sympathy for the Weimar Republic. He was fascinated by the history of Germans in West Prussia, and the scholarly work that qualified him for the professorship focused on that part of the world. He applauded the invasion of Poland, and in the late 1930s and early 1940s he produced historical explorations and future prognoses of Germany's role as a "force of order," the bearer of a unique cultural mission, in eastern Europe. Under the Nazis, he also directed a regional center for the study of the post–World War I history of East Prussia. After 1945, his methodological reflections on how to document the history of one German defeat could be transferred to his study of another.[11]

Schieder's Nazi party membership and his enthusiastic endorsement of Nazi expansion in eastern Europe in no way blocked his postwar career. Officially "denazified" by the Allies and publicly silent about his Nazi past, in 1947 he accepted a chair in modern history at the University of Cologne after the position was rejected by Hans Rosenberg, a German Jewish émigré who survived National Socialism by moving to the United States.[12] In 1957 Schieder became editor of the *Historische Zeitschrift* (Historical journal), the most prestigious historical periodical in the Federal Republic, and from 1967 to 1972 he served as head of the Association of Historians in Germany.

In the documentation project, Schieder's co-workers included Hans Rothfels, who had proposed Schieder to head the editorial staff when he had been approached for advice by officials in the Ministry of Expellees. Rothfels had long-standing ties with the "German east." He had taken a chair in Königsberg in 1926, establishing a career as a pathbreaking student of nationalism and multinational states at what he called the "frontier university" in East Prussia. He was a key influence on Schieder's intellectual development and the reason Schieder originally moved to Königsberg. Rothfels was forced out of Königsberg, however, not by the Red Army but by the Nazis. Although he had converted from Judaism to Protestantism before the First World War, served in the war, and saw himself as a loyal, patriotic German, particularly concerned to establish the significance of German cultural contributions in eastern Europe, he was removed from his position in 1934 and barred from teaching altogether a year later.[13] Rothfels's brief arrest after the "night of broken glass" in 1938 convinced him that the Nazis would classify him according to blood, not baptism or his conservative political con-

victions. He eventually emigrated to the United States, where he taught
first at Brown, then at the University of Chicago. He returned to a chair
at Tübingen University in 1951, well known for his study *The German
Opposition to Hitler,* which appeared in English in 1948 and in German translation a year later. In the postwar period, Rothfels was outspoken in his insistence that the historical profession directly confront
Germany's "most recent past" by writing "contemporary history." He
founded the Institute for Contemporary History in Munich, and he was
one of the two original editors of the *Vierteljahrshefte für Zeitgeschichte*
(Quarterly journal of contemporary history). Through these two structures, he exercised a significant influence on the writing of twentieth-
century German history in the Federal Republic.[14]

Also among the editors of the documentation project was Werner
Conze. A doctoral student of Rothfels in Königsberg under the Nazis,
he, too, had joined in celebrating the historical presence of Germans as
a positive force in the development of eastern Europe. Conze completed
his dissertation under Rothfels's direction before the latter's dismissal,
and Conze acknowledged Rothfels as a significant influence on his intellectual development. Conze ended the war not in Königsberg but in a
Soviet POW camp; while he had fought on the eastern front, his family
had fled to the west, where he was reunited with them after his release.
After the war, Conze moved first to Münster, then to Heidelberg, where
he emerged as one of the most influential advocates of social historical
methodology in the postwar period.[15]

Under this exceptionally distinguished supervision, the work on individual volumes was executed by a team of youthful assistants, including
Martin Broszat, who later went on to direct the Munich institute founded
by Rothfels, and, late in the project, Hans-Ulrich Wehler, a student of
Schieder's, who in the 1960s would emerge as West Germany's leading
practitioner of a "historical social science."[16] In the first decade after the
war, it would be difficult to imagine a more accomplished group.

The *Documentation* amassed an impressive mound of primary
sources.[17] Schieder insisted that the volumes go beyond a chronicle of
acts of inhumanity, the form favored by some within the Ministry of
Expellees, to include careful analyses of the political context in which
the expulsions had taken place.[18] The editors' lengthy introductory essays described the Red Army's advance westward at the war's end as
many Germans evacuated, the Allied decision at Potsdam to rid eastern Europe of ethnic Germans, and the official policies of expropriation and deportation carried out by Communist governments after

1945. In the volumes on Romania, Broszat's assignment, and Yugoslavia, for which Wehler wrote the introduction, there were also careful analyses of domestic collaboration with the Germans, Nazi plans for the ethnic homogenization of eastern Europe, and the German military occupation that had preceded liberation by the Red Army. These volumes thus offered some of the earliest systematic attempts by West Germans not only to document the history of the expulsion but also to describe the policies of German occupation in eastern Europe.

At the heart of the project were over seven hundred personal testimonies and eyewitness accounts, some complete, some extensively excerpted. Together with brief editorial introductions and a range of official government documents, the volumes on individual regions totaled more than 4,300 densely printed pages. This staggering collection represented only a fraction of the eleven thousand "reports of experience" assembled by the federal government with the cooperation of expellee interest groups and ultimately housed in the vaults of the new national archive. The sources included copies of letters to friends and relatives, diaries, testimonies dictated in response to questions from officials of regional expellee interest groups (most likely the case with Schwartz), and retrospective accounts written initially for the author's family or as a personal diary.[19]

Establishing the criteria for including some personal testimonies in the published volumes and eliminating others was essential not only for the project but also for outlining the most effective means to document "contemporary history." Writing in 1953, Rothfels laid out this methodological agenda in "Zeitgeschichte als Aufgabe" (Contemporary history as a task), the opening article in the inaugural issue of *Vierteljahrshefte für Zeitgeschichte.* Assembling documentary sources that would allow historians to write German history since 1917 was particularly difficult. Archival sources were dispersed, "homeless," because of the chaotic circumstances of the postwar years. The Institute for Contemporary History represented one attempt to address this problem, through its collecting of documentary materials relevant to the analysis of the recent past. In addition, historians must be willing to depart from the traditional conception that the only legitimate sources were those authored by state agencies and deposited in official archives. The scholarly project to document the expulsion represented an attempt to assemble sources of a different sort. Rothfels acknowledged that historians who sought to explain events from which they had so little distance faced a real challenge. However, he claimed, precisely such proximity made it easier in

some ways to fulfill the "task of historical understanding, to put one-
self in the place of the actors as well as the sufferers." Being implicated
in and painfully affected by the experiences they were describing could
give historians particular insights.[20]

Documentation like the first-person accounts of the expulsion, explained Martin Broszat, was not only appropriate but absolutely essential for historical research on events where official sources were likely to
be of dubious reliability because they were formulated according to the
"grammatical rules of a propagandistic or ideological nature."[21] When
governments might be lying or perverting the truth, it was crucial to
record faithfully the accounts of eyewitnesses. Broszat alluded to the
problems confronting anyone who sought to write a history of National
Socialism based exclusively on sources generated by the regime, but he
also did not trust eastern European successor states—which were governed by other "grammatical rules"—to provide the sources necessary
to write the story of Germans driven from their eastern European homes.
In his reflections on the methodological challenges of compiling the documentation, Broszat explained that taking seriously the testimonies of
individuals was an acknowledgment that in modern societies "the broad
mass, society in its entirety, has itself become in large measure the subject of history," not its object.[22] Such an approach, which allowed countless Anna Schwartzes to share in making their own history, was a dramatic departure from a historiographical tradition that had focused all
but exclusively on the stories of great men and nation states.[23]

Listening to eyewitnesses, however, did not mean suspending rigorous assessment of sources. Rothfels insisted that materials used to reconstruct Germany's "contemporary history" be subjected to the same
historical standards of measurement that had "developed over the
course of the last one hundred and fifty years."[24] The editors were
painfully aware that first-person accounts could not all be taken at face
value; it was their job to distinguish fact from fiction, dispassionate de-
scription from exaggeration. The process was made even more difficult
because many of those testifying recorded their memories only years after the events they documented. Schieder, who was directly involved in
virtually all aspects of the project, from securing a typewriter to hiring
secretarial help, also specified the criteria to be applied in determining
the reliability of such documentary accounts.[25] The work of sorting
through and classifying individual reports was left to a research staff,
but Schieder detailed review procedures. Assessing the value of the reports as the raw material for scholarly analysis should, he specified, fol-

low the same methods used in the inspection of all historical sources; it was critical to check documents against other documents, particularly official sources, and dismiss secondhand hearsay testimony.

According to Schieder, if there was any question at all about the accuracy of an account, if in any particular it failed to pass the rigorous "testing procedures" of the editors, then it was excluded in its entirety. The editors described their efforts to weed out the testimony of those who were particularly bitter and to exclude reports that tended toward "obvious exaggeration, unfounded speculation, [or] the amassing of statements that are polemical or ladened with resentment."[26] Confident that what remained after this painstaking "authentication and verification" was a record of the "entire process of the expulsion in [its] historical accuracy," the editors certified that the documentation was just as valuable and reliable as the archival sources and official government documents that had always been the starting point for German historians.[27] Their methods for verifying testimonies, they claimed, promised to transform subjective memory into unassailable fact. Unlike interest group publications that might be criticized as anti-Communist polemics, attempts to achieve "revenge and reprisal," or exercises in self-pity, the documentation was to serve as the basis for a "responsible confrontation with the most recent past" motivated only by an "incorruptible love for the truth."[28] In Broszat's words, the collected testimonies would provide "a true representation of the reality of what happened."[29]

A characteristically enthusiastic West German assessment of the volume that included Schwartz's testimony echoed Broszat's view. The fact that an editorial board of "four university professors from Cologne, Hamburg, and Tübingen, together with a high-ranking archival expert [*Oberarchivrat*] from Koblenz, has examined this vast material with painstaking objectivity and the most exacting evaluative standards banishes from the start any doubt of the absolute historical accuracy of its work."[30] Any West Germans who needed proof of what the "new citizens" in their midst had suffered now could consult the massive blue volumes published by the project.

Another important audience for the "contemporary history" presented in the documentation lay outside Germany. Publishing a record of the Red Army's crimes against Germans at the war's end, and the offenses committed by Soviets and eastern European Communists after May 1945, explained Schieder, would establish the expulsion as "one of the most momentous events in all of European history and one of the great catastrophes in the development of the German people." It was essential that the memory of this event be sustained "for the next generation and that it be made accessible, at least in part, to contemporaries at home and abroad." Publishing select documents would, he said, "emphatically make the world public aware of things that until now have been for the most part hushed up."[31]

For Schieder and ministry officials, more was at stake than eliciting sympathy and understanding. "At the right moment," Schieder elaborated, uncritically endorsing the ties between the work of professional historians and the Federal Republic's hope for some revision of the postwar boundary settlement, such a documentary record might also influence a "certain change of heart, for example, in the United States in favor of the German people, particularly in the question of the regions east of the Oder and Neisse"—a benefit that easily outweighed the potential liability of propagandistic responses from Communist eastern Europe.[32] As Adolf Diestelkamp, the official from the national archive who was part of the editorial team, put it, a sober, objective assessment of German experiences and losses could be a "decisive factor in our fight to win back the German east," in particular, territory that the postwar settlement had ceded to Poland.[33] The decision to publish substantial excerpts from the volumes in English-language translation, a project supervised by Rothfels, whose wartime experience in the United States qualified him for the task, was yet another indication that the project was aimed at readers beyond the Federal Republic's borders, in those western countries held accountable for the Potsdam agreement and the abandonment of eastern Europe to the Soviets.[34]

Readers abroad were vital, the editors and officials in the Foreign Ministry maintained, because there was little understanding outside Germany of the enormous consequences of the expulsion. A detailed account was essential, according to an official in the Ministry for Expellees, to counter the "false impression, produced by the propaganda of the opponent," that German forces of occupation in eastern Europe "had raped, robbed, terrorized, and butchered the population as long as Hitler was in power." This perverted version of the war's history already existed in documentation published by the Polish government, and anyone who questioned the potential power of such evidence needed look no further than the documentary publications after 1918 that had pinned blame for the First World War squarely on Germany.[35]

The project was also framed explicitly as a refutation of the belief, ascribed to the western Allies, that what had happened to Germans in eastern Europe at the war's end was no more than what they deserved. A detailed, factual response would set the record straight, reminding foreign readers "that the forefathers of the expellees were already in possession of rights to a home [*Heimatrecht*] in eastern and southeastern Europe at a time when America was not even discovered, that they were not robbers and pillagers but the upholders of culture [*Kulturträger*], who lived together with other populations of the same lands for centuries . . . and contributed significantly to the welfare of the host countries."[36]

The work of Schieder and his associates was not immune to criticism. East German historians charged that the project represented little more than an extension of Cold War anti-Communism, while expellee interest groups grumbled that the editorial staff was too soft, not hard, on Communism. Even though the project had relied heavily on interest groups to collect their sources, these organizations claimed that the editors had ultimately been unwilling to portray faithfully the true extent of Communist atrocities or to consult adequately with the real experts, most notably interest group leaders who had suffered personally from the expulsion. These people might lack the editors' academic credentials, but they claimed that their firsthand experience gave them authority of a different sort. Schieder, however, found in such politically motivated criticisms the proof that "the application of the strictest principles of the scientific advancement of the truth is the best politics."[37] The inability of the documentation to please all of the people all of the time delivered the evidence that the commission had done its job responsibly.

"Their only offense is that . . . German is their mother tongue"

The "true representation of the reality of what happened," the authenticated, official story that Schieder and his associates sought to tell, was outlined in Anna Schwartz's testimony. The thick volumes edited by Schieder and his colleagues overflowed with countless other individual tales of terror. This was the "mass fate" of Germans in eastern Europe, both those who had arrived relatively recently as part of Nazi resettlement initiatives that began with the transfer of ethnic Germans to parts of Poland in 1939, and millions more who were driven from land where their "families had been born, lived, and died, which [they] had loved, on which [they] had worked, and which [they] had defended against enemies."[38] Dr. Karl Grimm, a physician expelled from Czechoslovakia, expressed common sentiments when he mourned the destruction of a "region [*Land*] with a rich nature, an old culture, and a modern civilization . . . [a] people [*Volk*] blessed with children, a peasantry, a working class, a middle class, intellectuals, a vibrant, vital nation in a bountiful *Heimat*. That was a people, but it is a people no more, it is a chaotic mass of refugees, expellees, homeless, beggars," shipped like livestock from all parts of their former homes "into the unknown expanses of Germany and a distant uncertain fate."[39]

Even those eyewitnesses skeptical of the terrifying picture of the Bolshevik that Nazi propaganda painted and that was captured unceasingly in weekly newsreels in the last months of the war now testified to a reality that was even worse. Near the end of the war, Herr O. G., a butcher from Pomerania, had, "like anyone who thought and behaved decently," rejected "as Goebbels's propaganda the widespread reports in newspapers and on the radio of the Russian acts of terror." O. G. and his brother were not politically active, and "we treated our foreign workers in a humane fashion." With the arrival of the Red Army in his village, however, "quickly [my] credulity was bitterly disappointed."[40] The author of one of the project's full-length diaries, Hans Graf von Lehndorff, was an East Prussian doctor who traced his aristocratic ancestry back "many centuries" and established his credentials as an opponent of the Nazis by stressing his relations with some of those involved in the plot against Hitler in July 1944. Lehndorff compared the advance of the Red Army in the spring of 1945 to a "flood of rats that exceeded all of the Egyptian plagues."[41] Such images of animalistic hordes carrying disease, deployed in Nazi propaganda to describe Jews, could also be used to describe the Soviet advance. Goebbels's prediction had come true, and his rhetoric remained apposite.

The prejudice of Communists against Germans was fueled, the editors explained, not only by dramatic cultural and racial differences but also by ideology. Communists were driven by a "hatred of 'capitalists,' which stems from the traditions of the Russian revolution." Large estate owners and the lower classes alike were subject to indiscriminate torture; for ideologically charged Russians, mere home ownership was enough to justify murder, and a telephone was a clear sign that its owner was a "big capitalist."[42] Herr H., a former local official (*Bezirksbürgermeister*) from Breslau—an exceptional witness because he identified himself as both a Jew and an antifascist and because he had been named to his official post by the Soviet forces before he, too, fled westward— explained that "without any possessions, the great mass of the Soviets have no concept of property. It is thus understandable that they cannot acknowledge or respect the property of others. Quite openly, the Russians repeatedly stated that every German worker was a capitalist; in order to explain to the masses of Russian soldiers why German workers should have so much, they were told that all property was stolen."[43] As a Romanian German reported, the Russians believed that "anyone with property that could be expropriated qualified as a capitalist, regardless of whether at the time they were workers, white-collar employers, or even students."[44]

Like Anna Schwartz's, countless reports detailed how the Soviet occupation of eastern Europe commenced, literally and symbolically, with the forceful occupation of German women's bodies.[45] Accounts reported victims from nine to ninety, prepubescent girls and pregnant women. Because many men were dead or, still in uniform, separated from their homes in the last months of the war, stories of the German confrontation with the Red Army often told of women left to fend for themselves, guarded only by old men and boys mustered at the last minute into local defense militias (*Volkssturm*). Women's voices were legion in the documentation, and their stories of rape are especially horrifying. When women crossed paths with German soldiers in retreat, they realized that they shared a common fate; this war had erased the lines between battlefront and homefront. The scars of war that women bore, however, were the scars of rape by Red Army soldiers.[46]

For a housewife, A. F., from Königsberg, the fall of that city to the Russians was a time of terror. Mothers who attempted to sacrifice their own bodies to Red Army soldiers to protect their children could not save girls as young as ten from the fury of the Russians, and the "cries of despair of these children, mothers, or parents," horrifying evidence of "the war that was not yet over," still rang in Frau A. F.'s ears years later.[47] Ready to protect their honor with suicide, women described their decision to subject themselves instead to bodily violation so as not to abandon their children,[48] though in some cases mother love led women to kill their children, then themselves. Frau G. F., from the rural hinterland of the Silesian city Breslau, was prevented from taking this route as "twelve lads raped [her] so powerfully and forcefully that [she] constantly wanted to hang [herself] but had no opportunity, because the Russians constantly went in and out of the houses."[49] Although the largest number of reports of rape came from the areas in eastern Germany that lay along the Red Army's primary route to Berlin and that fell to Poland after the war, such stories appeared throughout the documentation. From all parts of eastern Europe, German expellees testified that once the Russians arrived, "no woman or girl was safe from the liberators."[50]

Some accounts of rape were told in categories familiar from Nazi propaganda. Although detailed information on the ethnic composition of the Red Army awaits a comprehensive social-historical account of the war's last months, evidence suggests that "Asiatic" troops were not overrepresented among those responsible for the Soviet army's worst acts against Germans.[51] However, "Mongols," the demonized Red Army soldiers of Goebbels's propaganda, lived on in German memories, and Asians in Red Army uniforms were not confined to Anna Schwartz's account. Herr A. S., driven from his home in Pomerania, testified that his servant girl was repeatedly raped by Russians, and vividly described the arrival in mid-February of "six Mongols" on horseback. According to his account, these soldiers tore children from the arms of women and girls and carried women off and raped them at gunpoint. Liberation came not from Russians but from an SS division that saved the honor of German women by recapturing his village. This brief "resurrection" was followed by a second crucifixion when the Red Army retook the town.[52]

In the memory of Frau Anitta Graeser from Czechoslovakia, the first Russians she encountered were all "Asians" who "rode camels [and] wore high, spiked, white fur hats and white fur coats. Their faces did not move, only the eyes were alive, and I will never forget that, how unbelievably wild they looked." To her knowledge, in the surrounding region, "at least in the areas where we were, there was not a single woman who was not raped. Yes, they even assaulted children, animals, and old people."[53] Seven years after the end of the war, Charlotte Hedrich, the wife of a salesman from West Prussia, testified that, though others were not so fortunate, she was able to "save herself from the worst because I showed no fear, and the danger gave me unbelievable strength. Even when they pointed the pistol at my breast, I didn't give in. I had nothing left to lose." She also told of a night when thirty drunken "Mongols" had come looking for women in the camp to which she and others from her village had been transported.[54]

In the introduction to volume 1, on the districts east of the Oder-Neisse line, the editors offered an analysis of the phenomenon of mass rape: "These rapes were the expression of a manner of behavior and mentality, which for European sensibilities is inconceivable and repulsive." Visions of Asiatic fury appeared again here. In part, the editors attributed the "particular boundlessness and savagery" of the mass rapes to the "traditions and notions that still exerted influence particularly in the Asiatic parts of Russia, according to which women are just as much the booty of the victor as jewelry, valuables, and property in housing and shops."[55]

In the western zones of occupation immediately following the war, observers often claimed difficulty in locating the boundaries that separated rape, prostitution, and fraternization with the victorious Allies. Sympathy for the rape victims of British, French, and American soldiers blurred with suspicion that women had succumbed to blandishments and material benefits offered by the victors. In the spring of 1945, the widespread impression that women in the western zones had resisted too little or not at all was a disturbing sign of a world in which German women's sexuality was outside German men's control. As Ernst Stecker, a politically active Ruhr metalworker who was forty at the end of the war, put it in 1983, recounting one of his most vivid memories from that time: "A Negro said: 'The German soldiers fought for six years, the German woman for only five minutes!' That's a fact from beginning to end. I was ashamed."[56]

The massive evidence of Red Army rapes, immortalized in the Schieder project, created no such confusion. Here, German women were victims, plain and simple. Valiant martyrs, not suspect fraternizers, they told tales of survival that described the brutality of war as dramatically as did the stories of men who had experienced another war at the front. In addition, in their accounts, rape *in* the "German east" became the rape *of* the "German east"; their experience symbolized the experience of all Germans, brutally violated by Red Army soldiers, and of a German nation, robbed of its honor and territory in eastern Europe.[57]

The farmer's wife I. K. from Pomerania recorded a night when Russians, having forced her and fourteen other townspeople out of a room in which they had been assembled, stayed behind with three young women, one of whom was in the advanced stages of pregnancy. When the Germans heard a shot fired they feared the worst, but after thirty minutes they were called back into the room. The women were still alive, but Frau I. K. learned from one of them what had transpired: "We suffered for you. During this time, I had three Russians."[58] Stories of rape in the documentation amounted to a moral balance sheet in which women's violated bodies took on an enormous emotional value, and women's suffering came to symbolize the victimization of all Germans.

In the Schieder documentation, other instruments of violence and terror joined rape to remind Germans of their complete subordination to the victor. There were reports of German women and men forced to shave their heads, to bear the sign of the swastika on their clothing or skin, or to march through the streets to be humiliated and ridiculed by local populations. Friedrich Graf Stolberg, a former large landowner and member of the Czech parliament, recalled that the armband forced on him by Czech partisans bore the swastika and the motto "We thank our Führer."[59] Frau A. L., who had worked for the signal corps in Prague, described how the Czechs shaved her hair and then doused her bald head with red paint after other partisans had already knocked out four of her teeth. "Rings were torn off swollen fingers with force," she continued; "still others saw to our shoes and clothing, so that finally we were all but naked, then they even tore off our underclothes, [and] young boys and men kicked us in the stomach."[60] In these and similar reports, the unbridled desire for revenge on the part of local populations often surpassed the brutality of Soviet soldiers, such that the appearance of Polish, Czech, or Yugoslav partisans could make the German population long for the Red Army.

Testimonies recorded how the world that eastern European Germans had known was transformed, as if the new political order were giving notice that "Yes, the times have changed; once you were the masters, now we are."[61] In expellees' accounts, the new regime distinguished itself in particular by inverting the established gender order, forcing women like Anna Schwartz to lay track or fell trees under the supervision of "female brigade-leaders, true beasts in the shape of humans."[62] Soviet women often appeared in expellees' memories as "pistol-packing mamas" (*Flintenweiber*), armed with guns and grenades, "at once terrifying and comical,"[63] an unambiguous symbol of the perverted values of Communism.

Other signs of a world turned upside down were abundant. Menial workers were now estate managers. "Gypsies" occupied farmhouses, the former owners now lived in day-laborers' huts, and erstwhile pigherders masqueraded as commandants. In Soviet forced labor camps, social hierarchies crumbled, and as Anna Schwartz recalled, "the high school teacher lay next to the factory worker, the farmer's wife next to the woman from the town, all united by the same fate."[64] The golden frame that had once held an oil painting of the ancestral home was now filled with a picture of Stalin, and a twenty-five-thousand-volume library, the heritage of the German presence in a Czechoslovak town, was torn from its shelves and severely damaged.[65] Medical students, ballet dancers, and opera singers filled jails to overflowing. Godless Communism's destruction of churches, recorded by Anna Schwartz, was another sign of changed times; Red Army soldiers had as little respect for Christian religion as they did for German culture, mindlessly transforming a prayer book into cigarette papers.[66]

In their recollections, eyewitnesses also focused on their uncertainty about what would happen next, as local German populations waited to find if they would be moved "'across the Oder' or 'to Siberia,'" expelled into the "Reich," or, like Schwartz, transported to the east to perform forced labor in the Soviet Union.[67] Accounts of the "trek" to the "Reich" were descriptions of "a province in the street, insanity and misery,"[68] roadways littered with the bodies of the dead and dotted with "prams [that] looked like gypsy wagons with all the children's wet diapers always hanging from their covers to dry during the journey."[69] No one could answer the "anxious unspoken question that was in the air, 'Is it forever or only for a few weeks?'"[70] Women, left unprotected by German men, appeared as courageous heroines, taking charge of wagons filled with personal belongings, children, and, "here and there, an old man or a soldier on leave."[71]

The Red Army's major advances in the winter of 1944 and spring of 1945 meant that for many, Christmas, Easter, Pentecost, and Ascension, moments for Christian reflection, marked intense memories in the midst of a godless Communism. Anna Schwartz's association of the passion of Christ with the passion of the expellees was no exception. Treks westward became a German "path of suffering" (*Leidensweg*),[72] the saddest imaginable "Corpus Christi procession,"[73] a road to Calvary.[74] These trials ended only with arrival in the "Reich," "where we were once again human and viewed as human. Who can empathize with this feeling? Truly, only the person who throughout all these months has gone with us through this hell, which we have now escaped."[75]

Annemarie Glück of Posen, a minister's wife, remembered "the last night in the *Heimat*," when she heard the Christmas message—for it was on Christmas Day that she and her children began their flight. Glück told how her children took the story of the baby Jesus with them on the trek, though, as one of her children remarked, "the Christ child was better off. He was allowed to live entirely alone with the animals and his parents in the stall, and he had as a bed his own manger (while we were packed in like sardines into the stalls and lay on the ground)." Sadness over their plight was, however, banished when they began to sing: "Jesus, you go ahead / Take us by the hand, into the Fatherland," a fatherland that they found not in the hereafter, but across the Oder in areas occupied by American troops.[76]

But neither were Americans always saviors. In the documentation, not only the Soviet Union but also the Soviets' wartime allies caused German suffering at the end of the war. The same critique of the postwar settlement that ran throughout discussions of compensation for expellees could be heard in reports describing the world that had been abandoned to the Soviets and their lackeys. Still unaware of the Potsdam agreement in the fall of 1945, Frau I. R. from Schreiberhau in Lower Silesia recalled that what had sustained Germans once Polish partisans had appeared was their abiding conviction in the justice that would prevail with the arrival of American and British troops, the "unshakable belief" that "this country was always German, thus the British and Americans are not suddenly going to allow it to become Polish." "'Asia has washed over us, the west will save us,'" was the general view, and it was one that she shared. "With this knowledge and confidence, we quite consciously constructed the last wall of humanity in the east," as they waited for the western Allies to shore them up. By the time she recorded these memories, Frau I. R. knew altogether too well that this wall had come tumbling down, and neither the Americans nor the British had done anything to stop it.[77]

Eberhard Schöpffer, a retired military man formerly of West Prussia, asked rhetorically how innocent Germans could have anticipated their fate in January 1945. Ignorant of wartime agreements among the Allies at Yalta, why should Germans have expected that "the British and Americans, Christian people who lived according to the law, would tolerate the complete evacuation of Germans from entire provinces where those Germans had lived for centuries?" Those who had dismissed threats of deportation to Siberia as "the propaganda of Goebbels," and until the last moment remained secure "in [their] faith in the Anglo-American sense of justice, experienced a horrifying fate that ended in untimely death" as propaganda came to life.[78]

In Hungary, "thousands and thousands of ethnic Germans" who had fled their homes were sent back by American troops to confront marauding Russians, or else were simply blocked from fleeing. In the memories of Otto Hölter, an engineer from Czechoslovakia, May 1946 registered permanently as "the beginning of an expulsion of the German population that was controlled by American officials." This was how Americans implemented the promise at Potsdam of humane treatment for ethnic Germans.[79]

Such testimonies, often written in the early 1950s, emphasized that the western Allies had been slow to recognize the horrors of Communism, a subject on which the expellees claimed particular expertise. The most powerful political lesson that those driven from eastern Europe extracted from their experience was that Communism was a corrupt, inefficient, and poisonous system that should be combated by every means possible. They had learned this lesson while Roosevelt sat with Stalin at Yalta and Truman sealed the fate of eastern Europe at Potsdam.

The editors of individual volumes in the documentation joined this anti-Communist chorus, offering additional insights from their historical perspective. In eastern Europe, they explained, Communism mixed with indigenous histories and traditions in particularly terrifying combinations. The superimposition of Soviet Marxism on Russian backwardness and a completely non-Western worldview had disastrous consequences; as Herr H., the local official from Breslau, reported, "The disregard, indeed, disdain, for human life is just as characteristic of the mentality of the Russians as their disregard for every form of personal property."[80] In their introduction to the volume on Hungary, the editors described the deadly mix of "Hungarian Communists and fanatical nationalists," which promoted a "destructive Magyar nationalism" and which sought to create a "homogenous Magyar nation."[81] Czechoslovakia, too, was characterized by the combination of a national and a social revolution, leavened by a general "psychosis of revenge" that turned Czechs against their former German friends.[82]

The arrival of Communism, not fascism, in eastern Europe marked the beginning of the "contemporary history" outlined in the documents. For the most part, eyewitness accounts began when good times turned bad, when Germans became victims, although "their only offense is that they have a German name and German is their mother tongue," that they were "born Germans."[83] The war narrated in the testimonies commenced in the summer of 1944 and continued through the winter of 1945, as the Red Army went on the offensive. The worst began just as national conflicts ceased. A German carpenter from Yugoslavia would forever remember 8 May 1945, not because of the war's end, but because it was the day when "hell was truly ripped open."[84] Those who rejoiced that the war was over quickly soon became aware that "now we really had to pass through hell."[85]

For those testifying in the documentation, the liberation of Europe, celebrated by the Allies, meant only "liberation" from possessions, homes, and, in some cases, loved ones. Freedom was only freedom to be subjected to the whim of the Red Army and local partisans. Matthias Kaiser, a salesman from the Yugoslav town of Hetin, sarcastically recalled Russians and partisans as the "true 'liberators,' why, they freed us from everything, they even freed many thousands from life itself."[86]

Few expellees reflected—or were asked by the editors to reflect—more than fleetingly on their relationship to a past that predated their own suffering. When eyewitnesses did evoke other memories of eastern Europe, it was to underscore themes that Schieder had developed in his own scholarship in the 1930s: the political, economic, intellectual, and social contributions that Germans had made to central Europe. They also pointed to the mutual respect and understanding that had characterized Germans' relations with other ethnic groups. Stressing a theme that was developed extensively in many of the scholarly accounts of the expellees in the 1950s, eyewitnesses stated that Germans were members of a "multinational community unlike any other in the world,"[87] joined together in a form of "unwritten solidarity among the unpolitical people of both nations . . . who had lived together here for years."[88] In the memories of expellees, these peaceful havens included no Jews, and the harmony of a multiethnic central Europe ended with the advance of the Red Army, not the earlier appearance of the Wehrmacht, German occupation, or the institution of collaborationist governments that were willing agents of Nazi rule.

The editors insisted that documentary evidence include a history of the expellees' experience that went beyond a litany of crimes carried out by Red Army soldiers and partisans,[89] but the testimonies they selected and their own editorial interventions did little to illuminate the crimes of Germans against eastern Europeans before the war's end. In 1955, Schieder proposed a concluding volume that would place the expulsion within the long-term context of late-nineteenth-century nationalism, forced population movements after World War I, the history of German minorities in eastern Europe in the interwar period, and Nazi "population policy" and population transfers. This idea, however, was rejected by the Ministry of Expellees, on the grounds that comparisons would make it impossible to claim the singularity of the expulsion.[90] Subsequently, neither Schieder nor the other editors pursued alternative means to publish the planned volume.

The books that did appear contained little evidence of German misdeeds. For example, neither eyewitnesses nor the editors commented on the exploitation of other nationalities as forced laborers by Germans.[91] Indeed, when foreign workers appeared in testimonies, they were often depicted as the gracious recipients of instruction from their German masters, no less eager than Germans to flee the Red Army and no more inclined to accept Communist liberation.[92] In the memory of one former regional Nazi peasant leader from West Prussia, thousands of prisoners and "eastern workers" (*Ostarbeiter*) had been staunch allies of the local German population as it prepared to flee before the advancing Red Army in January 1945. "They too had only one wish, not to fall into the hands of the Russians."[93] Germans expected nothing but loyalty from foreign workers, and an estate manager from East Prussia expressed astonishment that Poles, who "had nearly the same rights as a German worker" under Nazi rule, indiscriminately seized property and turned on their German masters once the Russians arrived.[94]

Those eyewitnesses who commented more explicitly on the Nazi past did so most often to distance themselves from it altogether, to register that they had "intensely hated the Nazi regime from the very beginning."[95] Many reports also emphasized clear lines of demarcation between big and small Nazis, evil perpetrators and innocent fellow travelers, thus challenging the vision of "collective guilt" that motivated Communist revenge and that informed western Allied policy immediately after the war. There were some bad Nazis in these accounts—typically opportunistic party bosses, the "gold birds," distinguished by their highly decorated uniforms—who postponed evacuation at the war's end, mouthing pronouncements of German victory while failing to note that the Red Army stood at the gates, then fleeing to save themselves, leaving their constituents behind.[96] Leading Nazis who had condemned as traitors those who questioned the Führer's will emerged as the biggest traitors of all. Indeed, the Nazi goal of creating a "community of the people" (*Volksgemeinschaft*) was achieved only at the war's end, "when all status differences were forgotten. . . . In these dark hours, everyone was just German, but it was unfortunately too late."[97] Adversity and the Red Army, not Hitler and Goebbels, had created the true *Volksgemeinschaft*. The expellees were thus victims twice over, prey first to scheming Nazis, then to marauding Communists.

In the testimonies, Soviets, Czechs, Poles, Hungarians, Yugoslavs, Romanians, and—by implication—Americans and the British, who immediately after the war had judged all Germans equally complicitous, mistakenly believed that all Nazis were bad. Expellees emphasized that membership in the League of German Girls, for example, did not imply a wholehearted embrace of Nazi ideology, and that German men were unwilling and in some cases unsuspecting last-minute conscripts into the Waffen-SS. At the local level Nazi officials were often heroes who, "true to their ideals, sacrificed themselves in the interests of the larger community."[98] Doubtless Schieder included himself among those expellees whose National Socialist sympathies indicated neither a flawed character nor evil intentions. Writing in 1960, he accepted that postwar Com-

munist excesses were a response to excesses of the Nazis, but he also criticized Communists for moving forcefully against Germans in eastern Europe "without any attempt to illuminate individual responsibility" for
Nazi misdeeds; virtually all Germans were deemed guilty.[99] The documentation painted the situation with equally broad strokes; in the testimonies it recorded, virtually all Germans were innocent.

Who was a fascist? Thirteen years after the end of the war, a pastor
expelled from Yugoslavia, Peter Fischer, recalled the criteria that returning partisans applied in his interrogation: "1. His parents have
moved away.—He's a fascist. 2. His brother was in the German army.—
He's a fascist. 3. He once said: What will become of us Germans?—He's
a fascist. 4. He ate and drank together with murderers. (I sometimes invited the local commandant to eat with me.)—He's a fascist."[100] The volumes made clear that misguided victorious Allies quite often asked not
which Germans were fascists, but how it was possible that any Germans
were not.

"Just as you have treated the Jews"

Eastern European Jews joined partisans and Red Army soldiers in some
of the expellees' accounts of the end of the war, but Jews were not invited
to speak for themselves. A rare exception to this rule was the testimony
of Herr H., the local official from Breslau cited earlier. In his testimony,
Herr H. shed no light on how he had spent the war years, but unlike most
of his fellow Germans in Breslau, he welcomed the Soviets' creation of an
"Anti-Fascist Freedom Movement" and a Jewish Committee. Hopes for
a better future were short-lived, however, for Soviet rule was quickly replaced by the reign of Polish Communists. Although Herr H. had sympathy for the armed youths, often the survivors of concentration camps,
whose excesses were driven by their desire for revenge, he was dismayed
when the new Polish rulers treated German Jews, "who had returned to
Breslau, their *Heimat,* from various concentration camps from Auschwitz
to Mauthausen," no less harshly than they treated other Germans. Herr
H. concluded that the Poles recognized "no difference between the Germans and German Jews," seeking indiscriminately to satisfy their desire
for revenge.[101] Doubtless Herr H. had other tales to tell of how Nazis had
distinguished between Jewish and non-Jewish Germans, but he was not
asked to reflect on a past that predated the arrival of the Red Army.

Elsewhere in the documentation, although Jews did not speak directly,
they certainly occupied German memories. In some cases, Germans,

about to flee in advance of the Red Army, recorded visions of treks of a very different sort, death transports of Jews who, unlike Germans, were following the "path into the Reich" on the instructions of SS guards. A former county administrator from the area north of Königsberg on the Baltic coast recalled how "many of the hundreds in the processions died from exhaustion, hunger, and maltreatment and remained unburied in the snow drifts, while the rest were driven . . . into the sea or shot by guards who were among [Germany's] foreign allies." Witnesses to this "insanity" were helpless in the face of police troops, who in turn were responding to orders from above.[102]

A retired mining official from Upper Silesia, Karl Wasner, recalled the death march of Jews from Auschwitz as they joined a chaotic cavalcade of British, French, and Soviet POWs, accompanied by SS soldiers. The Jews "crawled with frozen feet, wrapped in rags. Those who collapsed were shot and left lying on the ground." But in Wasner's memory, these living corpses were not inspired by the possibility of liberation by the Red Army. Rather, "they were all driven by only one thought: Forward to the west, don't fall into the hands of the Russians."[103] Seven years after the end of the war, Johannes Weidlein, former head of a high school in Budapest, could still envision the "endless columns of Jews who were driven westward," but in his memory they were not so bad off. Some, he remembered, were "quite well dressed, with raincoats and rucksacks." Those who collapsed were loaded onto a peasant cart, not shot. One sixty-year-old Jewish man, "with his old, heavy suitcase," begged a Hungarian soldier to end his misery, only to receive the soldier's assurance that "he was no murderer"; rather, he was there to offer the Jew a helping hand onto the cart.[104]

Udo Ritgen, a retired military man from West Prussia who had organized attempts to transport some ethnic Germans across the Baltic to western Germany as the Red Army approached in the spring of 1945—the evacuation expeditions that Anna Schwartz had missed—remembered conversations with 750 survivors of the concentration camp in Stutthof. They, too, wanted only "food and transport to the west." Confronted by the competing claims of "thousands of civilians who were waiting for the chance to depart," Ritgen recalled his difficulties overcoming a "psychological resistance" to meeting the survivors' demands. The Stutthof victims ultimately received priority because Ritgen feared that, were the Russians to win, any Germans who failed to flee would be left with "an extremely unreliable element" in their midst.[105]

For M. W., a woman from Lower Silesia, confrontation with the worst aspects of German anti-Semitism came when in the spring of 1946 she was forced by the local Polish militia to exhume Jewish corpses from mass graves for reburial in the local Jewish cemetery. The stripes on what tattered clothing remained signaled that these were victims of concentration camps. In graphic terms M. W. described the work, which left her "smelling like a corpse" and shedding "tears . . . that you couldn't wash away." The only alternative was to "stop crying, be brave, and thus assist in atoning for the crimes that were committed among our people."[106] Recorded in October 1951, a month after Adenauer's announcement of West Germany's willingness to enter serious negotiations with Israel over reparations, M. W.'s testimony echoed the chancellor's formulation of German complicity. Both she and Adenauer were ready to admit that atonement was essential for crimes that other Germans had committed; neither saw that they shared any responsibility for those crimes.

In other German memories, neither Israelis nor Russians nor Poles but eastern European Jews themselves determined the terms of atonement. In some reports, Jews appeared not in striped rags but Red Army uniforms, viciously leading interrogations or ruling over the camps established for ethnic Germans as they awaited deportation to the Soviet Union or transport to western Germany. Mathilde Maurer, a teacher from Transylvania, recalled how "Jews, Hungarians, and Communists were exercising a regime . . . of terror" against all Germans in the camp to which she was sent, and in Stefan Blum's memories of the war's end in Hungary the plundering Communists were "mostly Jews."[107] Hans Kreal, a retired library director from Czechoslovakia, testified that in the internment camp where he was detained he had met a former Jewish bank officer, who at the war's end exchanged his suit for a Czech officer's uniform. The head of all internment camps for Germans in the area after the war, this banker turned soldier, Kreal claimed, had survived under the Nazis because of his Christian wife, and he had found employment working in the agency that distributed seized Jewish property.[108] In Budapest after the war, a farmer claimed that the Jewish editor of one of the city's papers was behind the anti-German terror that commenced once the shooting stopped.[109] And Frau R. A. remembered an incident during her internment in August 1945, when Germans assembled for a Sunday worship service were locked in the church and a "Communist Jewess walked around the church with a lighted cigarette just as the priest consecrated Christ's sacrifice [Messopfer]."[110]

In one expellee memory, a Jew spoke English and wore an American uniform. F. J., from Czechoslovakia, described how Americans first occupied his town before abandoning it to the Soviets. He recalled a "tall, thin officer, blonde with blue eyes," who respectfully expressed sympathy when he noticed a picture of F. J.'s fallen son. This American's response contrasted sharply with the reaction of another officer, a medical doctor, who "tortured" him in German with cries of "*Hitlerschwein*" and "Nazi beast," charging that if he had not supported Hitler, his son would still be alive. This man "was particularly angry when he talked about concentration camps, particularly Buchenwald." When F. J. insisted that he had heard only of Dachau, the doctor responded: "In America, every child knows about it, and you pig, you claim not to know about Buchenwald?" With no explanation of the basis for his judgment, F. J. identified the reason for the officer's hostility: "He was a Jew."[111]

In other German memories, Jews sought not revenge but gain by exploiting the collapse of constituted authority. In the wake of the Red Army invasion of Czechoslovakia, Frau Wilhelmine von Hoffmann remembered her relatives' reports of how Jews "overran the towns" in the areas surrounding Theresienstadt. When former inmates of the concentration camp "could find alcohol there were the usual excesses, and women were seized from nearby houses."[112] Before his expulsion from Czechoslovakia, an engineer, Gustav Grüner, recalled that Jews—"who knows where they came from"—were active on the black market, doing a lively business in American cigarettes.[113] And B. F., a businessman from Breslau, remembered how Poles, "all Jews," rode their bicycles into the surrounding countryside, "their pockets always stuffed full of gold things," calling out: "We pay high prices for gold, rings, and so forth."[114] According to H. F., a civil engineer, the Jews of Pressburg in Czechoslovakia followed more orderly paths; by the spring of 1945 "Jewish owners were all once again in their businesses." Goods were readily available, H. F. recalled, "but compared with the levels at the beginning of 1945, the prices had increased many times over."[115]

In those rare testimonies where eyewitnesses commented explicitly on the systematic murder of European Jews, they did so to underscore their ignorance of what had transpired. Frau E. L. of Posen, in one of the longest individual accounts in the documentation, reported that during her detention in a Polish camp she asked the commandant of the local militia if she could see *Maidanek*, a film showing in a theater frequented by Poles and Russians. She recalled how the film presented the Soviet interrogation of the camp guards, testimony of survivors, "rooms labeled 'Baths,' which were declared to be gas chambers," and "piles of old clothes and shoes, etc." When the commandant asked her opinion, she

dismissed the film as "propaganda," an assessment that the commandant forcefully criticized. However, the editors of the Schieder documentation corroborated Frau E. L.'s ignorance, commenting that "the
answer of the author can be understood as a response to the enormity
of the horrors with which she had just been presented, which were unknown to the German people under the National Socialist regime until
the end of the war."[116]

Despite these claims of ignorance, in their testimonies some expellees
revealed that by the time they recorded what they had suffered, they
knew much of what had happened to Jews. "We are experiencing nothing unusual," mused Hans Graf von Lehndorff, "nothing different from
what millions of people have experienced in the past years." For Lehndorff, Nazi atrocities were no different from Communist crimes, both
emblematic of how the mid–twentieth century had spawned new ways
to express a brutal inhumanity.[117] History had repeated itself, once as
tragedy, once as farce, concluded Maria Zatschek, an expellee from
Czechoslovakia, who remarked, "What a bad comedy all this is: nothing is original, a copy of the Hitler regime, again and again we have to
hear: 'Just as you have treated the Jews.'"[118]

A university lecturer from Prague remembered that during his internment before he was deported, his Czech guards explained that the
model for the treatment of Germans was the Nazi concentration camp.
To make the comparison explicit, "pictures of [these camps] were displayed at the entrance [to the internment camp]. It would have been possible to make similar pictures in our camp as well."[119] The Schieder
project recorded precisely such pictures, in the form of detailed memories in which some Germans compared their suffering with the suffering
of Jews persecuted by Nazis. They provided images that associated the
"horrifying dream[s]" of Germans with other living nightmares.[120]

In their testimonies, some of the eyewitnesses in the Schieder collection acknowledged—directly or indirectly—the crimes committed by
Nazis, yet they did so by describing their own collective suffering, not their
collective accountability. Although ministry officials opposed Schieder's
plans for a concluding volume that would compare the expulsion to other
instances of twentieth-century inhumanity, some testimonies, as well as
some of the editorial commentary, nonetheless relied on such comparisons
to insist on the enormity of what Germans had endured. In seeking to
find parallels to their experience, some expellees settled on a powerful analogy: after the war, the conditions confronting eastern European Germans
"could not have been worse [than] a concentration camp."[121]

German suffering became the medium for describing Nazi atrocities and the moral coin for settling accounts, for "making good again" and atoning for the suffering of others.[122] In parliamentary debates over restitution for victims of the war, Germans and Jews were rhetorically equated. Some of the accounts provided in the documentation project, recorded even as German reparations to Israel filled newspaper headlines, stated the overwhelming similarity of the treatment of all victims and the moral equivalence of their suffering even more explicitly.

In late September 1951, Pastor Pöss recalled a September Sunday seven years earlier when his parishioners left Sunday mass only to be confronted by Czech partisans, now in charge, who instructed all males between sixteen and sixty to report to the local school. Loaded onto a train, they rode a short ways to the edge of a forest, where some fifteen of the strongest men were given shovels and told to dig a trench. When they had completed their work, the remaining forty-five men were ordered out of the train, and immediately recognized that they were being marched to a mass grave. Lined up in three rows, the Germans begged for mercy, but their pleas were met by the order of the Russian commissar, "dressed completely in leather," for the Czech partisans to open fire. With the first machine gun volley, Pöss fell into the grave, where he was buried alive by the bodies of other victims. As they picked over the bodies for valuables, robbing Pöss of a prized silver watch and money, the partisans did not realize that he lived. His benediction was uttered by one of the perpetrators: "You, pastor-whore, now even your Swabian Jesus cannot help you." The mistaken belief of the partisans and their Russian commander that their mission was complete allowed Pöss alone to survive.[123]

In Pöss's account and other stories in the documentation, the unmistakable parallels in the descriptions of German experience at the hands of Communists and Jewish experience at the hands of Germans remained implicit. Now the killing squads spoke Russian or another eastern European language; now the God defiled was Christian, not Jewish. Testimony of starvation so severe that it left its victims waiting only for death came from a German, not a Jewish, survivor.[124] In a town in Czechoslovakia, not Jews but all Germans were forced to identify themselves by "wear-[ing] the yellow armband and accept[ing] the Jewish [ration] card."[125] Russian, not German, camps were ruled by the mottoes "There are only the healthy and the dead"; "Whoever does not work does not need to eat."[126] The man who returned to Łódź in August 1945 "in torn clothes, spiritually completely destroyed, starved to skin and bones, head shaved, limping on crutches," was a German returning from a Soviet labor camp, not a Jew recently liberated from Auschwitz.[127] The youths in uniform who drove their prisoners on a death march with whips, shooting those who were sick or too weak to continue, wore Red Army, not SS or German, police uniforms, and their victims were German, not Soviet, soldiers.[128] The testimonies presented in the documentation depicted Germans not as perpetrators but as victims of "a crime against humanity,"[129] in scenes of families hastily rounded up and then torn apart by the same order heard at Auschwitz, sending "men to the left, women to the right,"[130] as they awaited deportation to unspecified destinations in overcrowded cattle cars that quickly filled with excrement and in which "thirst was worse than hunger."[131] And in the makeshift mortuaries for those who did not survive Soviet labor camps, it was German, not Jewish, teeth that were searched for gold crowns before corpses, "stark naked," were piled unceremoniously onto a wagon, arms and legs trailing from the sides, for transport to a mass grave.[132]

In some reports by Hungarian expellees, Jews worked as translators for the Red Army.[133] Yet even when not explicitly mentioned in German testimonies, Jews were an absent presence, providing the language with which Germans could describe their own experiences. If the campaigns of the Red Army and western Allies to "reeducate" Germans by confronting them with graphic evidence of the crimes of National Socialism did not convince expellees of their "collective guilt," they did provide them with a set of categories for evaluating and measuring their own collective experience as innocent victims.[134]

In 1952 Irene Kahl, from the district of Łódź, a part of Poland annexed to the Reich and, until 1944, site of one of the biggest Jewish ghettos, reported the arrival of the Russians in the winter of 1945. She told of how the Russians "locked us in chamber-like rooms (*Kammer*) . . . , but only the women. The men were sent to another chamber, and on the left, a bright fire burned. On the wall, there were pipes, and the fumes from this fire came into our chamber. Everyone started coughing. We thought we would suffocate. All of a sudden, the door opened, and they hauled me out. My mother screamed, but it did not help; I was raped. Then everyone was let out, everyone's eyes burned from the fumes."[135] Whose hell had Irene Kahl described?

In their commentary on the testimonies from Czechoslovakia, the editors suggested one answer to this question: "In some of [the former concentration] camps, particularly Theresienstadt, only the victims changed:

where Jewish prisoners had once suffered from the National Socialist system of oppression, Germans were now tortured and maltreated."[136] The formulation was important: Germans were punished not for crimes they had committed, but for crimes committed by a faceless regime. When the Czechs inscribed the entrance to one camp with the motto "Pravda vitezi" (Truth prevails), observed the editors, they were "consciously copy[ing] the practice and methods of the . . . National Socialist regime."[137] Innocent Jews, innocent Germans, the editors suggested, both had suffered unjustly.

The documents themselves and the editorial commentary satisfied the needs of some expellees, who agreed to testify as a response to the "constant reporting in the newspapers of the unbelievable charges that are raised against us" and believed that "it's high time that our case was brought to the public, just like that of the German concentration camps."[138] Jews and Germans demanded justice. "Without doubt innocent," a global verdict certified by the editors, "the mass of those affected" depicted themselves individually and collectively as victims of an ideology no less irrational than, and in its reduction of identity to ethnicity similar to, Nazi anti-Semitism.[139] The standard for measuring the sufferings of Germans thus became "the horrible crimes committed against the Jews in Hitler's concentration camps,"[140] while the goal of the Communists was taken to be nothing less than the "de-Germanization" (*Entgermanisierung*) of eastern Europe.[141]

If Jews provided the measure of crimes against Germans, they also occasionally appeared as teachers, willing to forgive, forget, and affirm the common humanity of all victims. Jews helped Germans to understand their fate, and Germans depicted themselves as particularly willing students. Eyewitnesses remembered many "good Jews" whose individual acts of personal generosity and kindness provided evidence of a boundless humanity. Despite their immeasurable losses, they sought not "an eye for an eye and a tooth for a tooth," but rather a world in which they could "live and let live," accepting that "we all have one God."[142]

In some expellee accounts, Jews were not the only erstwhile victims now ready to defend Germans and offer absolution. Although numerous testimonies did feature vengeful Polish commissars who now ruthlessly turned the tables on their former masters, backed by Russian "pistol-packing mamas," these horrifying images were contrasted with ones of forgiving Polish workers and Polish POWs who sought to protect Germans from menacing Red Army soldiers.[143]

Hans Hanel, a farmer imprisoned by the Czechs for a work detail af-

ter the war, recalled how Russian guards brutally beat youthful Germans
for donning the SS uniform late in the war. "Like vultures, they fell upon
them, stripping them, leaving them stark naked," and knocking them
senseless. But he also recalled that his Czech supervisor had greeted him
warmly: "I Communist, you now my brother. I sentenced to 2½ years in
a mine in Saxony, Hitler Germany quite good, regular work, much food,
cigarettes, booze, and much money. You have it good with me." Hanel
also remembered the Czech women who had illicitly passed him bread as
he trudged to his workplace, leading him to conclude, "There can be no
collective guilt for a people [*Volk*], no matter what language it speaks."[144]

In the testimonies of expellees, the forgiving Jew, the humane Russian,
the generous Pole, Czech, Hungarian, Yugoslavian, or Romanian, provided the important lesson that revenge was not inevitable. Their existence made existence of the good German a possibility as well. Reconciliation and forgiveness transcended ideology and ethnicity. Terror was
the product of totalitarian regimes, not individuals, who were able to recognize their common humanity as the basis for reconciliation, understanding, and moving beyond a troubling past in which some German
victims might also have been perpetrators.

"We can leave it to the victims themselves"

Survivors of expulsion, internment, and deportation, expellees were described and described themselves as profoundly changed, granted a privileged perspective by a difficult experience that gave them unique insights
into how best to build a new Germany. Alfred Karasek-Langer, an ethnographer who played a key role in recording the customs and traditions
of the expellees in the 1950s, referred to a German "diaspora," comparable to the "worldwide existence of Jewry." Marginalization and exclusion were transformative; they granted expellees a unique perspective on
the creation of a "new nation" and permitted them to "prepare the path
for a new order of life [*Lebensordnung*]" in West Germany.[145] Expellees
and Jews—both chosen people.

The methodological approach to "contemporary history" outlined by
Schieder and his colleagues granted eyewitnesses a privileged position.
The editors respected silence and selective memory, and they asked no
difficult questions of their sources. Never pausing to comment on the
ways in which testimony was solicited—almost always with the extensive assistance of expellee interest groups—they offered no reflections
on how memories of the past might be blurred by the present in which

they were recorded. Numerous accounts were collected as many as five, six, seven, or more years after the war's end, in a Germany that had changed enormously since 1945.[146] By the early 1950s, West Germans resolutely and all but universally rejected postwar reeducation campaigns intended to convince them that they were collectively responsible for the crimes of the Nazi state. As expellee interest groups met to solicit testimonies for the documentation project, the Cold War was intensifying and anti-Communism was a fundamental characteristic of the political culture of the Federal Republic. Reflections on loss and suffering were formulated against the backdrop of public policy debates over how to address the material needs of expellees, and memories filled with "Mongols" complemented the pronouncements of a chancellor who declared that "Asia begins at the Elbe."[147] Those editors who were themselves expellees also never suggested how their own experiences might influence their relationship to the project. They allowed hundreds of others to narrate the loss of the "German east" without commenting on the fact that this "mass fate" included their own loss and displacement.

"Contemporary history" as it was embodied in the documentation included no consideration of how expellees' stories might be affected by templates of remembrance shaped by the anti-Bolshevik, racist, and anti-Semitic categories of Goebbels's propaganda and Himmler's fantasies, or by shared narratives crafted on the trek, in work camps, or at the meetings of regional interest groups in the Federal Republic. The volumes amply recorded the brutality of the Red Army and the nightmarish justice meted out by postwar partisan governments. The catalogue of horrors thus recorded is staggering, a lasting record of what millions of Germans experienced in eastern Europe at the end of the Second World War. However, the editors never moved beyond what the testimonies recorded to question how their eyewitnesses described their experiences and which memories they chose to exclude.

Franz Neubauer, driven from Czechoslovakia, recalled 19 July 1945 as the "most horrible day" in the history of his community, the day "of expulsion from home and property [*Hof und Scholle*], one could say, the theft of the most precious goods that we owned, the *Heimat* that we loved. . . . In these minutes scenes were played out for which no words exist. . . . The only thing that we could take with us was all our memories, whether good or bad. This was the only thing that no one could steal from these people."[148] Neubauer exaggerated his speechlessness. In the documentation he and hundreds of other eyewitnesses found countless words to express their memories, which in turn were amplified by expert editorial commentary. The thick volumes, produced by some of West Germany's best-known historians and published by the West German state, were the official repositories of Neubauer's and countless others' pasts. The editors solemnly noted, "We can leave it to the victims of this period, who tell of their own experiences, to report with specific details what happened when the Red Army came. They do this with an urgency that would be impossible for anyone telling the story afterward to achieve."[149] Any further commentary was superfluous.

The documentation project, completed only in 1961 with the volume on Yugoslavia, occupied a small bookshelf, but it is unlikely that the weighty tomes filled the leisure hours of many West Germans. Despite print runs of between eight and ten thousand, sales were dismal.[150] However, at least two of the full-length autobiographical accounts that appeared as separate volumes, the diary of the East Prussian doctor Hans Graf von Lehndorff and Käthe von Normann's *Tagebuch aus Pommern, 1945–46* (Diary from Pomerania, 1945–46), quickly found their way into paperback editions and circulated widely. Lehndorff's account drew particular recognition, and remained near the top of the best-seller list in *Die Zeit* in late 1961 and early 1962.[151] In addition, for tens of thousands of expellees—and the millions more for whom they spoke—the very fact that they were asked to bear witness and that their testimonies were collected and preserved made it possible for these German victims to come to terms with one version of the past, grounded in intense personal memories that became crucial parts of public memory in the early history of the Federal Republic. Public commemoration and individual catharsis were thus parts of the same process.[152]

The volumes that documented how Germans had been driven from their historic homelands also sanctioned the accounts of expellee interest groups, journalists, and novelists, which did not carry the same scholarly credentials. Who could doubt popular fictionalized versions of similar stories when the editors cited them to corroborate the evidence they presented?[153] Who needed more footnotes, when the editors provided so many? The project did not include the only descriptions of the loss of the "German east" available in the Federal Republic, but as one newspaper reviewer expressed it, they delivered the "irrefutable proof of the accuracy of those [other] descriptions."[154] The work of Schieder and his colleagues thus amounted to a massive scholarly seal of approval for all accounts of the "expulsion of Germans from east-central Europe," even for readers who never opened the substantial blue-bound volumes in which this version of "contemporary history" rested.

"On the boundary between the real world and legend"

In introducing the final debates on the reparations treaty with Israel, Adenauer characterized ratification as a way to "end one of the saddest chapters in our history," not as the beginning of a process of locating that past in an understanding of long-term trends in modern German history. In the memories of Adenauer and most West Germans, the past to be overcome in the 1950s, the past to be incorporated systematically as part of the present, was not the past of German crimes but the past of German suffering. No institutional attempts were made to keep competing pasts present in the first decade of the Federal Republic's history. In Adenauer's cabinet, there was no Ministry for Survivors of Nazi Persecution and Nazi Concentration Camps, no prestigious team of historians to document the expulsion of Jews or other victims of the Nazis from east-central—or for that matter, western, southern, or northern—Europe. Neither West German historians nor the West German state thought it necessary to collect such eyewitness accounts as another vital source for writing "contemporary history." Jews, systematically excluded from German society after 1933 and from the parts of Europe occupied by the Nazis after 1938, were once again excluded, this time from the contemporary history of the Federal Republic.

To be sure, immediately after the war anyone who wanted to learn of Nazi atrocities needed look no further than Allied reeducation campaigns and the massive documentation compiled by the prosecutors for the Nuremberg trials and the series of Allied legal proceedings against a string of lesser Nazi officials and collaborators that followed Nuremberg. There were also a handful of studies that detailed some of the worst Nazi crimes and the ways in which the Nazi state had governed and carried out the "final solution" either directly or with the help of collaborationist governments in eastern Europe.[155] The work of the Institute for Contemporary History—headed by Rothfels and home to such talented co-workers as Broszat—included some of the earliest systematic analyses of the Nazi state and Nazi occupation policies in eastern Europe. However, even in these works, individual voices of the victims of Germans were rarely heard; suffering seldom had a face, name, or specific location.[156] Following a spate of survivor memoirs published in the western zones of occupation in the late 1940s, West Germans showed little interest in reading accounts of the victims of Germans. By the 1950s, the war stories that most interested them were those of German victims who were not also Jewish.[157]

For many West Germans, the next postwar confrontation with the personalized face of the Nazis' attempt to exterminate all European Jews was at performances of *The Diary of Anne Frank,* which came to the German stage in 1956. In an insightful exploration of the reception of Anne Frank in the Federal Republic, Alvin Rosenfeld describes the profound impact the play had on thousands of West Germans, and the Anne Frank youth clubs and commemorative services that it spawned. More than a decade after the war's end, West Germans showed a willingness to confront the face of Jewish suffering, a significant move toward an expanded discussion of the Nazi past and its consequences. Even in this context, however, the play considerably toned down the specifically Jewish characteristics of the story and transformed Anne Frank into a universalized symbol of all human suffering. Like the "good Jews" in the accounts of expellees, the Anne Frank of the play affirmed that it was still possible "to believe in the goodness of mankind," the line that also appeared on the cover of the 1955 German-language edition of the *Diary*.[158] In contrast, the pasts of the expellees were systematically recorded not as drama but as irrefutable fact, part of an authenticated public record that sought to establish not that humanity was fundamentally good, but that Soviet Communism was fundamentally bad.

Writing in 1955, the ethnographer Karasek-Langer remarked on the emergence of a new genre of "legend-like stories" in the postwar years, told by those who had been forced from their eastern European homes. They were the medium through which expellees offered a response to their experience. Many of these stories, "on the boundary between the real world and legend," emerged "out of the deepest subconscious, legends of the end of the world; predictions and prophesies, future-oriented dreams, signs from heaven and appearances of the virgin Mary, stories of guilt and atonement, punishments by God, curses and blessings, miraculous salvation, the return of the dead."[159] The accounts recorded in the Schieder documentation project included no appearances of Mary, but they did provide another view of "the end of the world." Another form of legend-building, they were enshrined as "contemporary history" by some of the Federal Republic's most important historians.

Expellees did not leave the past behind, and in some testimonies the past took literal form in a "handful of dirt, wrapped in a handkerchief, and carried into the unknown"; or, as the Romanian priest Friedrich Krauss reported, it was carried in the "museum wagon" that transported his lifelong work on local dialects, books on regional history, and a "bearskin, intended for the German hunting museum."[160] The multivolume documentation of the expulsion was another sort of museum, housing parts of the past that should not be forgotten or "mastered," but preserved.[161] An early review of the documentation asked, "Do we really want to forget what was far and away the most horrifying event of the last war?"[162] Schieder and his colleagues left West Germans with no doubts about which event should claim that status. Their collective efforts were intended as a guarantee that no one in the Federal Republic would forget.

CHAPTER FOUR

Prisoners of Public Memory

"Homecoming 1955"

"It is 44 minutes past midnight on Tuesday, October 11, 1955. 'Now the war is over.'" A newspaper reporter captured these reflections of a German soldier, Alois Bischof, who had just returned to Heidelberg after a lengthy involuntary stay in the Soviet Union. Bischof looked on in amazement as four policemen blocked traffic, making it possible for the little bus that carried him to thread its way through a jubilant throng of some 150 well-wishers of all ages. He had come home to "tread on the soil of Heidelberg . . . ten years after the end of hostilities." The account of this homecoming continued:

> Searching, the eyes of the returning POWs survey the mass of humanity. There—"Alois, A-l-o-i-s, my little boy,—now you're with your mother. Now everything is all right." The big man yells, "Mother," and twisting and turning their way through the crowd [mother and son] make their way to each other. Ten years have passed. Hardly anyone can control their emotions. A hug and kisses, embraces and mumbled words of love, and flowers, flowers.

Friends and neighbors respectfully withdrew, understanding that mother and son needed a moment alone. The reporter solemnly concluded, "He has come, he is there, home again, the returnee, and that is what is most important. It will be possible to see him later. Now is not the time to ask questions."[1]

Throughout the Federal Republic in the fall of 1955, the same scene was played out again and again. Bischof was only one of the "Ten Thousand," the last German prisoners of war to be released from Soviet camps. Although some returned to the German Democratic Republic, the overwhelming majority only passed through East Germany on their way to a final destination in the West. They were joined by several hundred women and eastern Germans deported to do forced labor in the Soviet Union or arrested on charges of spying in the Soviet zone of occupation after 1945. All had now been released as a consequence of negotiations between Chancellor Adenauer and his Soviet counterparts, conducted in Moscow in early September.

Ten years after the war's end, German soldiers captured headlines and the West German imagination without firing a shot. In countless reports in the daily press, illustrated magazines, and newsreels, their stories became Germany's stories.[2] Popular representations of returning prisoners of war emphasized that they were victims of show trials, sentenced for offenses they had never committed. As the press account of Alois Bischof's return emphasized, their homecoming marked the symbolic end of the war. In 1945, German soldiers had come home defeated. A decade later, those returning from the Soviet Union were depicted as the "last soldiers of the great war," courageous men who had fought and won the battle against Communist brutality.[3] However, these soldiers were also men who could cry, heroes of gentle strength, ready to rejoin their families and assume their part in building a strong but peaceful Germany.

Press accounts of the Moscow trip and its aftermath also featured Adenauer, himself a father and grandfather, as the "demagogic patriarch," a leader who by 1955 had won enormous favor with the western Allies and the West German electorate.[4] An army of journalists followed the West German chancellor to the Soviet capital in September 1955, using the trip as an occasion to review his record of accomplishment and his ability to perform effectively as a leader on the world stage. The popular press presented Adenauer as the right kind of leader for a new Germany. As the POWs returned in 1955, this forceful political leader, the "good father of Germany," stood at the head of the national family.[5]

The year 1955 proved an opportune time to reflect on all that West Germans had accomplished in the previous decade. In a series of special articles in the *Süddeutsche Zeitung* under the heading "Ten Years After," contributors affirmed that the Federal Republic had not only cleared away the rubble but had also permanently banished the political, economic, and social instability that had destroyed the Weimar Republic. Headlines announced what most West Germans acknowledged: "In Bonn, the Clocks Run Differently Than in Weimar." Although for many West Germans the promise and possibility of the "economic miracle" still exceeded the reality, Adenauer and his economics minister, Ludwig Erhard, had firmly established the authority of their Christian Democratic government by traveling along the "Path from Starvation to Prosperity."[6] Few questioned that the Federal Republic would continue along this route.

Returning POWs offered a critical perspective on this record of postwar accomplishment. The same newspapers that carried celebrations of the "economic miracle" presented returning soldiers as time travelers, "woolly mammoths who were locked eternally in the ice," Robinson Crusoes encountering a dramatically altered world.[7] Completely unprepared for a West Germany in the throes of rapid economic growth and expansion, POWs appeared as sage observers from another age. Men whose maturity and experience made them expert commentators on the dangers of Communism, they were also acutely attuned to the dangers of excess in an expanding consumer society. In the pages of daily newspapers, returning POWs offered their thoughts not only on what they had experienced in the Soviet Union but also on what they confronted in the Federal Republic.[8]

Historians of foreign relations have told a different story of the release of the last German POWs by the Soviets in the fall of 1955. In their account it is a geopolitical, not a domestic, drama that is played out, and the major actors were not German soldiers but Adenauer and the Soviet leaders, Nikolai Bulganin, Nikita Khrushchev, and Vyacheslav Molotov. This version of diplomatic wrangling and high politics goes something like this:

Adenauer traveled to Moscow in September 1955 to achieve better relations with the Soviets in order to pursue the long-term goal of Soviet acquiescence to the unification of a divided Germany. The trip was the chancellor's first major diplomatic act following the western Allies' suspension of the statute of occupation in May 1955, which ended most of their oversight of West German affairs. The Allies' act was the reward for the Federal Republic's willingness to enter the North Atlantic Treaty Organization (NATO); however, West Germany's agreement to rearm and enter a western European and North American anti-Communist military alliance headed by the United States drove even deeper the wedge between East and West Germany.[9]

When Adenauer arrived in the Soviet capital, German unity topped the agenda of no major power, and the West German chancellor was fully aware that he could not negotiate terms for reunification on his own. Meeting in Geneva in July 1955, the leaders of the Four Powers—France,

the United States, Britain, and the Soviet Union—had confirmed that German unification belonged to a distant, unspecified future. The Soviets,
for their part, had recognized the German Democratic Republic as an
independent nation and responded to West German entry into NATO
with the formal inclusion of East Germany in the Warsaw Pact, the East
Bloc counterpart to the western alliance. They now declared themselves
ready to accept two independent Germanys in place of Four-Power reg-
ulation of a Germany that would one day be unified. At Geneva, the Soviets made it clear that all future talks over German unification must include both German states. To underscore their stance toward East
Germany, on their way home from the talks the Soviet leaders stopped
off in East Berlin for an official state visit to sanctify the GDR's inclusion in the Warsaw Pact.[10]

Adenauer presented his trip to Moscow as a necessary step toward a
unified Germany. Rejecting charges that he was the "chancellor of the
Allies," whose forced march into the western alliance rigidified the Cold
War divide and jeopardized chances for German reunification, Adenauer
maintained that only by establishing diplomatic relations with Moscow
could West Germany enhance the chances of bringing together both Germanys, East and West. The possibility of accepting the existence of two
German embassies in Moscow was justified because this move might be
necessary to reunite Germany in the long term.[11]

In this chapter, I argue that Adenauer's trip and its aftermath, a central concern for historians of geopolitics and east-west relations and a
key marker in the development of Soviet–West German relations after
1945, had yet another set of meanings for contemporaries, meanings that
can be found not in diplomatic communiqués or the memoirs of those
who met in Moscow, but in the pages of the daily press. In accounts of
the POWs' return, Adenauer appears not only as a geopolitical strategist
but also as a compassionate, if forceful, father, insisting on the release
of the nation's sons. His trip is not only a diplomatic mission but also an
exploration of competing understandings of the Nazis' war in the Soviet
Union and a reflection on postwar modes of economic recovery. When
German soldiers return home in the fall of 1955, they are far more than
mere pawns in the diplomatic deal-making of great men and great powers; rather, the press gives them the best lines, permitting them to offer
commentaries on the meanings of the Second World War and postwar
development in the Federal Republic.[12]

"Homecoming 1955"—the return of the last POWs from the Soviet
Union—made for a riveting media event. It is difficult to imagine that

any West German was unaffected by the news. In addition to the large contingent of reporters who accompanied Adenauer to Moscow, the press was also ready at Friedland, the town in Lower Saxony through which returnees began to pass in October 1955, and from there reporters followed returnees as they journeyed to their homes throughout the Federal Republic. Announcements of the names of returnees over the radio became occasions for gatherings in local pubs, moments of celebration and reflection. Events surrounding the homecoming of the POWs were also staged as photo opportunities for the daily press and newsreel photographers; rich illustrations framed straight news accounts and feature stories, illuminating the personal fates of returning POWs and the families awaiting them.[13] The communication of these visual images by the press was still enormously important in an age when television remained a luxury available only to a small minority of West Germans and reading a daily paper and illustrated magazines was the one leisure activity in which most West Germans regularly indulged.[14]

From distinguished newspapers like the conservative *Frankfurter Allgemeine Zeitung* to illustrated weeklies like *Revue*, accounts were divided in assessing the significance of Adenauer's trip to Moscow for the future prospects of German unification. They also differed in their treatment of the event, ranging from the cool intellectual tone and hard-nosed political analysis of the liberal weekly *Die Zeit* to the sensationalism of publications like *Der Stern*. However, despite their political differences and the range of audiences they sought to address, these publications presented a remarkably homogeneous image of the "national homecoming" of the POWs, who reminded Germans that "they are not alone, rather, they belong to a nation [*Volk*]." The soldiers' return marked not just the reunion of individual families, but the "unity of the nation."[15] Prisoners for ten years and more in the Soviet Union, returning German soldiers became prisoners of public memory in the Federal Republic, conscripted this time to help West Germans order the past and critically assess the present.

"Father of Our Prisoners of War"

Fathers and sons awaited release in Soviet POW camps, and a father and grandfather flew to Moscow to bring them home. Adenauer was seventy-nine when he left for the Soviet capital. The dominant political presence in the 1950s, so powerful that the era is permanently associated with his name, Adenauer was a political leader who was known in intensely personal terms by the West German public. Particulars of Adenauer's life were no secret by the mid-1950s, and the Christian Democratic Union consciously sought to present the chancellor not only as an accomplished world leader but also as an approachable, humane man. The cult of personality surrounding Adenauer, crucial to CDU electoral strategies, included the image of Adenauer as a loving husband, father, and grandfather many times over. Anyone who followed the illustrated weeklies knew from the serialized version of Adenauer's "authorized biography" that his first wife, Emma, mother of three, had died young, the victim of kidney failure in 1916. With his second wife, Gussie, nineteen years his junior, he raised four more Adenauers. She suffered from a blood disease that led to her death in 1948, attended until the bitter end by her husband and children. As a nurse interviewed for the authorized biography confided to hundreds of thousands of West German readers, "perhaps it was a comfort for some of our other patients at the time simply to know that such families as the Adenauers existed."[16] Details of the chancellor's double loss and the comfort he received from his children and grandchildren were part of the public knowledge of the private man.

It is suggestive to compare this popular representation with that of the last German chancellor to contemplate a trip to Moscow. Propaganda attempts to portray Hitler's "human qualities" in the 1930s featured him clad in his "simple" uniform, adorned only with the Iron Cross that he had won as a "simple soldier," or offering bedside solace and "fatherly gentleness" not to a wife, but to a dying "Old Fighter," an early Nazi convert. His single status may have permitted Nazi propagandists to position him as a matinee idol, but when they pictured him surrounded by adoring children, the children were not his own.[17] Adenauer's public persona, in contrast, was not the product of a carefully orchestrated propaganda machine, but his well-publicized identity as a loving father and grandfather was based on lived, not imagined, relationships, allowing at least some West Germans to recognize in him a paternal empathy that a childless Führer could never have experienced.

It was perhaps this image of Adenauer that convinced some West Germans that they could address him directly with the concerns they wanted him to present to Soviet leaders once it was officially announced that he would travel to Moscow. Letter writers appealed to the chancellor not only as the head of the West German state, but as "a loving father," a man "who himself has daughters and will understand a worried mother."[18]

For other petitioners, Adenauer became not just one father among many, but the "father of our prisoners of war," who would know how to bring his sons home.[19]

In the summer of 1955, as Adenauer prepared for his visit with the Soviet leaders, loving mothers could tell the father of the nation about their children's accomplishments, confirming the character of the boys they had sent off to war. Liesel Hartmann boasted that her son, "the best fighter pilot in the world, was awarded the Knight's Cross." His "greatest achievements" included "356 kills in the space of one and a half years on the eastern front at the age of 22 and 23." Brave in war, Hartmann's son continued to fight battles of a different sort, "prov[ing] his character" despite all temptations presented by the Soviets. To promises of early release in return for cooperation with the Russians, he consistently gave the same response: "Not on your life, I am a German, and I'll remain a German, and I won't do anything for the Russians."[20] The typical POW, another patiently waiting wife explained to the chancellor, was like her husband, who was able to know his eleven-year-old daughter only from photographs because he "did his duty, and was true to his oath to defend his fatherland."[21]

Wives who had been "standing alone in the struggle of life for sixteen years" expressed their dismay that putative "widows and orphans should carry the burdens of the war for their entire lives" with no news of their husbands' fates. The woman who had lost one husband in the First World War did not want to lose a second. The mother who wanted only "once more to embrace my son, whom I love more than anything," reminded Adenauer that "a mother without a child is a lonely person."[22] Letter writers took the occasion to describe not only the predicament of loved ones but also their own circumstances and the impossibility of surviving on a pension that barely covered basic necessities. The "ten-year battle of a mother with children" paralleled the ten-year battle of husbands in Soviet camps, leaving some women to consider "leaving this life behind."[23] All appealed to the chancellor to use his trip to Moscow to determine what had become of their husbands and children and to make their families whole.

Adenauer also heard from children without fathers. A girl from Frankfurt, whose father had been missing for eleven years and who cried at her mother's reading of a letter from this man she knew only from photographs, explained to the chancellor that she would gladly travel to Russia in search of her father herself were she not "much too little and stupid." Instead she appealed to the taller and wiser chancellor to de-

termine her father's whereabouts.[24] Doubtless she would have agreed with
the eighteen-year-old who had last seen her father in June 1944 and exhorted Adenauer to "address the release of all POWs as the very most
important topic in Moscow," adding the special wish that the chancellor bring her father home with him on the plane.[25] In another instance,
elementary-school children in the town of Kisselbach appealed to the
chancellor on behalf of their classmate, an expellee from Upper Silesia
who had lost her father in the war and whose uncle was still in a Soviet
camp. They hoped the chancellor had the "strong nerves" he would need
as he "followed a difficult path [to Moscow] for Germany."[26]

The letters to Adenauer played out family dramas, describing relations
between wives and husbands, stoical "mothers standing alone," and children for whom fathers were distant strangers or completely unknown.
By 1955, these were familiar scripts for millions of women and children
who had experienced the separations and displacements of war. "The internal and external wounds of the war [are] now largely healed and life
[has] once again taken on meaning in recent years," one letter writer,
identifying herself as the "mother of a prisoner of war," conceded, but
she also reminded Adenauer that West Germans had not forgotten men
who had spent "the best years of life behind barbed wire" and women
whose prime was all but past.[27] Adenauer flew to Moscow as the head
of a sovereign state, entering negotiations with a major superpower over
the possibilities of normalizing relations, establishing formal diplomatic
contact, and achieving German unification. He also went as the "good
father of Germany," charged with ending the uncertainty of thousands
of families and reuniting fathers with children, husbands with wives, and
sons with parents.

Among appeals addressed to a kind, loving father, however, were more
critical voices that questioned whether the chancellor was up to the task.
An exasperated wife contrasted the "anxious avoidance of [the POW] question by the leading men of the government" with the steadfastness of
POWs, who "despite ten years of slavery, mistreatment, and starvation
still *have the courage to emphasize their innocence to their slaveholders.*"[28]
Another appeal ventured the view that the men in Bonn were permanently
paralyzed by their fear of losing prestige should they enter into direct negotiations with their former enemies. "We wives of POWs no longer understand the attitude of the government, after we've been comforted again
and again with instructions that any kind of intervention would worsen
the conditions of our men. Can they be made any worse?"[29] These and
other women could claim to speak for "thousands of women, mothers,

and children who have already waited for ten years and repeatedly have suspected that the government is more energetic in all other questions."[30] Individual writers received a form-letter response from the Foreign Ministry, assuring them that the chancellor had received "thousands of petitions" and would do everything in his power for the POWs; "there should be no doubt that all Germans expect an answer to this question as soon as possible."[31] However, this reassurance also suggested how acutely aware Adenauer's advisors were that doubts existed.

Erich Dombrowski, an editorial writer for the *Frankfurter Allgemeine Zeitung,* made it clear that the personal views expressed in petitions to Adenauer reflected widely held public concerns: "For us the fate of the POWs plays no small role. . . . Too much bodily and spiritual pain is associated with it." As Dombrowski doubtless knew, public opinion polls from 1955 indicated that 27 percent of respondents had a relative either missing in action on the eastern front or known to be in a Soviet POW camp. Another 15 percent claimed to have a personal acquaintance who fell into one of those categories.[32] For this reason, continued Dombrowski, raising his rhetorical level a notch, "a head of state has seldom . . . been accompanied by so many hopes and expectations of the simplest folk. Their wishes are not excessive, they don't want castles on the moon, rather, they want domesticity [*Häuslichkeit*], family life," presently unattainable because they are "constantly left in worry and fear because their loved ones are prevented from returning."[33] For many West Germans, then, the chancellor's charge in Moscow included not only national reunification but the restoration of "domesticity."

A Glimpse through the "Silk Curtain"

Press coverage of Adenauer's trip focused on the fact that competing economic systems were facing off in Moscow. A decade after defeat by the Red Army, West Germans were returning to the Soviet Union, this time armed with the symbols of capitalist affluence. If Adenauer was the "father of our POWs," he was also a patriarch who headed a successful market economy and had provided quite well for his family since the end of the war.

Newsreels featured the state-of-the-art Lufthansa aircraft that transported the chancellor and his entourage, two shining new "Super Constellations" that were among the first four-propeller planes purchased for a national fleet, licensed to ply the skies only since May.[34] The technological superiority of goods made not for but in West Germany was evident in Adenauer's demand that his personal Mercedes limousine meet him in Moscow, after being hauled to the Soviet capital on a specially chartered German train. Together with a second Mercedes, assigned to Foreign Minister Heinrich von Brentano, the car was celebrated in the illustrated magazine *Der Stern* as a genuine tourist attraction in Moscow, carrying not only West German political leaders but dreams of West German economic prosperity as well.[35] The West Germans' train also included a sophisticated "secure" car for secret discussions, dubbed the "embassy in the ghetto" by journalists, who were apparently unconcerned about the associations this metaphor might evoke only a little more than a decade after the Germans had first created, then destroyed, Jewish ghettos in Poland and other parts of eastern Europe.[36]

The contrast between postwar capitalist recovery and the dreariness of life under Communism was highlighted in a number of press reports that described Soviet department store windows displaying goods no Soviet citizen could afford at prices twice as high as those in West Germany. Massive expenditures on representative "monumental buildings"—not to be confused with massive expenditures on monumental Mercedes limousines—could not hide the "completely collapsed, premodern churches, the grey back alleys . . . , streets that were barely passable. Undifferentiated poverty begins twenty, at most fifty meters behind the whitewashed facades. Shocked children peer out, clad in dirty, undefined clothing," evidence of a society that produced "guns, not butter, [where] the standard of living of the population was reduced in order to invest everything in armaments."[37] Under such conditions, how could Soviets ever learn the lesson, pronounced by West Germany's economics minister Ludwig Erhard, that "free consumer choice" belonged to the "inalienable freedoms of humanity." Erhard's "will to consume" had permitted Germans to surpass the Soviets in a way that Hitler's "will to power" had not.[38] In Moscow, signs of Communist inefficiency and uniformity were everywhere: "Streetcars stumble through the outer districts, squeaking as if they were driving with five wet fingers over glass. And because all automobiles are of the same sort, the noise of honking horns and motors is uniform as well."[39] The contrast between the course of economic development since 1945 in a defeated Germany and a victorious Soviet Union could scarcely have been clearer.

What separated capitalism from Communism also registered in competing conceptions of women's proper place. In the streets of Moscow, reporters spotted women doing hard physical labor, "narrow-faced, thin women who mix cement in dusty machines, haul bricks, clear out foundations, paint the white lines on asphalt streets": such were the scenes of daily life "over which Lenin and Stalin stand guard." These images also conjured up German experience in the immediate postwar years when "women of the rubble" had rolled up their sleeves to clear away the past. Sentenced to live under a political order that permanently forced women into men's jobs, it was no wonder that "[Soviet] women understand nothing of how to put on a hat at a jaunty angle or the nuances of makeup." Even women who had the wherewithal to be consumers still seemed unable to get it right, appearing at the ballet in "tasteless dresses with crudely painted lips."[40]

These pictures affirmed that East and West were divided not just by an "iron curtain" that separated political systems. In addition, what the illustrated magazine Der Stern called a "silk curtain" cordoned off Communist command economies from capitalist worlds of fashion and elegance.[41] Reporters who followed the chancellor to Moscow noted the absence of "feminine souls who might tempt one to take a look."[42] A cityscape dominated by bearers of construction equipment, not sexual difference, meant that "Moscow seems sexless," not only because "everywhere women work as construction workers and on road crews and get the same wages for doing tough men's work" but also because the city was lacking "the scent of the feminine, a touch of the erotic."[43]

In his memoirs, Adenauer had nothing to say about "the scent of the feminine," but he did make implicit comparisons between Moscow in 1955 and German cities a decade earlier.[44] For many Germans, the early postwar years defined a world in upheaval, where women had done men's work. Looking back from the perspective of the mid-1950s, they saw women's employment in nonconventional jobs as an aberration, dictated by the exigencies of war and defeat. Restoration in the Federal Republic included the attempt to reconstruct woman's proper place. A West German woman should be a wife and mother, working in the home, not on a construction site, and spending the money that men earned. The SPD leader Carlo Schmid, who accompanied Adenauer to Moscow, was reported to reject even comparisons between 1955 Moscow and Germany in 1946; at least back then, he said, German "young women had always tried to look nice."[45] In the Soviet Union, however, circumstances considered abnormal by West Germans apparently defined the norm. Journalists who used Adenauer's visit to present a tale of two societies a decade after the war left little doubt about who had won the peace.

The "Triumph of Reason" and the "Conquest of Moscow"

West German press accounts of the Moscow visit focused on what distanced the postwar Federal Republic from the Soviet Union, but when formal meetings between Adenauer and Soviet leaders commenced on 9 September, Bulganin, Khrushchev, and Molotov made it clear that they were far more intent on remembering the war's devastation than on comparing modes of postwar economic recovery. In a series of exchanges that a *New York Times* reporter characterized as "meat-axe blunt" and a diplomatic parley that became little more than a "free exchange of blows," Adenauer and his counterparts rehearsed very different modes of "coming to terms with the past."[46]

All agreed that German and Soviet suffering in the Second World War defined a common interest in establishing the bases for peaceful coexistence. Adenauer emphasized the centrality of the POW question, an unresolved legacy of the war "that touches virtually every German family."[47] Bulganin, however, countered that Soviet families had their own memories of the four years of the "Great Patriotic War" and were not about to forget the "crimes of German militarism and fascism." He conceded that most Germans hated war as much as all Soviets, but those German soldiers still in the Soviet Union were genuine criminals, justly sentenced by Soviet courts. Although Bulganin provided no specifics to support this accusation, he made it clear that whatever Adenauer and the majority of West Germans might think, the men still under detention belonged behind barbed wire because they had "lost their honor. They are violent criminals, arsonists, murderers of women, children, and the elderly." Any discussion of the fate of these 9,626 war criminals, he insisted, must evoke memories of their victims, who numbered in the millions, "shot, gassed, and burned alive in German concentration camps"; "the 5.5 million innocent people killed in Majdanek and Auschwitz"; the "70,000 shot in Kiev and Babi Yar," death counts noticeably absent from West German reckoning of the cost of the war in the early 1950s. What Soviet citizen could forget the "tons of women's hair . . . taken from women tortured to death," the "burned cities and villages, and the women, youths, and children who were killed"? The German soldiers still in Soviet captivity were there precisely because "they [had] committed these horrifying acts."[48]

Although Adenauer insisted that he and Bulganin should avoid playing the role of "heralds of antiquity, who shout mutual recriminations at one another," and admitted the extent of Russian suffering, he also sought to draw a moral balance sheet, emphasizing that "in Germany as well, many bad things happened during the war" once the Red Army had pushed westward out of its own territory on the way to Berlin. In exceptional cases, German soldiers may have committed excesses, but even the western Allies had been willing to overturn sentences for war crimes, issued immediately after the war in an "atmosphere burdened by emotional feelings."[49] Adenauer called on the Soviets to follow this example.

Khrushchev, for his part, categorically rejected any suggestion that it was possible to establish a moral equivalence between German crimes against the Soviet Union and the Red Army's prosecution of the war against Germany. The round, bald Soviet leader little resembled a "herald of antiquity," but he had no difficulty assessing responsibility for the war's devastation, declaring that if "Hitler and his gang had not conjured up this calamity," the Red Army would never have appeared on German soil to "fulfill its holy obligation to its people with a great sacrifice of blood." German "war criminals" who were worried about their families should never have left home in the first place. Molotov echoed Khrushchev's sentiments, saying that "if Hitler's army had not attacked the Soviet Union, then the German people would have suffered nothing." Indeed, it was ultimately up to the Red Army to do what Germans could not: liberate the German people from Hitler.[50]

In this diplomatic point-counterpoint, Adenauer intoned another important theme in the postwar West German account of the triumph of National Socialism by insisting that the crucial question was why "after 1933 did the great powers allow Hitler to become so important?" With Molotov across from him, there is little doubt that Adenauer included the Soviet Union among the guilty parties; the nonaggression pact the Soviet minister had negotiated with Germany in 1939 had certainly enhanced Hitler's importance.[51] Molotov was "official witness to both visits, the old combatant of 1939," as one newspaper account characterized him, the survivor of power struggles in the wake of Stalin's death in 1953.[52] The West German chancellor also pointed to the 1936 Berlin Olympics as an example of unwarranted international acclaim that had elevated Hitler "in the eyes of many a stupid German."[53] German but not stupid, Adenauer emphasized that he had realized in the 1930s where things were heading. He came to Moscow as a German who had lived through the Third Reich but had consistently distanced himself from the Nazis.

Most West German papers chose not to publish the detailed accounts of Babi Yar and Kharkov, Auschwitz and Majdanek, that Bulganin provided. However, they did comment at length on the drama of the meeting and a prevailing "passion that was not common in international conference rooms."[54] Some reports also used the opportunity to state at length what Adenauer had only suggested, conjuring up pictures of the "many women and girls who came over the border, destroyed after many rapes, and others who were driven by fear into the seas of Mecklenburg." For "the sake of the dead," exhorted the *Frankfurter Allgemeine Zeitung*, it was essential for all Germans to remember what "millions of women and children would never forget."[55] Adenauer needed little more than a reference to "horrible things" to invoke a past that by 1955 was central to the public memory of the Federal Republic and was being cast in print in the massive documentation project edited by Schieder and his associates. As one commentator remarked, "Every German, however much he or she may condemn Hitler's aggressive war against the Soviet Union, knows that the chancellor was in the right when he made this point."[56]

Adenauer was also praised, however, for not dwelling unduly on the "evil spirit of the past."[57] Acknowledging the "weight of the past" without succumbing to the emotions that burdened it meant that the Moscow meeting could have a "purifying function."[58] In the midst of the heated exchange when Adenauer and his counterparts tallied their wartime losses, Khrushchev had warned that "we cannot allow ourselves to be overcome by passions," and contemporary accounts praised Adenauer for avoiding precisely such public displays of emotional excess.[59] On the contrary, he was depicted as a head of state who, by exercising self-restraint, "prov[ed] his strength of character."[60] The weekly illustrated magazine *Der Stern* credited Adenauer with "making the decisive contribution to the triumph of reason," and its banner headline pronounced that "In Moscow Reason Was the Winner."[61]

Many accounts of the Moscow trip commented extensively on the amount of alcohol consumed. Mitigating the effects of Russian vodka were healthy doses of olive oil, a home remedy administered by Hans Globke, one of Adenauer's most influential advisors, whose credentials also included doling out an important legal commentary on the Nazis' racist Nuremberg Laws. Globke's methods allowed the German delegation to keep up with the Russians; no one could take advantage of German men who were properly prepared.[62] Adenauer, in any case, could hold his own, able to drink without getting drunk. A sober leader of a sober Germany could be passionate without succumbing to his emotions.

Adenauer emphasized that "one cannot equate Hitler and his followers with the German people," and his self-controlled behavior was another indication that Germany was now headed by a different sort of man. Reporters made the point even more forcefully when they described how on the second day of talks the dance of diplomatic exchanges was followed by a performance of the ballet *Romeo and Juliet* in the evening. At the end, the Russian and German fathers rose and clasped hands, no longer warring Capulets and Montagues, but the reasonable heads of sovereign nations who sought to learn from past tragedies in order not to repeat them.[63]

Popular accounts praised Adenauer for his ability to control both his head and his heart; he had gone to Moscow to end the war that Hitler had begun, deploying not tanks but common sense. A cartoon in the *Süddeutsche Zeitung* depicted a diminutive "Soldier 1945" (*Landser*) being marched off, hands in the air, at the command of massive Red Army soldiers with fixed bayonets, and contrasted this image with that of a triumphant *Kanzler,* ten years later, receiving the salute of a Red Army honor guard, now at attention with bayonets pointing respectfully in the air (Fig. 20).[64] This new model of a German statesman controlled his temper, moderated his emotions, commanded respect, and knew when to renew his inner strength by attending a Sunday church service in a tiny Catholic chapel hidden away in the midst of a godless Moscow.[65] However, he also recognized when actions spoke louder than words. After two days of discussions with his Soviet counterparts, seeing no appreciable progress in any aspect of the negotiations, Adenauer determined that things were going nowhere fast. In a scene straight out of a Hollywood western, celebrated in contemporary accounts and raised to the status of legend in most standard treatments since, the chancellor proceeded to use an open telephone line—easily tapped by the Soviets—to order his plane to be readied for an early departure because of Soviet intransigence.[66]

Adenauer's memoir records that he told Bulganin explicitly that what most concerned him was the fate of the POWs, an issue of "particularly great psychological significance after everything the German people have endured." Without resolution of this question, Adenauer insisted that he could never convince his constituents to accept a normalization of relations between West Germany and the Soviet Union.[67] In the mythology of the Federal Republic, this show of single-minded determination prompted the Soviets to back down. By the end of the day, Bulganin was promising that nothing would stand in the way of the release of German POWs (Fig. 21).

"Like generals of opposing armies who have met in many battles and now with great uncertainty meet face to face to discuss a cease-fire for the first time," Adenauer and the Soviets had squared off.[68] The German chancellor who stared down the Soviets was not, as a reporter for the *Rheinischer Merkur* put it, an "old downtrodden horse—the comparison was made in a private discussion with a Moscow radio reporter— that in the twilight of its life sets to its task with gentleness and tractability." Rather, he had shown himself to be "robust as an old general of the guard," "full of vitality and resilience," the "man who, with kilometers of open terrain in front of him, was safely in control of the power of command and with impressive tenacity held the line at the front," an "indefatigable seventy-nine-year-old." This was the man who had achieved "the conquest of Moscow."[69]

Recent research has established that by the summer of 1955 the Soviets were more than ready to send home the last of the German POWs. The question was not whether, but when, and in exchange for what.[70] West Germans, however, did not know that, and the press attributed the Soviets' willingness to compromise entirely to Adenauer. "At the eleventh hour," the chancellor's decisive act had saved the day—this was the impression clearly articulated in "man-on-the-street" interviews in the *Süddeutsche Zeitung.* "It's simply fabulous, what he did. Now we can be at ease again. And it's amazing what the old guy put up with," exclaimed elementary-school teacher Helga Ney. A woman whose brother was still in a camp near Sverdlovsk, beyond the Urals, could not believe that "he did it! A fantastic achievement!"[71]

The consequence of the "old guy's" Moscow negotiations was not only the liberation of German POWs but also the de facto recognition of two German states, each with an embassy in the Soviet capital. Mere days after Adenauer's departure from Moscow, official representatives of the other Germany visited the Soviet capital. *Neues Deutschland,* the voice of the East German regime, reported: "In Germany there exist two states, one, a state of workers and peasants, the other, a state of militarists and factory bosses."[72] Adenauer's move toward accepting this political reality caused consternation within his own delegation and prompted critical responses in some press accounts and from foreign observers, particularly the U.S. ambassador to Moscow, Charles Bohlen, who informed the State Department that Adenauer's gesture represented the "complete collapse of the West German position." For the Soviets, he opined, the outcome represented "probably their greatest diplomatic victory in [the] post-war period."[73] Writing in the liberal weekly *Die Zeit,* Marion Gräfin Dönhoff condemned the "acceptance of the division of Germany" and terms that granted the "freedom of ten thousand [but] sealed the servitude of seventeen million [East Germans]."[74]

Most West Germans, however, did not judge their chancellor so harshly. Rather, by the time Adenauer returned to Bonn, journalists and editorial writers credited him with defeating not only Soviet opponents but also naysayers at home, who had charged him with "rigidity and traveling along a diplomatic one-way street. . . . In the moment of truth he proved himself to be far more flexible than many of his political opponents, [who] limp along behind fast-moving developments."[75] Even *Die Zeit*, which unremittingly criticized Adenauer for giving up so much in return for so little, expressed admiration for the man who had emerged from the "lion's den," remaining "cool, calm . . . always saying the right thing, exactly the right thing." This man, "who has experienced and lived through much following his motto, 'Just don't let yourself be frightened,'" was the one best able "in the present situation to ease, not resolve, the tensions between Germany and Soviet Russia."[76] If Adenauer lost his cool, it was only when he reportedly told Molotov that "were he ever to have met Hitler, he would have wrung his neck with his own hands."[77]

Social Democrats had long criticized Adenauer for subscribing to a "politics of strength" (*Politik der Stärke*), which was in fact a politics of weakness because it meant heavy dependence on the United States. In press accounts of the chancellor's Moscow trip, he emerged as the resolute, determined, shrewd master of a different sort of "politics of strength," one in which the "grand old man" had survived "the tough struggle."[78] Hitler's reputation had begun to collapse with the defeat of the Sixth Army at Stalingrad in the winter of 1943. Twelve years later, another German chancellor had "won the battle for the POWs in Moscow" without a single casualty. When the *Frankfurter Allgemeine Zeitung* asked, "Who won?" the question was rhetorical.[79] Adenauer's reputation was at an all-time high.[80]

The *Kölnische Rundschau* reported that when Adenauer's plane touched down on his return from the Soviet capital, his children and grandchildren greeted him; airport employees shouted out, addressing him by his nickname, "Thanks a lot Conny"; and a mother, darting from the crowd, knelt to kiss his hand, an image that was reproduced in myriad press reports and transmitted throughout West Germany in newsreel footage. With a son missing in Russia, this woman represented "the many mothers and married women in our German Fatherland, who for ten years and more have waited in vain for the return home from Soviet camps of their sons and husbands."[81] She had sensed the need "to express her thanks to this man before the entire world; the father of seven children, he risked everything in order to return to German mothers and wives what was most precious to them."[82] The "father of our POWs" had come home from Russia, mission accomplished. The sons soon followed.

"The *Heimat* Welcomes Its Sons"

A month after Adenauer's return, the first transport of German POWs reached the Federal Republic. As one newspaper account put it, in Friedland, the same town in Lower Saxony that since 1945 had been the "last stop of the great war" for countless returning POWs, "the bells of freedom are ringing."[83] Friedland, the "land of peace," had also been the entry point into West Germany for countless expellees and many of those fleeing the "Soviet zone of occupation." Reporters declared that the stories Friedland could tell were those of postwar Germans, and pictures from the town were "our picture[s]," pictures of Germany (Figs. 22 and 23).[84]

Among those pictures presented by the West German press in the fall of 1955 were scenes of women and children who had long suffered silently while their men languished behind barbed wire. Many accounts echoed the story in the *Kölnische Rundschau* that described "four brave women who never gave up hope": the mother, who hurried to get everything just right before "her little boy"—meanwhile turned thirty-five in a Russian POW camp—returned; the mother of three children "who lived through the previous twelve years in a matter of seconds" when she learned her husband was coming home; the wife who showed the reporter her purse in which she kept all her husband's letters; and the woman who was not home to answer the door when the reporter called "because she [had] to earn money," driven to work by her husband's extended absence.[85] These German Penelopes were the women who had waited faithfully, representatives of "the many German families to which providers are returning" (Fig. 24). They had sacrificed themselves to "hard lives and the worries of endless martyrdom" as their loved ones "suffered an unimaginable fate in an unimaginable distant place"; they "had struggled for many years for [their] economic existence while [they] were pushed aside by the hearty," fighting "many paper wars with public officials for a tiny pension."[86] Their men gone, they had taken on extraordinary responsibilities. With the return of husbands and fathers, women could proclaim to reporters: "Now he is here, now everything is good."[87]

This picture of the German woman "who[,] after a decade of separation" in which she had "remained resolutely faithful," now met her husband in Friedland provided a symbol of fidelity in a world "where there
is so much talk of infidelity."[88] She mirrored postwar images of German
women as the preservers of timeless values that had withstood the in-
fection of National Socialism, the falling bombs of the Allies, the invasion of the Red Army, the hardship of life amid the rubble, romantic temptations, and the competitive battles of the economic miracle.[89] These were
the women featured in stories that described wives who "persevered tire-
lessly" and whose "sacrifice, concern, [and] hard work" had sustained
the homes to which men could return.[90]

Marie Elisabeth Lüders, neither wife nor mother but a liberal feminist parliamentarian who had struggled since the 1920s for women's equal
rights, chose to address POWs in Friedland "as a woman," encouraging
her audience "to trust German women and to show goodwill to those
who have thought of you for ten years."[91] Although for POWs a difficult
transition was yet to come, commented one reporter, "the state can entrust this task to no better hands than the hands of families. Happy is
the state that has healthy families."[92] The very existence of such families, moreover, was testimony to West Germans' concerted efforts to make
the reconstruction of the family central to the reconstruction of Germany.[93]

The emphasis on healthy families implicitly articulated a critique of
families that were sick. Amid the joyous reunions reporters recorded
"tragedies . . . that are part of the norm in Friedland, the encounter of
the returning soldier and his wife, who has a small child in her arms,"
or the three-year-old girl who "stretched out her arms to reach the dark
face of the soldier and to grab his fur hat" and was rewarded only with
a look of despair as "the man stared steadily at the woman and went
on."[94] Hardened by trials in the Soviet Union, some POWs, who had
"learn[ed] to give in to fate," were now asked to withstand new tests at
home. One reporter speculated that to some extent the "newly won
confidence" that stemmed from surviving trials behind barbed wire
helped the POW overcome his disappointment and bitterness when he
first learned that his wife had filed for divorce from a "war criminal."[95]

Fortunately, too, good women were ready to replace bad. A feature
story in the daily *Westfälische Allgemeine Zeitung* told of the hundreds
of letters sent to Friedland by single women, who stated in conclusion:
"And so I would like to give a new home to a single, returning veteran."
Many a single woman declared that she could be "happy with a return-

ing veteran in my one-room apartment," within four walls that could re-place his "walls of barbed wire," or that she was ready to "fulfill all of his dreams."[96] The contrast between the woman who was loyal and pa-tient and the woman who was not played out another central theme in representations of women in the immediate postwar period, evoking mem-ories of "fraternization" and women who had not waited for their men to return, abandoning them for the Allied forces of occupation.[97] The spec-tacle in Friedland provided evidence that, even a decade after the war, there were still loyal German women willing to wait for German men who were loyal to the fatherland.

Politicians, public policymakers, and sociologists focused much at-tention on the fate of "women standing alone" (*alleinstehende Frauen*) and the "surplus of women" (*Frauenüberschuss*), the term used to de-scribe the demographic imbalance caused by the high rates of male death in the war. With the return of the POWs, however, press accounts im-plied that this "surplus" would ease. POWs not only diminished the "scarcity of men" (*Männermangel*) but also allowed men to stand next to women who were no longer forced to stand alone. Even the success-ful career woman need not be fulfilled only by her job, such as the "doc-tor from Godesberg" who wrote to Friedland saying that "it would be nice if he were blond, like my first husband who fell in the war."[98]

The promise of "happiness in a one-room apartment" and of dreams that could be fulfilled suggested that the reintegration of POWs was to be not only spiritual and moral, social and economic, but also sexual. Although the focus on children's needs and mothers' responsibilities in images of reunited families left little room for seeing the POW as a red-blooded, sexually active man, eager to find a red-blooded, sexually ac-tive woman, in other accounts commentators stressed that whatever else the POWs had suffered, their heterosexuality was intact. A reporter from the Berlin daily *Der Telegraf* followed twenty-eight-year-old Richard Schmidt as he joined in on the "first carefree stroll [*Bummel*] of his life," an outing in Berlin together with fourteen of his mates. He ended up a guest of a local dancehall proprietor whose own soldier son had not yet returned. There, Schmidt confided to the reporter that he had "last held a girl in his arms eight years ago, [and] it's been 2,918 endlessly long days since I danced."[99] The reporter left no doubt that Schmidt still knew how to lead.

For Heinz Kühn, thirty-two, who had "spent a third of his life behind barbed-wire" for the alleged theft of Soviet chickens, the reentry into heterosexuality meant meeting the girl of his dreams. Interviewed by a reporter in Berlin, Kühn expressed his passion for the film star Marika Rökk, who responded to the story by appearing at Kühn's apartment to take him to breakfast. Kühn had last seen Rökk on the silver screen in an improvised theater outside Budapest where he was serving in a tank division; he confessed that in person she looked even better. Rökk modestly accepted this compliment, rewarding Kühn and all other POWs who had returned to Berlin with tickets to her latest movie, *The Ministry Is Offended*[100]—though no ministry in Bonn could possibly take offense at this show of goodwill or the natural inclinations it expressed.

The medical and psychological problems of returning veterans had generated a mountain of studies in the early 1950s. In particular, attention focused on the problems of "dystrophy," the global diagnosis that described the physiological and psychological effects of starvation experienced by many POWs, especially in the late 1940s. Doctors soberly concluded that one potential consequence was sexual unresponsiveness, and they worried about the "impotent hero," plagued by a "eunuchlike lack of sexual desire."[101] Equally troubling, however, were medical reports that with improved nutrition for POWs in the early 1950s, reawakened sexual desire had sometimes tended in a homosexual direction; one study from the mid-1950s recorded that in some camps as many as 15–20 percent of the men engaged in homosexual relations.[102] The celebration of reunited heterosexual families and of single men eager to find the girl of their dreams indicated that homosexual tendencies, like ragged prison camp clothing, could be discarded once and for all.

Reentry, necessarily, involved readjustment. As another story of POWs in Berlin explained, the men who were good catches for single women were in no hurry, but rather were considering their options carefully, realizing that "reality didn't so easily measure up to their ideal picture of a future wife." They questioned, for instance, whether women "with painted lips could be decent women," and mistook a woman in seemingly invisible seamless nylons for a woman not fully dressed. The vision of a young woman speeding by on a moped "with high heels on her feet and a crash helmet on her head" prompted gasps of amazement, and "the hairstyles, 'ponytails with curly bangs, all so disheveled, as if it weren't even combed,'" distressed these men newly returned from another time and place. At least it was reassuring to learn that foxtrots and waltzes were still being danced, in addition to "Buggi" (boogie).[103]

The same Hamburg papers that carried stories of returning POWs provided accounts of West German performances of Louis "Satchmo" Armstrong, who in the fall of 1955 drew audiences of young women "with fire-engine red lips," clad in "pants, . . . with pony tails and bangs, young men with artists' goatees . . . and leather jackets."[104] These were the uniforms of jazz fans, a far cry from the "*Plennianzug*" (a combination of the Russian word for prisoner and the German word for suit), the overstuffed, ragged, Russian-issue jacket associated with the returnees. The young West Germans who destroyed an auditorium because of an inadequate sound system were veterans not of wars on the eastern front or against Communist oppressors, but of battles fought with stones hurled through windows and at policemen. The "scientific contributor" to one Hamburg daily offered an alarmist account of the jazz fans' "ecstasy of revolt" against "the petit-bourgeois order." Youthful rebellion, he asserted, was the product of a postwar society that had robbed young people of their childhood and provided them with few positive role models.[105] Similar concerns surrounded the fall 1955 West German premiere of the American movie *Blackboard Jungle,* featuring Bill Haley's "Rock around the Clock," an event that heralded the American rock 'n' roll invasion of Germany and presented models of masculinity defined by disaffection, rebelliousness, and androgyny.[106] The stories from Friedland, however, provided evidence that there were still proper German men, who had survived the loss of more than their youth, and who now sought domesticity, not street riots; order, not rebellion. They wanted women whose femininity was expressed in timeless values, not disposable nylons, who had withstood the enticements of an Americanized consumer culture as successfully as the POWs had resisted the temptation of early release in return for collaboration with their Soviet captors.

A feature story in the Hamburg daily, *Die Welt,* told of a POW, taken captive after the battle of Stalingrad, who returned to a Hamburg train station after reentry at Friedland. On the platform, the forty-two-year-old encountered a "gracious lady" to whom he introduced himself. "Then he leaned over the hand of the woman, raised it, and gave it a kiss, as if he stood not on a filthy train platform" but in far more elegant surroundings. With this act, he became "no longer a number among hundreds of thousands" but once again a man. Many years without "elegant women . . . decent clothing, parties, lights, glitter" had not "eternally damned him" nor transformed him into a "barbarian or a slave. . . . Unbowed and unchanged," his dignity was fully restored by kissing this woman's hand, a gesture that put the past behind him and allowed him "once again to become himself."[107] The moral of the story was easily fathomed: POWs wore a quiet dignity, not ducktails, and they sought the touch of a "gracious lady's" healing hands, not the scarlet lips of Americanized womanhood, to reaffirm their masculinity and reenter civilization.

This vision of elegant femininity stood in sharp contrast to the press accounts of several hundred of the *Heimat*'s daughters who floated home amid the sea of sons.[108] These returnees' "cheerless, dark clothing [and] hair that looked as if it hadn't been cared for in years" made them look like "Soviet women, like those we have lately seen in pictures, like completely exhausted beasts of burden." In Soviet Russia, this account continued, women's work included laying track; Ilse Hinzmann, a medical student from Berlin, told reporters that the "rail line was built with our sweat, sometimes our blood, and our tears."[109] Echoing reports of a Moscow bereft of the "scent of the feminine" that had framed Adenauer's visit, tales of the return of German women emphasized that under the Communists legal equality meant little more than the right to be treated like a draft animal. The Soviets' complete disregard for family life was reflected in the separation of mothers and their offspring, and women now returned to West Germany with children who could speak only Russian.[110] For these women, consumer culture defined a path back to the west and proper femininity. A reporter recommended the magic that began when women used "a bit of lipstick and an eyebrow pencil[,] put[ting] some color in pale faces." A beauty treatment could replace the dirty head scarf with "rings of modern curls" and soften the hands made rough by "hard labor in the mines of Workuta, carrying railroad tracks or sawing down trees at the Arctic circle." These were the tonics that could transform women "hardened by suffering" once again into real women.[111]

For the men who returned, however, the therapeutic effects of consumer culture apparently went only so far. Once the relatively small number of women had returned in October, reports of German homecomings focused exclusively on the potential dangers, not the advantages, of the "economic miracle." The woman in nylon stockings, flaunting her sexuality on the back of a moped, was only one symbol of a sexualized consumer culture; other stories described the POWs' astonishment at virtually every aspect of the "chrome-covered daily life, West German style."[112] Soldiers, whose last encounter with the home front might have been on a leave in 1944 and who remembered cities in rubble, now stood helpless in front of a radio, not comprehending the function of the pushbuttons. The "army of autos" jamming every intersection, the "overfilled shopwindows, illuminated with flaming electric signs"—this opulent urban landscape contrasted sharply with the image of an impoverished, deteriorating west portrayed in Communist propaganda in the POW camps.

Accounts depicted returnees negotiating feelings that ranged from a quiet sense of pride in German accomplishment to overwhelming feelings of bewilderment and dismay, mixed with concerns that pleasures could be dangerous.[113]

Compared with the east, West Germany's economy had thrived, but, the POWs cautioned, too much affluence, achieved too quickly, posed enormous problems. The reappearance of these men from a different age was a reminder that "we've allowed ourselves to be seduced by the exhilarating feeling of growing prosperity that has long drowned out anything unpleasant and disconcerting."[114] Returnees, asked to offer their impressions of a transformed Germany, commented on the "luxury cars, luxury restaurants, luxury women," and reflected that "in Siberia, we became calmer and more certain of our goals." Their experience granted them the insight that "happiness is something that is within people, not in an exalted standard of living," and newspaper accounts recorded their bemusement at their countrymen, who seemed to buy "their cars, their families, and their happiness on the installment plan," living at a hectic, American pace.[115] The POWs could reinvigorate the country, replenishing "the energies that have been spent in the ten years of the 'economic miracle,'" but they also could reinject "much of the idealism that has been wasted." They were bearers of a "pioneer spirit," lost by those "in their elegant cars [who] have forgotten what it was like to walk" and oblivious to the accident of fate that put them in the driver's seat, not behind barbed wire for ten years or more.[116]

"You've come late, but you've not come too late," pronounced the minister president of Lower Saxony, Heinrich Hellwege, at the ceremony to greet the first transport from the Soviet Union. "As you see," he explained to the returning POWs, "we're in the midst of reconstruction, and we can never have too many helping hands. We need you in our collective efforts."[117] Reporters hastened to caution that not all POWs would make the transition effortlessly. Some would need help finding jobs, reintegrating into families, and negotiating dramatically altered surroundings. West Germans should realize that for some, the "inner transformation from gray, mass object into an individual" would not be accomplished simply with flowers and new clothes.[118] However, with time and love, all would be ready to contribute their unique talents to rebuilding Germany. Uncorrupted by consumer culture, unburdened by immodest desires, and familiar with hardship, POWs were uniquely positioned to add a "moral renewal" to the "economic renewal" that was already under way.[119]

If the POW could recognize the excesses of the economic miracle, he was also well qualified to comment on another clear and present danger: the threat of Soviet aggression. Any hopes that the Soviet Union had changed after the death of Stalin turned out to be unfounded. Russia proved that "dictatorship outlives the dictator," a rule to which West Germany was clearly an exception.[120]

In press accounts, POWs testified volumes about the horrors of the red brand of totalitarian rule, captured nowhere more powerfully than in stories of unjust accusations, show trials, arbitrary sentences, and inhumane treatment. Insisting that they were soldiers and prisoners of war, not war criminals, returnees told of charges by false witnesses, trials that lasted mere seconds, and sentences that reflected not justice or the rule of law but ideological frenzy. How could a general have blown up a bridge he had never been near? What was the crime of the divisional translator, "who never fired a shot and never gave an order to fire"?[121] How could a soldier have killed partisans when he was already incarcerated in a POW camp at the time? No prisoner had committed a crime, all were brave soldiers who had dutifully carried out orders. According to one widely published story, "Professor Dr. Schenk, the doctor in the camp in Sverdlovsk," exhorted his comrades in Friedland to join him in an oath: "Before the German people and before the dead of the German and Soviet armies, we swear that we have not killed, profaned, and plundered." Lest anyone think that he was protesting too much, he added: "If we caused misery and suffering to other people, it all took place according to the rules of war."[122]

Some West German commentators warned that claims of "collective innocence" were no more justified than the Allied claims of German "collective guilt."[123] Among the returnees, the Auschwitz doctor Karl Clauberg, renowned for sterilization experiments, was a case in point, and West German authorities moved quickly to arrest and charge him. Social Democratic papers and the trade union press in particular insisted that known camp guards like "Iron Gustav Sorge," an SS officer who had served at Sachsenhausen, should also be brought to justice, despite Sorge's claims that he had "committed no crimes . . . [had] only carried out orders . . . [and] would welcome a trial."[124] The insistence of press accounts that West German courts would go after the truly guilty, however, left no doubt that by 1955 Germans were fully capable of judging their own and knew far better than the victorious Allies how to assess culpability for crimes against humanity. These calls to prosecute the real criminals also made it clear that it was completely misguided to equate a tiny group of true "concentration camp beasts with the millions of honest German soldiers." Only in the GDR were the returning POWs presumed guilty; there East Germans, attempting to be "more Soviet than the Soviets," followed Moscow's lead. In Bonn, however, an entirely different spirit reigned.[125] West German authorities, having declared that they would act aggressively once they received incriminating evidence from Moscow, considered the absence of such evidence only further proof that the majority of German soldiers had been unjustly accused. In 1955, the presumed innocence of all but a few POWs was the presumed innocence of all but a few Germans.

Dramatic accounts of the POWs' journey home emphasized that the battle against Communist injustice and false accusations did not end at the Soviet border. Press reports described how POWs forcefully confronted agents of the East German security police who boarded the transport train and attempted to rip up bedsheets, transformed into political posters, bearing the slogans "Everything for Germany: Germany, We Are Yours" and "We Thank You Dr. Adenauer." The returnees, according to these accounts, sprang from the train "onto the platform, attacking the security officials, leveling one" and sending the others fleeing.[126] These German soldiers reached Friedland as part of a "triumphal procession" (*Triumphzug*) of men who had survived the struggle against Communism, "won the propaganda battle for the Federal Republic," and resisted brainwashing techniques reminiscent of those used by the Red Chinese and North Koreans on American POWs.[127]

Pictures of brave men willing to defend the "father of our POWs" and the fatherland, warriors who stood up against Soviet prison guards and East German police, were a sharp contrast to images from the immediate postwar years of infantalized, demoralized, disabled veterans who straggled home to families they had unsuccessfully protected.[128] Valiant fighters against Communism this time around, the returning POWs of 1955 had never "stooped silently in submission."[129] Dubbed "Hitler's strongest soldiers," they had fought on for ten more years, and this time they were victors in the struggle against "Soviet inhumanity and Bolshevik propaganda," reminders that constant vigilance against the Communist threat was essential.[130]

The POW did not "walk, he marche[d]," without any "inferiority complexes,"[131] an implicit comparison with those who had stooped to accept Communist blandishments. The West German press, in fact, devoted far more attention to those charged with betraying the fatherland than to those charged with crimes against humanity. A case in point was

General Walter von Seydlitz, among the POWs in the first transport that
arrived in Friedland (Fig. 25). In 1943, when he was captured after the
German defeat at Stalingrad, he had been a founder of the League of
German Officers and since then had served as a leading member of the
National Committee for a Free Germany. Most West Germans viewed
these organizations, which had recruited antifascist forces among German POWs, as little more than traitorous associations, and their members as collaborationists who had abetted the cause of the Soviets and
the Communist leaders of the Soviet zone of occupation.[132]

Seydlitz, explained *Der Tagesspiegel*, had not come with the other
POWs from a camp, but from a special prison in Moscow, transported
in a sleeping car, his very presence casting a "shadow over the reunions"
in Friedland.[133] A reporter described how he encountered considerable
hostility from returnees who were unwilling even to remain in the same
room with him, a Judas whose "thirty pieces of silver had yielded [no]
interest."[134] Without commentary, the *Süddeutsche Zeitung* reported that
"one man in a white doctor's coat approached Seydlitz and called to him:
'And what became of the hundreds of thousands of German soldiers, Herr
von Seydlitz, whom you betrayed in Stalingrad, who through your . . .
fliers were encouraged to desert and then disappeared into the depths?'"
"Please emphasize," commented another POW, "that what Seydlitz says
is not our opinion." Almost all journalists made clear that it was not their
opinion either.[135]

In a manner befitting a national traitor, Seydlitz, the general who had
abandoned his men in Stalingrad, abandoned them again in Friedland,
carried off, as *Der Tagesspiegel* reported, "in a black limousine, driven
by a chauffeur."[136] It was up to a retired general, the former head of a
tank division, a "lovable old guy, . . . a seventy-year-old with a white
goatee," to remind Seydlitz that "a general who writes to other generals, 'Come on over, you'll be the first to be released from POW camp,'"
was no longer truly a soldier.[137]

Erich Kuby, a columnist for the *Süddeutsche Zeitung*, offered a rare
critique of those who presumed to judge Seydlitz, a "tragic idealist, who
had the courage not to be opportunistic—in Stalingrad, after Stalingrad,
and today." Kuby, who by the early 1960s would be something of a pre-
cursor to the West German "new left," reminded his readers in the fall
of 1955 that "it is the terrifying, bitter truth that the triumph of [the generals who now criticized Seydlitz] would have been the triumph of Hitler;
if they had won, most of those individuals, to whom we now entrust the
care of the nation by democratic means, would have been sitting in con-

centration camps." However, Kuby's regret that sensationalist reporting about Friedland had been used to "satisfy the public desire for spectacle" and to "warm up all sorts of political brews" was decidedly exceptional, as was made clear by a reader's response that compared Kuby with the "Allied prosecutors in Nuremberg" and condemned Seydlitz as a "base opportunist who would sell his fatherland for a bowl of lentil soup."[138]

Seydlitz's presence among the returning POWs allowed West Germans to replay postwar battles over who was honorable, who was not; who had followed orders loyally, who had counseled cowardly surrender; who was ready to starve for Germany, and who could be seduced by an extra ration. In the process, it was apparent that clear boundaries already separated resistance and betrayal; loyal soldiers struggling to survive a fate they did not choose and opportunists who only looked out for themselves; courageous men and cowards. Kuby called for a critical reexamination of these boundaries, but in the fall of 1955 most West Germans did not wish to complicate the past.

In remarks directed to an early transport of returning POWs and widely reported in the press, the president of the Federal Republic, Theodor Heuss, insisted that now was the time to reflect on the "spiritual fate of those who have once again been given their freedom," not to "speak of where to locate guilt, right and wrong."[139] The Federal Republic was ready to reassure "all who had done their duty as soldiers" that they "need not feel like outcasts." Few questioned that almost all returning POWs had done their duty and nothing more.[140] In the press accounts from Friedland, the exceptions were men like Seydlitz, who had committed crimes against Germans; those who were identified as having committed crimes against Jews were few in number, and those who were guilty of crimes against Soviets and other eastern Europeans did not exist.

Unified in their innocence, POWs were also united by common experiences of war and imprisonment, which erased the social and political distinctions that had separated them before they had set out to conduct a racist war against the Soviet Union. "Former regional Nazi leaders [*Gauleiter*], former KPD leaders, [and] heavily decorated generals" appeared in the press sharing common feelings and turning in their rough Russian fashions for a new suit of clothes.[141] When the official in Friedland called out the name "Von Bohlen—Harald, born 1916," the youngest brother of Alfried Krupp stepped forward, clad in the *Plennianzug*: "dark brown, frayed fur vest and a turtleneck sweater, his hands dug deep into his pockets." Newspaper accounts of Harald's return left much of his fam-

ily's history untold. Alfried had headed the Krupp armaments-manufac-
turing branch and contributed mightily to the Nazi war buildup. In 1943
he had assumed the directorship of all the firm's operations. Employer of
foreign slave labor, pillager of German occupied countries, and war
profiteer, the elder Krupp had also done time, having been sentenced at
Nuremberg to twelve years. Unlike his brother, he had served only three,
amnestied in 1951 by U.S. High Commissioner McCloy and granted not
only his freedom but also the return of property confiscated at the time
of his conviction.[142]

In 1955 the focus was not on Alfried's past, but on Harald's. "Slim,
with a thin face, framed by a red beard, his feet stuck in oversized rub-
ber boots," the younger Krupp told of his interrogation in Moscow by
the Soviet secret police and his years of work in a laundry and on a team
that built apartments for Russians. His professional aspiration as a free
German citizen? The "former student" offered himself as a "perfect laundry or construction worker." His hopes? "For now, to restore my nerves.
My most intimate wish: a room where I can be completely alone." However, fulfilling that wish could wait. In Friedland he spent his first night
in freedom with his "comrades in a poorly lit room of the barracks . . .
where the camp beds stood next to one another, . . . like his 600 comrades of whom he is one, like all the rest," partaking of the "final memory of the community of the barracks that [had] lasted for more than a
decade."[143]

Krupp's experience was a powerful symbol of how POWs, "whether
awaited by poverty or prosperity, a big house or a single room, whether
they were picked up in Friedland or found themselves at the beginning
of a painstaking journey home, essentially all experienced the same
homecoming—and their wives and mothers all cried the same tears."[144]
Barbed wire was the great leveler. If a perverse preservation of class distinctions had survived the war, it was in the Soviet Union, where German generals had been released before common soldiers.[145] By the mid-
1950s, the notion that West Germany was no longer riddled with the
socioeconomic differences that had hastened the demise of the Weimar
Republic had become a staple of political rhetoric and sociological analysis. United by their common loss and misery, West Germans were now
part of what the sociologist Helmut Schelsky called a "leveled-out petit-
bourgeois middle-class society."[146] Mythical classless POWs could thus
fit easily into a mythical classless Federal Republic.

The West Germany that greeted the returnees was also a nation fully capable of integrating *all* Germans, including those whose former homes had now disappeared behind the iron curtain. Adenauer's recognition of the Soviet Union had represented an acknowledgment of the postwar division of Europe with a divided Germany at its center. However, the accounts of returning POWs underscored both the diplomatic fiction that the Federal Republic was the official voice of all Germans and the domestic political fiction that the West German state was prepared to integrate Germans from all parts of the Thousand Year Reich without complaint.

In Friedland "it is possible to hear all the dialects of Germany," reported the *Frankfurter Rundschau*,[147] a formulation that uncannily evokes the scene in Leni Riefenstahl's *Triumph of the Will* where mobilized Nazi workers at the Nuremberg party rally of 1934 responded to the question "Woher stammst du, Kamerad?" (Where do you come from, comrade?) with a lexicon of German place-names ranging from the Baltic to Bavaria. Over twenty years later, POWs from Danzig—now in Poland—from Königsberg—now called Kaliningrad—from the Sudetenland—once again part of Czechoslovakia—or from parts of the Reich that were now in the "Soviet zone" could all name the Federal Republic as their *Heimat,* and West Germany presented itself as the *Heimat* to which all Germans could return.

Press accounts left no doubt that the men who came home were not the same men who had left. War and imprisonment had taught them important lessons. Although they had "experienced the low point of humanity" at the hands of their captors, their long stay in the Soviet Union had given them ample time to gain insight and knowledge that uniquely equipped them to make a contribution to the Federal Republic.[148] On the front pages of newspapers all over Germany, these "free German citizens" shared their emotions with the nation that awaited them. In a speech at ceremonies to greet returning POWs in Friedland, repeated endlessly in the print press and newsreels, Hans Herzog, a returnee from Hamburg, confessed that his heart was beating fast as he addressed his listeners: "Ten long years, we didn't cry one single time, but today tears came into our eyes because there is so much love and loyalty."[149] The same message was captured over and over again in the photographs that accompanied news stories. Men, weeping or close to tears, embraced mothers, wives, and children (Fig. 26). The caption of a photo in one mass-circulation illustrated magazine quoted a returnee who asked those at home to "forgive us if we are not yet completely in control of [ourselves]. But our hearts have not hardened. On the contrary: The love you have shown us on this, our first day at home, shattered the band shaped by bitter injustice around our hearts."[150]

As they were presented in the daily press, Herzog and his tearful comrades were not like the veterans of the First World War, cut off from civil society and able to find solace only in a homosocial paramilitary formation or a brown uniform, nor were they the silent men of a "lost generation," for whom the ersatz family of the trenches was the only family they knew.[151] In Friedland, soldier met soldier, but in images captured repeatedly in newspaper stories, photographs, and newsreel footage husbands also were reunited with wives, fathers became reacquainted with children, and teary-eyed sons embraced sobbing mothers. These individual stories became a national drama as "the *Heimat* welcome[d] its sons,"[152] a homecoming that revealed "a feeling of togetherness that was little diminished by a long period of the most bitter injustice" and articulated the "idea of the *Volksgemeinschaft*." In this moment, "the real Germany," a "unique nation," was there for all to see.[153] As returning POWs intoned "Now Thank We All Our God" before the newsreel cameras in Friedland, there was also no question that this "real" Germany was a Christian nation, part of the "occident" (*Abendland*), not the godless east.[154]

Reunited with their own families and the family of the nation, and restored to a *Heimat* in the "Christian west," POWs desperately sought to share their thoughts and feelings. As one reporter described a returnee, "The experiences of the years of separation had built up so that now it's as if a waterfall were spurting out of him. Hour after hour. He talks and talks. Finally he can talk! Finally he can share everything in his soul that has so oppressed him."[155] What POWs had to say did not "dishonor [their] fate in the Soviet Union by transforming it into adventure stories, rather [they] sought to transform their experiences of a variety of forms of humiliation and the scarcity of material goods and love into a solemn lesson about the dignity of man."[156] This was a story that could be told at home. The soldiers who marched across the front pages of West German papers in late 1955 were not the rabid warriors of the trenches depicted by Ernst Jünger, nor were they the broken youths of Erich Remarque. These men were strong, but they were definitely not silent. Theirs was a "gentle strength," expressed in tears and testimony, the strength of sons, fathers, and husbands overcome by the need to share their emotions with mothers, children, and wives.[157]

Writing in *Der Tagesspiegel* that same fall of 1955, Alexander Mitscherlich employed the categories of a popularized psychoanalysis to describe the "divided father" and "generational conflict in the modern world," both products, Mitscherlich explained, of the "invisibility of the father." Fathers no longer had work that allowed them to demonstrate their abilities, a situation that resulted in the "removal of the father" (*Entväterlichung*) from society. Distant or altogether absent fathers produced rebellious sons.[158] In Friedland, at least as presented by the media, fatherhood was restored. The picture of the caring man, anything but distant from his children, was epitomized by the "unknown POW who choked back tears" as he confided to a reporter, "Since I ended up in prison in Stalingrad thirteen years ago, it was my most moving experience finally to be able to hug a German child."[159] Friedland offered evidence that some German fathers were quite visible; they had returned, restoring balance and order and providing role models for German youth.

The same papers that carried stories heralding the arrival of "two big transports" of POWs also announced: "[The] Bundestag debates the conscription law." Even as the last generals were returning home, "the first general can be named" in the new West German army.[160] A cartoon depicted the army volunteer emerging from a recruiting office in his new uniform and the returned POW leaving Friedland in civilian clothing; "two souls with one thought," both proclaimed that they could "finally [wear] respectable clothes."[161] Although the West German public was deeply divided over the prospect of a Germany rearmed only a decade after the end of the Second World War, the returnees from the Soviet Union represented a chastened, wiser masculinity, a model for those who would join a new army of "citizens in uniform." Emotional, yet like their chancellor in Moscow, in control of their feelings, and enjoying the domesticity of a healthy family, they represented a German manhood that could enter a reformed West German army. The soldier who would represent Germany in a European army would be free of the symbols, ceremonies, and mystification that had characterized the German military in the past, a man whose strong arms could carry a gun but could also embrace a wife and child, a man surrounded by his loved ones.[162]

"One of the great, memorable days . . . in the postwar history of the German people"

Some contemporary critics and some of Adenauer's own political allies judged harshly the outcome of the chancellor's negotiations in Moscow, measuring the return of the POWs against the uncertain future of those other "prisoners," East Germans who were now cut off more than ever from the Germans across their western border. However, the popular response to Adenauer's trip and its results overwhelmingly highlighted the "untold joy of those reunited," not the consequences for those for whom reunification had become unattainable in the short term.[163]

The judgment that the return of the first POW transport marked "one of the great, memorable days . . . in the postwar history of the German people" was no hyperbole.[164] "Homecoming 1955" continued to lend a warm glow to the Adenauer era long after the octogenarian chancellor stepped down in 1963. In May 1967, shortly after his death, 75 percent of those questioned in a public opinion survey placed the release of the last POWs from the Soviet Union at the top of the list of the first chancellor's accomplishments. In 1975, two decades after Adenauer's trip to Moscow, the figure still stood at 66 percent.[165] What West Germans recalled was not the geopolitical machinations that have preoccupied historians of the postwar period, but rather memories of men returning to families and, finally, an end to the war. Adenauer's Moscow negotiations may have signaled the short-term impossibility of joining East and West, but they made possible the symbolic unification of the West German body politic.

Unlike the chancellor immediately before him, Adenauer had never worn a uniform; however, his trip to Moscow made it clear that he did not need to don one to establish his authority. As he explained to reporters, he had accomplished what a former general, Eisenhower, had failed to do: he had won the release of the POWs.[166] He had bested his opponents on the eastern front, winning a diplomatic war with words and reason, not by sending millions of German soldiers to death or prisoner-of-war camps. The popular biography of Adenauer that first appeared in serialized form in the illustrated press even as the last POWs were coming home told the story of a "Christian head of state," a "model for young people," and was offered as an alternative to the "literature of the soldier."[167] In January 1956, on the occasion of his eightieth birthday, tributes to the chancellor candidly acknowledged his "patriarchal quality," which allowed him to present to the younger generation "the figure of a ruling grandfather" and "exhibit . . . authority without losing freedom."[168] His performance in Moscow was irrefutable evidence of his courage, compassion, and determination, his willingness to talk and his ability to use reason, not shrill threats and invective; these qualities had permitted "a nation [Volk] to get its sons again," men who now pledged to be "the most faithful sons of the fatherland."[169]

Not all West Germans shared in this celebration of national unity. Communists and German Jewish organizations protested the enthusiastic welcome given returning soldiers who were implicated not only in a destructive war in the east but also in the attempt to murder all European Jews. They contrasted the homecoming of the POWs with West Germans' chilly reception of concentration camp survivors at the end of the war, the endless accounts of the suffering of POWs with the general silence about the suffering of Jews under National Socialism, and the bounty bestowed on POWs by the West German state with the federal government's penurious response to other victims.[170] These protests, however, did not come from the "real Germany" revealed at Friedland; they were the voices of outsiders—outsiders in the Third Reich and outsiders in the Bonn Republic.[171]

The tale of national unity that played itself out in Moscow and Friedland in the fall of 1955 reviewed key scenes of the war's end, but it also indicated some of the ways in which postwar West Germans were ready to distance themselves from the Germany of World War I, Weimar, and National Socialism. The historian Elisabeth Domansky describes how the First World War militarized German society, redefining relations between women and men: "Men's dominance over women derived no longer from their role as *fathers* but from their role as *soldiers.*"[172] Gisela Bock insists that the Nazis pursued a "modern cult of fatherhood," but in the context of "Nordic patriarchalism," fatherhood began and ended with ejaculation; in this sense, there can be little doubt that the Nazis promoted an exaggerated form of what Domansky calls "the new militarized system of male supremacy."[173] In 1955, soldiers returned from the Soviet Union with their honor intact, but in postwar West Germany the uniform could no longer be the basis of male authority, and sperm alone could not a father make. *Die Zeit,* describing the simple, unadorned uniform of the new West German army, observed that the pre–World War I hit song "The soldier, the soldier, he's the handsomest man in the entire country" would have no fans in a democratic Germany. It was time to take off the highly polished "boots . . . , the symbol of a form of domination that the best representatives of the German army never wanted."[174] Returning POWs provided evidence that the German man had removed his boots and was at home, part of a reconstructed family, sobered and enlightened, not hardened or alienated, by his experience of war and its aftermath. They powerfully indicated that the new West German man was best clothed in the civilian dress POWs were handed upon their return home. Strong but gentle, the returnee was a citizen-father, defined by his relations to parents, wife, and children. He would put on a uniform to defend the fatherland, not to establish his rights as a patriarch.

The "Ten Thousand" who appeared in newsreels and all over the daily press in the fall of 1955 embodied precisely those qualities that West Germany needed as it continued along the tightrope spanning economic prosperity and materialistic excess. They were "writing the last chapter of the Second World War," but they also provided the occasion for a critical inspection of the route West Germany had traveled since 1945.[175] In this sense, as one headline announced, "Friedland [Had] Become German History."[176] In scenes of homecomings all over the Federal Republic, POWs appeared as wise observers who demonstrated discipline, honor, and dignity; they tied the West Germany of the economic miracle to a past that was German, not National Socialist, a repository of values that would prevent Germany from becoming another America. Finally home, they "vividly represent[ed] our own history, our own fate, our own poverty," and in the pages of the popular press they became commentators on how history, fate, and poverty had been processed, analyzed, and surmounted in the decade since the war's end.[177]

Fig. 1. Defeat of the German army at Stalingrad in February 1943 was followed for tens of thousands of German soldiers by the long march into Soviet prisoner-of-war camps. Courtesy of Bildarchiv preussischer Kulturbesitz.

Fig. 2. In the early summer of 1943, some 52,000 German soldiers were marched through the streets of Moscow on their way to prisoner-of-war camps. According to contemporary estimates, more than 3 million German soldiers spent some time in Soviet captivity. Courtesy of Bundesarchiv, Koblenz, Bild 183/E 0406/22/9.

Fig. 3. As the Red Army approached Königsberg at the end of the Second World War, civilians fled the city with whatever possessions they could carry, as shown in this photograph taken in April 1945 by Arkadi Shaykhet. Courtesy of Bildarchiv preussischer Kulturbesitz.

Fig. 4. In the treks of Germans from those parts of the Reich that were ceded to postwar Poland and other parts of eastern Europe, women were overrepresented. These women have reached Potsdam after fleeing Silesia in the spring of 1945. Photograph by Hilmar Pabel. Courtesy of Bildarchiv preussischer Kulturbesitz.

Fig. 5. Images like this profoundly shaped the individual memories of millions of expellees, who made their homes in West Germany in the 1950s. They also shaped public memory of the Second World War in the Federal Republic. Courtesy of Bundesarchiv, Koblenz, Bild 146/76/137/8A.

Fig. 6. "Expellees: Your Misery Is Our Misery." This poster, issued by the Christian Democratic Union, represents the direct appeals that postwar West German political parties made to victim groups. The use of a female image to symbolize the fate of the expellee also reminds the viewer that, among those driven out of eastern Europe at the end of the war, women and children were in the majority. Courtesy of Bundesarchiv, Koblenz, Plak 4/8/27.

Vergeßt sie nicht . . .

. . . **die Einsamsten unseres Volkes**

. . . **die Kriegsgefangenen in aller Welt**

. . . **die Vertriebenen und die Heimatlosen**

Fig. 7. This poster was reproduced from a special Christmas 1947 edition of a daily newspaper. The caption reads, "Don't forget them / The loneliest of our people / The prisoners of war throughout the world / The expellees and the homeless." Courtesy of Bundesarchiv, Koblenz, Plak 4/7/6.

Fig. 8. At the annual Day of the Germans in September 1955, expellees dedicated an eternal flame in Berlin, calling for "Freedom, Justice, and Peace" and insisting that "the east too is [part of the] European fatherland." Courtesy of Landesbildstelle Berlin.

Fig. 9. Annual celebrations like this one in Berlin in 1955 permitted expellees to come together with their countrymen. Banners announce the provenance of individual groups as participants parade in folk costumes. Courtesy of Landesbildstelle Berlin.

Fig. 10. The refusal of the Soviet Union to provide an accurate count of German soldiers and civilians held captive after the war allowed West German estimates to escalate. This poster, issued by the Social Democratic Party, refers to the "5,000,000 [Who] Are Missing" and calls on the Soviet government to "Release Them." Courtesy of Bundesarchiv, Koblenz, Plak 4/7/1.

Fig. 11. The German POW in Soviet hands became an important symbol of postwar Communist brutality against Germans, as this poster suggests, with its caption stating, "Our Prisoners of War and the [Civilian Prisoners] Deported by Soviet Terror Accuse." Courtesy of Bundesarchiv, Koblenz, Plak 5/47/49.

Fig. 12. As part of the "remembrance week" for POWs staged in Berlin in 1953, city officials unveiled this plaque, which bore the inscription "You Are Not Forgotten." Courtesy of Landesbildstelle Berlin.

Fig. 13. This poster advertised a 1953 traveling exhibition sponsored by the League of Returning Veterans, POWs, and Relatives of Those Missing in Action. It reads. "We Admonish: The Prisoner-of-War Camp as Experience and Lesson." Courtesy of Bundesarchiv, Koblenz, Plak 5/47/45.

Fig. 14. This poster from 1946 called for a day of remembrance for the "Victims of Fascism." By the early 1950s, however, most West Germans associated barbed wire with the victims of Soviet barbarism, not German fascism. Courtesy of Bundesarchiv Koblenz, Plak 4/57/14.

Fig. 15. In 1952, the Berlin organizers of an informational exhibition about the fate of German prisoners of war created a model of a Soviet POW camp. Courtesy of Landesbildstelle Berlin.

Fig. 16. In the early 1950s, West Germans called for the release of all remaining prisoners of war at annual "remembrance weeks" (*Gedenkwochen*). In this picture, taken in October 1952, Vice-Chancellor Franz Blücher addresses a meeting in Berlin. The banner calls for the Soviets to "release our prisoners of war," and signs cry out that there are still 85,405 German soldiers in Soviet hands. The truncated poster on the left claims 1,320,966 missing in action, of whom 1,200,000 are assumed to be in "East Bloc countries." Courtesy of Landesbildstelle Berlin.

Fig. 17. The assembly of care packages for German POWs in the Soviet Union served as a community event—another reminder of those for whom the war in the east had not yet come to an end. The picture was taken in West Berlin in 1954. Courtesy of Landesbildstelle Berlin.

Fig. 18. In this photograph of the remembrance week for POWs, expellees, and other war victims staged in Berlin in 1952 and sponsored by the German Red Cross, the large candle, a symbolic beacon to guide home German detainees, was lit by the mayor of West Berlin, Ernst Reuter. Courtesy of Landesbildstelle Berlin.

Fig. 19. Young torchbearers in the 1953 remembrance week's nationwide marathon, at Ernst-Reuter-Platz in Berlin. Courtesy of Landesbildstelle Berlin.

Fig. 20. In September 1955, when Konrad Adenauer arrived in Moscow, he was greeted by the Soviet leader Nikolai Bulganin and saluted by a military honor guard. This photograph, taken by Ernst Grossar, appeared in a photo essay in *Der Stern*, 18 September 1955. Courtesy of Bildarchiv preussischer Kulturbesitz.

Fig. 21. A large contingent of press photographers accompanied Adenauer to Moscow, and the chancellor provided the press corps with frequent photo opportunities. Here he is pictured with Nikolai Bulganin (*left*) and Nikita Khrushchev (*right*); missing is Vyacheslav Molotov, the third principal negotiator. Photograph by Hanns Hubmann. Courtesy of Bildarchiv preussischer Kulturbesitz.

Fig. 22. The return of the "last soldiers of the great war" in October 1955 was the occasion for national celebration. Arriving in special chartered buses after their long train ride from the Soviet Union, POWs were greeted by an enthusiastic crowd. The photograph was taken by Robert Lebeck. Courtesy of Bildarchiv preussischer Kulturbesitz.

Fig. 23. These soldiers, part of the first transport from the Soviet Union in October 1955, were greeted as a conquering army that had survived Soviet barbarism, returning to West Germany with their dignity and honor intact. Courtesy of Bundesarchiv, Koblenz, Bild 146/85/24/14.

Fig. 24. Relatives seeking information about missing loved ones appeared to greet the "Ten Thousand" in Friedland, hopeful that one of the returning POWs would have news of a father, husband, or son. Photograph by Robert Lebeck. Courtesy of Bildarchiv preussischer Kulturbesitz.

Fig. 25. Among the first POWs to arrive in Friedland was General Walter von Seydlitz, whom many West Germans considered a Soviet collaborator because of his participation in the League of German Officers and the National Committee for a Free Germany. Here his wife attempts to shield him from hostile press photographers. The picture, taken by Gerhard Gronefeld, appeared in the illustrated weekly *Quick* on 22 October 1955. Courtesy of Bildarchiv preussischer Kulturbesitz.

Fig. 26. This picture by Robert Lebeck of a mother greeting her son was on the cover of a special issue of the illustrated magazine *Revue* (22 October 1955) devoted to the POWs' homecoming. The caption read, "Here no words are necessary. After a decade of torturous uncertainty Frau Adergold from Hanover has her son Willi again. Like her, thousands of mothers experienced an inexpressible happiness in Friedland." Courtesy of Bildarchiv preussischer Kulturbesitz.

Fig. 27. In *Grün ist die Heide,* the forester, Walter (Rudolf Prack), and the beautiful young expellee from Pomerania, Helga (Sonja Ziemann), have just heard a shot in the forest, signaling a poacher whom Walter suspects to be Helga's father, Lüders. Courtesy of Deutsches Filminstitut.

Fig. 28. In *Grün ist die Heide,* the local judge (Willy Fritsch, left) falls in love with Nora (Maria Holst), an expellee horsewoman who appears in town as part of the Serrano Circus. Courtesy of Deutsches Filminstitut.

Fig. 29. In *Waldwinter,* Marianne (Sabine Bethmann) wins Martin's (Claus Holm) heart for the *Heimat* by introducing him to an expellee family from Silesia, experts in glassblowing. The gray-haired father explains to his children and grandchildren that the delicate bubbles he puts into his glass objects are the tears of Holy Hedwig, the patron saint of Silesia, who "weeps for all the people who have lost their homes." Courtesy of Deutsches Filminstitut.

Fig. 30. In *Ännchen von Tharau,* Utz (Klaus-Ulrich Krause) enjoys a free ride on the bumper cars that Ulrich (Heinz Engelmann) manages for the traveling carnival. Courtesy of Deutsches Filminstitut.

Fig. 31. In *Ännchen von Tharau*, Anna (Ilsa Werner), representing the "new woman" of 1950s West Germany, serves the carnival owner, the "new woman" of Weimar, who has lost her charms in the altered world of postwar Germany. Courtesy of Stiftung Deutsche Kinemathek.

Fig. 32. *Suchkind 312* opens in the lap of bourgeois luxury as Ursula (Inge Egger) serves breakfast to her husband, Robert (Paul Klinger). Courtesy of Deutsches Filminstitut.

Fig. 33. *Suchkind 312* described circumstances familiar to many Germans who knew scenes like this one, in which children and parents study Red Cross advertisements of "Parents seeking their lost children" and "Lost children seeking their parents." Photograph by Hilmar Pabel. Courtesy of Bildarchiv preussischer Kulturbesitz.

Fig. 34. In *Suchkind 312,* Achim (Paul Klinger) and Martina (Ingrid Simon) have happily set up house in Ursula's absence. Courtesy of Stiftung Deutsche Kinemathek.

Fig. 35. *Hunde, wollt ihr ewig leben?* a 1959 movie that examined the Wehrmacht's complete defeat at Stalingrad in February 1943, ended with soldiers being marched off to prisoner-of-war camps. Courtesy of Deutsches Filminstitut.

Fig. 36. In *Der Arzt von Stalingrad,* the young assistant of the good doctor Böhler, his former student Sellnow (Walter Reyer), falls passionately in love with their Soviet superior, Comrade Alexandra Kasalinskaja (Eva Bartok). Here Sellnow is caught in the act by Pjotr Markow (Hannes Messemer), Kasalinskaja's Red Army lover. Courtesy Stiftung Deutsche Kinemathek.

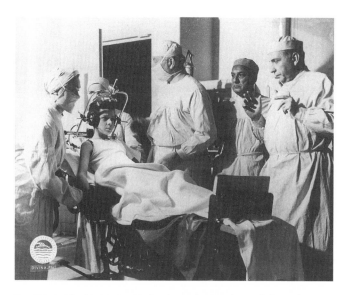

Fig. 37. Böhler (O. E. Hasse), the doctor from Stalingrad (*far right*), prepares to operate on the son of the Soviet commandant. Assisting him is his Soviet counterpart, Major Dr. Kresin (*center*). Courtesy of Stiftung Deutsche Kinemathek.

Fig. 38. In *Taiga,* Hanna (Ruth Leuwerik) stops a fellow prisoner from committing suicide. Her act of compassion and courage wins the hearts of the men in the camp. Courtesy of Deutsches Filminstitut.

Fig. 39. The poster advertising *Taiga* depicted Hanna (Leuwerik) observing herself in a mirror, admired by Ernst Roeder (Hannes Messemer). Courtesy of Bundesarchiv, Filmarchiv, Berlin.

Fig. 40. In *Taiga,* Hanna completes her return to civilization when her comrades fashion her a dress. Courtesy of Stiftung Deutsche Kinemathek.

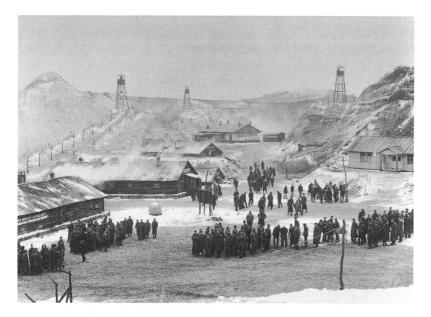

Fig. 41. *Der Teufel spielte Balalaika* tells the story of a Soviet POW camp that housed both Japanese and German prisoners, sentenced to long terms breaking rocks in a stone quarry. Courtesy of Deutsches Filminstitut.

Fig. 42. As *Der Teufel spielte Balalaika* ends, Elena Seidenwar (Anna Smolik) is framed by barbed wire as she watches the departure of a German she has befriended, on his way home, and of her husband, a Soviet political officer, being taken off for interrogation. Courtesy of Stiftung Deutsche Kinemathek.

CHAPTER FIVE

Heimat, Barbed Wire, and "Papa's Kino"

Expellees and POWs at the Movies

In some West German stories of the 1950s, the fates of expellees and POWs intersected. In the winter of 1945 Anna Wittkuhn, a refugee from East Prussia, crossed the Weichsel, the river that emptied into the Baltic near Danzig, barely eluding the advancing Red Army as she fled into western Germany. She settled in a small town on the banks of the Main River and quickly found employment in a restaurant that featured the finest wines of local vintners. With her came a baby boy, Utz, who was not her biological child but the offspring of another woman who lost her life on the trek and entrusted Anna with the care of the boy. Eight years after the war's end, Wittkuhn had still not revealed this secret to Utz, whom Wittkuhn's neighbors assumed to be the illegitimate consequence of a wartime passion. Only Wittkuhn knew that the boy's real father was dead on the eastern front, or so Utz's mother had told Anna shortly before she passed away.

Wittkuhn, a "new citizen," was completely integrated into West Germany by the early 1950s. Good at her job, a prized employee, she had also sparked romantic overtures from Adrian Rotenbach, the heir apparent to a profitable vineyard on the banks of the Main. Her new countrymen also respected her past, calling her Ännchen von Tharau, an allusion to an epic-length poem of the nineteenth century that celebrated the values of nature, rural life, and *Heimat*. In 1945, however, Tharau had been occupied by the Soviets; once south of Königsberg, the city renamed Kaliningrad, it was no longer a German *Heimat*.

In the 1950s, the arrival of a carnival in a West German town disrupted normal routines temporarily, but for Anna one carnival in particular brought permanent changes. Into her life walked Ulrich Lessau, manager of the main attraction, a bumper-car racecourse, the *Autosuperrennbahn.* Lessau, an attractive man roughly Anna's age, had been a fighter pilot in the war, shot down and taken prisoner by the Soviets only months before German capitulation. Only recently returned from "six years in the big men's barracks in Asia," he now found himself lost among people who act "as if nothing had happened."[1] Utz was immediately attracted to the pint-sized autos and was drawn even more to the man running the racecourse. Convinced that she knew Lessau's name from somewhere, Anna searched for a connection in the drawerful of memories she had salvaged from the trek. Among them was a picture of Utz's father given to her by the child's biological mother. There was no doubt: the man in the photograph was Ulrich Lessau.

Wittkuhn's story was not among the "reports from experience" collected by Schieder and his associates, nor one of the sociological accounts that traced expellees' integration in the Federal Republic, and Lessau did not march into West German homes on the front page of a newspaper announcing the release of POWs from behind the Urals. Rather, they met in a 1954 movie called *Ännchen von Tharau,* one of a string of films that offered West Germans the opportunity to reflect on the legacy of the Second World War. To hear tales of the "expulsion from the east" or to learn the lessons of the "barbed-wire university," West Germans did not need to follow debates in the Bundestag, read "contemporary history," or peruse the daily paper; they needed only to go to the movies.

In her superb study of postwar cinema in the Federal Republic, Heide Fehrenbach demonstrates that movies contributed mightily to "reconstructing national identity after Hitler."[2] West German producers and directors confronted a flood of foreign, particularly American, films, to which they responded aggressively by offering a uniquely German product. Movie audiences, in turn, expressed their preference for productions of German origin. In the decade before televisions kept audiences in their living rooms, when more West Germans than ever before—or since—sought entertainment at the movies, the film industry churned out comedies, adventure films, costume dramas that carried their audiences back to an age of Kaisers and kings, and movies that conjured up an imagined German past of rural idylls and harmonious communities.[3] Among the products on offer were also many versions of the Second World War.

In this chapter, I do not explore the so-called rubble films of the immediate postwar years, which showed Germans what they could see all around them—leveled cities and shattered lives.[4] Some of these movies, such as Wolfgang Staudte's famous *Die Mörder sind unter uns* (The murderers are among us), raised difficult questions of German responsibility for the mass murder of innocent civilians in Poland. In Wolfgang Liebeneiner's *Liebe 47* (Love 47)—a film version of the Wolfgang Borchert play *Draussen vor der Tür* (translated as *The Man Outside*), which Liebeneiner had also directed—one of the central characters, a POW returning from the Soviet Union, is tortured by the knowledge that by following orders he sent men under his command to their death. By the end of the 1940s, however, movies that presented this part of the past so relentlessly and raised such difficult questions about blame and responsibility were ceasing to be big draws, leading reviewers to conclude that audiences were sated with stories that focused only on the "hopelessness of the first postwar years." As one reviewer put it, it was "time for spiritual restoration. We have had enough of violent emotions."[5]

However, even if the physical ruins of destroyed cities and souls were less prominent in German theaters, the "troubling exigencies of the postwar years" remained a staple of the film industry. As Fehrenbach writes, even when there were no gunshots or falling bombs, the war and its consequences remained "part of an unportrayed past. Like a natural catastrophe, it has no author but unsettling repercussions."[6] Among those "unsettling repercussions" were Germans driven from eastern Europe to new homes in West Germany, and prisoners of war in the Soviet Union. These key symbols of German suffering now became central elements of many West German movies.

In this chapter, I focus on seven movies that directly addressed the experiences of these two groups.[7] I have chosen movies that aimed to reach a mass audience. They did not signal aesthetic or cinematic breakthroughs, nor is it likely that they will ever be included in a retrospective of "great" German movies, save as a negative point of reference for films of the "Young German Cinema," the artistic revolt of the "sons" of the 1960s against the work of "fathers" whose political and aesthetic predilections still reeked of Nazi "blood and soil." The films presented in this chapter were products of "Papa's Kino," the label attached by the Young German Cinema to most movies of the 1950s. Whatever their artistic merits, however, these films belonged to a popular culture that in straightforward terms reinforced certain conceptions of the war and its aftermath and articulated lessons for the present in terms of the past.

In two movies, expellees are at center stage. *Grün ist die Heide* (The heath is green), a 1951 film directed by Hans Deppe illuminating the integration of East Elbian refugees into West German society, was phenomenally popular, among the top three draws the year it opened and the biggest box office film the next year. By 1959 some nineteen million West Germans had seen it; it was the most successful *Heimatfilm* of the decade.[8] In the 1956 movie *Waldwinter: Glocken der Heimat* (Forest in winter: The bells of home), Liebeneiner, one of the best-known directors of the 1950s, moved decidedly away from the neorealist aesthetic of *Liebe 47* as he followed expellees from snow-covered landscapes in Silesia to snow-covered landscapes in Bavaria.

In *Ännchen von Tharau*, directed by Wolfgang Schleif, the confrontation of expellee and POW suggests the ways in which the experiences of these two groups were readily linked in popular consciousness in the early 1950s. Both characters are victims of circumstances beyond their control. POW and expellee fates also merge in the 1955 film *Suchkind 312* (Lost child 312). Directed by Gustav Machaty, the movie was based on a novel of the same name, first serialized in the popular weekly radio program guide *Hörzu* (Listen up) and written by that publication's founder and chief editor, Eduard Rudolf Rhein, writing under his pseudonym, Hans-Ulrich Horster. In it Rhein told a story of the chaos of the war's end, difficult reunions, adults caught between past and present, and children in search of their parents. The book is still available in Germany in an inexpensive paperback edition.[9]

In three other movies I discuss, Germans in uniform moving east, rather than Germans routed from their homes moving west, were the principal subjects. In "rubble movies" and in some films of the first half of the 1950s, although the returning POWs were featured roles, their experiences of war and postwar imprisonment did not appear explicitly on screen. The protagonists bore the scars of dashed dreams and interrupted lives, but the shooting war was in the background. In the second half of the decade, with all POWs safely returned from Soviet camps, filmmakers were increasingly ready to revisit the battlefields, and the POWs' "barbed-wire university" came to the silver screen as well. Soviet jailers in Red Army uniforms communicated an ideological message that established still more links between the anti-Bolshevik demonology of the Third Reich and the fundamental anti-Communism of the Bonn Republic. However, by this time West Germans were also inching toward "peaceful coexistence" with Moscow. Movies that presented enemies from a Stalinist past also included visions of another, kinder and more compassionate, post-Stalinist Russia with which better relations were possible.

Often based on serialized novels that first appeared in popular illustrated magazines, movies that explored the experience of German POWs billed themselves as powerful reminders of the devastation of war. *Der Arzt von Stalingrad* (The doctor from Stalingrad), a 1958 movie directed by Geza von Radvanyi, closely followed the novel of the same name by Heinz Konsalik, the book that, by his own account, established his reputation as an extremely successful author of reams of pulp fiction.[10] Playing the good doctor was O. E. Hasse, a familiar face for West German film audiences. The movie also featured Eva Bartok, a Hungarian émigrée whose personal life, four marriages, and as many divorces made her a favorite with magazine writers, and Hannes Messemer, another well-known actor.[11] *Taiga,* another Liebeneiner film, was based on a novel that first appeared week after endless week in *Revue,* a mass-circulation illustrated weekly. The author of the novel and the screenplay, Herbert Reinecker, had a well-established reputation as a writer of adventure tales, including such National Socialist favorites as *Pimpfenwelt* (World of [Nazi] youth).[12] In *Liebe 47,* a returning POW fretted endlessly over causing the death of men under his charge; in *Taiga,* a 1958 production, POWs were "three hundred forgotten men" in Siberia, and only Russians committed inhuman deeds. The movie also starred Messemer, who played opposite Ruth Leuwerik. One of the biggest box office draws of the late 1950s, Leuwerik continued to top fan ratings throughout the decade.[13] Finally, *Der Teufel spielte Balalaika* (The devil played the balalaika), a 1961 movie that depicted Germans and Japanese POWs forced to break rocks in a Soviet quarry, was widely discussed as a powerful cautionary tale about the insanity of war in a nuclear age.

These were not the only movies in which the "newly arrived" eastern Germans and prisoners of war appeared,[14] but measured by the high profile of their directors and stars and the press responses they generated, they were the best-known films that addressed these themes. They dramatized parts of the past that West Germans wanted to see, and they represented another important context in which memories of the war on the eastern front and its outcome shaped West German public memory in the 1950s. The movies did not invent these stories of noble survivors, and they drew on themes and characters that were familiar to most West Germans in the 1950s. Abandoning any concern with guilt and complicity, they depicted melodramatic confrontations between unambiguous heroes and villains and offered clear moral lessons from experiences

shared by millions of Germans. For the most part, the "spiritual restoration" that West German tales of expellees and POWs offered emerged
not from explorations of the "violent emotions" of the war but from the
revelation that loss and suffering were redemptive and the insistence that
Germans had successfully withstood the virus of the Third Reich and the
barbarism of Soviet Communism. They told stories with happy endings
and few complications, stories many West Germans were ready to hear.[15]

There's No Place Like *Heimat*

Tales of the expellees' discovery of a new home in the Federal Republic
became a central theme of one of the most popular movie genres in the
1950s, the *Heimatfilm*. Of all movies produced in West Germany between
1950 and 1962, roughly one in five was a *Heimatfilm;* for the early 1950s,
the ratio was even higher.[16] These movies, featuring unsullied natural landscapes in which the camera lingered endlessly on charming bunnies and
stately deer or followed noble eagles to their nests high in snow-covered
mountains, reproduced scenes that had been the bread and butter not only
of Nazi cinema but also of theatrical and literary traditions that stretched
back to late-nineteenth-century celebrations of rural society and tradition.
The *Heimat* represented hearth and home, local culture and identity, values that postwar *Heimatfilme* could portray as a German bedrock that had
escaped the devastation of war and National Socialism. As Celia Applegate writes in her study of the "German idea of *Heimat*," after 1945 the
concept "came to embody the political and social community that could
be salvaged from the Nazi ruins."[17] This *Heimat* was the real Germany,
distinct from the aberrational epiphenomenon of the Third Reich. Because
everyone could claim a *Heimat,* it also defined a rhetoric of a universal experience that took on specific, individual forms, what Alon Confino has
described as a "common denominator of variousness."[18] By representing
German communi*ties*, something that everyone had, the concept of *Heimat*
could thus also represent *the* German community, the nation as sum of
many unique parts.

Heimatfilme of the 1950s that focused on expellees made the explicit
point that in the postwar era many Germans were *heimatlos*—uprooted,
without a sense of connectedness to locality or nation—because they had
been separated from their homes. The experience of expellees could thus
stand in for the fate of those evacuated or bombed out of cities, who fled
East Germany to find refuge in the west, or who were quickly exiting a
declining agrarian sector for work in urban areas.[19] There were many

forms of "homelessness" in the postwar era, many audiences who could see themselves in tales of new beginnings. The stories of Germans displaced by the past, in search of a home, and seeking to determine what parts of their traditions could be integrated, what parts jettisoned, were not just the stories of expellees.

Later generations of filmmakers and critics excoriated the *Heimatfilm* as prima facie evidence of the abject state of the West German movie industry in the 1950s, an embarrassment on the way to the Young German Cinema of the early 1960s, and expressing a hopelessly nostalgic longing for the past. But *Heimatfilme* offered more than straightforward escapism or a rural reverie that could stand in for a concept of nationalism delegitimated in the wake of National Socialism. Not just myths of innocence unearthed from times past, *Heimatfilme* were also stories of West Germany's present. The expellees of *Heimatfilme* sought no return to days gone by. Rather, they exhibited how traditional values and modernity could happily join hands, each enriching the other.[20]

The director of *Grün ist die Heide* (1951), a *Heimatfilm* par excellence, was Hans Deppe, who had made some twenty musicals under the Nazis. The film was a quick attempt to capitalize on the unanticipated success of Deppe's *Schwarzwaldmädl* (Girl of the Black Forest, 1950), the first big postwar *Heimatfilm,* which exceeded all expectations at the box office.[21] *Grün ist die Heide,* a remake of a 1932 film of the same title, featured Rudolf Prack and Sonja Ziemann, the same pair of romantic stars that appeared in *Schwarzwaldmädl.* Both were favorites of West German audiences. Ziemann plays Helga Lüdersen, the adult daughter of an expropriated Pomeranian large landowner, Lüders (Hans Stüwe), whose home is now occupied by the Poles. Father and daughter have landed in green pastures, however, since Lüders has a relative who owns a big house in the Lüneburger Heide, the region in Lower Saxony from which the film takes its title, where Lüders and Helga are welcome guests.

Lüders has lost his wife due to circumstances the film never elucidates, but his other losses—most notably, his estate and a private forest where he could hunt for game to his heart's content—are no secrets. Indeed, his inability to set aside his gun in his new West German home and his desire to shoot game in a nearby forest where such activity is strictly prohibited are the source of enormous difficulties. To be sure, Lüders is no poacher in the usual sense. As one reviewer noted, this was not an "American-style gangster film of crime for crime's sake"; rather, the displaced landowner was "a victim of his lack of inhibition—a condition that stemmed largely from a difficult human fate."[22] He also has redeeming qualities, and he has distinguished himself by applying his estate management skills to increase the profitability of his relative's agricultural property. What drives this otherwise upstanding German to break the law is the past; poaching is a drug to ease the pain of suffering and loss. Still, mitigating circumstances notwithstanding, a Germany in the midst of restoration cannot afford to have its forests devastated. Lüders has not yet proven that he can be the right kind of "new citizen."

Enforcing the rules of the new order is Walter Rainer, played by Prack. Relatively new to the area, he is the assistant to the forest and game warden, an older man who is a trusted native. Awaiting retirement, this seasoned veteran is grooming Walter to be his replacement. Walter is frustrated by the poacher, "who would simply shoot everything away, after we have taken such pains to rebuild the forest and game." He comes to suspect Lüders but turns a blind eye to the father's crimes because he has fallen in love with the daughter (Fig. 27). Helga fears she cannot reform her father, and she sees no escape route except to the anonymous city, a prospect that completely demoralizes the elder Lüdersen but that seems to be the only option.

Paralleling the troubled romance of Helga and Walter is a nascent love affair between the local judge (Willy Fritsch) and a friend of Helga's, Nora (Maria Holst), similarly displaced from eastern Germany and bereft of material goods, but still amply outfitted with beauty, wit, and a keen sense of social etiquette (Fig. 28). Nora and Helga have lost touch since "those times," but now Nora rides into town with the circus. A skilled horsewoman who once galloped over the Pomeranian hinterland for pleasure, Nora now earns her living with her English saddle and a stunning white steed. There is never any doubt that the beautiful, blonde Nora, possibly once at home in the League of German Girls, is decidedly out of place in the nomadic life of the Serrano Circus, a world peopled by dwarves, clowns, and dark-skinned acrobats who speak with heavy accents. Her association with this world, however, is purely instrumental, a way to get to a new beginning in America, the circus's next port of call.

The judge, old enough to have served as a civil servant under an earlier German regime, has taken responsibility for the care of expellees in the village. He understands that "homesickness can be a serious illness." Nora, "a little reticent and skeptical, like all young people who, as refugees, have to find their way" (as publicity materials for the film put it),[23] at first playfully deflects the judge's romantic forays. Gradually, however, she shows signs that she is not immune to the healing powers of a genuine *Heimat* and a man mature enough to have learned some of life's lessons.

Helga and her father are ready to leave for urban anonymity, but at Helga's urging Lüders agrees to attend the annual local festival (*Schützen-fest*) to say his good-byes; his daughter in turn is assured of one more meeting with Walter. The folk songs of the festival are a counterpoint to the hurly-burly of the music from the circus; the camera moves back and forth between Germans dancing in folk costume on one stage and wild west riders in cowboy outfits, and jugglers and tumblers prancing about wildly in harem pants and fezzes, on another. The only moment of repose in this exotic world comes when an immaculately clad Nora takes her turn around the ring on her snow-white horse.

Leaving no mystery about the movie's central message is Lüders's farewell speech at the festival, which he delivers

> not for me alone, but for the many others who have found a second home [*Heimat*] here among you. I will never forget the days I was allowed to be with you in the *Heide*, in the *Heide* that has also become my second home.
>
> Don't be too hard on the people who have fled to you. Whoever has not been compelled to leave his home cannot know what it means to be without one [*heimatlos*]. I know that we also have not always been as we should. But we have been most severely punished. . . .
>
> I thank you. I thank you from the bottom of my heart for all the good things you have permitted me to know.[24]

This is a tough act to follow, but a group of musicians that appears throughout the movie, carefree wandering souls who live from the beneficence of the village, tries. At the bidding of the judge, one of them leads the assembled masses, decked out in traditional dress, in a folk song from Silesia that trumpets the glories of the "Riesengebirge, German mountains, you, my beloved homeland," though since 1945, as the audience well knows, the region's beloved mountains have been Polish, not German. The song, the judge emphasizes, is not just for Silesians, but for all who are homeless, just as Lüders's story is not just for Pomeranian large landowners, but for all expellees.[25] As the minstrel sings, the camera lingers on the faces of the Silesians, "faces," as one otherwise critical review put it, "that still bear pain."[26]

Shots in the forest disrupt the pathos, and Walter takes off in search of the poacher. Helga, fearing her father has still not contained his passions, dispatches Nora as well, who follows on horseback. Lüders, meanwhile, in pursuit of his honor, is also searching for the poacher, not a deer, but when he catches the miscreant in the act the poacher shoots, leveling him, just as, simultaneously, Nora is leveled when she is thrown from her horse. The villain is no local; rather, he is the animal trainer from the circus, who has slaughtered deer to feed his lion and killed a local gendarme who got in his way. A suspicious character, he is marked from the moment the circus rolls into town and, on registering with the local police, is unable to produce a passport. He is, as one reviewer commented, easily recognizable as the criminal "because he's the one without identity papers."[27] A man with no identifiable *Heimat* to lose is, by definition, a shady character. With the poacher safely in custody, it is clear that Lüders and Nora will both need long periods of recuperation, and while their physical injuries mend there will be ample opportunity for love, heather, and *Heimat* to bloom.

Fehrenbach, in her insightful analysis, points to the film's presentation of the theme that both "old" and "new" citizens must make compromises in order to shape a new West German version of *Heimat*. Lüders Lüdersen stands in not only for the singing Silesians but for all Germans who have experienced downward mobility because of the war; a common fate here supersedes class and regional differences.[28] The movie suggests the ways in which, by the early 1950s, the displacement of eastern European Germans had come to symbolize the general displacement brought on by the war.

Integration, not surprisingly, takes different forms for women and men. Lüders can truly become part of a new *Heimat* only when he has accepted the rule of law. But for Nora and Helga, the rule of a man—a clear preview of marriage and domesticity—is the path to the future. Women also are emotional managers of the older generation. Helga first secures her father's place in his new surroundings and only then pursues her own happiness. Nora and Helga also more readily negotiate the past, gracefully transcending "those times" with good spirits and good looks.

The movie spends no time addressing the social conflicts between "old" and "new" citizens that beset the western zones of occupation in the late 1940s and West Germany after its founding in 1949.[29] In this *Heimat,* the social contract is defined by mutual understanding. When the movie opened in Berlin the city's former mayor, the Social Democrat Louise Schroeder, praised it as a reminder of the "community created during the [1948] blockade [of Berlin by the Soviets], which must continue to survive."[30] That community, according to *Grün ist die Heide,* should embrace all Germans, including those "new citizens" competing for jobs and other resources in the Federal Republic. To be sure, the movie evoked the atmosphere of an older generation of *Heimatfilme,* but then, as one reviewer put it, "there was a big, undivided Germany, there were not millions of refugees, expellees driven from their homes, and people who had been uprooted."[31] Although another critic charged that no sentimental color film could ever capture the expellees' "path to Golgotha,"[32] far more common was the view that in this updated variation the *Heimatfilm* could "directly touch the hearts of all those who are forced to live far from their homes."[33]

The movie emphasizes that a preoccupation with the past is no way to overcome pain and suffering. Nora does not race her white horse backward in time, and her initial plan is to ride all the way to the home of modernity, the United States. By the end of the movie, she has come to appreciate that the *Heimat* is where she belongs. She also understands, however, that this new home is no re-creation of a past she has left behind. Her red lips and fashionable clothes signal that she is not an old-fashioned girl, and precisely this quality is what attracts the local judge.

Lüders, for his part, redeems himself by going not in search of memories and his beloved deer but after the criminal. When the film begins, Lüders, like the poacher, has no clear identity. Yet he is able to find his way to a new home—and a rehabilitated sense of self—by helping to enforce the social contract of a reconstructed Germany. The terms of that contract are set by Walter and Helga, the younger generation who will define a new West German future. Where Walter spent the war years is never clear, though his age leaves little question that he has "served"; still, he provides convincing evidence that in the postwar world Germans can bear arms and wear a uniform with a sense of dignity and honor—as most German men had before 1945. Against the background of the outbreak of the Korean War and the national discussion of West Germany's potential entry into a western European military alliance, Walter is a responsible German(y) rearmed, the "citizen in uniform" who anticipates the army of honorable men who will fill the ranks of the Bundeswehr in the second half of the decade.[34] His is not the only uniform, however. The folk costumes that flood the closing scenes of the *Schützenfest* represent the national uniform of *Heimat,* festive and multicolored, not brown, German, not fascist.

Other untainted German pasts take center stage as well. The judiciary, defamed by the victors immediately after the war as a hotbed of National Socialism, emerges here as the soul of decency, epitomized by the judge, who feeds the roving minstrels and eases the entry of those expelled from the east into their new home. And even as the Bundestag debated the provisions of the "131 law," the measure that would reinstate National Socialist civil servants who had lost their jobs at the end of the war because of their politics, the judge offered moviegoers additional evidence that under Hitler the German civil service had done nothing wrong.[35]

Although many reviews bemoaned the film's sticky-sweet sentimentality, *Grün ist die Heide* was praised as an indication that German film audiences were tired of "American wild west movies" and longed for dramatic forms that "confronted the problems of the present and tried to solve them, rather than avoiding them."[36] By 1951, the problems of the present were the problems of German victims, not of those Germany had victimized. And they were solved by limitless goodwill, sympathy, generosity, as well as an understanding, acceptance, and transcendence of the past.

How You Gonna Keep 'Em Back in Paree after They've Seen the Farm?

The redeeming power of a world that had been lost behind the iron curtain but that could be found again in the west was also a central theme of *Waldwinter: Glocken der Heimat* (1956), which followed expelled Silesians to a new home in Bavaria. The movie's director, Wolfgang Liebeneiner, was himself a Silesian, but he had left home at a relatively young age to pursue his professional ambitions as an actor. After a successful transition from stage to screen in the 1920s he rose to a position of prominence under the Nazis, heading the artistic faculty of the German Film Academy and picked by Goebbels in 1943 to be director of production for Ufa, the Nazi film agency.[37] Liebeneiner's credits during these years included writing and directing *Ich klage an* (I accuse), a dramatic justification of euthanasia, produced at a time when the Nazis were enlisting all possible means to convince Germans that it was necessary to eliminate "worthless lives."[38] Goebbels, Liebeneiner's boss, praised the film as "wonderfully made and truly National Socialist," and his enthusiasm for Liebeneiner's "artistic contributions to political propaganda during the war" led him to recommend Liebeneiner for an honorary professorship.[39] Liebeneiner survived National Socialism unscathed to reemerge as a major contributor to a new postwar West German film industry.

A director for all seasons, Liebeneiner saw in *Waldwinter* the chance to make a "typically German production," a *Heimatfilm*, a genre he considered to have strong appeal because "in no other film-producing nation of the world has such an exceptionally large part of the population been homeless." *Heimatfilme*, however, he explained, spoke not only to the literally displaced, but also to those who, despite having left home to find new jobs in West Germany's geographically mobile postwar economy, would never abandon the "desire for a true *Heimat* and all the emotions associated with it."[40] No "sentimental little story" that simply sought to "fill the box office quickly," concluded one reviewer, this was a movie that was "honest, neat, and lively."[41]

Like *Grün ist die Heide, Waldwinter* focused on a reconstructed present, not a devastated past. It opens in Silesia, where villagers are celebrating that ur-German holiday, Christmas, in a rustic wooden church. The overrepresentation of adult women is a clear indication that able-bodied men have long since vanished to the front. Only one man in uniform is in the church, Hartwig, played by a young Klaus Kinski, who communicates a sense of fear, bewilderment, and shell shock as he tries to comfort a girl some years his junior. Otherwise, there are no signs that Germany is in the sixth year of the war.

As the villagers exit the church they are met by a Wehrmacht officer who speeds up on his motorcycle. The officer is Martin (Claus Holm); he has rushed from the front to tell his grandparents, the baron (Rudolf Forster) and baroness (Helene Thimig), and all the villagers that the Red Army's arrival is imminent. "Won't it end soon?" asks the trusted old servant of the baron, who recognizes him immediately. Martin replies, "It ended a long time ago, but no one knows when it will really finally be over." He advises the villagers to depart immediately for the baron's castle in Bavaria. "Who knows if we will ever see Silesia again," muses Martin's grandmother. As audiences were aware, this was a question for which irredentist Silesians and the West German government still had no definitive answer in early 1956, when the movie was released.

The villagers are out of Silesia before the Red Army appears. They thus bear the psychological scars of displacement, but, as one reviewer commented, the "horrifying days of the destruction of Silesia"—the stuff that filled the pages of the Schieder documentation and other expellee accounts—were not part of Liebeneiner's story.[42] Marauding Russians had no place in the *Heimatfilm*, though a decade after the war viewers certainly did not need explicit references to know the manifold meanings of expulsion from the east. Liebeneiner's expellees appear again in the snow a decade later in a Bavarian, not Silesian, winter. The baron's connections have made possible the relocation of the entire village to the town of Falkenstein, nestled safely in the Bavarian forest near the border with Czechoslovakia.

Things, however, are not as simple as they seem. The baron faces bankruptcy. He has sought to expand the local artisanal glassmaking industry—an attempt to "rescue a piece of Silesia . . . and to build it anew with unspeakable sacrifice and effort"[43]—by buying a huge, modern generator, but the bank has refused him credit. Not the business naïveté of the baron, but an evil estate manager is at fault. Behind his back, the estate manager has been selling off the baron's forest to lumber interests and keeping the proceeds. The manager hopes thereby to force the sale of the baron's palatial home in order to transform it into a luxury resort hotel, and he will use the money he's stolen from the baron to make the purchase. If his plan works, it will be the rich of Munich, not the honest Silesians, who enjoy the natural beauties of the forest in winter. The manager is spurred on by his wife, a dangerously fashionable woman whose red hair, ambition, and desire clearly exceed the confines of this new Bavarian *Heimat*.[44]

The baron calls on his grandson for advice. Martin, last seen in a Wehrmacht uniform as he urged the villagers to flee the Red Army, is now sporting the uniform of the sophisticated international businessman. The baron's telegram reaches him in Paris, where his French lover, Simone (Erica Beer), runs an haute couture hat boutique. Martin's return to straighten out his grandfather's finances means a postponement of the pair's planned vacation to Egypt and the pyramids. This destination never reached by Rommel's tanks is now easily achieved by a Germany armed with the almighty DM.

Martin rolls into the snow-covered Bavarian town in a big car that carries the symbolic weight of modernity and success in the postwar economy. At first he is more bemused than charmed by his resettled fellow countrymen. His eye, however, is immediately caught by Marianne (Sabine Bethmann), a foster child of the baron and baroness since the unexplained death of her parents; a young girl of fifteen when last he saw her, she is now a fully grown woman. Still, even this potential romance cannot blunt Martin's business acumen. After studying the baron's account books, he begins to believe that his grandfather might have to enter a partnership, to which the baron ruefully responds that he already has one—with the state, which has given him something, but not nearly enough, under the terms of the "law to equalize the burdens" (*Lastenausgleichsgesetz*).

Facing these dismal facts, Martin concludes that his grandfather has no option but to sell off the forest and his castle and move to a new life in the city, leaving his fellow Silesians to fend for themselves. "And lose their home a second time?" protests Marianne, reminding Martin that it is not only the baron's welfare that is at stake. "Their *Heimat*," says Martin, who clearly has forgotten the meaning of the word, "is in the east. Where they earn their money really should make no difference to them." Marianne, outraged at how little Martin understands, realizes that she and the baron will nonetheless need his business sense to save the day. What follows is the taming of the shrewd.

While Marianne tries to win Martin's head for the village and the values of "*Heimat,* obligation, and responsibility," Martin tries to win Marianne's heart for himself. Martin is also pursued by Inge (Susanne Cramer), the daughter of the local pub owner. She, too, has blossomed since the last time Martin saw her, a shy girl in the Silesian church, but Hartwig, the young soldier who tried to comfort her a decade earlier, is still watching her every move. Withdrawn and reticent, possessed of an otherworldly air that suggests he did not escape the war without lasting consequences, he communicates primarily by playing on a Silesian zither and exploding occasionally out of insane jealousy of Martin, even though the urban intruder has in no way encouraged Inge's advances. Inflamed by his resentment of Martin, Hartwig denounces the baron, charging both grandfather and grandson with colluding to sell off the newly established *Heimat* to the highest bidder. Ejected for such heresy and defeatism from the pub where Inge works, he races off into the night, apparently armed and dangerous.

Slowly but surely, Martin begins to realize that something is amiss in the baron's business affairs, but he also comes to understand that with the right kind of management, the glassworkers could enter a mass-export market. Much contributes to this turnaround: he takes a long walk through the snowy landscape accompanied by the local forester (Gert Fröbe), a man who would have prevented any tree harvesting "if I had not been a prisoner of war"; he looks in on an artisanal family, busy making hand-carved figurines for Christmas; and together with Marianne he spends an afternoon with a glassmaker who explains to his children and grandchildren that the delicate bubbles he puts into his glass objects are the tears of Holy Hedwig, the patron saint of Silesia, who "weeps for all the people who have lost their homes" (Fig. 29). Martin slowly comes to understand that in the *Heimat,* more than the bottom line is at stake.

Before he can untangle his grandfather's finances and lead the *Heimat* into the future, however, he must confront his own present. Simone has arrived from Paris, on the day of the annual village festival and dance. Martin is in her hotel room, where, fresh from the bath, she has just put on her robe, when in walks Marianne. Scandalized—and clearly jealous—

Marianne storms from the room, although by now Martin's unaccustomed awkwardness and inhibition have made Simone realize that, for him, there is no place like home. She concedes that her "time to disappear" has come.

Before Martin patches up things with Marianne, he sets off to solve the mystery of the baron's affairs. On his way to get new information from a local informant, however, he is shot. A jealous Hartwig is the prime suspect. Marianne, meanwhile reassured by Simone that Martin's heart belongs to her and the *Heimat,* learns of Martin's injury. Together with the baron she rushes off to find him. Before they arrive, Martin's informant, a crusty old farmer, has taken him in, dressed his wound, and offered evidence of the manager's crimes. The baron and Marianne arrive just as the local gendarme appears with Hartwig in tow, but they quickly realize that Hartwig was not pursuing Martin; rather, he had traveled to Poland to visit their Silesian village. Originally planning to retrieve official documents left behind when he fled so that he could emigrate, leaving the old memories behind forever, Hartwig has now returned to his true home, his new *Heimat* in Bavaria, to report that under Polish control, Silesia is in a state of complete collapse; the work of generations of Germans has crumbled in a mere decade. After a wild chase up and down snow-covered hillsides in pursuit of Martin's assailant, foresters and police finally catch the manager, just as he and his wife attempt to cross into Communist Czechoslovakia—that safe haven for all criminals, the other side of the border between West and East.

The way is now clear for Martin's union with Marianne, who is convinced that Martin has left Paris behind once and for all. The time has also arrived for the village's union with modernity. The entire population marches into town to celebrate the arrival of the new generator, the village band oompahing away, in a scene that is a mixture of a religious processional and a Soviet rural festival of the 1930s extolling the five-year plan and the electrification of the countryside. The baron, who for much of the movie has bumbled more than led, now takes charge as he did a decade earlier, the restored patriarch, with Martin, the heir apparent, by his side. "My dear friends from the old and new *Heimat,* today we celebrate the start of a new chapter that will carry us a bit further. All beginnings are difficult, we Silesians know that. But we have fought our way through." Armed with the latest technology, they will continue to fight. And lest the audience miss this enthusiastic endorsement of the merger of old and new, as the generator arrives, so too does a package for Marianne: Simone has sent her a wildly fashionable Parisian hat and a bridal veil. There is nothing backward about this *Heimat.*[45]

Premiering five years after *Grün ist die Heide, Waldwinter* focused not on the problems of integrating "new citizens" but on their contributions to the *Heimat* that had taken them in. Transported to Bavaria, Silesians were ready to rebuild not only their own lives but also a new Germany. They were not troubled souls, still working through a disturbing past by poaching in protected forests, nor were they freeloaders riding on a wave of economic prosperity; rather, their numerous talents, hard work, and solid values were part of what was making prosperity and continued growth possible.[46] An initial helping hand from the state thus seemed a small price to pay. At a moment when the "economic miracle" was finally becoming a reality for West Germany, registering in an expanded range of consumer goods and a rising standard of living, the movie made it clear that expellees could also claim responsibility for these developments.[47]

Silesians, ready to embrace modernity, had brought with them unique values; as one reviewer put it, "Their mystics and visionaries, their poets and storytellers, [were] altogether a vast wealth of intelligence and memory" that commanded respect.[48] In the movie's final scene, the entire village assembles once again at a church—an exact replica of the one they left behind in Silesia, which at this point seems a gratuitous reminder that the old can indeed be restored in a new context. The very title of the film makes the same point. *Waldwinter,* originally a novel written at the turn of the century by a regional Silesian novelist, Paul Keller, had made it once before into the movie theaters, produced under the Nazis in 1936.[49] Tradition did not mean it was necessary to reject generators, world markets, or Parisian fashion. Just as an old story from the turn of the century or a movie from the 1930s could take on new meanings in a transformed context, in the right hands artisanally produced Silesian glass could turn a profit and reach well beyond West Germany's borders. The market for tradition was limitless. The problems of economic integration were not ignorance or a resistance to new things; rather, it was wheeler-dealers like the estate manager, rotten individuals who had chosen not to put *Gemeinnutz vor Eigennutz* (common good before individual interest), who erected the barricades on the road to success. These are the lessons Martin must learn. Once restored to the *Heimat,* he, too, grasps how to wed tradition and modernity. The evil manager ultimately seeks refuge in the land of criminals behind the iron curtain.

The film makes it clear that the manager, the only real lawbreaker in the movie, has no military past. In contrast, explains the baron's wife to Marianne, Martin "was in the war, and he lost his parents. Then he was a prisoner of war, after he had been lied to and deceived along with the rest of us." And Martin himself, whose aspirations to become a surgeon were interrupted by a command performance driving a German tank, declares that he has turned to business after the war as a way to forget—the model of what more than a decade later the Mitscherlichs would describe as West Germany's flight into economic expansion as a way to avoid confronting the past.[50] Under Marianne's gentle, therapeutic guidance, however, Martin comes to understand that another past exists, one of unvarnished honesty and truth.

A year after the suspension of the western Allied statute of occupation and West Germany's entry into NATO, the movie also emphasized that France and Germany could be friends, if not lovers. Love and money were not the same. West Germans could do business in Paris, but when it came to looking for hearth and home, Germans sought Germans, and the French knew when to retreat graciously.

Like Martin's, Marianne's parents are dead; indeed, the movie is conveniently silent about the generation that would have participated most actively in and gained most significantly from National Socialism. Instead the tough work of postwar reconstruction is entrusted to the generation that was socialized in the Kaiserreich—the baron "is approaching seventy"—or the one that was too young to know better under the Nazis and had already atoned with material losses or detention as a POW. The new Germany would build only on the best of the old, with incriminating parts of the past simply going unmentioned.

Heimat Is Where the Heart Is

Ännchen von Tharau, a drama that "presented the problems that confronted thousands of people robbed of their *Heimat,*" appeared two years before *Waldwinter.*[51] Anna Wittkuhn (Ilsa Werner), like Marianne, shows herself able to do the hard work of sinking economic roots into new soil. And like Marianne, she is capable of physically and psychologically rehabilitating men, though Ulrich Lessau (Heinz Engelmann) is no successful entrepreneur who needs to be reminded of the values of home. A skilled machine-builder schooled in engineering and physics, he has chosen a nomadic existence, but when he enters Anna's life his cheerful exterior hides a gnawing uncertainty. As in *Grün ist die Heide,* the carnival serves as a symbol of disorder and instability, a world from which Anna initially wants to shield her son, Utz (Klaus-Ulrich Krause).

When Ulrich asks Anna whether she ever thinks Utz might need a father, it is obvious that he needs a son; as Ulrich admits, he "has no one who would make it all worthwhile." Anna understands that her secret knowledge of his identity would give meaning to Ulrich's existence, but she fears losing her own reason for living. Even so, she cannot deny the attraction between Utz and Ulrich (Fig. 30). As the publicity materials for the film explained, "the man and child are curiously attracted to each other; they do not understand that 'the voice of blood' has spoken."[52]

Ulrich is also attracted to the boy's mother, and his growing affection for Anna leads him to share parts of his past. He tells her, for instance, that he was in East Prussia shortly before he was shot down on the eastern front, the first step on the way to a POW camp behind the Urals. The more Anna is in turn drawn to Ulrich, the less attractive are the entreaties of her other suitor, the heir to the local vineyard.

Ulrich is ready to settle down. His technical expertise becomes known to a contractor finishing preliminary surveys for a project to dredge the Main, thereby making it accessible to larger ships and world markets. Silesian glass and Mainzer wines are uniquely German products that everyone wants. On the spot, Ulrich is offered a job: in the midst of the economic miracle, there is work for everyone. By now, it is obvious that more than steady employment inclines Ulrich to stay, but offhand gossip misinforms him about Anna's marital intentions, leading him abruptly to change his plans and head off to rejoin the carnival, which has already left for its next port of call.

A son needs his father, however, and Utz sets off upriver, following Ulrich's trail to Würzburg. When Anna finds that Utz is missing, she panics. Informed by the contractor that the boy has hitched a ride on a barge heading up the Main, she quickly enlists Adrian Rotenbach, who, though disappointed in love, owns a car and is ready to be a friend. Together they drive off to retrieve Utz. She finds the boy sound asleep in Ulrich's bed and finally tells him what the "voice of blood" told the audience long ago. Ulrich, though, asserts no a priori parental rights; he wants to marry Anna and earn his place as a father, an offer Anna and Utz readily accept.

In *Ännchen von Tharau*, Ulrich realizes that the way to overcome his ennui and reestablish his manhood is through fatherhood, marriage, and the full application of his talents in West Germany's sustained march into the world economy. Utz's legitimacy is never at issue in the movie; he simply represents the confusion of those troubled times, when love was abruptly interrupted by air raid sirens or the call back to arms and children were not blamed for their parents' brief moments of passion. Utz's biological mother is completely absent, a distant memory who vanishes after delivering her newborn to Anna. She does not have to fret about whether to wait for the return of a soldier-father presumed dead, nor does she inhabit any space in Ulrich's heart or mind. That part of the past poses no problems.

For Anna, biology is not destiny; rather, the war's end has shaped her fate, and like the Madonna—seen frequently in the background of scenes where she appears—she is without sin. In the postwar world she inhabits, women may outnumber men, but for the right kind of woman there is an ample supply of eligible bachelors. Put off by a suitor too young to have known the real meanings of war and too rich to appreciate what it takes to create an existence from scratch, she ultimately finds happiness with a fellow traveler. Both she and Ulrich "have been marked by the small and big worries of the postwar years."[53] She shares his suffering, and he in turn sees straight into her heart.

Anna is precisely what her town—and the Federal Republic—need, embodying as she does the values of hard work and a willingness to accommodate and adjust without complaint. The other central female character in the film is the manager of the traveling carnival, a woman old enough to be Anna's mother, whose décolletage and excessive makeup identify her as a "new woman" of the old sort, a representative of the sexually charged 1920s (Fig. 31). In the 1950s, now completely gone to seed, she is out of place; she can charm the older generation at the wine restaurant's *Stammtisch,* but she is definitely not Germany's future. Anna is the "new woman" of the Adenauer era; she can take care of herself and Utz, but without marriage her life is not complete.

Biology does not tie Anna to Utz, but there is never any question that she is the real mother; she has cared for her son, and she will care for his father. Similarly, paternity alone does not a father make, and the "voice of blood" barks no orders. Anna and Ulrich will enjoy the companionate marriage in which women and men were different but equal, the form of modern union celebrated by postwar sociologists of the family and institutionalized in the reformed Civil Code that was making its way through the Bundestag even as audiences watched this movie couple achieve happiness.[54]

Neither Anna nor Ulrich, any more than Lüders and Helga Lüdersen or the transported Silesians of *Waldwinter,* finds any fulfillment by retreating into fantasies of the world they have lost; rather, they embrace the new. Modernity figures comically in a running gag about the local tavern owner's plans to bring in business by sponsoring a film festival; it is launched by a special evening for expellees, where they watch a movie about the breeds of horses in the East Prussian region they have left behind. Other expellees also charge headlong into the spirit of the economic miracle. An older couple, burgeoning entrepreneurs, start a thriving business with an ice cream pushcart. And a lovable old drunk, who weeps for joy when he sees his beloved East Prussian horses on the silver screen, inherits a broken-down horse, which he rehabilitates and which rehabilitates him, providing the means to establish a light hauling service that builds his self-respect. Even quaint expellees are industrious, needing little startup capital to get going.

Elsewhere in the film, modernity is no laughing matter. The town universally endorses the project to dredge the Main, which promises to bring German wine to the world, "from the Black Sea to the North Sea." The age of *Heimat* is not the age of environmental anxiety, and when one local worries that the fumes from passing ships will spoil the best wine-growing regions, he is assured that elsewhere, precisely where the air is worst, the grapes grow best. Those who might fear the excesses of the economic miracle are reminded that even modernity's exhaust can be a good thing.

A modern economy and a modern marriage also require mobility; when the movie ends, a blissful Anna declares that she and Utz will follow Ulrich anywhere. It is hearts and hard work that make the *Heimat*, not the opposite.

Little Girl Lost

Suchkind 312, which premiered in 1955, is set not in the mountains, a pristine forest, or along the picturesque banks of the Main but in the lap of bourgeois luxury. In its opening sequence, Ursula Gothe (Inge Egger), an expellee who has found a new life in Wiesbaden, is assisted by a maid as she busily sets the breakfast table for her husband, Robert (Paul Klinger), and son, Hellmuth, in a morning room that was well beyond the dreams of most West Germans in the early 1950s (Fig. 32). This is the "economic miracle" imagined, not lived. Robert, a prim, exacting martinet, briskly tells Ursula how she should spend her day improving his life and prettying herself for an evening with his immediate supervisor, a social event with clear professional implications. When Ursula recalls that her husband's boss, on his last visit, burned a cigarette hole in her couch, Robert blithely suggests that such mishaps should trouble their insurance agent, not them. Ursula expresses her amazement that even the upholstery is insured, whereupon Robert assures her that they "are insured for virtually everything. . . . Nothing can happen to us." Little does he know.

Ursula has a past that no insurance can make whole. With Robert off to work, she is riveted by a local newspaper that she had stashed away while Robert was in the room, and she studies a picture of a girl seeking her parents. In the late 1940s and 1950s, the "search service" (*Suchdienst*) of the German Red Cross sought to reunite families divided as they fled eastern Europe at the war's end (Fig. 33).[55] Ursula is a part of this history. She has a daughter, Martina (Ingrid Simon), from a romance late in the war, but she and the child became separated in their flight from the Red Army. She presumes that her lover, Achim Lenau (Alexander Kerst), sent to the eastern front late in the war, remained there for eternity. Their child's whereabouts are unknown; after five years of unsuccessful searching, Ursula had given up hope. Now Martina stares at her from the front page of the illustrated press. Ursula has said nothing of her child to her husband because she fears his response; Robert is a man of the future, the West German civil servant who has cleared away the war's ruins and thinks that a secure present will ward off any problems from the past. But the newspaper picture now prompts her to tell all to Robert's sister, Jo, the owner of an antique store, who trafficks in memories and is ready to help Ursula reunite with Martina. Using Jo's address, she writes to the Red Cross, asking for more information about the child.

Ursula is not the only one making inquiries. Achim Lenau, like Ulrich Lessau, has returned from the dead and appears in the Red Cross office, demanding to see his daughter. Achim has little patience for bureaucratic formalities. How can a man who has been in Siberia for six years have all the identity papers these officials require? What Achim mistakes for hard-heartedness, however, is necessary if Martina's true parents are to be identified; so far there have been three other inquiries about her. Determining Martina's biological origin will require a thorough examination by a professor from the Institute of Anthropology. After a bevy of blood tests and the assessment of physical characteristics, this man will establish whose child she is. Once again, the "voice of blood" will have the last word.

Achim manages to get Jo's address from the official, and he soon appears on her doorstep. The reunion with Ursula follows, with Achim ready to start over where they left off. His six years in Siberia have only intensified his love for Ursula; thoughts of her are all that kept him going, and he never lost the compass she gave him, engraved with the message "So that you will always find the way to me." Ursula is also ready to follow her heart, but holding her back is her commitment to her marriage and, especially, Hellmuth.

Robert realizes that something is amiss when Ursula, neglecting her housewifely responsibilities, begins to steal time for secret meetings with Achim. He pushes for an explanation, and she holds nothing back. Outraged, Robert informs Ursula that if she reclaims her child, there will be no choice but to send Martina away to school in Sweden or Switzerland; any revelation of this scandal will mean his professional ruin. Ursula counters with the past, rhetorically asking how Robert can pretend to sit in judgment when "he has never experienced flight, starvation, homelessness." He is spoiled by affluence, she says, having inherited his house from his uncle and been put through university by his parents. Still, Hellmuth stops Ursula from fleeing: as she bolts from the house, she trips on one of the boy's toys and ends up in the hospital, her reunion with Achim delayed.

Difficulties are compounded when Martina goes missing. Having been delivered by her foster parents to a threatening, anonymous municipal dormitory where she is to spend the night before her "anthropological" test, she flees and wanders about the Hamburg docks; there she is picked up by a kindly crew of precinct police. Knowing only that Martina is lost, Ursula rushes to Hamburg where the police reunite mother and daughter. Achim soon follows. A short time later, with their anthropological bona fides established, the family is made whole. Blood has triumphed yet again. The adorable Martina innocently adjusts to the complexities of this new arrangement. Her last name is now Hanka—from her foster parents—her father is Lenau, and her mother is Gothe; if this creates no problems for Martina, why should it for anyone else?

The reconstituted family retreats to Hanover and the tidy, modest company bungalow that Achim has secured, a benefit from his job as an electrical engineer and an expression of the child-friendly face of West German capitalism. Ursula, however, is still torn between her past and present, and in a fit of conscience, she returns to Robert and her son. Completely unsympathetic to her plight, Robert guarantees that divorce will result in her losing custody of Hellmuth.

While Ursula works at sorting things out, Achim and Martina are happily setting up house; in the mother's absence, the daughter provides an air of domesticity that Achim alone could never achieve (Fig. 34). However, the daughter's desire to be an even better housekeeper by finding the right implement to drain noodles for her father's dinner leads her into risky territory: a department store, a realm of pleasure and danger in which she is truly an innocent abroad. Although she focuses exclusively on housewares, when her back is turned a stylishly dressed female shoplifter drops a stolen nylon blouse, an unambiguous symbol of consumer excess, into Martina's bag. The house detectives suspect collusion and arrest Martina. Achim quickly appears and insists on his daughter's innocence, but the store officials, baffled by the multiple last names of this family, report the case to the local youth affairs office.

An investigation establishes that because only Ursula has legal custody of Martina, Achim will have to surrender the girl to foster care unless her mother appears or abdicates her parental rights to Achim. Ursula is ready to accept the latter of these impossible choices, but before she can get to Hanover to tell Achim, Hellmuth falls ill. Torn between her two children, Ursula delegates Jo to go in her stead and explain things to Martina and Achim. Achim, sensing Martina's need for a motherly presence, asks Jo to stay. She agrees to do so temporarily in order to restore domestic order, but an aunt is no mother. The youth affairs office insists that Ursula join her daughter. Ready to surrender full custody to Achim, she ultimately appears at his door unannounced, bringing a sleeping Hellmuth with her. She spins a tale of moving to start over in a different city with Robert, but when she hastily exits she sets out to end her life completely, not begin a new one. Jo and Achim intervene to prevent her suicide and assist in negotiating a reconciliation with Robert, who confesses his "jealousy about [her] past" but also passionately proclaims his abiding love and his willingness to change. Achim is prepared to step aside. He cannot destroy a marriage, and Ursula must return to Robert, remaining loyal and giving her husband a chance to create a true home that will also include Martina.

Suchkind 312 was based on a book that appeared first in serialized form in a popular radio program guide that reached more West Germans than any other weekly magazine by the mid-1950s, then as a novel.[56] The publicity promoting the movie stressed the director's difficulty in finding a child to play Martina when the Martina of the illustrated magazine, advertised on light poles throughout West Germany, was already so firmly established in the public's mind. The young actress he finally chose, Ingrid Simon, herself a refugee child, filled the bill; life merged with art.[57] The tale of children separated from parents in the chaos of the war's end was a familiar one; as one reviewer reminded readers, there were 97,000 Martinas who since 1945 had been reunited with their families by the press and radio advertisements of the Red Cross.[58] Even reviewers who criticized the "overcooked, sloppy" tone of the film agreed that it addressed a theme of enormous significance in the postwar world; it illuminated the fate of "homeless children lost on the flight [from the east], carried off by strangers, left waiting for father and mother in hygienic but hapless institutional homes, without names or birthdates."[59] For those who judged the movie favorably, it, like the novel on which it was based, was a "timely protest on behalf of all children who were left over as victims of the last war."[60]

Robert, jealous of Ursula's past, has raced too quickly into the future. He studied while Achim fought, but he failed to learn much about the most important things in life. The perverted values of a timeless, rigid, upper middle class, conformism without compassion, and a false security that masks soullessness prevent him from seeing beyond form to substance. Precisely these values, the movie implies, have gotten Germans in trouble before, as the movie's POW and expellee well know.

Other dangers await West Germans in the early 1950s. Robert's well-appointed home is a sign that he has become lost in external expressions of success, and Martina's brush with consumer culture becomes a brush with the law. Money can even be a way to buy love, and one of Martina's would-be mothers arrives at her foster home in a huge convertible, bribes her with chocolates, and offers her foster parents 10,000 DM to surrender the child without the inconvenience of bureaucratic paperwork.

Not all expressions of consumer society are bad, of course. The movie reminds the audience that by exploiting the illustrated press and the radio, the Red Cross has reunited many children and parents. *Suchkind 312* in both movie and print versions also suggests how the media of mass culture can be used to communicate important commentaries on the legacies of the war. But dangers will emerge when desire exceeds need and the law. As in *Waldwinter,* expellees and POWs seem particularly well positioned to recognize when the economic miracle threatens to be too much of a good thing.

Achim has rebounded from his prisoner-of-war experience with apparent success, but his financial stability has not led to conspicuous consumption. His entry into the economic miracle is marked by moderation. After six years in Siberia, Achim knows things that Robert begins to understand only when he confronts his own personal crisis and potential loss. Indeed, Achim must also instruct Ursula. When a marriage still exists, it has to be preserved. This message was communicated not only by *Suchkind 312* but also by West German courts that proclaimed it was not the state's responsibility to sort out abnormal relationships when they constituted a "conscious attack on the institution of marriage."

The marriages that needed protecting were those sanctioned by church and state.[61] If the confusion of the war permitted the suspension of dominant moral norms, by the early 1950s it was time to return to that completely redeemable part of the status quo.

Achim, though an instant father, still cannot make a house a home. A husband with no wife is a man in trouble. Achim's respect for the institution of marriage exceeds his longing to fulfill his fantasy of a family with Ursula, but in their time together Jo and Achim identify much that joins a man who understands his past and a woman whose business is collecting memories. Indeed, there is a strong suggestion (spelled out explicitly in the serialized novel) that this woman "standing alone" has met the right man. Frau and Herr Gothe are given another chance to preserve an established marriage, while Jo and Achim can look forward to creating a new one. Expellee and POW both enjoy happy endings, each integrated by different means into a West Germany ready to learn from their experiences.

Winning the Battle of Stalingrad

In movies that focused on the expellees, the shooting war usually served only as background. In a raft of other 1950s movies, shots were fired not by poachers or gendarmes racing up and down snow-covered hills in hot pursuit, but by soldiers of the Wehrmacht on battlefields from North Africa to Stalingrad.[62] These movies invariably told a story of noble German men who had been sent to fight battles they could not win. Although doctrinaire Nazis were certainly present, depicted as a mix of corruption, comic blundering, and blind fanaticism, the true German man wore a uniform because he had to; meanwhile, he sought to outsmart commanding officers at every turn, wanting only to protect fellow comrades and return to hearth and home. He fought bravely but only to ensure that the Russians would not make homecoming impossible. The nation he represented was not National Socialist but German, and the territory he defended was not the Führer's bunker but the *Heimat*—the Lüneburger Heide, the Bavarian countryside, and the Silesian mountains. The rehabilitation of the German military on the screen thus closely paralleled the rehabilitation of the German military by the western Allies and the Bundestag, as West Germans, chastened by their experiences, once again put on uniforms, profoundly aware that not all orders should be followed unquestioningly. Hungry for peace and sta-

bility, not power or territory in eastern Europe, they were still ready to
take up arms against the Soviet army, the same opponent featured in so
many war movies.

Dramatic presentations of the war in the east also made explicit the
ties between defeat and imprisonment for thousands of German soldiers.
Hunde, wollt ihr ewig leben? (Dogs, do you want to live forever?), a 1959
movie that examined the Wehrmacht's overwhelming defeat at Stalingrad in February 1943, ended with newsreel footage of soldiers being
marched off to prisoner-of-war camps. Directed by Frank Wisbar, a German who had left in 1938 and returned from a career in movies and television in the United States in 1955, the film was judged the second-best
West German movie of 1959, and it was awarded a prize of 100,000
DM from the Interior Ministry. Wisbar was praised for his extraordinary accomplishment, and in the same year that Theodor Adorno won
the prize in literature from the League of West Berlin Critics, Wisbar won
the league's film prize for *Hunde*.[63] Celebrating it as a pacifist movie that
"represented a monument to the innocent victims of the war," critics concluded that packed theaters were a clear indication that "even movie audiences were now ready to contribute to the so-called 'mastering of the
past.'" The movie was a "German Requiem" in which those mourned
were soldiers in Wehrmacht uniforms who lay dead in the rubble of Stalingrad or who survived as part of the "kilometer-long caravan of suffering" that led to Soviet POW camps (Fig. 35).[64]

Der Arzt von Stalingrad, which premiered in 1958, picked up the tune
where the "German Requiem" left off, following defeated Germans to
incarceration behind barbed wire. The director, Geza von Radvanyi, a
Hungarian who had moved to Paris in the 1920s, described the film as
the last part of a trilogy about the war. At the start of the decade, he
had directed *Frauen ohne Namen* (Women without names), a fictional
story of an international group of women, without homes or identity
papers, in a holding camp outside Trieste at the end of the war; and *Irgendwo in Europa* (Somewhere in Europe), the tale of a gang of children, victims of the fascists, left homeless orphans in wartorn Hungary.[65]
In this new work, the detainees were Germans in uniform, not civilians,
and the war's victims were German men, not eastern European boys. A
widely acclaimed director, Radvanyi had only disdain for the "*Heimat-
kitsch*" produced by his contemporaries, movies that "you could direct
from bed by telephone," and ranted against the threat to quality films
that television represented.[66] This was a serious director for a serious
theme.

Heinz Konsalik's best-selling book on which the movie was based is still available in Germany in an inexpensive paperback edition.[67] It tells the story of Dr. Hans Böhler, a character based on Otmar Kohler, a Wehrmacht doctor made legendary by accounts in the illustrated press that described how he had voluntarily stayed on in Soviet prisoner-of-war camps healing German wounds until he returned to head a Bavarian hospital in the 1950s.[68] In the movie, Böhler is played by O. E. Hasse, whose credits included a number of other war films. For example, he played the noble military resister to the insanity of Nazi orders in the 1955 film *Canaris,* and the good-natured, wise commanding officer on the eastern front in part two of *08/15,* a movie that opened in August 1955 just as Adenauer was preparing to travel to Moscow.[69] Based on the middle book in Hans Helmut Kirst's best-selling trilogy *08/15,* the story traced the odyssey of a common soldier in the Third Reich, beginning in Germany on the eve of the war and continuing in the snowbound Soviet Union.[70] Hasse's persona as a hard-headed, soft-hearted military man was therefore well established before he ever picked up the scalpel in Stalingrad.

Der Arzt von Stalingrad opens as Germans at home sip beer in a pub and listen to Hitler's voice blaring from a radio, assuring them that he will never surrender. Newsreel footage of roaring anti-aircraft guns and a burning plane plummeting from the sky are evidence that in fact there is little reason for optimism; the war has come home to Germany. The scene switches to the basement of a bombed-out building in Stalingrad, where things look even worse. From a radio mounted on the wall, Hitler's voice still encourages Germans to fight to the end, but Böhler and his comrades know that they have lost their war. Russians bearing a wounded comrade storm into the cellar and demand that Böhler scrub up and move from the German victim he is tending to their fellow soldier. Unhesitatingly, Böhler complies. This is a man of medicine, after all, not a man of war; his trade is preserving life, not ending it. The Red Army soldiers—and later the guards in the POW camp to which Böhler will be delivered—are played in large part by Asians, émigrés from western Mongolia who fled westward with the German army in the last years of the war.[71] The "Mongols," who still dominated the memories of expellees, appear here as well.

Böhler becomes the chief German doctor for a large POW facility, housed in a former church that godless Soviets have allowed to decay. The old Russia looks out from the walls in icons of saints, which frame the work of this angelic doctor; Böhler remarks that they are working in a "church where miracles have happened; we are in the best of company." In such surroundings, the good doctor will be accomplishing a few miracles of his own.

Böhler is subordinate to Soviet officials whose rooms are decorated with pictures of devils, not saints: Stalin is everywhere. The good doctor's immediate supervisor is Dr. Alexandra Kasalinskaja (Eva Bartok), a Red Army captain renowned for her heartless medical assessments that send German after German from the infirmary back to hard labor, in scenes accompanied by the music of the Red Army chorus. Böhler is assisted by a younger German doctor, Sellnow (Walter Reyer); from Böhler, Sellnow has learned medicine, not patience, and he blusters loudly about the impossible conditions under which they must work. Böhler simply carries on with solemn dignity, accomplishing the job at hand and reminding Sellnow: "You forget that we are not exactly well liked; we just have no luck with world history, it happens to us every twenty-five years." Böhler is clearly old enough to know whereof he speaks. Indeed, he too has suffered personal loss, for his daughter fell victim to a bombing raid during the war. His wife is absent altogether, even from his memories. With no one waiting for him at home, he is effectively positioned to be the caring father of the homosocial family of POWs.

Comrade Kasalinskaja is not just a doctor, she is a woman. To make the point, the camera follows her into her private quarters where she undresses behind a curtain; a German prisoner, detailed to stoke her fire, looks on, as her shapely silhouette in turn stokes his. Her lover is the camp commandant, Pjotr Markow (Hannes Messemer), whose war experiences have given him only a bitter heart and a lame arm with a prosthetic hand. But Markow is not her only suitor. The charged exchanges between Kasalinskaja and Sellnow over inadequate medical supplies are also the elixir of love, and in no time it is Sellnow, not Markow, who is appearing in the comrade doctor's bedroom. Kasalinskaja confronts Sellnow with her past sufferings and lets him know precisely how deep her bitterness toward Germans runs; she has lost her fiancé, also a doctor, who was left by the Germans to starve to death, and she shares the outrage of "millions who have lost everything. . . . I hate all of you, all of you." But if she successfully resists the romantic onslaught of the enemy at first, Sellnow's tough love, rugged good looks, and two good arms soon convince her that there is more to life than seeking revenge. When he forcefully embraces her, she orders him: "Let go! Let go! This is an order!" But unlike fanatical Nazis, Sellnow does not do everything his superiors command. As the film magazine *STAR-Revue* explained to its readers, "Love for Dr. Sellnow transforms [Kasalinskaja] into a woman who sees the human being behind the enemy" (Fig. 36).[72]

Böhler understands that he cannot surgically remove Sellnow's desire, but he does have a medical expertise that the Soviets desperately seek. Kasalinskaja's superior is the distinguished, gray-haired Major Dr. Kresin (Leonard Steckel), who knows Böhler from a past in the 1930s when their shared passion for science was far more important than Hitler and Stalin. Kresin enlists Böhler to take on a patient, the son of a silent, kind-eyed Red Army general whose chest full of medals testifies to the war he has seen but who bears no grudge; unlike Markow, he has not continued the battlefield fight behind barbed wire. The general's son is also a representative of the other Russia, a highly gifted musician who appears not in a Red Army tunic but in the folk costume of a cossack, and who plays tunes of Tchaikovsky and Russian folk melodies, not military march music. Even some Russians in uniform and their progeny, the movie implies, have survived the ideological invasions of the Communist regime. Yet the good seem destined to die young: the boy has a brain tumor. Böhler knows how to remove it, however, and Kresin offers him the chance "to repair in a small way what world history has destroyed in a big way." Finding himself in a strong bargaining position, Böhler insists on quid quo pro: he demands that the Soviets go ahead with plans to release a number of his comrades, momentarily interrupted because of reports of sabotage in the camp and the murder of an informer.

Transported to a hospital in Stalingrad—all white tiles and shiny stainless steel, precisely what Böhler lacks in the camp—the doctor and his Soviet admirer now don surgical scrubs, the uniforms they love best (Fig. 37). Turning to what is dearest and most honorable in their two cultures, they save the boy, who will live to play the violin another day. Böhler, however, cannot save Sellnow, who, unable to abandon either his men or his desire for Kasalinskaja, refuses to join the transport home. When Markow discovers Sellnow and the comrade doctor in a passionate embrace, he shoots Sellnow on the spot. As the trucks carrying off the released prisoners roll out of the camp, Kasalinskaja is taken away by "Mongolian" guards; she, too, has become a prisoner behind barbed wire. Forbidden love comes at a high price.

As Böhler asks his departing mates, "Well boys, all set?" a Soviet directs the good doctor's attention to the placard bedecking the transport truck: "No More War." "That is good," Böhler remarks, "but the Russians also should not forget it, the next time it comes around." In 1958, the "it" that might return was another catastrophe brought on by ideological systems out of control, this time armed with nuclear weapons. West Germans, restricted to a defensive role within NATO, could point a warning finger at Cold War giants not similarly contained; the brown danger of 1939 had been replaced by the red danger of the late 1950s, a Soviet Union that could drop atomic bombs. Fanaticism, not people, was the problem, and fanaticism was unique to no one nation.

The film reminded West German audiences of other familiar themes. German doctors, judged by the victorious Allies for their crimes against concentration camp victims and their participation in the Nazis' euthanasia program, appear here as compassionate, caring, and capable of healing deep wounds—of soldiers and of nations. *Der Arzt von Stalingrad* thus repeated a key message of other 1950s doctor films, this time played out in a Soviet POW camp.[73] The movie also made the point that Germans had maintained their good humor, camaraderie, and honor in the camps. The exaggerated exception, a cowardly informer, merely gets what he deserves. Böhler realizes that killing camp spies is bad business, but even he is willing to forgive such slips. War is hell, even when it is fought behind barbed wire.

German soldiers have also not lost their taste for a shapely figure, and the movie emphasizes that this homosocial world continues to rotate on a heterosexual axis. The camp scrounger, dispatched by Böhler to steal a silk scarf (a source of ersatz sutures) from female guards enjoying an after-work sauna, ogles the women endlessly before purloining their wraps. And Kasalinskaja is at the center of the fantasies of the entire camp. When Markow asks the informer what the prisoners say about her, he reports that they call her a whore. However, this in no way diminishes her charms. As one prisoner quips to another, "I'd prefer her naked in bed to you in tails and a top hat." Kasalinskaja is never naked, but she does nicely fill her uniform and her luxurious white fur-lined coat, and with both Markow and Sellnow she removes her stylish fur pillbox hat to let her hair down.

The film's explicit sexual references triggered debates within the industry's self-censorship agency (the Freiwillige Selbstkontrolle der Filmwirtschaft, or FSK) about whether such scenes endangered the morals of viewers younger than eighteen. The FSK, instituted to monitor the age appropriateness of films and made up of representatives from the industry, state cultural ministries, youth offices, and churches, also objected to a proposed poster that featured "a romantic pair, intensely kissing and embracing," because, it felt, it would detract from the "horrible occurrences in Stalingrad." The film's distributors responded to this charge with the argument that life in the camp was far removed from the fighting and that the movie could not detract from what happened in Stalingrad in any case because it did not attempt to portray those events. Critics failed to appreciate fully that the poster also featured Böhler separated by a red line from the young doctors in love.[74] Announcing a movie about a noble medical man, the poster proclaimed that a healthy German heterosexuality had not been killed, either in Stalingrad or in the camps.

From the start it is obvious that Sellnow and Kasalinskaja are star-crossed lovers, but their affair provides ample opportunity to underscore that even German men who are humiliated, reduced, starved, and disarmed still have red-blooded appetites, ones that cannot be sated with improved camp rations or care packages from home. To be sure, the move from fantasy to reality is dangerous. Böhler repeatedly warns Sellnow that by pursuing his passion he betrays his comrades, and the movie makes clear that the Nazis were not the only ones who rewarded sexual transgression with death. Indeed, imprisonment and interrogation by the Soviet secret police might be worse. For Soviets, crossing ideological lines was just as serious as crossing racial lines under National Socialism.

For affections of a purer sort, the movie leaves some space. Böhler and Kresin are a romantic odd couple, but their mutual fondness is sublimated, translated into expertise in the operating theater. Also paralleling the stormy passions of Sellnow and Kasalinskaja is the chaste hand-holding of another Russian female camp officer and a German prisoner; her attention, care, and affection are the right recuperative protocol after Böhler has saved the young soldier's life, conducting an appendectomy armed only with a pocket knife. A sketch artist, the recovering soldier depicts the Soviet in her uniform—"Nicht gut"—and then in a modest frock—"Das ist gut." The masked femininity of the Soviet comrade can flourish in the right kind of western fashion. Shorn of ideology, in suitable clothes, and remaining at the level of an innocent kiss, love need know no national boundaries.

All Soviets are not alike, of course. Some listen to the Red Army chorus, others prefer tunes from the great Russian *Heimat*. Some, like Kresin, have lived through enough regime changes and disappointed hopes to have learned patience. The generation of the 1917 revolution and the generation of Weimar embodied in Böhler understand many of the same things; neither bears responsibility for the extremes of their respective national histories. The grandfather generation is guiltless, the message symbolically represented by Grandfather Adenauer throughout the 1950s. Even some parts of the Nazi past could be reformed and put to good use. This was a theme implicit in stories on the making of the film, which noted that Radvanyi's Soviet camp and the church that now functioned as a hospital were constructed in the former studio of the infamous Nazi sculptor Joseph Thorak, the creator of grotesque forty-five-foot statues once slated to adorn Hitler's autobahn.[75]

Pictures of Stalin are ubiquitous in the Soviet camp offices, but by 1958 Khrushchev's denunciation of Stalin's crimes and a general easing of Cold War tensions had allowed West Germans and Soviets, in a world aspiring toward "peaceful coexistence," to have some enemies in common. By honestly acknowledging their troubled history, Böhler and Kresin can define a basis for cooperation. Working together, these men heal the past and sew up the future.

Favorable reviews praised Radvanyi for delivering a "demanding, good German movie," a welcome departure from the usual kitsch offered by the production company that made the film.[76] Other critics were less generous, taking Radvanyi to task for a "tone of sentimental calamity that did not ring true" and dismissing the film as a cliché-ridden expression of the movie industry's attempt to make money by exploiting the "nameless misery, the tragic suffering, of the POWs."[77] The movie that the POW experience deserved, one reviewer objected, would not allow the "terror of the Russians and the resistance of the Germans, the hunger and the sickness," to serve as an excuse for Eva Bartok to "romp about with cheerful sexuality."[78] However, even critics who insisted that Radvanyi's method was misguided agreed that his message was crucial; West Germans should not forget the "collective suffering" of POWs, a suffering that tied them to those "martyred in concentration camps."[79] The movie made it clear that thirteen years after the end of the war, Stalingrad "a symbol of German defeat that we so successfully have overcome," remained part of "our reality, even when some would have us believe that it is already long since past and forgotten."[80] Even those who thought Radvanyi had recalled Stalingrad inappropriately applauded his commitment to commemorate this German tragedy.

Snow White and the Seven Dwarves

In a Red Army uniform, the eternal feminine creates problems for Sellnow, but in the 1958 movie *Taiga*, with a German face, it works wonders.[81] With Liebeneiner again behind the camera, this tale of a "camp for three hundred men, the forgotten of the war," opens like a typical *Heimatfilm* as the camera moves slowly across a vast expanse of evergreens and the best of Germany's cultural heritage, Bach's third Brandenburg Concerto, plays in the background. But this is not the baron's endangered forest in *Waldwinter*, neither Silesia nor Bavaria, and it is presented in black and white, not the pastels of many *Heimatfilme*. Rather, this stand of timber is behind the Urals. As the camera moves down from the treetops, barbed wire disrupts a picture of tranquillity, and where it stops there is no Bach, only men at rock bottom—dispirited, demoralized, divided. Condemned to clear the endless forest, the men share a common misery, but the bonds of comradeship have loosened; one team, skilled woodcutters in civilian life, is exceeding the norm in the race for extra rations. The pastor is too demoralized to save souls, and even the doctor is sick, unable to heal himself, let alone others. Things could hardly be worse. Hannes Messemer, the vengeful Pjotr Markow of *Der Arzt von Stalingrad*, appears here as Ernst Roeder, a lone voice of reason, who tries unsuccessfully to stop this collective dissolution.

Into this mess steps Hanna Dietrich (Ruth Leuwerik), a doctor assigned to replace her sick comrade. Leuwerik was well known to West German film audiences for her portrayal of Maria in *Die Trapp-Familie* (the basis for the American musical and movie *The Sound of Music*), in which the erstwhile nun softens the edges of the brusque but kindhearted Austrian Baron von Trapp; evades evil Nazis; and escapes with her instant family to a new home in America, where she, the baron, and his musically talented children win international recognition and recording contracts for a mix of German and American folk music.[82]

In *Taiga*, there are no evil Nazis, but Leuwerik's character is once again confronted by extraordinary challenges. Billed by a film magazine as the "Angel from Siberia,"[83] she is the "woman for three hundred men," not singing children and an Austrian baron, though the Soviet commandant states in no uncertain terms that she is there to minister to their physical illnesses, not their libidos. At first, the order is all but unnecessary, and, completely unaware of her appearance, dressed in the same standard-issue *Plennianzug* as the men, her hair shorn, chain-smoking and picking the thick-cut Russian tobacco from her teeth, Hanna is ready to give up. Romance is the farthest thing from her mind. She has been transferred to this desolate location because she broke a bottle over the head of the commandant in another camp when he demanded more from her than medicine. "For a long time, you have enough strength, then it is gone. . . . Resistance, yes, that is the only thing that gives meaning to my life," she says, and she is not certain of even that any more. She speculates that this camp will be the last stop for her. Even in this state, Hanna excites the sexual lust of one rate-busting woodcutter, but she finds she has a protector in Ernst Roeder, who tucks her into a safe corner of the barracks. She will sleep safely next to him. His name—*ernst* is the German word for serious, grave, earnest—fits.

Only gradually do woman and men find their way back to western civilization. Without medicines, Hanna declares there is little she can do, but her fellow prisoners quickly show her how wrong she is. In one dramatic scene, she prevents a desperate prisoner from running into the barbed wire and meeting certain death (Fig. 38). She also proves that listening is the best therapy as the men begin to tell her stories of home, the children they know and the children they have never met, the women who are waiting and the women about whom nothing is known. Still, Hanna remains skeptical of the grandfatherly prisoner who assures her that she has given them what they most need; for her, *Liebe* is just a five-letter word. Other meanings of love she learned from the six Russians in one camp who raped her, the two prisoners who came to blows over her, and the guards in another camp who forced her to strip. Her rough exterior begins to soften only when, borrowing a mirror, she sees with her own eyes how low she has sunk. Armed with a comb and surrounded by reverential admirers, she starts the long climb up from the bottom (Fig. 39).

By the next day, after sawing wood from dawn to dusk, the prisoners return not to cold barracks, but to a happy home: Snow White awaits the Seven Dwarves. Hanna has set water to boil so the men can all wash up, and her overstuffed jacket is gone, replaced by a gauzy blouse. "Mom's going to stick us all in the bath," jokes a prisoner, but not everyone senses only a maternal warmth. When Hanna goes to fetch more wood for the fire, the overachieving woodcutter pursues her; she resists his advances, however, and crowns him with a log. The outraged men of the barracks call for blood, demanding that the offender run the gauntlet, to be driven into the fence and the deadly gunfire of the guards. Hanna is astonished; she has defended herself and "that's enough for me, but you want to kill him. . . . Have you gone crazy?" She forgives the offender, shakes his hand, and draws him back into the reformed community, which now tightly revolves around her.

One comrade offers to make her a dress, another to clean her shoes, and all agree, "You have many fathers here, yes, and some brothers too, if you want." When Hanna protests that a dress is insane in a POW camp, the barracks' sage grandfather responds that it is by no means crazy for her to "look like a woman should look." What is wrong, rather, "is the life we are living, that is crazy, that is not normal. . . . We must remember, we all have wives, and they look just like you, and that's what they're like, at home, on the street, that's what they're like" (Fig. 40). Crawling into bed next to Ernst, she makes it clear that fathers and brothers are not the only men she needs in her life; a new coiffure and the promise of a dress and clean shoes have made her "alive again, and you feel like you're alive, and you can't sleep." But Ernst's drives are still tightly capped; he is not ready to be touched by an angel.

Fortunately, fate lends romance a helping hand. Ernst and Hanna are riding in the back of a Russian truck, assigned to accompany an injured comrade from the forest work detail. The backfiring truck—a tribute to Russian technical ability, as Ernst wryly comments—jerkily comes to a halt, providing Ernst and Hanna with a private moment for a passionate embrace. Showering her with kisses, Ernst dubs her "my dachshund, my beautiful little dachshund," an outburst Hanna correctly interprets as an expression of affection. Snow White has met her prince, and the family of the barracks is now complete. Hanna and Ernst retreat to their corner to tell stories of their prewar lives and to imagine a postwar future; despair has given way to pillow talk. Hanna gets the love she needs, and Ernst is once again a man.

The prince, Snow White, and the dwarves settle into comfortable domestic rituals, until one night when Hanna is summoned to the commandant's quarters. The brave men of the camp, knowing that Russians have only one thing on their minds when they see a German woman, are not about to leave Hanna defenseless, and, three hundred strong, they assemble to rescue her. What awaits Hanna, however, is no threat to her honor, but the news that she will soon be released. "Thoughts know no distances," Ernst reassures her, and they will one day be reunited. As she departs, the camera follows her through the barbed wire out into the endless forest, and a voice-over offers a benediction: "A year later the men were also released and returned home. At the border, waiting for them along with many others, was a woman, a woman to whom they owed so much: their lives, and more than their lives, for hope and faith are more than life."

Some critics praised the relentless realism of Liebeneiner's movie, his ability to capture the "genuine squeaking of the boots in the mud, the exhausted march through the gate of the camp, and the nocturnal scream of the infirm, whose nerves have snapped."[84] Critics who feared that Leuwerik was "good, somewhat too good," just as Messmer was "too noble" but admitted that the last word belonged to those "who know the reality," discovered that among the movie's most enthusiastic

fans was the League of Returning Veterans, POWs, and Relatives of Those
Missing in Action, which had been involved in advising Reinecker on
the screenplay.[85] A spokesman for the league, which in 1955 claimed a
membership of half a million, acknowledged the potential power of
movies to "accomplish a broad, penetrating work and an educational
function that should not be underestimated." Precisely movies like *Taiga*
could serve as a "jarring source of self-reflection for large parts of the
German people," teaching them about an experience that had profoundly
marked their fathers, grandfathers, brothers, and uncles.[86] The movie offered important lessons to an ignorant postwar generation of young
people. Individual league members showered Leuwerik with fan mail and
presents, and at a special premiere for former POWs a leader of the organization celebrated the movie as a "deeply moving condemnation of
the elevated slogans of our twentieth century."[87] Four years after *Taiga*
opened, the league still judged it "the best film about the theme of the
POW experience since the end of the war."[88]

In its unabashed affirmation of the healing powers of femininity and
domesticity, however, *Taiga* described the then-dominant ideology of
hearth and home far more effectively than it did conditions in a Soviet
prisoner-of-war camp. In its portrayal of Hanna as a woman who was
feminine but also tough, self-reliant, and able to take care of herself, the
movie echoed the ways in which the housewife and mother of the postwar era—the veteran of bomb attacks and postwar privation—was capable of many things. Like Anna/Ännchen, Hanna is a "new woman"
of the Federal, not the Weimar, Republic. Leuwerik, when interviewed
about her transformation into Hanna, commented that she actually liked
the look of the "matchstick-long haircut" that was required for the part.[89]
But even if "new women" of another era lurked within Leuwerik and
potentially appealed to some female viewers in the 1950s, for most West
Germans androgynous short haircuts were definitely not in. Hanna is not
the feminist doctor of the Weimar sex reform movement, the independent woman who can survive without a man.[90] In the movie, when she
finally looks in the mirror she is appalled by her appearance, and her
physical transformation is the first step toward her psychological, emotional, and sexual recovery. Her attraction to Ernst is triggered by his
eagerness to protect her, and a new frock seems to free her even of her
nicotine habit. Her fondest memories are of home, her sisters, and her
father, a doctor who spends his evenings playing cards with the local phar-
macist and the keeper of the graveyard; in talking with Ernst she spins
out scenes of the *Heimat* very similar to those depicted in other movies

of the 1950s. Her mother is altogether absent. Her father's example has led her to medicine, and his words ring in her ears: "Since I wanted to study medicine, he said to me, 'My child, a human being is God's miracle, and who has not understood that can never be a good doctor.'" Faith and hope, not politics, have brought Hanna to the healing profession. Indeed, once her transformation has taken place, she seems not even to frequent the camp sick ward; her healing powers come from her maternal instincts, not her medical knowledge.

Hanna helps the men, but they help her as well. The same images of men filled with love for family, not the camaraderie of the front, seen everywhere in Friedland in the fall of 1955 are here in excess. When Hanna's "fathers" and "brothers" are released by the Soviets, they will head to their loved ones, not to nostalgic reunions with former comrades. Longing for domesticity, they are ready to share their emotions. What has riddled their souls is not their crimes against humanity, but the inhumane conditions of the camp. The stories they rush to tell Hanna are not of exploits in battle; rather, they are tales of "*Heimat,* wife, and children, [of] loving and being loved."[91]

Ernst, afraid of his own emotions, is at first reluctant to pursue intimacy with Hanna in the barracks, which would be tantamount to a primal scene in front of assembled fathers and brothers, but when the time is right, he is ready for love. Along with him, all German men are prepared to defend the reputation of a German woman. The movie implicitly revisits postwar memories of "Frau, komm," the demand of the Red Army soldier to the unprotected German woman, the victim of the victor's revenge, in order to banish those memories, another indication of how vivid they remained long after the war. In *Taiga,* the commandant's "Frau, komm" is met with a determined show of force, evidence that, the second time around, German men would not leave mothers, daughters, wives, and lovers at risk. For Hanna, resistance may be the only thing that gives meaning to her life when the film begins, but by the end life's meaning rests in love and heterosexual union. For the men in the camp as well, love is a healing balm, but the end of the film indicates clearly that rediscovering the ability to resist is central to the meaning of a restored and renewed German masculinity.

Anne Frank behind the Urals

Billed as a balanced assessment of the POW experience, one in which neither heroes nor villains wore only one uniform, and a necessary reminder to a younger generation that threatened to forget what the POWs had suffered, *Der Teufel spielte Balalaika,* directed by Leopold Lahola, was released in 1961.[92] Though the movie was shot in the Lüneburger Heide, there was nothing green about the heath where Lahola filmed his musical devil, and once again the Germans behind barbed wire were depicted in black and white (Fig. 41). The movie tells the story of a camp that houses both German and Japanese prisoners, sentenced to long terms breaking rocks in a Soviet quarry. Into this bleak world comes a woman, this time neither German nor Russian. Elena Seidenwar (Anna Smolik) is a Viennese Jew who has joined the Red Army as a translator after her liberation from a Nazi concentration camp; gratitude and political conviction have also led to marriage with a Russian, a Red Army political officer.

Elena translates Russian into the Germans' native tongue, and she knows that "without words, people cannot understand one another." She also translates German experience into the terms of Jewish suffering. Analogies between Elena's past and that of the German POWs are not left to the imagination. She has arrived slightly in advance of her husband, and on her first night in the barracks she is awakened by terrifying nightmares in which the visions of her past invade the present and appear on the screen. As she later explains to her husband, "I dreamed this barbed wire is my barbed wire, this imprisonment is my imprisonment." Brown or red, barbarism is barbarism.

Elena's husband, understanding that mindless vengeance serves no purpose in the camp, seeks instead to use his insights into human nature to create a more equitable order. However, he constantly confronts opposition from the camp commandant, Lieutenant Fusow (Pierre Parel), who takes solace in the bottle and whose arbitrary cruelty makes him despised by all. Seidenwar (Charles Millot), the camp political officer, has no sympathy for the system of brute force institutionalized by his drunken compatriot and reinforced by the German Antifa (antifascist) officer, Gellert (Günter Jerschke), a corrupt martinet who misuses the many talents of his German charges. Though far from forgetting why the Germans are there, Seidenwar nevertheless is able to see the senselessness of demanding an eye for an eye; he therefore proposes a regime that makes the most of German know-how. He also shows compassion and respect for an elderly, mentally imbalanced admiral, who seeks only to take to his grave his World War I medal, awarded by the Kaiser. And when the tyrannical Lieutenant Fusow demands that another prisoner surrender a picture of his family because it depicts the loving father in a German uniform,

Seidenwar intervenes, simply cutting out militarized paternity and allowing the man to keep his wife and children.

Elena and her husband find that their most willing student in this
"barbed-wire university" is Peter Joost (Götz George), a voice of reason
and respectability in the German barracks. On the night of her horrifying dream as she seeks to flee her demons, Elena unwittingly races into
the men's barracks—and straight into Peter's arms, where she finds reassurance in ample measure. He is not the sort of German who sent her
to a concentration camp; rather, he is suffering through his own living
nightmare. In Peter's exchanges with Elena, the movie hammers home
the equivalence of German victims and victims of Germans. If anything,
opines Peter, Germans are worse off. "Yes, you were under arrest, but
all over the world people were fighting for you; that was right, I know,
but what of us? No one loses sleep because of us, and perhaps that [too]
is just." But Elena withholds judgment: "Whoever has truly suffered for-
gets how to hate," she responds, uttering a line that was featured prominently in promotional materials for the film, just as Anne Frank's benediction, "In spite of everything I still believe that people are really good
at heart," had been celebrated as her central message when her story came
to the German stage in 1956.[93]

The understanding Peter seeks from Elena is never sexual, but their
intimacy is enough to lead her to share cigarettes and secrets about the
upcoming transport home of some Germans. Some of Joost's mates, however, believe that he has given, not received, information; specifically, they
suspect he has disclosed their escape plans. They lie in wait for him in
the quarry and arrange for a hauling cart to careen off the tracks, badly
injuring him; they place him in jeopardy as well by hiding their escape
map in his bandages while he recovers in the barracks. Seidenwar, accompanied by Gellert, conducts a search that reveals the map, prima facie grounds for naming Joost as an accomplice. In addition, Seidenwar
senses that Joost has learned of the coming transport and that Elena is
his source. Planning an escape is a political crime, but instead of reporting
Joost, Seidenwar—who like Elena has suffered enough to stop hating—
exercises his reason, contains his jealousy, and adds Joost's name to the
list of those who will be sent home, explaining that he "is one of the few
who has learned something." Soon Joost is preparing to leave, but not
before Fusow, tipped off by Gellert, the Antifa informer, discovers that
he was once in possession of the escapees' map, a fact that Seidenwar
has kept to himself. It is too late to stop the transport, though, and within
a short time Joost is on his way back to Germany. As the movie ends,

Seidenwar is also leaving. However, he is not heading home but to an interrogation cell of the secret police. In tears, Elena watches from within the camp, framed by barbed wire, as the two men in her life depart, one free, the other on his way to prison (Fig. 42).

Der Teufel spielte Balalaika brought accolades to the producer, Peter Bamberger, himself a six-year veteran of Soviet POW camps, who won praise for his courageous willingness to address an important topic, "an appeal to humanity" and "a piece of our national past," in an unsentimental, uncompromising fashion.[94] For most West Germans in 1961, the search for truth included remarkably forceful, explicit comparisons of Jewish and German victims. After his encounter with Elena, where the analogy between concentration camp and POW camp is at center stage, Joost retreats to the barracks and asks his mate, "Say, have you ever known a Jew?" Whatever else Joost did during the war in the east, meeting Jews—at the end of his rifle or in other contexts—was apparently not among his assignments, nor was he acquainted with any of the German Jews who fled Germany after 1933 or were deported eastward in the early 1940s. The Jew he meets—forgiving, compassionate, understanding, like the Jew in some of the accounts in the Schieder documentation and like the Anne Frank introduced to West Germans in the 1950s—was the Jew willing to give Germans solace. Set in 1950 after most German POWs had been released and those remaining were the defendants in trials for particularly egregious offenses, the movie did not need to state explicitly what most West Germans never questioned, that no matter how long Stalin kept them behind the Urals, German POWs were innocent. The circumstances of these soldiers' detainment are never explored. When Joost finally meets a Jew, he receives absolution even though he committed no sins.

The movie unabashedly reiterated another common understanding of the German past: Communism, at least in its Stalinist variant (again announced by the ubiquitous portraits of Papa Joe in the camp), was no different from Nazism. Elena, for one, has been imprisoned by both variants of twentieth-century totalitarianism. However, another Russia peeks through. In an interview, the producer, Bamberger, commented that the film revolved around the contrast between Fusow and Seidenwar: "There are countless Seidenwars in Russia . . . we should know that they exist." Soviets agreed. A special showing of the movie at the 1961 Cannes Film Festival won praise from Soviet representatives, who commented on the film's honesty and fairness.[95]

In 1961, no devils, either musical or tone deaf, reigned in the Soviet

Union; eight years after Stalin's death and five years after Khrushchev's revelation of Stalin's excesses, Bonn was moving gradually toward better relations with Moscow. Presumably, the steadily expanding trade relations of the late 1950s between West Germany and the Soviet Union were with the Seidenwars, not the Fusows.[96] Good Germans and good Russians had existed in the past, and they certainly existed in 1961; reviews celebrated the movie as an attempt to stress a common humanity and to build a bridge between peoples. Continued improvement in German-Soviet relations perhaps explains why German POWs behind Soviet barbed wire ceased to be a topic filmmakers sought to address.

More or less grudging accommodation with those other Germans across the border to the east was not so simple, however. The real devil in the movie is the groveling, corrupt German Antifa officer Gellert, who could ultimately find a happy home in only one place: the German Democratic Republic. Seidenwar recognizes that Gellert is capable only of following orders; his constant heel-clicking salutes prompt nothing but disdain from Seidenwar, who associates Gellert with mindless Prussianism, mindless Nazism, and, implicitly, mindless Communism as practiced in East Germany, where the Berlin Wall would be erected only a few months after Gellert and Seidenwar went head to head on West German movie screens.

The other distant continent that enters Lahola's movie is Asia, even farther beyond the Elbe than Stalingrad or Siberia. This time, it is figured not only as stony-faced "Mongol" guards. Here, Asians are also prisoners; indeed, they are the true fascists. They follow the orders of their leaders without thinking, obediently filling the norm, refusing to participate in German-led work stoppages, and showing none of the emotional range of their German counterparts. The one Japanese prisoner who consorts with the Germans who are attempting to escape knows what to do when he is found out. Before Fusow can fetch him from the barracks, he commits ritualistic suicide, binding his head in the flag of the Rising Sun, while his fellow prisoners silently look on. This east is a world in which honor has meaning, but it is a meaning Germans cannot begin to understand. To make the point, the movie leaves extensive passages of dialogue among the Japanese prisoners untranslated. There is no Elena around to help; Asia remains decidedly foreign.

This drama of Germans in postwar Soviet hands appeared just as another German was taken into custody in Israel. In the spring and summer of 1961, the attention of many West Germans was riveted on the trial of Adolf Eichmann in Jerusalem, with newsreels showing Germany on trial before Jewish judges who listened patiently to a recounting of personal tragedies and indicated little willingness to forgive. In the feature film, in contrast, Elena emphasizes how little is achieved by standing in judgment, and Seidenwar sacrifices himself for the well-being of a Wehrmacht soldier. As a sympathetic review of the movie in the prestigious *Frankfurter Allgemeine Zeitung* pointed out, the international public was doubtless astonished to see "soldiers of the German Wehrmacht as prisoners, the refuse of the war, beaten in a lockup; the proud conquerors and ruthless oppressors as the oppressed." This reminder could be no more timely, since "recently . . . international film screens have so often been filled with the horrifying acts of the German occupation." Unlike the sensationalist accounts of the POW experience in illustrated magazines and pulp fiction, *Der Teufel spielte Balalaika* was "a German contribution to our most recent history that should be taken very seriously."[97] By 1961, however, it had little to add to modes for understanding that history that were already firmly in place.

Letters from the Past to the West German Present

In *Taiga,* Ruth Leuwerik forever secures her place in the hearts of her fellow prisoners one night when she tells them stories, fantasies of home. She calms a prisoner, driven to the brink by the Soviet interdiction of mail from relatives, by explaining that she eludes despair by dreaming up her own letters from the loved ones she left behind, and she proceeds to conjure up just such a vision for the ailing "lieber Franz." Later in the movie, another prisoner awakens, terrified that he has lost his imagined letter in the prison yard; fantasy has become reality. Hanna comforts him by participating in the delusion she has encouraged, rocking him back to sleep, assuring him that he will get the letter back. By the early 1950s, the films in which hardworking eastern Germans found a place in a new West Germany and noble POWs suffered with dignity were another brand of fantasy that had become reality. These movies were comforting; they created an imagined past that few West Germans wanted to shatter.

Reviewers and the censorship board of the film industry worried at length about whether movies truly captured the essence of the expellee experience or deposited enough mud of the right consistency on the grounds of the studios' Soviet camps.[98] What movies were getting right, however, was not Soviet muck but stories of a past selectively remembered, told and retold many times—in public policy debates, official histories, and the pages of the daily press and illustrated magazines that serialized the stories on which some of the the films were based. This past had long since become part of West Germany's public memory of the Second World War. Much of it could be left unsaid. By the early 1950s, the devastating consequences of the war were an accepted part of the past; there was no need to dwell on them. When Adenauer visited Moscow in 1955, he had only to mention that "in Germany as well, many bad things happened during the war," and West Germans knew what he meant. Moviemakers, similarly, did not need to depict the last days of the war on the eastern front in living color; that history was common knowledge.

Other signs of wartime devastation were ubiquitous, however. Movies featured the scarred bodies and minds of women and men and secrets of a postwar chaos in which normal moral expectations and plans for the future were suspended. In many war movies, although blood and death were everywhere, the victims wore the uniforms of the Wehrmacht, not those of the western Allies or the Red Army or the striped suit of the concentration camp inmate.

The movies also glossed over the ways in which the war's devastation had come home. The West German *Heimat* depicted here knew nothing of the deep divide between "new" and "old" citizens and the insurmountable difficulties that some expellees confronted in finding a place in West German society. The POWs who came home on movie screens were hale and hearty, and even when the war marked them—disrupting career paths or creating a sense of estrangement—they recovered quickly.

Back in the *Heimat*, followers of Hitler seemed to have disappeared altogether. Nazis did appear in movies that focused on the shooting war and the men taken prisoner once the shooting had stopped, but they were Nazis etched in black and white, the first to leave when the going got tough, the first, when caught, to collaborate with the Soviets, maniacally clicking their heels, saluting, and following orders of another totalitarian regime. In the POW camps, those whose critique of fascism led them to sympathize with Communism exhibited only their unreliability, not a moral transformation. Most men in uniform, in these depictions, had fought a war they did not choose, and even in that war they had done nothing of which they need be ashamed. Once at home, they were busy apprehending potential poachers and guaranteeing the return of wildlife to the German forest. Although some "rubble films" of the early postwar years had explored questions of German responsibility for crimes against others, by the 1950s only the *real* Nazis were accountable, and they could be counted on relatively few fingers. They had sent soldiers to their death at Stalingrad, just as they had sent Jews to their death at Auschwitz, though the murder of these non–"Aryan" victims was never shown on the screen.

As some film historians have noted, the war movies of the 1950s were part of the restoration of the German military in the face of widespread popular opposition to rearmament.[99] And movies that presented heroic survivors, Erich Kuby acerbically added, were also a means of retelling war stories with different outcomes in which Germans were the ultimate victors. Writing of the 1959 Stalingrad blockbuster *Hunde, wollt ihr ewig leben?* Kuby reflected that "our life in West Germany since 1950 can only be comprehended if we understand that this time around every single German wants to win the war he lost. The German man cannot tolerate having a lost war in his past."[100] Movies filled with heroes who despised Nazism and triumphed over Communism and then came home to a compassionate Federal Republic were an effective way to describe how West Germany had moved beyond the emotional and ideological rubble of the Third Reich.

In films of the 1950s, loyal defense of the fatherland and the ability to take out a Red Army tank still defined German manhood; men who had not served in the 1940s were suspect. However, not just soldiers unwilling to succumb to Communist barbarism but also compassionate, caring husbands and fathers abounded behind barbed wire. Veterans who returned home chastened had learned that the interests of the *Heimat* were best achieved with economic know-how, not military might. These virtuous, enlightened German men still knew a beautiful woman when they saw one, but what they most longed for was home; those who pursued other pleasures and transgressed ideological, national, or racial lines betrayed their comrades.

Movies also spread thick the balm of maternity, though in the 1950s good women not only cared for men, children, and childlike men, they could also take care of themselves. Hanna, in *Taiga*, fights back against German and Russian rapists; Jo of *Suchkind 312* is a successful businesswoman; Anna/Ännchen supports herself and her son; and Marianne of *Waldwinter* has crafted a strategy to send Silesian glass into the world marketplace. Missing in each case, however, was a man. The "new woman" of the Adenauer era, able to wear a dirndl or a Parisian hat with equal grace and style, was self-reliant. But she needed a husband to complete the picture.

Expellees and POWs both offered cautionary tales about the potential dangers inherent in the economic miracle. Martin, in Liebeneiner's

Waldwinter, requires remedial lessons to understand that a generator and German quality handiwork can coexist under one roof, but he is quick to learn how easily tradition can complement modernity. In *Suchkind 312,* however, too much of a good thing can prove to be dangerous. Robert, the martinet, has to learn that family means more than just stability and bourgeois comforts, and when Martina goes shopping, she immediately gets into trouble. Repositories of traditional values, expellees and returned POWs showed their ability to change yet at the same time be able to resist the siren call of excessive consumption, and they counseled viewers to follow their example. They reminded West Germans, caught up in the hustle and bustle of the economic miracle, that morality, tradition, and modernity were not mutually exclusive; old values need not block economic growth, but they could ensure that consumer culture did not run amok. Movies suggested that eastern Germans, like the POWs who returned in 1955, could help keep western Germans from becoming Americans.

Heimat was important, but in an era when geographic mobility was increasing dramatically and more and more West Germans commuted to work, *Heimat* was clearly depicted as a movable feast.[101] Tradition and values were rooted in Germans, not in specific locations in Germany. *Heimatfilme* that featured tales of expellees were directed at the new West Germans whose stories they told. For example, advertising tips from the production company that distributed *Waldwinter* reminded theater owners that it was "important for propaganda" to target the "2,204,460 Silesians who live in the area of the Federal Republic."[102] The displacement of expellees, however, also symbolized the wartime displacement of all Germans and the postwar displacement of West Germans, driven from their prewar homes not by the Red Army but by the destruction of urban housing stock during the war and, in the 1950s, by the search for better jobs. An imagined *Heimat* did not appeal only to expellees.

The movies also commented on foreign as well as domestic relations. The Germany that successfully integrated expellees and welcomed home innocent POWs was the only Germany with a rightful claim to the name. It was a Germany that could provide refuge for eastern Germans as well as for fleeing East Germans who were not the robotic graduates of an Antifa education. However, although Communism was evil, by the late 1950s POWs were able to announce that Soviets could be friends, if not allies. Movies thus provided an interpretation of both the end of the shooting war and the easing of the Cold War.

"The German film can hardly be better"

Interviewed in 1961 by a film magazine about the making of *Der Teufel spielte Balalaika,* the producer, Peter Bamberger, decried contemporary German moviemakers who continued "to make films similar to the films made several years ago." Too many West German filmmakers had "no relationship to the present and no answers to the questions of the times." If offered nothing better, Bamberger speculated, West Germans would simply stay home and watch television. "Film will be forced to do something different from television. . . . We must produce fewer and better films. If that does not happen, I fear the worst. What we need, quite simply, is more modernity and quality if we are not going to stay stuck on the same track."[103]

Only slightly more than a year later, the "Oberhausen manifesto," the credo of the Young German Cinema, the group of filmmakers who demanded a complete break with "Papa's Kino" and something entirely new, echoed many of the same sentiments. They boldly announced that "the old film is dead. We believe in the new one." As Fehrenbach argues, the Oberhausen manifesto did not simply mark a generational shift; rather, it built on demands, already voiced in the 1950s, that *Kultur* should not take second place to commercial concerns.[104] However, the movies that the progenitors of the Young German Cinema would direct were a far cry from *Der Teufel spielte Balalaika,* and their makers had only disdain for the outmoded genre of the *Heimatfilm;* they might have agreed with Bamberger's prognostication and recommendations, but they would hardly see Bamberger's movie as heralding the future they proclaimed.

Some alternative ways of viewing the past had assumed far greater importance by the late 1950s. Even before the arrival of the Young German Cinema, Wolfgang Staudte's 1957 movie *Rose Bernd,* a retelling of a Gerhart Hauptmann story, transformed Rose into a Silesian expellee, abused and mistreated by an inhospitable West German society and ostracized in a rural environment that exudes none of the compassion and comfort of the *Heimat.* And in Falk Harnack's film *Unruhige Nacht* (Restless night), a soldier on the eastern front emerges not as the noble survivor of a POW camp but as a victim of German military justice, condemned to death for betraying military secrets to the enemy and seeking refuge with a Russian woman before being run to ground.[105] By the early 1960s, more and more West Germans were unwilling to settle for stories in which only Germans were victims. The explicit equation of concentration camp and POW camp in movies like *Der Teufel spielte Bal-*

alaika, together with the account they gave of Jewish forgiveness and German innocence, was also not acceptable to everyone in the Federal Republic; it represented, as one critic remarked, "the dubious tendency to
diminish guilt by transforming it into a general global phenomenon."[106]
Another reviewer, charging that *Teufel* was trapped within clichéd understandings of the war and the POW experience, asked why Germans
were always so eager to be granted forgiveness by the former inmates of
concentration camps.[107]

To be sure, some exceptional films of the late 1950s, as well as ones
produced in the following decades by representatives of the Young German Cinema, offered a more complex range of perspectives on the war
and its aftermath; however, their message reached only a tiny fraction
of the West German audience. The critical acclaim accorded Harnack's
Unruhige Nacht, for example, did not translate into good box office.
There are also no indications that West German audiences in the Federal Republic's first decade were frustrated or disappointed by the take
on the past that celluloid tales of POWs and expellees offered. In a blis-
tering critique of West German movies published in 1961, Joe Hembus
mockingly proclaimed that "the German film can hardly be better."[108]
When it came to movies depicting the experience of displaced eastern
Germans and soldiers detained in the Soviet Union, many West Germans
may not have appreciated his irony. The tales told at the movies strove
to clear away messy memories, celebrate uniquely German values, and
present a reassuring version of the past. Indeed, as West Germans re-
treated into forms of leisure that took place at home, not in theaters,
they could see this same past repeated again and again on the small screens
in their living rooms, with movies from the 1950s remaining a staple of
German television. The 1960s and 1970s would offer different accounts
of the war, but in the 1950s few West Germans questioned that "Papa's
Kino" knew best.

Epilogue

In 1955, Hans Rothfels, editor of the *Vierteljahrshefte für Zeitgeschichte,* offered readers an assessment of the meaning of the war "ten years after" (*zehn Jahre danach*). The article was a revised version of a speech originally given to a student organization at the University of Tübingen, where West Germany's postwar youth had asked this senior historian, a representative of their grandparents' generation, to offer his reflections on the meanings of 1945. Rothfels, who had spent that year in emigration in the United States, effectively summarized how competing memories of the war's outcome had become part of the history of the Federal Republic.

Emphasizing the epochal significance of Germany's defeat, "the deep paradox of May 9," and a war that "erased the boundaries between front and *Heimat,* between soldier and civilian," Rothfels recalled both the "horrible things that took place in occupied areas, particularly in the east," and what was done "to real and imagined opponents in concentration camps."[1] Although he had little to say about the Germans' war against the Jews, he described in detail the "eastern side of the defeat, that is, the expulsion and separation, the loss of a thousand-year-old history and the loss of German unity." These consequences of the war were "justifiably foremost in the memories of today." Drawing on the federally funded documentation of the expulsion of Germans from eastern Europe that he had helped to edit, Rothfels offered vivid images of the atrocities committed against Germans by partisans and the Red Army, citing a death toll of 1.6 million Germans in "areas of the Reich east of the Oder and Neisse," while referring only once to those "whose families may have been gassed at Auschwitz," a fate that Rothfels escaped only because he left Germany in 1938. He waxed eloquent about the sacrifices made "in defense of home territory[,] . . . the maintenance of a protective buffer in the southeast that were accomplished with the fulfillment of soldierly duty," and the valiant attempts by "navy details and the military leadership, as well as they could, to save threatened individuals, those in flight, and entire military units from the Russian advance." West Germans should not forget these heroic moments in their past, he counseled. In the context of the "much-discussed German miracle" of rapid economic recovery following the war, Rothfels encouraged his readers to remember that amid "all the chaos and signs of decline and moral endangerment" a decade earlier there were also countless "manifestations of unprecedented generosity and helpfulness." Rothfels's comments appeared on the eve of Adenauer's trip to Moscow, and readers were well aware that for some of those military men, generosity and helpfulness had ended in Soviet captivity. For those Germans still behind barbed wire, the German miracle had not yet begun.

Germans who sought to confront the past crimes of Germans against others should not, he cautioned, follow the route prescribed by the victorious allies. Highly critical of the postwar settlement, he warned against the dangers of "ideological wars" and "crusades" in which one "became infected with the same poison against which one fought." The "collective desire for revenge," exemplified by Morgenthau, could not ensure peace, and the thesis of "collective guilt" smacked of "biological methods of classification that were previewed by National Socialism."

The way to mark 9 May 1945, the day "the complete capitulation of Germany went into effect," Rothfels concluded, was with an "hour of commemoration" for all victims, including those killed by Germans as well as those Germans "murdered after the end of hostilities, those who drowned or perished in the snow as they attempted to flee, who froze or starved, who did not survive the forced marches or forced labor camps [Zwangslager]." He also recalled "those women who, after the deepest humiliation, took their own lives, or their husbands, who resisted this disgrace," an unambiguous reminder of the literal rapes that heralded the symbolic rape of eastern Germany and eastern Europe by the Red Army. When Rothfels evoked the "inferno of the people of the east," he alluded not to the ovens of Auschwitz but to the devastation and destruction wrought by the Red Army on its way to Berlin. Mourning German victims should not, warned Rothfels (himself a victim of Nazi anti-Semitism), diminish memories of the suffering of others. However, a complete tally could only be one that captured "reality in its horrifying totality."

This book has discussed some of the ways in which West Germans described, commemorated, understood, and remembered the "horrifying totality" of the past. That totality included at best a partial account of the years between 1933 and 1945, in which Germans systematically marginalized and persecuted other Germans and, after 1939, countless other Europeans who did not conform to the racial, political, religious, and sexual prescription of the Nazi state. But for most West Germans in the 1950s, the suffering of Germans who were not victims of Nazi persecution dramatically eclipsed the suffering of these groups. Expellees and POWs captured by the Soviets tied the Bonn Republic to the Third Reich without demanding painful reflection on the origins of National Socialism, the mass support the regime garnered, or the brutal war on the eastern front in which millions of Germans participated. Their experiences demonstrated that, if nothing else, National Socialism had correctly identified the diabolical nature of Soviet Communism. Germans driven from their eastern European homes or forced to labor in Soviet camps also corroborated the widespread belief that whatever suffering *some* Germans had caused, millions of other Germans had sustained enormous losses and made incalculable sacrifices. They represented a Germany doubly victimized, first by a Nazi regime run amok, then by Communists, and they allowed all West Germans to order the past in mutually exclusive categories in which perpetrators and victims were never the same people.

In West German public memory of the 1950s, expellees and POWs provided ample evidence that German values had survived National Socialism and the devastation of the war. After ten years and more of separation from the *Heimat*, POWs recognized its worth. As presented in newspapers, newsreels, and movies, they also brought with them models of a chastened masculinity that was happiest at home. With expellees from the east came a rich past of peaceful coexistence in a multicultural central Europe and a willingness to work hard at rebuilding what they had lost. And both groups, though ready to embrace and contribute to the "economic miracle," also harbored a healthy skepticism of the dangers of a consumer society that threatened to careen out of control.

Stories of survivors, ennobled by suffering, did not fully describe the experience of those eastern European Germans who had participated in and benefited from repressive regimes in Nazi-occupied Europe; who were forever separated from loved ones, careers, property, and a set of cultural values rooted in a specific place—losses that could not be restored with material compensation or rhetorical flourishes; or who remained outsiders in the Federal Republic, unable to attain the standard of living of other West Germans throughout the 1950s. Nor did they leave much room for the memories of those POWs for whom overcoming physical and emotional disability was an attenuated process; who harbored right-wing political views that left them deeply alienated from the Federal Republic; who had experienced death on an unprecedented scale; or who lived with disturbing memories of their participation in a racial war on the eastern front and the "final solution." Some of the individual memories of POWs and expellees became part of the Federal Republic's public memory; others were stories that few people wanted to hear. It is not the purpose of this book to chart dimensions of the experience of POWs and expellees that were not captured in the public memory of the 1950s. Rather, I have traced how some war stories were represented and incorporated into the founding myths of the Federal Republic and how the past of National Socialism and devastating defeat in war became part of the West German present.

In recent years, oral historians have sought to unearth other memories of unresolved trauma, pain, and loss, and of a quotidian not adequately captured in the forms of public memory described in this book. However, these historians should not overlook the extent to which what Germans recalled of their wartime experiences in the 1970s, 1980s, and 1990s was necessarily filtered through the forms of public memory that emerged in the Federal Republic's early history.[2] Any call for Germans to mourn their losses in the present must take into consideration how they mourned their losses in the past. In the 1950s, few Germans acknowledged their responsibility for the crimes of the Third Reich or the extent of their identification with Hitler and National Socialism. They did not engage in the therapeutic "work of mourning" called for by the Mitscherlichs, but there was much else for which Germans demonstrated a striking ability to mourn.

By the late 1950s and early 1960s, increasing numbers of West Germans were ready to hear a more complex account of the National Socialist regime and the war. The past in which Germans were victims receded, displaced by a history of the Third Reich in which Nazi atrocities took center stage. A full explanation of what accomplished this complication of public memory exceeds the scope of this book. Here I will suggest only some of the most important signposts along the path to a different understanding of the Third Reich, though I will also point to representative reminders that other pasts never completely disappeared from view.[3]

Complicating Public Memory

Among historians, the rapidly growing commitment to identifying National Socialism as a system deeply rooted in German history and politics, not as a "catastrophe" or the demonic projection of a small elite, was signaled by the coming of age of a group of scholars more likely to have experienced Nazism as adolescents than as young adults and largely trained after 1945. Many, strongly influenced by Werner Conze and Theodor Schieder, two of the editors of the project to document the expulsion, moved away from the focus on high politics that had long dominated German historiography and began to explore the appropriateness of methodologies borrowed from the social sciences. Particularly important was the work of historians who turned an older, conservative emphasis on German exceptionalism—a *Sonderweg*—on its head. The *Sonderweg* explained not the triumph of Germany as a major power and a preeminent *Kulturstaat* in Europe, but the peculiar route from an authoritarian Kaiserreich to an authoritarian Third Reich. In their accounts, May 1945 represented a *Stunde Null* (zero hour), a complete rupture that dramatically separated the Third Reich from the Bonn Republic. By the late 1960s, a new generation of radical students, children of the rubble who had little or no direct experience of National Socialism and who had been raised on tales of a suffering Germany, added its critical voice. Reviving Marxist analyses of fascism, they discovered a path that had not ended in 1945; rather, the capitalist system that had brought fascism to Germany tied Hitler's Germany to Adenauer's. What unified these diverse approaches was their commitment to a far more complete and troubling account of National Socialism.

The new version of the German past that began to emerge in the 1970s analyzed the popular bases of Nazi support and the success of the state's efforts to invade and transform German society; it emphasized the virtual absence of German resistance to Nazi racism, terrorism, and expansionist aggression, and the broad support for the regime, at least until the war turned sour after the German defeat at Stalingrad in 1943; and it charted the history of German anti-Semitism and the persecution of the Jews, including the participation of the Wehrmacht in the murder of Jews and other civilians. These critical historians focused not on German suffering but on the crimes committed by Germans against others, and they explained the Second World War, particularly the war on the eastern front, as a logical outgrowth of National Socialist ideology, not an aberration attributable to Hitler alone.

This historiographical shift took place against a broad political background that included the trial of Adolf Eichmann in Jerusalem, which received extensive coverage in the Federal Republic, and, even closer to home, major trials of Nazi war criminals in West Germany, among them Gustav Sorge and Wilhelm Schubert, two of the "ten thousand" who had returned triumphantly in late 1955. Arrested in February 1956, they went on trial in Bonn in 1958, and both received multiple life sentences for murders committed as guards in Sachsenhausen.[4] In the same year, the West German government established an office in Ludwigsburg whose task was the collection of materials for use in criminal prosecutions of German citizens who, like Schubert and Sorge, had carried out acts of murder and violence wearing a German uniform. In December 1963, twenty Auschwitz guards went on trial in Frankfurt, and for the next twenty months West Germans could read daily reports that left little mystery about what had taken place at this extermination facility in occupied Poland.[5]

The crimes of Germans were also repeatedly the stuff of parliamentary debates over extending the statute of limitations for prosecution on murder charges—in particular, mass murder committed between 1939 and 1945—until finally, in 1979, all limitations on prosecution for this crime were suspended once and for all. Critics charged that sentences for convicted criminals were too mild and that the judicial pursuit of Nazi criminals should be more aggressive. However, no one could deny the shift in public attitudes from the 1950s when the "amnesty lobby" had prevailed.[6]

By the late 1960s, after two decades of uninterrupted rule by Christian Democratic chancellors, many West German voters were ready for a dramatic political change at the national level and, in 1969, elected a chancellor who had spent the war not in "internal migration" or a Wehrmacht uniform, but fighting Germans in the Norwegian resistance. Willy Brandt openly held his fellow citizens collectively accountable for their past as perpetrators. The 1950s preoccupation with the crimes of Communists against Germans was dramatically eclipsed by Brandt's public acknowledgment of the crimes of Germans against Poles and Jews during his December 1970 trip to Warsaw. In this highly symbolic visit,

Brandt concluded treaty negotiations that marked the postwar normalization of relations with Poland, the recognition of the Oder-Neisse line
as Poland's western border, and the state's official abandonment of expellees' claims to their former *Heimat*. When Brandt fell to his knees at
the monument to the 1943 Warsaw Ghetto uprising, he drew international attention by commemorating another past, one that West Germans
had seldom directly addressed in the 1950s. His *Ostpolitik* at once expressed the Federal Republic's ability to assert itself as an independent
geopolitical actor in the present and acknowledged the disastrous consequences of Nazi Germany's independent foreign policy in the past. It
was not surprising that, in this context, rhetorics of German victimization figured far less prominently than heretofore.[7]

"Contemporary History" Revised

The fate of a federally funded project to record the experience of German prisoners of war mirrored these major shifts in perspective, revealing how a past in which Germans were victims was displaced by one in
which many Germans had committed crimes. The proposal to collect first-
person accounts of the experience of POWs as evidence of another "mass
fate" of the Second World War was conceived as a companion to the
Schieder project and emerged from the Ministry for Expellees in 1956,
shortly after the last POW had returned from the Soviet Union.[8] Because
the project directly addressed one of the most important representatives
of German victimhood of the 1950s, it deserves consideration in detail.

Coordinating the project and contributing the introductions to several volumes was Erich Maschke, another of Rothfels's students in
Königsberg, who became a chairholder at the University of Jena under
the Nazis. An outspoken propagandist for German expansion in eastern
Europe, he celebrated a "German right to the east" and practiced a variety of history that was riddled with racist conceptions of Germany's
eastward expansion as part of the necessary "growth of the German national body," a place to be filled with German "blood and the best of
[Germany's] soul."[9] His academic career was interrupted by military service that allowed him to battle what he had identified as the "Asiatic powers" behind Soviet expansion,[10] but German inability to contain those
powers resulted in his capture by the Soviets and a lengthy stint as a prisoner of war that ended only with his release in 1953. Although dismissed
from his university position on political grounds in 1945,[11] in the 1950s
he was named to a professorship in social and economic history at the

University of Heidelberg. Maschke did not have the same high professional status as the editors of the expellee project, but he was well situated; entrusting the official chronicle of the POW experience to him was therefore a clear sign that a "scientific" account, free of any claims of partisan bias or self-pity, was the goal.

Of the twenty-two volumes published, the majority described the areas where the treatment of German POWs had been worst and where they had remained imprisoned the longest—the Soviet Union, Poland, Czechoslovakia, and Yugoslavia.[12] Hans Koch, director of the East European Institute in Munich who headed the project until his death in 1959, justified the significance of documenting the POW experience by emphasizing that "there is constant talk about the crimes committed by the German people, but no one will talk about how much the German people [Volk] have suffered."[13] The project sought to offer a more balanced account of the war's consequences.

In his introduction to the first two volumes, on Yugoslavia, Maschke echoed the intentions of the Schieder project, presenting the POW experience as "one of the greatest mass fates of the present," a collective experience that was "typical of our age and that has shaped it."[14] Like his counterparts who had compiled the expellee testimonies, he promised "strict objectivity and scientific clarity" as he and his co-workers sought to distill "what was typical out of the plenitude of individual fates" in order to offer a "balanced, strictly factual presentation . . . that should take into consideration all aspects of [the POWs'] lives."[15] Drawing on thousands of reports and hundreds of tape-recorded accounts from POWs, collected with the assistance of the German Red Cross and church-affiliated groups that had helped returning POWs, the project staff also enlisted the League of Returning Veterans, POWs, and Relatives of Those Missing in Action, soliciting responses to questionnaires and lengthy first-person accounts from members willing to put their experiences in writing or on tape. This was the opportunity for "prisoners of war to write their history."[16] Like Schieder, Maschke claimed that in its combination of document, analysis, and synthesis, picture, narrative, and statistic, the project not only captured the experience of POWs, but also outlined a method and mode of presentation that could be taken as a model "for the social historical investigation of mass fates in the context of contemporary history."[17]

The volumes in the POW project presented countless tales of barbaric Soviet cruelty and the valor of innocent Germans, stories that West Germans had long since been able to see at the movies, hear at annual days of remembrance for POWs prior to their final return in 1955, and read in novels, memoirs, the daily press, illustrated weeklies, and publications of veterans' organizations. As these sources made clear, the physical and psychological troubles of returning veterans were the symptoms of a "barbed-wire sickness" brought on by capture and Communist atrocities.[18] Neither individual eyewitnesses nor the project editors considered that the etiology of this disease might lie in even earlier experiences of participation in a war of mass destruction whose explicit goals included the extermination of European Jewry, elimination of the menace of "Judeo-Bolshevism," and subordination of the "inferior races" of eastern Europe and the Soviet Union in order to provide "living space" (*Lebensraum*) for Germans. If Nazis were villainous, Maschke concluded, their crimes against humanity paled by comparison with what Soviets had inflicted on Germans after 1945. Totalitarian Communists had honed to perfection methods that totalitarian fascists also tried to implement.[19] The real German criminals in the camps were denunciators and collaborators, ready to sell out a comrade for a piece of bread; in the Maschke documentation, they were depicted in the same harsh light used in *Der Arzt von Stalingrad* and *Der Teufel spielte Balalaika*.

Speaking in 1960 to an audience of returned prisoners of war in an attempt to win their support for the project, Maschke stressed that "your history is a part of German history; without it our most recent past is unimaginable."[20] However, by the time that Maschke and his associates completed their work a decade later, the Federal Government was far less eager to have only this version of its "most recent past" appear as an account officially sanctioned by the state for dissemination at home and abroad. The time for showcasing tales of German victims in uniform had passed.

From the start, the publication of individual volumes had been subject to approval by the West German Foreign Ministry, and ministry officials took seriously their charge to review the work of the project. By the early 1960s, when the first volumes were nearing completion, the government expressed its concern that given the trials of German war criminals then under way, documentation of what Germans had suffered during the war would likely be misinterpreted and would prompt only intensified scrutiny of what Germans had done to others. Ministry officials were far from swayed by arguments that a complete accounting of German suffering would clear the air and promote international understanding.[21] Because the volumes addressed German experiences in both west and east, the potential was too great that longtime friends, as well as foes with whom "peaceful coexistence" seemed a genuine possibility, would be offended. By 1969, the person who headed the Foreign Ministry was Willy Brandt, then on his way to the chancellorship and his journey to Warsaw.

The history the POW volumes told was not new; it was the conventional wisdom of the 1950s. But the domestic and geopolitical context had changed, and by the late 1960s the West German government sought to restrict the endless tales of suffering POWs and brutal Communists to a limited public of professional historians who could be trusted to read the documentation critically. Among competing war stories, Maschke's was not the "contemporary history" that Bonn sought to package for domestic and international consumption.[22] Two decades after the war's end, the West German state recognized the need for a more complicated past.

The Never Quite Completely Repressed

Even in the late 1960s and 1970s, however, as a different official history took shape, other pasts had not vanished. The Foreign Ministry could limit the circulation of Maschke's bound volumes to libraries and professional historians, but in March 1972—just as the Bundestag began debating ratification of the "Eastern Treaties," negotiated by the Brandt government to normalize relations with Warsaw and Moscow—no one in Bonn could prevent the mass-market weekly *Quick* from running a series of articles, allegedly leaked in part from the Maschke project, that presented a historical perspective on the "eastern bloc." While parliamentarians called for peaceful coexistence, *Quick* offered its readers stories of Russians who amputated arms with nail files, of vengeful partisans, of the "white hell" of POWs shipped behind the Urals, of marriage rings exchanged for bread rations, of heroes behind barbed wire, horror stories all verified in the "secret documents in *Quick*," accounts that were "simple and straightforward, a piece of history."[23] The government might choose not to tell this story far and wide, but the reading public had other sources.

Stories of victimized Germans also continued to circulate in inexpensive paperback editions. Two of the three diaries published by the expellee project were reissued periodically, and by the mid-1960s, 235,000 copies of Hans Graf von Lehndorff's *Bericht aus Ost- und Westpreussen* (Report from East and West Prussia) were in print.[24] The supply of eyewitness accounts of the expulsion was constantly renewed, and those testifying insisted that they would not allow the voices of German suffering to be silenced, not that silence had prevailed thus far.[25]

The West German government, though loath to allow Maschke's stories a broad circulation, also continued to generate a documentary record of the losses of civilians and of Bonn's success in integrating the "new citizens" into a democratic Federal Republic. In the late 1960s, the Ministry for Expellees, Refugees, and the War-Damaged published another bookshelf full of volumes that recorded in detail the destruction of German life and property by Allied bombs. A similarly massive documentation, celebrating West Germans' ability to clear away the rubble, recorded the Allies' reluctance to acknowledge the extent of the losses of German expellees and republished sources dealing with the "law for the equalization of burdens" from parliamentary debates, newspaper accounts, and interest group statements.[26]

Institutes of east European research further contributed to West Germans' awareness of the lost "German east." At least in the 1950s and 1960s, the work of the scholars in these institutes focused primarily on the social, economic, political, and cultural contributions of German-speaking communities and on the harmonious mix of ethnicities and cultures that had characterized eastern Europe before the Versailles treaty injected a xenophobic nationalism into this multicultural idyll. Jews were virtually absent in the "east-central Europe in German historical consciousness" presented in this scholarship.[27]

Told with an explicitly political inflection, a similar version of the history of Germans in eastern Europe was repeated in the political lobbying of expellee interest groups that railed against any conciliatory gestures in West German–eastern European relations.[28] Although by the late 1950s most West German politicians paid only lip service to claims that Germany's borders should be shifted eastward, they continued to appear at annual meetings of expellee groups, acknowledging the importance of these voters and the symbolic significance of the loss of the "German east." Political opposition from expellee groups to any moves toward better relations with eastern European countries in the 1970s emphasized that "Germans had suffered too" by pointing to the authoritative documentation that Schieder and his co-workers had assembled in the 1950s and asserting that "Auschwitz is only half of the truth, according to the findings of the documentation of the crimes committed during the expulsion."[29] The fact that the "right to a home" (*Recht auf Heimat*) in the east was increasingly illusory for a generation whose only home was in the west meant no end to the juxtaposition of victims of Germans and

German victims, together with a virulent anti-Communism, among those whose memories included expulsion and expropriation. The fate of German minorities whose homes were still literally in the east also remained an item on the agenda of virtually every negotiating round between West Germany and its eastern European neighbors.[30]

Sustaining memories of German victimization was by no means the exclusive preserve of irredentist special-interest groups. The West German television broadcast of the U.S. miniseries *Holocaust* in 1979, frequently cited as a high point in West Germans' confrontation with the individual faces of mass extermination,[31] was followed two years later by *Flucht und Vertreibung* (Flight and expulsion), a three-part series on West German television, accompanied by a large-format book filled with pictures, that documented a different sort of German tragedy. A combination of historical analysis, documentary footage, and personal memories captured in interviews, the series advertised itself as a courageous attempt to address directly a topic "as good as taboo" in the Federal Republic, a "consequence of our lack of historical consciousness."[32] Critically praised as a much-needed record of "personal suffering and collective fate," *Flucht und Vertreibung* self-consciously chose to illuminate its subject with dramatic documentary film clips and a mixture of "history and stories" (*Geschichte und Geschichten*), personal testimonies framed by objective scholarly analysis. Without acknowledging the obvious parallels with the editorial introduction to the Schieder project, those responsible for the series denied any desire to "make accusations or reckon guilt against guilt"; their intent was only to "address this devastating chapter of German history," "to present what happened, to show how it was."[33]

In 1987, another televised variant of the same story was aired, this time in a three-part version of Arno Surminski's novel *Jokehnen*. A fictionalized tale of daily life in an East Prussian village of the same name, it offered an account of German history from Hitler's triumph to German defeat and the expulsion of the village's inhabitants westward.[34] The cast of characters—the "good" Jew; the reliable, steadfast Nazi mayor (played by Armin Müller Stahl); the disillusioned aristocratic resister; the warm-hearted Polish and Soviet forced laborers; the evil Nazi bosses who exploit every opportunity to avoid service at the front; the predacious Red Army soldiers—had not changed since the early 1950s. As the drama ends, a voice-over narration describes the fate of the characters at the center of the miniseries. Although viewers learn that the Jew dies in Auschwitz and a Russian POW returns home to extraordinary devastation and the loss of many loved ones, as in the tallies of Adenauer in 1949 and Rothfels in 1955, the list of German victims far exceeds the count of the victims of Germans. The young female teacher, sent to fill in for a Nazi enthusiast conscripted late in the war, is "raped to death." The mayor, finally disillusioned by the last days of the war, receives no clemency from the Red Army and perishes "in a camp on the border between Europe and Asia." Others never return from the front, languish in POW camps, or go to watery graves on ships, sunk by Soviet bombs as they attempt to escape East Prussia late in the war.

The story of the expellees was not only told on television and in coffee table books, but it remained the stuff of scholarly analysis as well. In 1984, an inexpensive paperback edition of the documentation originally edited by Schieder and his colleagues was reissued. In a highly favorable review in the *Frankfurter Allgemeine Zeitung,* Gotthold Rhode recommended that as West Germans commemorated the fortieth anniversary of the war's end they hear the "voice of those . . . whose time of suffering only really began once the weapons were silenced."[35] New works accompanied the restoration of old ones, and by the late 1980s research into the integration of the expellees emerged as an important focus of a younger generation's attempt to write a full account of the social history of the Federal Republic.[36] POWs also received their due; the editors of a 1981 collection that drew on the Maschke documentation, for example, insisted that "everyone who experienced great suffering has a right to speak about it, regardless of whether this pain is the consequence of sources that can be explained, whether or not it is viewed as just or unjust punishment." Such testimony was necessary because the older generation "had not come to terms with what they had suffered." Stories of POWs had remained "far from the public sphere." Mourning German suffering was the essential prerequisite for Germans to mourn the suffering of others.[37]

The intention to unleash silenced memories was also behind the efforts in the late 1970s and 1980s of an eclectic mix of professional historians and grassroots "history workshop" (*Geschichtswerkstatt*) movements that sought to capture the "history of daily life" under the Nazis. Local groups often led the way in documenting the history of concentration camps and the persecution of "asocials" and in restoring the memory of other "non-Aryan" victims, largely erased in the 1950s. However, participants in oral history projects also encouraged the generation that had experienced the war to record testimonies that did not probe the "quiet [*verschwiegen*] everyday history of racism," but focused instead on what Germans, not others, had suffered during the "bad times" of the forties.[38] In many instances, the memories of POWs and expellees collected in the 1980s began—as had memories from the 1950s—in a hail of falling bombs, at the moment of capture on the eastern front or the first appearance of the Red Army, and in the drama of forced deportation to the Soviet Union or forced expulsion to the west.[39]

Movies by some of West Germany's most important directors also addressed a past of German loss. By the late 1970s, the "Young German Cinema," the progressive artistic movement that had only harsh words for "Papa's Kino," was offering empathetic reflections on what fathers— and mothers—had suffered during the war.[40] Three examples illustrate the Young German Cinema's preoccupation with war stories that were not entirely new. In *Deutschland, bleiche Mutter* (Germany, pale mother), first shown in 1979, the feminist director Helma Sanders-Brahms told a daughter's story of her mother's odyssey from Hitler's Germany to Adenauer's. In Sanders-Brahms's account, the Second World War liberated German women, revealing their strength and resourcefulness in the absence of men; for women, the real war began in 1945, when rape by Allied soldiers and the return of German men brutally transformed them from self-reliant agents into victims. However, the film's powerful images of the decaying corpse of a German soldier and bombed-out cities were not only the backdrop for the heroic acts of the mother and daughter at the center of the movie; they were also forceful reminders of the devastation of Germany brought on by the Nazis' war. In one of the most extended sequences in the movie, mother and daughter find refuge in an abandoned factory, where smokestacks and ovens in the background suggest the fate of different victims.[41]

In the political context of the late 1970s, with anti-Americanism high on the agenda of the West German left, it is not surprising that when a rapist attacks Sanders-Brahms's heroine, he is an American, not a Red Army, soldier. However, if, on an allegorical level, the rape is intended to suggest, as Anton Kaes argues, that "postwar Germany is the innocent victim of rape by America," the scene also evoked memories of other rapes, both literal and allegorical, recorded in memoirs and described throughout the official documentation of the expulsion. Much of the war experienced by the mother and daughter also takes place in an unspecified German east, where they escape the bombs falling on Berlin. The mother sings a traditional German folk song that juxtaposes a sleeping child with a "Pomerania burned to the ground," the same Pomerania from which many Germans had fled westward, escaping the Red Army in 1945. And a homeless boy, incorporated into the film with original documentary footage, is a representative of the innocents who lost home and family during the expulsion. Indeed, the same footage was used in the television series *Flucht und Vertreibung.*[42] The film thus called forth strong memories of the war in both west and east.

In Alexander Kluge's 1979 movie *Die Patriotin* (The patriot), the war in the east, particularly the German defeat at Stalingrad, figures not as background but as a central thread, weaving in and out of the story of a West German high school teacher "who has sympathy with the dead of the Reich" and who searches for ways to present German history to her students. Kluge, long fascinated with this dramatic turning point in the war, makes much use of documentary film footage of the battle of Stalingrad, the decisive event that for thousands of soldiers led not to death but to a long stay in Soviet captivity.[43] He also draws implicitly on a set of memories of the aftermath of German defeat by making the narrator of his movie a "German knee," all that remains of a soldier killed at Stalingrad in late January 1943.[44] The knee, borrowed from a poem by the German poet Christian Morgenstern, was also an allusion to other dramatic narratives of Stalingrad and the Second World War. In Wolfgang Borchert's 1947 drama *The Man Outside,* a play widely known in the late 1950s and 1960s and the basis for Wolfgang Liebeneiner's movie *Liebe 47,* Borchert's central character is a veteran of the war on the eastern front, a POW, "one of the many" returning from the Soviet Union, who has "waited outside in the cold for a thousand days. And as entrance fee he's paid with his knee-cap."[45] In the play, the confused survivor, Beckmann, is tortured because he followed orders, setting out on an impossible mission and leading to their death the men under his command. Kluge goes a step further, suggesting that Germans also killed others by opening his film with the background music composed for the movie *Night and Fog.* This 1955 documentary on the concentration camps by the French director Alain Resnais had been seen by some West Germans in movie theaters in the second half of the 1950s, but it was available to many more when it was premiered on West German television a year before the opening of Kluge's film. In his analysis of the movie, Kaes suggests that this choice "may hint at a consciousness that does not want to exclude Auschwitz from the patriotic *Trauerarbeit* [work of mourning]" in the film. However, as in Borchert's play and Liebeneiner's movie, it may also suggest a consciousness in which all of the war's victims are equated. And even Kluge, depicting the war from the enlightened perspective of the late 1970s, presents Jews killed by Germans only as a subtle musical reference, while the fallen dead at Stalingrad and bombed German cities are vividly portrayed.[46]

Edgar Reitz's *Heimat,* the saga of one German town from the end of the First World War until the early 1980s, aired on West German television in eleven episodes in 1984. Reitz painstakingly presented a past not of Nazi crimes or even the banality of evil, but of a German society cloaked in ignorance and innocence, caught in patterns of daily life that seemed entirely normal. An adherent of the Oberhausen manifesto and a critic of "Papa's Kino," he nonetheless made it clear that he had seen many a *Heimat* film in the 1950s; his *Heimat* drew on some of the same themes and visual elements that were on movie screens three decades earlier in West Germany and four decades earlier in Nazi Germany.[47] At least twenty-five million West Germans watched at least one part of the series, and it was the subject of extensive media attention. Although set in western Germany, the title of Reitz's film evoked memories linked since the war's end with a German *Heimat* in eastern Europe that had been literally, not metaphorically, lost. The miniseries opens on 9 May 1919, as one of the central characters, Paul Simon, returns from a French prisoner-of-war camp, a "survivor of the western front."[48] Surely few West Germans could miss the reference to another war that ended in May and to other survivors—survivors of an eastern, not western, front. When Reitz's saga moves into the thirties and forties, his focus remains on what one reviewer called a "history of small people who live their lives in dignity," but there is little room in his drama for the history of other small people denied the right to life of any sort.[49]

Sanders-Brahms, Kluge, and Reitz insisted on the necessity, validity, and in some ways superiority of a subjective perspective—the history of the war and postwar years as seen through a daughter's eyes, a soldier's suffering, the daily lives of common people. They were responding to what they perceived to be the erasure of individual experience and personal voices in historical accounts that focused on ideologies, structures, and institutions. As in the Schieder and Maschke projects and most of the oral history efforts of the late 1970s and 1980s, the actors in their historical dramas spoke German and were not Jewish. These filmmakers did not choose to tell subjective stories of other victims of the war.

The Repressed Returns

The *Wende,* the turn, is now a term most closely associated with the monumental changes of 1989 that led to the unification of the two Germanys.

In the early 1980s, however, the *Wende* described West Germany's political shift rightward, as the Free Democratic Party dropped its alliance with Social Democrats for a coalition with the Christian Democratic Union and the chancellorship of Helmut Kohl. Under this conservative political constellation, pasts of German suffering, never entirely absent from political discourse and popular culture, took on far greater significance. Paying no heed to tales of German victims that had dominated public memory in the 1950s, many West Germans demanded a usable past that did not collapse modern German history into an extended prologue to the horrors of National Socialism. Forceful reminders that Germans, too, had been victims of the Nazis' war paralleled West German self-assertion on the international political stage. In the spring of 1985, forty years after the end of the Second World War in Europe, competing German pasts became the focus of intense debate, particularly in the Federal Republic, the United States, and Israel.

Memories of victims were linked that May when U.S. president Ronald Reagan joined West German chancellor Kohl in a day of commemoration that began at Bergen-Belsen, the site of a Nazi concentration camp, and continued with a visit to a military cemetery in Bitburg, where, among others, soldiers of the SS were buried. At ceremonies following the cemetery visit, Kohl called for remembrance of the "infinite suffering that the war and totalitarianism inflicted on nations."[50] For his part, Reagan, at a press conference prior to his departure for the Federal Republic, had asserted that the German dead at Bitburg "are victims of Nazism also. . . . They were victims, just as surely as [were] the victims in the concentration camps."[51]

Bitburg and Bergen-Belsen were not the only controversial sites of commemoration that spring. In comments to the Bundestag on 8 May, Richard von Weizsäcker, then president of the Federal Republic, remembered "the six million Jews who were murdered in German concentration camps" and reminded his fellow citizens who chose to focus on their own suffering that "the 8th of May was a day of liberation. It liberated all of us from the inhumanity and tyranny of the National Socialist regime."[52] In other venues, however, "liberation" received different interpretations. Kohl followed Bitburg and Bergen-Belsen with a visit to Hanover for the annual rally of the national organization representing those Germans expelled from Silesia at the end of the Second World War.[53] For them, 1985 marked the fortieth anniversary not of "liberation" from National Socialism, but of expulsion from their homes. Despite assurances that they would tone down their outspokenly national-

ist rhetoric in return for Kohl's participation, some of those present at
the Hanover meeting raised banners at the moment the chancellor appeared which proclaimed that "Silesia Remains Ours" (*Schlesien bleibt
unser*). Although public opinion polls revealed that this was a minority
view, that 76 percent of all West Germans were ready to live with the
postwar border, still, nearly one in four was not.[54] Even for West Germans who conceded that Silesia was no longer "ours," commemorating
the loss of a German homeland in the east invoked a familiar moral balance sheet that equated different forms of hardship and suffering.

Historians had not defined the terms of this public debate over the
German past, and their claims in the mid-1980s to a privileged role in
"shaping identity" (*Identitätsstiftung*) largely reflected an exaggerated
sense of their own significance and a narrow conception of the potential arenas in which identity takes shape. However, the "historians' controversy" (*Historikerstreit*)—a scholarly debate over the place and significance of National Socialism and the Holocaust in the narrative of
modern German history, which ultimately involved a "who's who" of
senior male historians in the Federal Republic and many students of Germany elsewhere—did focus discussions over the relationship between history and politics that Kohl and others had forcefully placed on the agenda.

The historians' controversy generated a mountain of books and articles, and by the late 1980s a small cottage industry was churning out
commentaries on West German historians' tortured search for a histor-
ically grounded national identity.[55] However, like memories of wars,
memories of scholarly controversies can fade; over a decade after the fact,
it is perhaps useful briefly to review some of the key events in this particular dispute in order to situate it within the larger frameworks for understanding the meanings of 8 May that already existed.

In one of the most important interventions in the *Historikerstreit,* Andreas Hillgruber, in his book *Zweierlei Untergang: Die Zerschlagung
des deutschen Reiches und das Ende des europäischen Judentums* (Two
sorts of demise: The destruction of the German Reich and the end of
the European Jewry), brought together expanded versions of two talks
given in 1984 and 1985.[56] Hillgruber had long been a student of eastern Europe. His dissertation was a study of German-Romanian relations
in the years 1938–44, and the book that earned him a professorship analyzed Hitler's planning for the war in the east. Hillgruber's scholarship
had also done much to illuminate the relationship between the Wehrmacht's last-ditch attempt to hold back the Red Army in 1944 and 1945,
on the one hand, and the aggressive pursuit of the "final solution," on

the other. In the early 1970s, he was among the first to challenge accepted claims that the Wehrmacht's war in the east was in no way linked
to the brutal murder of many Soviets and the campaign to exterminate
European Jews, and he also consistently emphasized the centrality of
anti-Semitism in Hitler's strategy.[57] Thus, when *Zweierlei Untergang* was
published he had a well-established reputation as one of the leading German historians of Nazi war strategy and foreign policy. Research into
the war, however, also meant reflecting on a chapter in his own history.
Born in 1925 and raised in Königsberg, where his father, a schoolteacher,
was removed from his post by the Nazis, he had been old enough to be
drafted into the German army late in the war. From 1945 to 1948 he
was a POW, a captive of the French and the Americans. Much of his
professional career was thus dedicated to fighting over the meanings of
the war that he had experienced firsthand. His ties to the east doubtless
also connected Hillgruber to Theodor Schieder, who chose him for a
position in Cologne.[58]

In his short book, Hillgruber devoted most of his attention to the first
of his "demises": the collapse of the German front in East Prussia in the
winter of 1944–45 and the "expulsion of Germans from east-central Europe," events that for Hillgruber defined "the destruction of the German
Reich." The historian considering the war's end and searching for a point
of empathetic identification must, argued Hillgruber,

> identify himself with the concrete fate of the German population in the east
> and with the desperate and sacrificial exertions of the German army of the
> east and the German fleet in the Baltic, which sought to defend the population
> of the German east from the orgy of revenge of the Red Army, mass rapes,
> arbitrary killing, and compulsory deportations.[59]

As if to underscore where his readers' empathy should lie, Hillgruber provided far more detailed descriptions of the circumstances of Germans in
the east than of the suffering of Jews, his second "demise." In the pointed
formulation of the historian Charles Maier, "If indeed these two experiences are two sorts of destruction, one is presented, so to speak, in tech-
nicolor, the other in black, gray, and white."[60]

What joined the expulsion of ethnic Germans from eastern Europe
and Nazi efforts to murder all European Jews in Hillgruber's analysis
was the fact that both phenomena originated in the same kind of political extremism; measured by what motivated them, the two "demises"
were different only in degree, not in kind. From this perspective, the advance of the Red Army could be called a "liberation" for those victims

of the Nazis released from concentration camps and prisons, but for Germans, "'liberation' does not capture the reality of the spring of 1945."[61] He was particularly critical of the postwar settlement that destroyed Germany's ability to serve as a bridge between east and west in central Europe, leaving Germany eclipsed by the Cold War superpowers. For Hillgruber, the past that had vanished included "the good coexistence of German and Slavic peoples in the center of Europe in the time before the First World War and to some extent between the wars"; he reminded his readers of how "close together the representatives of these nations belonged." Jews appeared in this "center of Europe" in Hillgruber's other "demise" only on their way to killing facilities in the east.[62]

In his contribution to the historians' controversy, Ernst Nolte also stressed the comparability of the Nazis' extermination of the Jews and other forms of state terror in the twentieth century. Nolte was best known for a major work, *Der Faschismus in seiner Epoche* (Fascism in its epoch), published in 1963, which had established a comparative framework for the study of National Socialism. His analysis of the German case placed particular emphasis on anti-Semitism and the Holocaust as uniquely defining characteristics of German fascism.[63] Indeed, *Der Faschismus* was of such import that Theodor Schieder had encouraged Nolte to submit it to the University of Cologne as a *Habilitationsschrift*, the second major research project required for a German professorship.[64]

In his comparative study of fascism, Nolte had described the war in the east as the "most horrifying war of conquest, enslavement, and destruction of the modern period."[65] Twenty years later, other horrors seemed to loom just as large. Now Nolte sought comparisons not among fascist systems and ideologies, but between totalitarian systems and the crimes of Hitler and Stalin. The "final solution," he argued, was not in any way sui generis, but was rather an expression of extremism and politically motivated violence that could be traced back at least to the "reign of terror" of the French Revolution and had reached a twentieth-century high point with the Gulag and mass murders under Stalin. Nolte's emphasis on the atrocities of Stalinism was familiar to those who knew his work, but what sparked controversy in the 1980s was the comparison of Stalin's and Hitler's crimes, a clear challenge to those who claimed the singularity of Auschwitz.[66] New with the Nazis, Nolte maintained, was only the "technical process of gassing," but all other crimes committed by the National Socialists—"mass deportations and executions, torture, death camps, the extermination of entire groups following strictly objective selection criteria, [and] public demands for the annihi-

lation of millions of guiltless people who were viewed as 'enemies'"—
were anticipated by the excesses of the Soviet Union. Nolte already knew
the answer when he asked, "Did the National Socialists, did Hitler, perhaps commit an 'Asiatic' deed only because they saw themselves and those
like them to be potential or actual victims of an 'Asiatic' deed?"[67]

What went largely unnoticed in the paper wars that surrounded the
historians' controversy was that the battle lines drawn by Hillgruber,
Nolte, and the politics of Bitburg had long histories, stretching back to
the Federal Republic's first decade.[68] Saul Friedländer chastised Hillgruber for equating the Holocaust and the expulsion, thus elevating to "an
element of learned discourse" an "image of the past carried by part of
the West German population," and he criticized Nolte for transforming
German perpetrators and bystanders into victims.[69] But neither he nor
any other commentator on the historians' controversy appreciated to
what extent learned discourse and popular consciousness had reinforced
such an "image of the past" in the public memory of the Federal Republic long before Hillgruber joined the "two demises" and Nolte
equated the victims of Hitler and Stalin. Rothfels had linked victims' fates
not forty, but "ten years after," pointing not only to a "system that had
liquidated alleged class enemies just as thoroughly as National Socialism had [liquidated] alleged racial enemies," but also to the crimes per-
petrated by Soviets against Germans at the end of the war.[70] And like
Hillgruber, Rothfels had used a palette of vivid colors to depict German
victims, while those "gassed at Auschwitz" appeared in black and white.

When Nolte asked if Germans in the east needed to fear becoming the
victims of an "'Asiatic' deed" at the end of the war, his question was also
not new, and there were already countless responses in the 1950s testimonies of POWs and expellees. Behind Nolte's designation "Asiatic"—
though safely tucked between quotation marks—were also undertones
of a racist anti-Communism that transformed all Russians into "Mongols" and that was central to Nazi propaganda, but that had also survived in public pronouncements of the first West German chancellor and
the memories of Germans who had experienced the end of the war on
the eastern front.[71]

Nolte's call for a comparative approach to totalitarian terrorism, his
insistence that the "final solution" was not unique, also found parallels
in the first postwar decade. The heated historical controversy in the mid-
1980s over whether Nazi crimes were unique or could be compared with
other instances of mass murder in the twentieth century represented a
return to familiar ground. POWs in Soviet captivity and expellees alike

compared the Nazi persecution of the Jews with Communist persecution of Germans; the "final solution" had long since been "relativized."[72] In his 1955 essay "Ten Years After," Rothfels emphasized that if anything distinguished the excesses of red and brown totalitarianism, it was that National Socialism grew out of a culture grounded in "occidentalism," not "orientalism," making Germany's crimes more horrifying but, in their essence, no different from those of Stalinism.[73]

The musings of Michael Stürmer and others in the mid-1980s that after the war West Germans had suffered a "loss of history" completely disregarded the selective "contemporary history" written in the first postwar decade. Stürmer's claim that a German history capable of "shaping identity" was possible only once Germans had mourned "for the victims and the pain of what was lost" took no note of how much mourning of this variety had already taken place.[74] When Joachim Fest fretted that "the public sphere, despite all encouragement from the political side, has still not emerged from the shadow cast by Hitler and the crimes committed under him," he also seemed to have suffered a "loss of history," the history of the 1950s, in which the crimes committed by Germans had received far less systematic scrutiny than the crimes committed against Germans.[75] Remarkably, even Broszat, whose contribution to the historians' controversy, "A Plea for a Historicization of National Socialism," expressed a desire to understand German society in the Third Reich and at the same time achieve a critical self-distancing from National Socialism, did not reflect on how his own work of compiling expellee memories from Romania thirty years earlier had been motivated by the same intentions and represented another form of the "historicization" of the war's end, nor did Hillgruber note that he was thoroughly familiar with the Schieder documentation project.[76] And Hans-Ulrich Wehler, who had also worked on the Schieder project and was among the most active participants in the historians' controversy, made no mention of how an insistence on German suffering in the 1980s seemed eerily to echo the insistence on German suffering three decades before. Those participants in the controversy who called for West Germans to escape the "shadow of Hitler" did not consider that in the 1950s Hitler's shadow barely obscured a West German landscape that was filled with German suffering and accounts in which the "real heroes" were survivors of Communist aggression, not survivors of concentration camps.[77]

The recapitulation of postwar history in this scholarly conflict was rooted at least in part in the biographies of the protagonists. The generation of the fathers now reasserted itself in the return to tropes of German history that had been firmly established in the 1950s. As the novelist and social critic Peter Schneider remarked, "When German historians address the past, they do so not only as scholars, but necessarily as participants too."[78] However, opposing sides were not defined solely by generation. Michael Stürmer, thirteen years the junior of Hillgruber, who himself was sixty at the time, lined up with those seeking a German history that could escape Hitler's shadow and would respect the innocence of the "cellar children, to which I, born in 1938, was damned," as well as that of the "refugee children, like my wife," who had survived "by the grace of God." For Stürmer, the "blessing of a late birth," the absolution claimed by Kohl for himself and other Germans who came of age only after 1945, did not erase childhood memories of a postwar generation that had not "asked to be born in Hitler's Germany."[79]

The call in the mid-1980s to link victims of Germans and German victims triggered vehement responses from many who protested Reagan's Bitburg visit, aggressively contested Hillgruber's juxtaposition of two "demises," and denounced Nolte's rejection of the singularity of Auschwitz. Jürgen Habermas, for one, questioned the motives of "whoever insists on mourning collective fates, without distinguishing between culprits and victims."[80] Habermas's position also had an intellectual lineage that extended back to the immediate postwar period, echoing as it did the views of Eugen Kogon, Karl Jaspers, and others who had criticized Germans who sought to mitigate their culpability for National Socialism by emphasizing their own suffering and who did not recognize the "blessing of defeat."[81] Four decades later, a broad spectrum of West German historians, intellectuals, and the president of the Federal Republic himself endorsed such critical views, defining one major difference between 1980s debates over competing pasts and those of the late 1940s and early 1950s. The past of Nazi crimes emphasized by some critical observers in the first postwar decade had moved from the margins to center stage. Still, it was by no means the only actor. The past of German victimization did not have to be scripted anew, because it was already in place. It had been written in the 1950s not only at the *Stammtisch* and in organizations of veterans and expellees; it had also been shaped by the rhetoric of high politics and the formulation of public policy, stories in the daily press, the work of distinguished historians, and movie melodramas.

Assessments in the late 1980s that the historians' controversy was over proved premature. By the early 1990s, following the *Wende* of 1989–90 and the unification of West and East Germany, it had become apparent that the Bitburg controversy and the issues raised in the rancorous exchanges among Hillgruber, Nolte, and their allies and critics were not isolated incidents but rather were all part of a protracted debate over the relationship between history and memory in Germany. The search for a usable past, it seemed, remained no less pressing in 1990 than it had been in the immediate postwar years or the *Wende* of the early 1980s.[82]

Even before May 1995, when the fiftieth anniversary of the war's end unleashed a flood of commemorative events, it was evident that the pasts of German victims and of the victims of Germans were still vying for space and recognition in public consciousness. When Helmut Kohl addressed the first meeting of the parliament of a reunified Germany in October 1990, he began by calling for a moment's silence in honor of the victims of Nazism, then moved without pause to call for the same measure of respect for the victims of Communism.[83] The controversy surrounding a memorial in Berlin that would commemorate victims of Nazi terror alongside German victims of the war provided additional proof that Germans were still far from unified on whether they should "insist on mourning collective fates."[84] A memorial of another sort, the House of German History, a permanent exhibition of the history of the Federal Republic housed in a massive new building on the "museum mile" in Bonn, planned long before unification, opened in June 1994. On entering the exhibition, what first captures the visitor's attention is a huge video screen that displays an endless film loop depicting the treks of expellees, pushing on across ice and snow in the winter of 1945. In this telling, postwar German history begins not with Auschwitz or even with Adenauer, but with the expulsion of Germans from areas near the Baltic in late 1944 and early 1945.[85]

Competing pasts also continued to face off in movie theaters. Steven Spielberg's *Schindler's List* opened in a unified Germany a year after Helke Sanders's *BeFreier und Befreite* (Liberators take liberties), which focused on the experience of women raped at the end of the war by Red Army soldiers. Once again proclaiming to break the silence, Sanders's film retold stories that were crucial to defining the experience of expellees and that had been rehearsed with endless variation in the late 1940s and early 1950s.[86] In a review in *Der Tagesspiegel,* Gabriele Riedle claimed: "Germans as victims of Russians—no sane person could claim that up until now. We generally saw that as taboo."[87] Riedle's study of the past did not include the first postwar decade.

With some variations, other histories repeated themselves. The screening of Joseph Vilsmaier's film *Stalingrad* marked the fiftieth anniversary of the Soviet defeat of the Germans at that city on the Volga. Another form of commemoration, it attracted nearly one and a half million German viewers in 1993 alone. The movie begins in August 1942 in Italy, where Wehrmacht soldiers, lounging on the beach, are soon mustered for a war in colder climes. An enthusiastic young lieutenant, scion of an aristocratic military family ready to earn his spurs—or his Iron Cross— on the eastern front, is shocked by the brutality of the war in that arena. Horrified by the mistreatment of Soviet POWs and the Soviet civilian population, he is soon at odds with his jaded, ideologically crazed superiors. His battle-worn men know better than to share his initial enthusiasm; as his disillusionment grows, however, they quickly discover the bases on which they can create a community of survivors.

Like filmic re-creations of the war in the east from the 1950s, Vilsmaier's movie can also not resist introducing the eternal feminine. The lieutenant's ability to preserve a sense of honor in the midst of chaos and moral collapse is symbolized by his valiant protection of a female Red Army fighter, found bound to a bed in an abandoned officers' quarters. Having been raped by Nazis, she is protected by this noble German, who guarantees that his men will not add insult to injury. The Russian, whose mother was German, realizes a strange kinship with her enemies and joins them in their vain attempt to escape through the Soviet lines, until she is shot dead by her own troops in a desolate, snowbound landscape. The good Russian and the good German transcend ideological systems to join forces, both ultimately victims of the insanity of war. Although the film graphically presents the horror of a war that claims countless Soviets, including civilians and unarmed POWs, it is ultimately a movie that, in the words of *Zeit* columnist Andreas Kilb, "shows the Germans just as they most like to see themselves: as victims"[88]—victims of crazed Nazis, the Red Army, the Russian winter, and a war they never wanted to fight.

Many of the same themes are also present in *Mein Krieg,* a 1990 movie that appeared against the backdrop of German unification. Directed by Harriet Eder and Thomas Kufus, it presents documentary footage shot by a number of Wehrmacht soldiers. These "amateur filmmakers," explain the directors, "filmed their departure and the invasion of the Soviet Union."[89] Interviewed by the directors years after the events they captured on film, the former soldiers reflect on their experiences, presenting the war, as the literary theorist Marcia Klotz explains, in many of the same terms used by Hillgruber to describe the most dramatic of his two "demises."[90] One eyewitness complicates the account by expressing remorse, and credits a stay in a Soviet POW camp for his enlightenment as to the extent of German crimes in the war, but for the most part the film repeats tales of German innocence and naïveté and of soldiers who lack any understanding of the larger context that gives meaning to their acts. There was little new about these war stories.

Against this background, it is not surprising that the call for Germans not to forget the past of their own victimization was heard yet again in May 1995. We have come full circle. Yet by that point, the international context framing commemoration had changed dramatically. The passing of the Cold War meant that fifty years after the war's end, Bill Clinton's dilemma was not how to cram visits to Bergen-Belsen and Bitburg into a few hours, or how to exploit a solemn moment to blast the evils of Communism, but rather how to be at Arlington National Cemetery on the morning of one day and make it to Moscow by the next. The geopolitical politics of war and peace had shifted, and 1995 was a year for the United States to acknowledge other alliances, other pasts.

Still, the events of the spring of 1995 made it apparent that the end of the Second World War continues to be a central arena for debates over the relationship between history and political identity in a post–Cold War unified Germany. In his famous 1985 address to parliament, Weizsäcker intoned a ritualistic call for German-German unity, maintaining that "Germans are one people and one nation . . . because [we] have lived through the same past."[91] Fifty years after the war's end, however, in a Germany now unified, the past looked no more one-dimensional than it did in 1945. A series in the liberal weekly *Die Zeit*, titled "*1945 und heute*" (1945 and today), included installments on the Holocaust, soldiers, deserters, trials of Nazi war criminals, and crimes committed against Germans. In his contribution on the Holocaust, "The Elimination of a People," Elie Wiesel argued that the "Germans' attempt to kill the Jews of Europe remains a unique crime." He warned against attempts to "water down" the meaning of the Holocaust, a term that should be applied only to the attempts of Germans to eliminate European Jewry. Use of the term *Völkermord*, the "intention to exterminate an entire people," also called for particular care. "We must be careful with words," Wiesel advised. "Language is very important, we must use it with care."[92] Contrary to Wiesel, Peter Glotz, writing on "the sickness of nationalism" and the expulsion of Germans from eastern Europe, invoked a familiar comparison when he insisted that "the destruction of the Jewish people, planned by Hitler, was not the only genocide [*Völkermord*]" of the twentieth century. "Genocidal" as well were all "expulsions that are carried out against the will of the population and without the possibility that [that population] can be resettled altogether in one place."[93]

Many Germans agreed with Glotz, not Wiesel. In the midst of the historians' controversy, Nolte bemoaned the "past that will not pass." The
forms of remembering the war's end ten years later revealed that there
was more than one past that refused to vanish.[94]

In his May 1985 speech, Weizsäcker insisted that it was essential for Germans to commemorate the war's end "among themselves." That internal process of introspection has become decidedly easier since the dramatic transformation of relations between East and West beginning in
the late 1980s; as a front-page headline in *Die Zeit* announced in September 1994, with the withdrawal of the last Russian troops from Germany, "only now is the war over."[95] Perhaps this definitive end of the
Cold War will enable Germans to find new ways to sort through the
memories of the Nazis' war that preceded it.

To be sure, how Germans and post-Communist nations in eastern Europe remember the war that ended in 1945 will continue to shape their
relations. Before 1989, Hillgruber's invocation of a history in which Germany served as a bridge—rather than a dividing line—between east and
west could be called a "geopolitics of nostalgia," and, in the midst of the
historians' controversy, no one would have predicted that the bridge
would be reconstructed quite so rapidly.[96] Now it is in place. As Germans and their eastern European neighbors confront this dramatically
altered reality, it will be important to see whether the legacy of Nazi occupation and the ravages of the SS and the Wehrmacht will inevitably be
juxtaposed to the legacy of the expulsion.[97] As new democracies to Germany's east leave the shadow of the former Soviet Union, they will re-
assess their own histories of occupation by the Nazis, their experiences
as collaborators and resisters, and their participation in the expulsion of
Germans from eastern Europe.[98] Former East Germans will also unearth
their history as victims of the war and of postwar Soviet occupation, a
past erased by a Communist regime that euphemistically referred to the
Soviet imprisonment of German soldiers as "antifascist reeducation" and
called the postwar expulsion a "policy of resettlement."[99] How Germans
and eastern Europeans come to terms with their intersecting pasts will
have an important influence on both foreign diplomacy and the shape
of new domestic political identities.

More than fifty years after the war's end, it must also be noted, categories of complicity and responsibility do not carry the same highly personal meanings for all Germans. To be sure, some myths die hard. Echoes
of older claims of the "clean Wehrmacht" could be heard in protests

against a traveling exhibition of photographic evidence of the "crimes of the German army" that began touring Germany as part of the events surrounding the fiftieth anniversary of the war's end. Despite over two decades of scholarship that left no question of the participation of regular army troops in the murder of Jews, other noncombatants, and Soviet POWs, this history still provoked heated controversy.[100] However, 1995 could well be the last major commemoration of the end of the Second World War in which large numbers of participants will be alive to claim the authority of eyewitnesses and troop out a set of meanings of the war that were established almost as soon as the shooting stopped. The second postwar generation participates in a national identity powerfully shaped by historical memory, but fewer and fewer Germans alive today were in uniform, in exile, in flight before the onslaught of the Red Army, in cities where they dodged falling bombs, in hiding, or in concentration camps where they hoped for liberation in the early 1940s.

Nevertheless, finding new positions from which to offer balanced assessments of the war's end is not easy; it involves the problems inherent in the binary oppositions of perpetrator and victim, guilt and innocence. In the 1950s, most West Germans were able to interpret their experience only in absolute moral categories: a nation of German victims had confronted a handful of Nazis perpetrators and a multitude of brutally vengeful Communist victors. Choosing between the positions of perpetrator and victim was the option Hillgruber offered Germans in his mid-1980s call for historical empathy, the same choice that confronted most West Germans in the 1950s. But in the Third Reich, if some Germans lived such absolute choices, most did not. An account of Germany in May 1945 that moved beyond this binary would deny no victim the ability to mourn, but it would also follow Habermas in insisting that "mourning collective fates" is inappropriate. It would avoid any tendency to establish the moral equivalence of the victims of Germans and German victims, just as it would reject an analysis that explained the suffering of all Germans as the quid pro quo for the suffering inflicted on others by the National Socialist state. It would also move beyond a language in which the categories of victim and perpetrator were mutually exclusive. Instead it would seek to capture the complexities of individual lives and "mass fates" by exploring how, during the 1940s, it was possible both to suffer and to cause suffering in others.

Notes

Abbreviations Used Frequently in Notes

BAK	Bundesarchiv (Koblenz)
BVFK	Bundesministerium für Vertriebene, Flüchtlinge und Kriegsgeschädigte
CDU	Christlich-Demokratische Union Deutschlands
CSU	Christlich-Soziale Union
DFI	Deutsches Filminstitut
DP	Deutsche Partei
FDP	Freie Demokratische Partei
FRUS	*Foreign Relations of the United States*
KPD	Kommunistische Partei Deutschlands
NA	National Archives
OMGUS	Office of Military Government U.S.
PAAA	Politisches Archiv des Auswärtigen Amts
PIB	Presse- und Informationsamt der Bundesregierung
SED	Sozialistische Einheitspartei Deutschlands
SPD	Sozialdemokratische Partei Deutschlands
US HICOG	U.S. High Commission for Germany
VDB	*Verhandlungen des deutschen Bundestags*
VdH	Verband der Heimkehrer, Kriegsgefangenen und Vermisstenangehörigen

Chapter One

1. See Richard H. Kohn, "History and the Culture Wars: The Case of the Smithsonian Institution's *Enola Gay* Exhibition," *Journal of American History* 82 (1995): 1036–63, part of a special issue of the journal that devoted consid-

erable space to a discussion of the controversy; also Nicholas D. Kristof, "The Bomb: An Act that Haunts Japan and America," *New York Times*, 6 Aug. 1995; and Ian Buruma, "The War over the Bomb," *New York Review of Books* 42, no. 14 (21 Sept. 1995): 26–34.

2. Nicholas D. Kristof, "Japan Divided on Apology to Asians," *New York Times*, 6 Mar. 1995; idem, "Japan Confronting Gruesome War Atrocity," *New York Times*, 17 Mar. 1995; idem, "Why Japan Hasn't Said That Word," *New York Times*, 7 May 1995; Teresa Watanabe and Mary Williams Walsh, "Facing the Demons of War Guilt," *Los Angeles Times*, 13 Aug. 1995; and Charles Smith, "War and Remembrance," *Far Eastern Economic Review*, 25 Aug. 1994, 22–26. My thanks to Katherine Ragsdale for calling my attention to these articles. See also John W. Dower, "Triumphal and Tragic Narratives of the War in Asia," *Journal of American History* 82 (1995): 1130–31; Michael J. Hogan, ed., *Hiroshima in History and Memory* (New York: Cambridge University Press, 1996); and Kai Bird and Lawrence Lifschultz, eds., *Hiroshima's Shadow* (Stony Creek, Conn.: Pamphleteer's Press, 1998).

3. "8. Mai 1945: Gegen das Vergessen," *Frankfurter Allgemeine Zeitung*, 7 Apr. 1995. My thanks to Thomas Schmitz for calling my attention to the ad. See also Edgar Wolfrum, "Zwischen Geschichtsschreibung und Geschichtspolitik: Forschungen zu Flucht und Vertreibung nach dem Zweiten Weltkrieg," *Archiv für Sozialgeschichte* 36 (1996): 501–2.

4. Stephen Kinzer, "Germans More Willing to Confront Nazi Crimes," *New York Times*, 1 May 1995; and "Lust am Erinnern," *Spiegel*, 24 Apr. 1995, 18–21. For less optimistic analyses of the "Initiative 8. Mai 1945," the group responsible for the 7 April advertisement, see Ralph Giordano, "Auch die Unfähigkeit zu trauern ist unteilbar," *Tageszeitung*, 18 Apr. 1995; Richard Herzigen, "Strategen der Retourkutsche," ibid., 15–16 April 1995; and Mary Williams Walsh, "V-E Day Events Present Paradox for German Psyche," *Los Angeles Times*, 5 May 1995; and in general, the interesting analysis of press accounts in Klaus Naumann, "Die Rhetorik des Schweigens: Die Lagerbefreiungen im Gedächtnisraum der Presse 1995," *Mittelweg 36* 5, no. 3 (1996): 23–30; idem, "Im Sog des Endes: Umrisse einer Printmedienanalyse zur deutschen Erinnerungspolitik im Gedenkjahr 1995," *Relation* 3 (1996): 175–96; idem, *Der Krieg als Text: Das Jahr 1945 im kulturellen Gedächtnis der Presse* (Hamburg: Hamburger Edition, 1998).

5. See "Die Jungen denken anders," *Spiegel*, 8 May 1995, 76–77; also William Tuohy, "German Leader Stirs Flap as Britons Recall Beating Nazis," *Los Angeles Times*, 7 May 1995; Roger Boyes, "What Did You Do in the War, Hans?" *The Times* (London), 6 May 1995; Stephen Kinzer, "Allies and Former Enemies Gather to Pledge Peace," *New York Times*, 9 May 1995; and the review of press coverage of the expulsion in Klaus Naumann, "Die Mutter, das Pferd und die Juden: Flucht und Vertreibung als Themen deutscher Erinnerungspolitik," *Mittelweg 36* 5, no. 4 (1996): 70–83; and idem, *Der Krieg als Text*, 72–90.

6. For a comparative perspective on the late 1940s and 1950s in the two Germanys, see Jürgen Danyel, "Die geteilte Vergangenheit: Gesellschaftliche Ausgangslagen und politische Dispositionen für den Umgang mit Nationalsozialismus und Widerstand in beiden deutschen Staaten nach 1949," in *Historische*

DDR-Forschung: Aufsätze und Studien, ed. Jürgen Kocka (Berlin: Akademie Verlag, 1993), 129–47; and Werner Bergmann, Rainer Erb, and Albert Lichtblau, eds., *Schwieriges Erbe: Der Umgang mit dem Nationalsozialismus und Antisemitismus in Österreich, der DDR und der Bundesrepublik Deutschland* (Frankfurt am Main: Campus, 1995).

7. For statistics on expellees, see Gerhard Reichling, *Die deutschen Vertriebenen in Zahlen,* pt. 1: *Umsiedler, Verschleppte, Vertriebene, Aussiedler, 1945–1985* (Bonn: Kulturstiftung der deutschen Vertriebenen, 1986), 26–27; idem, ibid., pt. 2: *40 Jahre Eingliederung in der Bundesrepublik Deutschland* (Bonn: Kulturstiftung der deutschen Vertriebenen, 1989), 14, 30–31; idem, "Flucht und Vertreibung der Deutschen: Statistische Grundlage und terminologische Probleme," in *Flüchtlinge und Vertriebene in der westdeutschen Nachkriegsgeschichte: Bilanzierung der Forschung und Perspektiven für die künftige Forschungsarbeit,* ed. Rainer Schulze, Doris von der Brelie-Lewien, and Helga Grebing (Hildesheim: August Lax, 1987), 46–56. Nearly 57 percent (4,541,000) came from East Prussia, Brandenburg, Pomerania, Lower Silesia, and Upper Silesia; 24 percent (1,918,000) from Czechoslovakia; 8.2 percent (650,000) from Poland, including Danzig; and another 8 percent (639,000) from other parts of southern and eastern Europe. The contemporary claim of some two million German deaths caused by the expulsion is probably greatly exaggerated. See the assessment of the available statistics in Rüdiger Overmans, "Personelle Verluste der deutschen Bevölkerung durch Flucht und Vertreibung," *Djieje najnowsze* 26 (1994): 51–65; idem, "'Amtlich und wissenschaftlich erarbeiten': Zur Diskussion über die Verluste während Flucht und Vertreibung der Deutschen aus der ČSR," in *Erzwungene Trennung: Vertreibungen und Aussiedlungen in und aus der Tschechoslowakei, 1938–1947, im Vergleich mit Polen, Ungarn und Jugoslawien,* ed. Detlef Brandes, Edita Ivaničková, and Jiří Pešek (Essen: Klartext, 1999), 149–77; and idem, *Deutsche militärische Verluste im Zweiten Weltkrieg* (Munich: R. Oldenbourg, 1999), 299. Good general overviews of the process of expulsion are provided by Pertti Tapio Ahonen, "The Expellee Organizations and West German Ostpolitik, 1949–1969" (Ph.D. diss., Yale University, 1999), 12–24; Michael R. Marrus, *The Unwanted: European Refugees in the Twentieth Century* (New York: Oxford University Press, 1985), 325–31; Eugene M. Kulischer, *Europe on the Move: War and Population Changes, 1917–47* (New York: Columbia University Press, 1948), 282–90; and, a study that also makes use of Polish sources, Philipp Ther, *Deutsche und polnische Vertriebene: Gesellschaft und Vertriebenenpolitik in der SBZ/DDR und in Polen, 1945–1956* (Göttingen: Vandenhoeck & Ruprecht, 1998), 50–66. On the POWs, see Kurt W. Böhme, *Die deutschen Kriegsgefangenen in sowjetischer Hand: Eine Bilanz* (Bielefeld: Ernst & Werner Gieseking, 1966), 151. A lower estimate of between 2.3 and 2.8 million is offered by Stefan Karner, "Verlorene Jahre: Deutsche Kriegsgefangene und Internierte im Archipel GUPWI," in *Kriegsgefangene-Voennoeplennye: Sowjetische Kriegsgefangene in Deutschland, Deutsche Kriegsgefangene in der Sowjetunion,* ed. Haus der Geschichte der Bundesrepublik (Düsseldorf: Droste, 1995), 59; also idem, *Im Archipel GUPVI: Kriegsgefangenschaft und Internierung in der Sowjetunion, 1941–1956* (Munich: R. Oldenbourg, 1995), 9. This corresponds to official Soviet figures of 2,389,560; see Anatolij Chorkow, "Zur Organisation des Kriegs-

gefangenenwesens in der UdSSR," in *Deutsch-russische Zeitenwende: Krieg und Frieden, 1941–1995,* ed. Hans-Adolf Jacobsen et al. (Baden-Baden: Nomos, 1995), 456; Stefan Karner, "Die sowjetische Hauptverwaltung für Kriegsgefangene und Internierte," *Vierteljahrshefte für Zeitgeschichte* 42 (1994): 447–71; and in general, Peter Steinbach, "Jenseits von Zeit und Raum: Kriegsgefangenschaft in der Frühgeschichte der Bundesrepublik Deutschland," *Universitas* 7 (1990): 637–49; idem, "Zur Sozialgeschichte der deutschen Kriegsgefangenschaft in der Sowjetunion im zweiten Weltkrieg und in der Frühgeschichte der Bundesrepublik Deutschland: Ein Beitrag zum Problem der historischen Kontinuität," *Zeitgeschichte* 17 (1989): 1–18; idem, "Die sozialgeschichtliche Dimension der Kreigsheimkehrer," in *Heimkehr 1948,* ed. Annette Kaminsky (Munich: C. H. Beck, 1998), 325–40; and Wolfgang Benz and Angelika Schardt, eds., *Deutsche Kriegsgefangene im Zweiten Weltkrieg: Erinnerungen* (Frankfurt am Main: Fischer, 1995). On the reliability of the numbers from German sources, see Rüdiger Overmans, "German Historiography, the War Losses, and the Prisoners of War," in *Eisenhower and the German POWS: Facts against Falsehood,* ed. Günter Bischof and Stephen E. Ambrose (Baton Rouge: Louisiana State University Press, 1992), 127–69; and idem, "55 Millionen Opfer des Zweiten Weltkrieges? Zum Stand der Forschung nach mehr als 40 Jahren," *Militärgeschichtliche Mitteilungen* 48 (1990): 103–21. Recent revelations in Russian archives may call for an upward revision of the number of prisoners of war and suggest that all previous counts are estimates at best. See Günther Wagenlehner, "Zweimal einem Wahn geopfert," *Parlament,* 28 Apr./5 May 1995.

8. Gerhard L. Weinberg's *A World at Arms: A Global History of World War II* (New York: Cambridge University Press, 1994) is a stunning achievement, but it remains fixed largely on political, military, and economic history.

9. Eugen Kogon, *Der NS-Staat: Das System der deutschen Konzentrationslager* (Munich: Alber, 1946). By 1947 a second edition was in print, and there were 100,000 copies in circulation.

10. Eugen Kogon, "Gericht und Gewissen," *Frankfurter Hefte* 1, no. 1 (1946): 29–31; and idem, "Über die Situation," *Frankfurter Hefte* 2, no. 1(1947): 29, 34. On Kogon's background and the history of the *Frankfurter Hefte,* see Karl Prümm, "Entwürfe einer zweiten Republik: Zukunftsprogramme in den 'Frankfurter Heften,' 1946–1949," in *Deutschland nach Hitler: Zukunftspläne im Exil und aus der Besatzungszeit, 1939–1949,* ed. Thomas Koebner, Gert Sautermeister, and Sigrid Schneider (Opladen: Westdeutscher Verlag, 1987), 330–43. A critical perspective was also offered by the émigré Hannah Arendt, "The Aftermath of Nazi Rule: Report from Germany," *Commentary* 10 (1950): 342–53.

11. Karl Jaspers, *The Question of German Guilt,* trans. E. B. Ashton (New York: Capricorn Books, 1961), 21, 114. The German edition of Jaspers's book appeared in 1946. See also Anson Rabinbach, *In the Shadow of Catastrophe: German Intellectuals between Apocalypse and Enlightenment* (Berkeley and Los Angeles: University of California Press, 1997), 129–65.

12. In general, see Frank Stern, *The Whitewashing of the Yellow Badge: Antisemitism and Philosemitism in Postwar Germany,* trans. William Templer (Oxford: Pergamon, 1992); Michael Brenner, *Nach dem Holocaust: Juden in Deutschland, 1945–1950* (Munich: C. H. Beck, 1995); and Atina Grossmann, "Trauma,

Memory, and Motherhood: Germans and Jewish Displaced Persons in Post-Nazi Germany, 1945–1949," *Archiv für Sozialgeschichte* 39 (1998): 215–39. On the West German Communist Party, see Patrick Major, *The Death of the KPD: Communism and Anti-Communism in West Germany, 1945–1956* (Oxford: Clarendon Press, 1997); and on the immediate postwar period before the creation of two Germanys, see Eric D. Weitz, *Creating German Communism, 1890–1990: From Popular Protests to Socialist State* (Princeton: Princeton University Press, 1997), 313–27.

13. Here I consciously echo the title of Anson Rabinbach's insightful essay, "The Jewish Question in the German Question," in *Reworking the Past: Hitler, the Holocaust, and the Historians' Debate,* ed. Peter Baldwin (Boston: Beacon Press, 1990), esp. 45–53. See also the thoughtful reflections of Omer Bartov, "'Seit die Juden weg sind . . .': Germany, History, and Representations of Absence," in *A User's Guide to German Cultural Studies,* ed. Scott Denham, Irene Kacandes, and Jonathan Petropoulos (Ann Arbor: University of Michigan Press, 1997), 209–26; idem, "Defining Enemies, Making Victims: Germans, Jews, and the Holocaust," *American Historical Review* 103 (1998): 771–816; and idem, *Mirrors of Destruction: War, Genocide, and Modern Identity* (New York: Oxford University Press, 2000), esp. 104–18.

14. Benedict Anderson, *Imagined Communities: Reflections on the Origin and Spread of Nationalism,* rev. ed. (London: Verso, 1991), 7.

15. See, e.g., Ute Frevert, "Die Sprache des Volkes und die Rhetorik der Nation: Identitätssplitter in der deutschen Nachkriegszeit," in *Doppelte Zeitgeschichte: Deutsch-deutsche Beziehungen, 1945–1990,* ed. Arnd Bauerkämper, Martin Sabrow, and Bernd Stöver (Bonn: J. H. W. Dietz Nachf., 1998), 18–31.

16. Martin Broszat, Klaus-Dietmar Henke, and Hans Woller, eds., *Von Stalingrad zur Währungsreform: Zur Sozialgeschichte des Umbruchs in Deutschland* (Munich: R. Oldenbourg, 1988); Lutz Niethammer, "Privat-Wirtschaft: Erinnerungsfragmente einer anderen Umerziehung," in *"Hinterher merkt man, dass es richtig war, dass es schiefgegangen ist": Nachkriegs-Erfahrungen im Ruhrgebiet,* ed. Lutz Niethammer (Berlin: J. H. W. Dietz Nachf., 1983), 79–82.

17. See the insightful discussion in Helmut Dubiel, *Niemand ist frei von der Geschichte: Die nationalsozialistische Herrschaft in den Debatten des Deutschen Bundestages* (Munich: Carl Hanser, 1999), 72–74.

18. Bruno Wasser, *Himmlers Raumplanung im Osten: Der Generalplan Ost in Polen 1940–1944* (Basel: Birkhäuser, 1993). See also Hans Umbreit, *Deutsche Militärverwaltungen 1938/39: Die militärische Besetzung der Tschechoslowakei und Polens* (Stuttgart: Deutsche Verlags-Anstalt, 1977), esp. 190–221; Czesław Madajczyk, *Die Okkupationspolitik Nazideutschlands in Polen, 1939–1945* (Berlin: Akademie Verlag, 1987); Jürgen Förster, "The Relation between Operation Barbarossa as an Ideological War of Extermination and the Final Solution," in *The Final Solution: Origins and Implementation,* ed. David Cesarani (London: Routledge, 1994), 87–88; Valdis O. Lumans, *Himmler's Auxiliaries: The Volksdeutsche Mittelstelle and the German National Minorities of Europe, 1933–1945* (Chapel Hill: University of North Carolina Press, 1993), esp. 161–65; Robert L. Koehl, *RKFDV: German Resettlement and Population Policy, 1939–1945* (Cambridge, Mass.: Harvard University Press, 1957); Horst Rohde, "Hitler's First

Blitzkrieg and Its Consequences for North-eastern Europe," in *Germany and the Second World War*, vol 2: *Germany's Initial Conquests of Europe*, ed. Militärgeschichtliches Forschungsamt (Oxford: Clarendon Press, 1991), 67–150.

19. See the insightful analysis of the rapid development of Nazi racial policy in John Connelly, "Nazis and Slavs: From Racial Theory to Racist Practice," *Central European History* 32 (1999): 1–33.

20. See, e.g., Israel [Yisrael] Gutman, *Resistance: The Warsaw Ghetto Uprising* (Boston: Houghton Mifflin, 1994); idem, *The Jews of Warsaw, 1939–1943: Ghetto, Underground, Revolt* (Bloomington: Indiana University Press, 1982); Ezra Mendelsohn, *The Jews of East Central Europe between the World Wars* (Bloomington: Indiana University Press, 1983), 23–24; and Lucjan Dobroszycki, ed., *The Chronicle of the Łódź Ghetto, 1941–1944*, trans. Richard Lourie et al. (New Haven: Yale University Press, 1984).

21. Gotthold Rhode, "The Protectorate of Bohemia and Moravia," in *A History of the Czechoslovak Republic, 1918–1948*, ed. Victor S. Mamatey and Radomír Luža (Princeton: Princeton University Press, 1973), 296–321; Detlef Brandes, *Die Tschechen unter deutschem Protektorat*, pt. 1: *Besatzungspolitik, Kollaboration und Widerstand im Protektorat Böhmen und Mähren bis Heydrichs Tod (1939–1942)* (Munich: R. Oldenbourg, 1969); and idem, ibid., pt. 2: *Besatzungspolitik, Kollaboration und Widerstand im Protektorat Böhmen und Mähren von Heydrichs Tod bis zum Prager Aufstand (1942–1945)* (Munich: R. Oldenbourg, 1975); Detlef Brandes and Václav Kural, eds., *Der Weg in die Katastrophe: Deutsch-tschechoslowakische Beziehungen, 1938–1947* (Essen: Klartext, 1994); Loránd Tilkovszky, "The Late Interwar Years and World War II," in *A History of Hungary*, ed. Peter F. Sugar, Péter Hanák, and Tibor Frank (Bloomington: Indiana University Press, 1990), 346–55; Jörg K. Hoensch, *A History of Modern Hungary, 1867–1986*, trans. by Kim Traynor (London: Longman 1988), 146–60; idem, "The Slovak Republic, 1939–1945," in Mamatey and Luža (eds.), *History of the Czechoslovak Republic*, 271–95; Sheila Grant Duff, *A German Protectorate: The Czechs under Nazi Rule* (London: Frank Cass, 1970); Detlef Vogel, "German Intervention in the Balkans," in *Germany and the Second World War*, vol. 3: *The Mediterranean, South-east Europe, and North Africa, 1939–1941*, ed. Militärgeschichtliches Forschungsamt (Oxford: Clarendon Press, 1995), 479–526; Valdis O. Lumans, "The Ethnic German Minority of Slovakia and the Third Reich, 1938–45," *Central European History* 15 (1982): 266–97; Vojtech Mastny, *The Czechs under Nazi Rule: The Failure of National Resistance, 1939–1942* (New York: Columbia University Press, 1971); and Alan E. Steinweis, "German Cultural Imperialism in Czechoslovakia and Poland, 1938–1945," *International History Review* 13 (1991): 466–80. An important perspective on how German occupation enhanced the status of "Volksdeutsche" and intensified anti-Semitism is offered by Doris L. Bergen, "The Nazi Concept of 'Volksdeutsche' and the Exacerbation of Anti-Semitism in Eastern Europe, 1939–1945," *Journal of Contemporary History* 29 (1994): 569–82.

22. Quoted in Jürgen Förster, "The German Army and the Ideological War against the Soviet Union," in *The Policies of Genocide: Jews and Soviet Prisoners of War in Nazi Germany*, ed. Gerhard Hirschfeld (London: Allen & Unwin, 1986), 17. For an excellent introduction to the vast literature on the Ger-

man attack on the Soviet Union, see Horst Boog et al., *Der Angriff auf die Sowjetunion* (Frankfurt am Main: Fischer Taschenbuch Verlag, 1991). See also Manfred Messerschmidt, *Die Wehrmacht im NS-Staat: Zeit der Indoktrination* (Hamburg: R. v. Decker, 1969); Omer Bartov, *Hitler's Army: Soldiers, Nazis, and War in the Third Reich* (New York: Oxford University Press, 1992); idem, *The Eastern Front, 1941–45: German Troops and the Barbarisation of Warfare* (Houndmills, Basingstoke, Hampshire: Macmillan Press, 1985); idem, "The Conduct of War: Soldiers and the Barbarization of Warfare," *Journal of Modern History* 64 suppl. (1992): S32–S45; Peter Jahn and Reinhard Rürup, eds., *Eroberung und Vernichtung: Der Krieg gegen die Sowjetunion* (Berlin: Argon, 1991); Christian Streit, "Ostkrieg, Antibolschewismus und 'Endlösung,'" *Geschichte und Gesellschaft* 17 (1991): 242–55; idem, "The German Army and the Policies of Genocide," in Hirschfeld (ed.), *Policies of Genocide*, 1–14; idem, *Keine Kameraden: Die Wehrmacht und die sowjetischen Kriegsgefangenen, 1941–1945* (Stuttgart: Deutsche Verlags-Anstalt, 1978); Theo J. Schulte, *The German Army and Nazi Policies in Occupied Russia* (Oxford: Berg, 1989); Ernst Klee, Willi Dressen, and Volker Riess, eds., *"The Good Old Days": The Holocaust As Seen by Its Perpetrators and Bystanders*, trans. Deborah Burnstone (New York: Free Press, 1991); and Hannes Heer and Klaus Naumann, eds., *Vernichtungskrieg: Verbrechen der Wehrmacht, 1941–1944* (Hamburg: Hamburger Edition, 1995).

23. See, e.g., Michael Kumpfmüller, *Die Schlacht von Stalingrad: Metamorphosen eines deutschen Mythos* (Munich: Wilhelm Fink, 1995); Wolfram Wette and Gerd R. Ueberschär, *Stalingrad: Mythos und Wirklichkeit einer Schlacht* (Frankfurt am Main: Fischer Taschenbuch Verlag, 1992); and *SOWI* 22 (1993), a special issue dedicated entirely to "Stalingrad: Erinnerung und Identitätssuche," ed. Alf Lüdtke. Recent estimates place the total number of German soldiers taken prisoner at Stalingrad at 110,000, of whom some 17,000 died on the way to the camps. See Manfred Hettling, "Täter und Opfer? Die deutschen Soldaten in Stalingrad," *Archiv für Sozialgeschichte* 35 (1995): 515–31, esp. 524n.34.

24. Yeshayahu A. Jelinek, *The Lust for Power: Nationalism, Slovakia, and the Communists, 1918–1945* (Boulder, Colo.: East European Monographs, 1983), 68–77; and Anna Josko, "The Slovak Resistance Movement," in Mamatey and Luźa (eds.), *History of the Czechoslovak Republic*, 362–84.

25. See the recent study of Manfred Zeidler, *Kriegsende im Osten: Die Rote Armee und die Besetzung Deutschlands östlich von Oder und Neisse, 1944/45* (Munich: R. Oldenbourg, 1996).

26. For a recent general introduction, see Robert Streibel, ed., *Flucht und Vertreibung: Zwischen Aufrechnung und Verdrängung* (Vienna: Picus, 1994), which includes general discussions as well as specific essays on Yugoslavia and Czechoslovakia; and Richard G. Plaschka et al., eds., *Nationale Frage und Vertreibung in der Tschechoslowakei und Ungarn 1938–1948* (Vienna: Verlag der Österreichischen Akademie der Wissenschaften, 1997).

27. Lumans, *Himmler's Auxiliaries*, 18.

28. Weinberg, *World at Arms*, 264.

29. John Barber and Mark Harrison, *The Soviet Home Front, 1941–1945: A Social and Economic History of the USSR in World War II* (London: Longman, 1991), 40–41.

30. Streit, *Keine Kameraden,* 245–46. Streit estimates the number of Soviet POW deaths at 3.3 million.

31. Here my analysis diverges from the thoughtful comments of Michael Geyer, "The Place of the Second World War in German Memory and History," *New German Critique,* no. 71 (1997): 17.

32. Iwona Irwin-Zarecka, *Frames of Remembrance: The Dynamics of Collective Memory* (New Brunswick, N.J.: Transaction, 1994), chap. 3, "Communities of Memory," 47–65. See also Ulrich Herbert, "'Die guten und die schlechten Zeiten': Überlegungen zur diachronen Analyse lebensgeschichtlicher Interviews," in *"Die Jahre weiss man nicht, wo man die heute hinsetzen soll": Faschismus-Erfahrungen im Ruhrgebiet,* ed. Lutz Niethammer (Berlin: J. H. W. Dietz Nachf., 1983), 67–96; and Gabriele Rosenthal, "Vom Krieg erzählen, von den Verbrechen schweigen," in Heer and Naumann (eds.), *Vernichtungskrieg,* 651–63.

33. Maurice Halbwachs, *On Collective Memory,* trans. Lewis A. Coser (Chicago: University of Chicago Press, 1992), 5. I have found very useful the reviews of the literature on collective memory provided by Alon Confino, *The Nation as a Local Metaphor: Württemberg, Imperial Germany, and National Memory, 1871–1918* (Chapel Hill: University of North Carolina Press, 1997), 10–13; and Rudy Koshar, *Germany's Transient Pasts: Preservation and National Memory in the Twentieth Century* (Chapel Hill: University of North Carolina Press, 1998), 4–11; also Confino, "Collective Memory and Cultural History: Problems of Method," *American Historical Review* 102 (1997): 1386–1403; and Susan A. Crane, "Writing the Individual Back into Collective Memory," ibid., 1372–85.

34. See, e.g., several of the essays in John R. Gillis, ed., *Commemorations: The Politics of National Identity* (Princeton: Princeton University Press, 1994); George L. Mosse, *Fallen Soldiers: Reshaping the Memory of the World Wars* (New York: Oxford University Press, 1990); Joanna Bourke, *Dismembering the Male: Men's Bodies, Britain, and the Great War* (London: Reaktion Books, 1996), 210–52; G. Kurt Piehler, *Remembering War the American Way* (Washington: Smithsonian Institution Press, 1995); Daniel J. Sherman, "Monuments, Mourning, and Masculinity in France after World War I," *Gender and History* 8 (1996): 82–107; idem, "Bodies and Names: The Emergence of Commemoration in Interwar France," *American Historical Review* 103 (1998): 443–66; and Peter Reichel, *Politik mit der Erinnerung: Gedächtnisorte im Streit um die national-sozialistische Vergangenheit* (Munich: Carl Hanser, 1995).

35. See the important recent work of Koshar, *Germany's Transient Pasts.*

36. See, e.g., Niethammer, "Privat-Wirtschaft," 17–105.

37. See, e.g., James E. Young, *The Texture of Memory: Holocaust Memorials and Meaning* (New Haven: Yale University Press, 1993); Harold Marcuse, "Das ehemalige Konzentrationslager Dachau: Der mühevolle Weg zur Gedenkstätte, 1945–1968," *Dachauer Hefte* 6 (1990): 182–205; and idem, *Legacies of Dachau: The Uses and Abuses of a Concentration Camp, 1933–2001* (Cambridge: Cambridge University Press, forthcoming).

38. Irwin-Zarecka, *Frames of Remembrance,* 13–14.

39. See Helmut Peitsch, "Towards a History of *Vergangenheitsbewältigung:*

East and West German War Novels of the 1950s," *Monatshefte* 87 (1995): 287–308; Heinz Brüdigam, *Der Schoss ist fruchtbar noch . . . : Neonazistische, militaristische, nationalistische Literatur und Publizistik in der Bundesrepublik,* 2d ed. (Frankfurt am Main: Röderberg, 1965); Michael Schornstheimer, *Die leuchtenden Augen der Frontsoldaten: Nationalsozialismus und Krieg in den Illustriertenromanen der fünfziger Jahre* (Berlin: Metropol, 1995); and idem, "'Harmlose Idealisten und draufgängerische Soldaten': Militär und Krieg in den Illustriertenromanen der fünfziger Jahre," in Heer and Naumann (eds.), *Vernichtungskrieg,* 634–50. On "expellee literature," see Louis Ferdinand Helbig, *Der ungeheuere Verlust: Flucht und Vertreibung in der deutschsprachigen Belletristik der Nachkriegszeit* (Wiesbaden: Otto Harrassowitz, 1988); Klaus Weigelt, ed., *Flucht und Vertreibung in der Nachkriegsliteratur: Formen ostdeutscher Kulturförderung* (Melle: Ernst Knoth, 1986); and Zohar Shavit, "Aus Kindermund: Historisches Bewusstsein und nationaler Diskurs in Deutschland nach 1945," *Neue Sammlung* 36 (1996): 355–74.

40. "Dokumente des Grauens," *Stuttgarter Zeitung,* 2 Sept. 1954, copy in Bundesarchiv (Koblenz), B150/5641 [hereafter cited as BAK]; and "Die deutsche Tragödie," *Westfälische Zeitung,* 30 Oct. 1957, copy in BAK, B150/5643. The project is discussed in Chapter 3.

41. Profoundly influential on my thinking about movies in the 1950s is Heide Fehrenbach, *Cinema in Democratizing Germany: Reconstructing National Identity after Hitler* (Chapel Hill: University of North Carolina Press, 1995).

42. Theodor W. Adorno, "What Does Coming to Terms with the Past Mean?" in *Bitburg in Moral and Political Perspective,* ed. Geoffrey H. Hartman (Bloomington: Indiana University Press, 1986), 124.

43. Ibid.

44. Alexander Mitscherlich and Margarete Mitscherlich, *Die Unfähigkeit zu trauern: Grundlagen kollektiven Verhaltens* (Munich: Piper, 1967), 19. See also Hartmut Berghoff, "Zwischen Verdrändung und Aufarbeitung," *Geschichte in Wissenschaft und Unterricht* 49 (1998): 96–114; and Eric L. Santner, *Stranded Objects: Mourning, Memory, and Film in Postwar Germany* (Ithaca, N.Y.: Cornell University Press, 1990), 1–6.

45. See, e.g., the characteristic formulation of this position in Wolfgang Benz, "Postwar Society and National Socialism: Remembrance, Amnesia, Rejection," *Tel Aviver Jahrbuch für deutsche Geschichte* 19 (1990): 2. For critical perspectives, see Hermann Graml, "Die verdrängte Auseinandersetzung mit dem Nationalsozialismus," in *Zäsuren nach 1945: Essays zur Periodisierung der deutschen Nachkriegsgeschichte,* ed. Martin Broszat (Munich: R. Oldenbourg, 1990), 169–83; Manfred Kittel, *Die Legende von der "zweiten Schuld": Vergangenheitsbewältigung in der Ära Adenauer* (Frankurt am Main: Ullstein, 1993); Christa Hoffmann, *Stunden Null? Vergangenheitsbewältigung in Deutschland, 1945 bis 1989* (Bonn: Bouvier, 1992); Udo Wengst, "Geschichtswissenschaft und 'Vergangenheitsbewältigung' in Deutschland nach 1945 und nach 1989/90," *Geschichte in Wissenschaft und Unterricht* 46 (1995): 189–205; and, focusing particularly on the ways in which women's experiences as victims became central to the definition of a West German national identity in the early

postwar years, Elizabeth Heineman, "The Hour of the Woman: Memories of Germany's 'Crisis Years' and West German National Identity," *American Historical Review* 101 (1996): 354–95.

46. Hermann Lübbe, "Der Nationalsozialismus im politischen Bewusstsein der Gegenwart," in *Deutschlands Weg in die Diktatur: Internationale Konferenz zur nationalsozialistischen Machtübernahme im Reichstagsgebäude zu Berlin,* ed. Martin Broszat et al. (Berlin: Siedler, 1983), 329–49, esp. 334–35.

47. Jeffrey Herf, *Divided Memory: The Nazi Past in the Two Germanys* (Cambridge, Mass.: Harvard University Press, 1997), 225. My thoughts on this topic have been greatly influenced by discussions with Frank Biess of the University of California, San Diego. See Biess's thoughtful review of Herf's book in *German Politics and Society* 17 (1999): 144–51.

48. "Saddest chapter": *Verhandlungen des deutschen Bundestags* (Bonn: Universitäts-Buchdruckerei Gebr. Scheur, 1950) [hereafter cited as *VDB*], (1.) Deutscher Bundestag, 252. Sitzung, 4 March 1953, 12092.

49. Herf, *Divided Memory,* 3, and in general, Chap. 8, "Atonement, Restitution, and Justice Delayed: West Germany, 1949–1963," 267–333.

50. These topics are discussed at greater length in Chapter 2 below.

51. Norbert Frei, *Vergangenheitspolitik: Die Anfänge der Bundesrepublik und die NS-Vergangenheit* (Munich: C. H. Beck, 1996).

52. Curt Garner, "Public Service Personnel in West Germany in the 1950s: Controversial Policy Decisions and their Effects on Social Composition, Gender Structure, and the Role of Former Nazis," in *West Germany Under Construction: Politics, Society, and Culture in the Adenauer Era,* ed. Robert G. Moeller (Ann Arbor: University of Michigan Press, 1997), 135–95; idem, "Schlussfolgerungen aus der Vergangenheit? Die Auseinandersetzungen um die Zukunft des deutschen Berufsbeamtentums nach dem Ende des Zweiten Weltkrieges," in *Ende des Dritten Reiches—Ende des Zweiten Weltkrieges: Eine perspektivistische Rückschau,* ed. Hans-Ulrich Volkmann (Munich: Piper, 1995), 607–74; James M. Diehl, *The Thanks of the Fatherland: German Veterans after the Second World War* (Chapel Hill: University of North Carolina Press, 1993); and Ulrich Brochhagen, *Nach Nürnberg: Vergangenheitsbewältigung und Westintegration in der Ära Adenauer* (Hamburg: Junius, 1994).

53. S. Jonathan Wiesen, "Overcoming Nazism: Big Business, Public Relations, and the Politics of Memory,1945–1950," *Central European History* 29 (1996): 201–26; idem, "Reconstruction and Recollection: West German Industry and the Challenge of the Nazi Past, 1945–1955" (Ph.D. diss., Brown University, 1998).

54. Michael L. Hughes, *Shouldering the Burdens of Defeat: West Germany and the Reconstruction of Social Justice* (Chapel Hill: University of North Carolina Press, 1999).

55. For a useful introduction, see Gerd R. Ueberschär, ed., *Der 20. Juli 1944: Bewertung und Rezeption des deutschen Widerstands gegen das NS-Regime* (Cologne: Bund-Verlag, 1994); also Norbert Frei, "Erinnerungskampf: Zur Legitimationsproblematik des 20. Juli 1944 im Nachkriegsdeutschland," in *Von der Aufgabe der Freiheit: Politische Verantwortung und bürgerliche Gesellschaft im 19. und 20. Jahrhundert,* ed. Christian Jansen, Lutz Niethammer, and Bernd Weis-

brod (Berlin: Akademie Verlag, 1995), 493–504; and in general, for a much fuller sense of the range of resistance, Peter Steinbach and Johannes Tuchel, eds., *Widerstand gegen den Nationalsozialismus* (Berlin: Akademie Verlag, 1994).

56. Michael Krause, *Flucht vor dem Bombenkrieg: "Umquartierungen" im zweiten Weltkrieg und die Wiedereingliederung der Evakuierten in Deutschland, 1943–1963* (Düsseldorf: Droste, 1997); and Gregory Frederick Schroeder, "The Long Road Home: German Evacuees of the Second World War, Postwar Victim Identities, and Social Policy in the Federal Republic" (Ph.D. diss., Indiana University, 1997).

57. The quotations are from Bernhard Winkelheide, a spokesman for the Christian Democratic Union (hereafter CDU), in *VDB*, (1.) Deutscher Bundestag, 162. Sitzung, 13 Sept. 1951, 6959; and Winkelheide, "Warum Familienausgleichskassen?" *Soziale Arbeit* 1 (1951): 100.

58. On women and the family, see Robert G. Moeller, *Protecting Motherhood: Women and the Family in the Politics of Postwar West Germany* (Berkeley and Los Angeles: University of California Press, 1993); Elizabeth Heineman, "Complete Families, Half Families, No Families at All: Female-Headed Households and the Reconstruction of the Family in the Early Federal Republic," *Central European History* 29 (1996): 29–60; idem, *What Difference Does a Husband Make? Marital Status in Germany, 1933–1961* (Berkeley and Los Angeles: University of California Press, 1999); idem, "Hour of the Woman"; Sibylle Meyer and Eva Schulze, *Wie wir das alles geschafft haben: Alleinstehende Frauen berichten über ihr Leben nach 1945* (Munich: C. H. Beck, 1985); and idem, *Von Liebe sprach damals keiner: Familienalltag in der Nachkriegszeit* (Munich: C. H. Beck, 1985). On youth culture, see the pathbreaking work of Uta G. Poiger, *Jazz, Rock, and Rebels: Cold War Politics and American Culture in a Divided Germany* (Berkeley and Los Angeles: University of California Press, 2000); idem, "Rebels with a Cause? American Popular Culture, the 1956 Youth Riots, and New Conceptions of Masculinity in East and West Germany," in *The American Impact on Postwar Germany*, ed. Reiner Pommerin (Providence, R.I.: Berghahn Books, 1995), 93–124; idem, "Rock 'n' Roll, Female Sexuality, and the Cold War Battle over German Identities," in Moeller (ed.), *West Germany Under Construction*, 373–410; and Kaspar Maase, *BRAVO Amerika: Erkundungen zur Jugendkultur der Bundesrepublik in den fünfziger Jahren* (Hamburg: Junius, 1992). Even when contemporaries concluded that youth discontent would not spill over into fascist extremes as it had in Weimar, National Socialism was a constant point of reference; see, e.g., Helmut Schelsky, *Die skeptische Generation: Eine Soziologie der deutschen Jugend* (Frankurt am Main: Ullstein, [1957] 1984).

59. Ahonen, "Expellee Organizations"; also idem, "Domestic Constraints on West German Ostpolitik: The Role of the Expellee Organizations in the Adenauer Era," *Central European History* 31 (1998): 31–63.

60. Frank P. Biess, "The Protracted War: Returning POWs and the Making of East and West German Citizens, 1945–1955" (Ph.D. diss., Brown University, 2000); also idem, "'Pioneers of a New Germany': Returning POWs from the Soviet Union and the Making of East German Citizens, 1945–1950," *Central European History* 32 (1999): 143–80; idem, "Survivors of Totalitarianism: Returning POWs and the Reconstruction of Masculine Citizenship in West Germany,

1945–1955," in *The Miracle Years Revisited: A Cultural History of West Germany,* ed. Hanna Schissler (Princeton: Princeton University Press, 2000). Biess, Ahonen, and I were all completing our studies at roughly the same time. They both read all relevant parts of the penultimate version of this book and in turn shared with me their work. Because we worked with some of the same sources, there are similarities in some of the conclusions we reach, but each of us has pushed the material in different directions. See also the early formulations of some of the themes I develop in this book in my article "War Stories: The Search for a Usable Past in the Federal Republic of Germany," *American Historical Review* 101 (1996): 1008–48.

61. On the possibilities for German-German comparison, see Norbert Frei, "NS-Vergangenheit unter Ulbricht und Adenauer: Gesichtspunkte einer 'vergleichenden Bewältigungsforschung,'" in *Die geteilte Vergangenheit: Zum Umgang mit Nationalsozialismus und Widerstand in beiden deutschen Staaten,* ed. Jürgen Danyel (Berlin: Akademie Verlag, 1995), 125–32; Jürgen Danyel, "Die beiden deutschen Staaten und ihre nationalsozialistische Vergangenheit: Elitenwechsel und Vergangenheitspolitik," in *Deutsche Vergangenheiten—eine gemeinsame Herausforderung: Der schwierige Umgang mit der doppelten Nachkriegsgeschichte,* ed. Christoph Klessmann, Hans Misselwitz, and Günter Wichert (Berlin: Ch. Links, 1999), 128–38; and for the first systematic comparison, see Herf, *Divided Memory.*

62. Norman M. Naimark, *The Russians in Germany: A History of the Soviet Zone of Occupation, 1945–1949* (Cambridge, Mass.: Harvard University Press, 1995), 419 (quotation), 148–49 (on "settlers"). See also Herf, *Divided Memory;* Jürgen Danyel, Olaf Groehler, and Mario Kessler, "Antifaschismus und Verdrängung: Zum Umgang mit der NS-Vergangenheit in der DDR," in *Die DDR als Geschichte: Fragen—Hypothesen—Perspektiven,* ed. Jürgen Kocka and Martin Sabrow (Berlin: Akademie Verlag, 1994), 148–52; Danyel (ed.), *Geteilte Vergangenheit.* On treatment of expellees in the GDR, see Philipp Ther, "The Integration of Expellees in Germany and Poland after World War II: A Historical Reassessment," *Slavic Review* 55 (1996): 792–96; idem, *Deutsche und polnische Vertriebene;* Michael Schwarz, "Vertreibung und Vergangenheitspolitik: Ein Versuch über geteilte deutsche Nachkriegsidentitäten," *Deutschlandarchiv* 30 (1997): 177–95; Alexander von Plato and Wolfgang Meinicke, *Alte Heimat—neue Zeit: Flüchtlinge, Umgesiedelte, Vertriebene in der sowjetischen Besatzungszone und in der DDR* (Berlin: Verlags-Anstalt Union, 1991); Manfred Wille, Johannes Hoffmann, and Wolfgang Meinicke, eds., *Sie hatten alles verloren: Flüchtlinge und Vertriebene in der sowjetischen Besatzungszone Deutschlands* (Wiesbaden: Harrassowitz, 1993); and the review of recent literature in Wolfrum, "Geschichtsschreibung," 511–13. On POWs, see the work of Biess; also several of the essays in Annette Kaminsky, ed., *Heimkehr 1948* (Munich: C. H. Beck, 1998).

63. A useful introduction to this broad topic is offered in Ian Buruma, *The Wages of Guilt: Memories of War in Germany and Japan* (New York: Penguin Books, 1994). Possibilities for comparisons with the Japanese case, explicit in Buruma, are implicit in John W. Dower, *Embracing Defeat: Japan in the Wake of World War II* (New York: W. W. Norton, 1999), esp. 485–521.

Chapter Two

1. *VDB*, (1.) Deutscher Bundestag, 5. Sitzung, 20 Sept. 1949, 27–28. See also the pathbreaking work on postwar West German anti-Semitism by Frank Stern, *Whitewashing*, 341–42; idem, "The Historic Triangle: Occupiers, Germans, and Jews in Postwar Germany," in Moeller (ed.), *West Germany Under Construction*, 199–229; idem, "Philosemitism: The Whitewashing of the Yellow Badge in West Germany, 1945–1952," *Holocaust and Genocide Studies* 4 (1989): 463–77; and Constantin Goschler, "The Attitude towards Jews in Bavaria after the Second World War," in Moeller (ed.), *West Germany Under Construction*, 231–49. On the Jewish community in postwar Germany, see Brenner, *Nach dem Holocaust*.

2. VDB, (1.) Deutscher Bundestag, 5. Sitzung, 20 Sept. 1949, 27, 29.

3. Extracts from the "Report of the Tripartite Conference Berlin (Potsdam), 17 July–2 Aug. 1945" appear in Beate Ruhm von Oppen, ed., *Documents on Germany under Occupation, 1945–1954* (London: Oxford University Press, 1955), 49.

4. *VDB*, (1.) Deutscher Bundestag, 5. Sitzung, 20 Sept. 1949, 23, 27–29; and in general, Dubiel, *Niemand ist frei*, 44–45. Adenauer's reference to the millions of dead expellees overstated the case considerably. See Overmans, "55 Millionen Opfer," 110; and idem, *Deutsche militärische Verluste*, 299. In general, on the political organization of the "war-damaged" and the politics of distributing the costs of compensation, see the excellent study by Michael L. Hughes, *Shouldering the Burdens of Defeat*.

5. For useful introductions to the history of the CDU/CSU, see Geoffrey Pridham, *Christian Democracy in Western Germany: The CDU/CSU in Government and Opposition, 1945–1976* (London: Croom Helm, 1977); Rudolf Uertz, *Christentum und Sozialismus in der frühen CDU: Grundlagen und Wirkungen der christlich-sozialen Ideen in der Union, 1945–1949* (Stuttgart: Deutsche Verlags-Anstalt, 1981); Noel D. Cary, *The Path to Christian Democracy: German Catholics and the Party System from Windthorst to Adenauer* (Cambridge, Mass.: Harvard University Press, 1996); and Maria Mitchell, "Materialism and Secularism: CDU Politicians and National Socialism, 1945–1949," *Journal of Modern History* 67 (1995): 273–308. On the early history of the FDP, see Jörg Michael Gutscher, *Die Entwicklung der FDP von ihren Anfängen bis 1961* (Meisenheim am Glan: Anton Hain, 1967); and Dieter Hein, *Zwischen liberaler Milieupartei und nationaler Sammlungsbewegung: Gründung, Entwicklung und Struktur der Freien Demokratischen Partei, 1945–1949* (Düsseldorf: Droste, 1985).

6. Major, *Death of the KPD*.

7. There is an extensive literature on the party's early history. See, e.g., Kurt Klotzbach, *Der Weg zur Staatspartei: Programmatik, praktische Politik und Organisation der deutschen Sozialdemokratie, 1945 bis 1965* (Bonn: J. H. W. Dietz Nachf., 1982); Douglas A. Chalmers, *The Social Democratic Party of Germany: From Working-Class Movement to Modern Political Party* (New Haven: Yale University Press, 1964); and the useful summary and extensive bibliography in Siegfried Heimann, "Die Sozialdemokratische Partei Deutschlands," in *Parteien-Handbuch: Die Parteien der Bundesrepublik Deutschland, 1945–1980*, vol. 2, ed.

Richard Stöss (Opladen: Westdeutscher Verlag, 1984), 2025–30, 2042–50, 2127–30. See also Hans-Jürgen Schröder, "Kanzler der Alliierten? Die Bedeutung der USA für die Aussenpolitik Adenauers," in *Adenauer und die deutsche Frage,* ed. Josef Foschepoth (Göttingen: Vandenhoeck & Ruprecht, 1988), 118–45.

8. *VDB,* (1.) Deutscher Bundestag, 6. Sitzung, 21 Sept. 1949, 36. In general, see Herf, *Divided Memory,* 271–88.

9. Willy Albrecht, *Kurt Schumacher: Ein Leben für den demokratischen Sozialismus* (Bonn: Neue Gesellschaft, 1985), 34–36.

10. In my discussion of debates over reparations, I draw heavily on the substantial secondary literature on this topic. I am particularly indebted to Stern's superb study, *The Whitewashing of the Yellow Badge.* For other good accounts, see Lily Gardner Feldman, *The Special Relationship between West Germany and Israel* (Boston: George Allen & Unwin, 1984), 32–86; Kai von Jena, "Versöhnung mit Israel? Die deutsch-israelischen Verhandlungen bis zum Wiedergutmachungsabkommen von 1952," *Vierteljahrshefte für Zeitgeschichte* 34 (1986): 457–80; Yeshayahu A. Jelinek, "Political Acumen, Altruism, Foreign Pressure, or Moral Debt: Konrad Adenauer and the 'Shilumim,'" *Tel Aviver Jahrbuch für deutsche Geschichte* 19 (1990): 77–102; Axel Frohn, ed., *Holocaust and Shilumim: The Policy of Wiedergutmachung in the Early 1950s* (Washington, D.C.: German Historical Institute, 1991); Tom Segev, *The Seventh Million: The Israelis and the Holocaust,* trans. Haim Watzman (New York: Hill & Wang, 1994), 189–252; and the discussion and collection of primary sources in Yeshayahu A. Jelinek, ed., *Zwischen Moral and Realpolitik: Deutsch-israelische Beziehungen, 1945–1965* (Gerlingen: Bleicher, 1997). See also Y. Michael Bodemann, with a contribution by Jael Geis, *Gedächtnistheater: Die jüdische Gemeinschaft und ihre deutsche Erfindung* (Hamburg: Rotbuch, 1996).

11. Dagmar Barnouw, *Germany 1945: Views of War and Violence* (Bloomington: Indiana University Press, 1996), esp. 1–41; Cornelia Brink, *Ikonen der Vernichtung: Öffentlicher Gebrauch von Fotografien aus nationalsozialistischen Konzentrationslagern nach 1945* (Berlin: Akademie, 1998), 23–123; Marcuse, *Legacies of Dachau;* idem, "Konzentrationslager Dachau"; Morris Janowitz, "German Reactions to Nazi Atrocities," *American Journal of Sociology* 52 (1946): 141–46; David Culbert, "American Film Policy in the Re-Education of Germany after 1945," in *The Political Re-Education of Germany and Her Allies after World War II,* ed. Nicholas Pronay and Keith Wilson (London: Croom Helm, 1985), 173–81; Dubiel, *Niemand ist frei,* 71; Norbert Frei, "'Wir waren blind, ungläubig und langsam': Buchenwald, Dachau und die amerikanischen Medien im Frühjahr 1945," *Vierteljahrshefte für Zeitgeschichte* 35 (1987): 385–401; Robert H. Abzug, *Inside the Vicious Heart: Americans and the Liberation of Nazi Concentration Camps* (New York: Oxford University Press, 1985); Barbie Zelizer, *Remembering to Forget: Holocaust Memory through the Camera's Eye* (Chicago: University of Chicago Press, 1998); Brewster S. Chamberlin, "Todesmühlen: Ein früher Versuch zur Massen-'Umerziehung' im besetzten Deutschland, 1945–1946," *Vierteljahrshefte für Zeitgeschichte* 29 (1981): 420–36; Michael Hoenisch, "Film as an Instrument of the U.S. Reeducation Program in Germany after 1945 and the Example of *Todesmühlen,*" in *The Role of the United States in the Reconstruction of Italy and West Germany, 1943–1949,* ed. Ekkehart Krippendorff

(Berlin: Zentrale Universitätsdruckerei der Freien Universität, 1981), 127–57, including a transcript of the narration that accompanied the images; "The Atrocity Film in Bavaria," Office of Military Goverment, United States (OMGUS), Information Control: Intelligence Summary, no. 30, 9 Feb. 1946, National Archives [hereafter cited as NA], RG260, OMGUS, Records of the Information Control Division, Records of the Motion Picture Branch, Motion Picture Production and Distribution 1945–1949, Film Intelligence Reports, box 281, folder 21; and "German Prisoner Reactions to a Film on Atrocities," ibid., box 290, folder 4; Volker Ullrich, "'Wir haben nichts gewusst': Ein deutsches Trauma," *1999: Zeitschrift für Sozialgeschichte des 20. und 21. Jahrhunderts* 6 (1991): 11–46; and, by way of comparison, Ron Robin, *The Barbed-Wire College: Reeducating German POWs in the United States During World War II* (Princeton: Princeton University Press, 1995).

12. Diehl, *Thanks of the Fatherland*, 54–55.

13. Josef Foschepoth, "German Reaction to Defeat and Occupation," in Moeller (ed.), *West Germany Under Construction*, 73–89.

14. Norbert Frei, "Von deutscher Erfindungskraft, oder: Die Kollektivschuldthese in der Nachkriegszeit," *Rechtshistorisches Journal* 17 (1997): 621–34. There is a vast literature on the Allied move toward integrating Germany into a military alliance and rearming Germans. See, e.g., Gerhard Wettig, *Entmilitarisierung und Wiederbewaffnung in Deutschland, 1943–1955: Internationale Auseinandersetzungen um die Rolle der Deutschen in Europa* (Munich: R. Oldenbourg, 1967); Arnulf Baring, *Aussenpolitik in Adenauers Kanzlerdemokratie: Bonns Beitrag zur europäischen Verteidigungsgemeinschaft* (Munich: R. Oldenbourg, 1969); Roland G. Foerster et al., *Von der Kapitulation bis zum Pleven-Plan*, vol. 1 of *Anfänge westdeutscher Sicherheitspolitik, 1945–1956*, ed. Militärgeschichtliches Forschungsamt (Munich: R. Oldenbourg, 1982); Donald Abenheim, *Reforging the Iron Cross: The Search for Tradition in the West German Armed Forces* (Princeton: Princeton University Press, 1988); and David Clay Large, *Germans to the Front: West German Rearmament in the Adenauer Era* (Chapel Hill: University of North Carolina Press, 1996).

15. Adenauer's remarks to the Bundestag are republished in R. Vogel (ed.), *Deutschlands Weg nach Israel*, 36.

16. Gardner Feldman, *Special Relationship*, 54–56, provides a good account of the unofficial contacts in 1950–51 that preceded these talks; see also Jena, "Versöhnung mit Israel?" 461–62; and, in general, Stern, *Whitewashing*.

17. For the view that Adenauer had little to gain from the Allies and acted out of genuine moral conviction, see Michael Wolffsohn, e.g., "Globalentschädigung für Israel und die Juden? Adenauer und die Opposition in der Bundesregierung," in *Wiedergutmachung in der Bundesrepublik Deutschland*, ed. Ludolf Herbst and Constantin Goschler (Munich: R. Oldenbourg, 1989), 161–90; "Das deutsch-israelische Wiedergutmachungsabkommen von 1952 im internationalen Zusammenhang," *Vierteljahrshefte für Zeitgeschichte* 36 (1988): 693–731; and on the broader willingness of West Germans to accept Adenauer's position in the late 1950s, "Von der verordneten zur freiwilligen 'Vergangenheitsbewältigung'? Eine Skizze der bundesdeutschen Entwicklung 1955/1965 (Zugleich eine Dokumentation über die Krisensitzung des Bundeskabinetts vom

4. und 5. März 1965 und die Böhm-Schäffer-Kontroverse 1957/1958)," *German Studies Review* 12 (1989): 111–37. Most other interpretations place greater emphasis on the international context in general and American pressure in particular: e.g., Stern, *Whitewashing,* 352, 367, 382; Yeshayahu A. Jelinek, "Die Krise der Shilumim/Wiedergutmachungs-Verhandlungen im Sommer 1952," *Vierteljahrshefte für Zeitgeschichte* 38 (1990): 113–39; idem "Political Acumen," 77–102; and Jena, "Versöhnung mit Israel?" 457–80. In general, see also Constantin Goschler, *Wiedergutmachung: Westdeutschland und die Verfolgten des Nationalsozialismus (1950–1954)* (Munich: R. Oldenbourg, 1992), 257–85; Norbert Frei, "Die deutsche Wiedergutmachungspolitik gegenüber Israel im Urteil der öffentlichen Meinung der USA," in Herbst and Goschler (eds.), *Wiedergutmachung,* 215, 223; Feldman, *Special Relationship,* 39–41, 50–89; Nicholas Balabkins, *West German Reparations to Israel* (New Brunswick, N.J.: Rutgers University Press, 1971), 119, 132, 140–41; Nana Sagi, *German Reparations: A History of the Negotiations* (New York: St. Martin's Press, 1986); and Kurt R. Grossmann, *Die Ehrenschuld: Kurzgeschichte der Wiedergutmachung* (Frankfurt am Main: Ullstein, 1967). For a thorough look at the American position, see Thomas Alan Schwartz, *America's Germany: John J. McCloy and the Federal Republic of Germany* (Cambridge, Mass.: Harvard University Press, 1991), 176–84.

18. Stern, *Whitewashing,* 372; Michael Wolffsohn, "Das Wiedergutmachungsabkommen mit Israel: Eine Untersuchung bundesdeutscher und ausländischer Umfragen," in *Westdeutschland, 1945–1955: Unterwerfung, Kontrolle, Integration,* ed. Ludolf Herbst (Munich: R. Oldenbourg, 1986), 206; idem, "Globalentschädigung," 171; Goschler, *Wiedergutmachung,* 213–14; Rainer Erb, "Die Rückerstattung: Ein Kristallisationspunkt für den Antisemitismus," in *Antisemitismus in der politischen Kultur nach 1945,* ed. Werner Bergmann and Rainer Erb (Opladen: Westdeutscher Verlag, 1990), 238–52; Werner Bergmann and Rainer Erb, *Anti-Semitism in Germany: The Post-Nazi Epoch since 1945,* trans. Belinda Cooper and Allison Brown (New Brunswick, N.J.: Transaction, 1997), 1–3; and Karl W. Deutsch and Lewis J. Edinger, *Germany Rejoins the Powers: Mass Opinion, Interest Groups, and Elites in Contemporary German Foreign Policy* (Stanford: Stanford University Press, 1959), 169–70.

19. On attitudes within the CDU, see Ute Schmidt, "Hitler ist tot und Ulbricht lebt: Die CDU, der Nationalsozialismus und der Holocaust," in Bergmann, Erb, and Lichtblau (eds.), *Schwieriges Erbe,* 65–101.

20. See in particular Jena, "Versöhnung mit Israel?" 470–72. Debates over reparations in Israel were no less contentious; see Segev, *Seventh Million.*

21. Dehler, in an address to German Jewish jurists in December 1951, quoted in Wolffsohn, "Globalentschädigung," 164.

22. *VDB,* (1.) Deutscher Bundestag, 252. Sitzung, 4 Mar. 1953, 12092. Walther Hasemann of the FDP similarly defended the treaty as the means to "mark the end point of one of the darkest chapters of German history"; ibid., 12278.

23. Ibid., 254. Sitzung, 18 Mar. 1953, comments of von Thadden, 12280; Hans-Joachim von Merkatz (DP), 12279; Hugo Decker (Bayernpartei), 12281; and Oskar Müller (KPD), 12280.

24. This point has been forcefully made most recently by Herf, *Divided Memory,* 284–88; see also Schlomo Shafir, "Die SPD und die Wiedergutmachung gegenüber Israel," in Herbst and Goschler (eds.), *Wiedergutmachung,* 191–203.

25. *VDB* (1.) Wahlperiode, 254. Sitzung, 18 Mar. 1953, 12290–93; Herf, *Divided Memory,* 288.

26. In what follows, I draw heavily on the excellent study of Goschler, *Wiedergutmachung.* Goschler's excellent analysis is an important corrective to the largely self-congratulatory review of the politics of "Wiedergutmachung" that was published under the auspices of the Finance Ministry in the 1980s; see Ernst Féaux de la Croix and Helmut Rumpf, *Der Werdegang des Entschädigungsrechts unter national- und völkerrechtlichem und politologischem Aspekt* (Munich: C. H. Beck, 1985) (vol. 3 of a series entitled *Die Wiedergutmachung nationalsozialistischen Unrechts durch die Bundesrepublik Deutschland,* ed. Bundesministerium der Finanzen). See also Christian Pross, *Wiedergutmachung: Der Kleinkrieg gegen die Opfer* (Frankfurt am Main: Athenäum, 1988); and for a useful overview of the terms of compensation, Walter Schwarz, "Die Wiedergutmachung nationalsozialistischen Unrechts durch die Bundesrepublik Deutschland: Ein Überblick," in Herbst and Goschler (eds.), *Wiedergutmachung,* 33–54.

27. Goschler, *Wiedergutmachung;* also idem, "Attitude towards Jews"; and Marcuse, *Legacies of Dachau.*

28. Hans Giessler, "Die Grundsatzbestimmungen des Entschädigungsrechts," in Walter Brunn et al., *Das Bundesentschädigungsgesetz: Erster Teil (§§1 bis 50 BEG)* (Munich: C. H. Beck, 1981), 52–54 (vol. 4 of Bundesministerium der Finanzen [ed.], *Wiedergutmachung nationalsozialistischen Unrechts*); Herbert, "Nicht entschädigungsfähig," 273; and Ludorf Herbst, "Einleitung," in Herbst and Goschler (eds.), *Wiedergutmachung,* 26.

29. In general, see Robert G. Moeller, "The Homosexual Man Is a 'Man,' the Homosexual Woman Is a 'Woman': Sex, Society, and the Law in Postwar West Germany," in Moeller (ed.), *West Germany Under Construction,* 251–84.

30. See Norbert Schmacke and Hans-Georg Güse, *Zwangssterilisiert, verleugnet, vergessen: Zur Geschichte der nationalsozialistischen Rassenhygiene am Beispiel Bremen* (Bremen: Brockkamp, 1984); Wolfgang Ayass, *"Asoziale" im Nationalsozialismus* (Stuttgart: Klett-Cotta, 1995); and in general the comprehensive overviews of Michael Burleigh and Wolfgang Wippermann, *The Racial State: Germany, 1933–1945* (Cambridge: Cambridge University Press, 1991); and Michael Berenbaum, ed., *A Mosaic of Victims: Non-Jews Persecuted and Murdered by the Nazis* (New York: New York University Press, 1990).

31. Arnold Spitta, "Entschädigung für Zigeuner? Geschichte eines Vorurteils," in Herbst and Goschler (eds.), *Wiedergutmachung,* 385–401. In 1956, the Bundesgerichtshof determined that after 1 March 1943, when Sinti and Roma were also persecuted because of their race, they became racial victims of the regime, and as a consequence they were entitled to compensation for suffering endured after this date. On continuities in policies restricting Sinti and Roma after 1945, see Gilad Margalit, "Die deutsche Zigeunerpolitik nach 1945," *Vierteljahrshefte für Zeitgeschichte* 45 (1997): 557–88.

32. Goschler, *Wiedergutmachung,* 156–59. See also Gotthard Jasper, "Die disqualifizierten Opfer: Der Kalte Krieg und die Entschädigung für Kommu-

nisten," in Herbst and Goschler (eds.), *Wiedergutmachung,* 361–69; Pross, *Wiedergutmachung,* 272–74.

33. In general, see Pross, *Wiedergutmachung;* also Alf Lüdtke, "'Coming to Terms with the Past': Illusions of Remembering, Ways of Forgetting Nazism in West Germany," *Journal of Modern History* 65 (1993): 566–69; and Helga Fischer-Hübner and Hermann Fischer-Hübner, *Die Kehrseite der "Wiedergutmachung": Das Leiden von NS-Verfolgten in den Entschädigungsverfahren* (Gerlingen: Bleicher, 1990).

34. See, e.g., Ulrich Herbert, *Fremdarbeiter: Politik und Praxis des "Ausländer-Einsatzes" in der Kriegswirtschaft des Dritten Reiches* (Bonn: J. H. W. Dietz Nachf., 1985); also Alf Lüdtke, "The Appeal of Exterminating 'Others': German Workers and the Limits of Resistance," *Journal of Modern History* 64 suppl. (1992): S46–S67; and Walter Struve, "The Wartime Economy: Foreign Workers, 'Half Jews,' and Other Prisoners in a German Town, 1939–1945," *German Studies Review* 16 (1993): 463–82.

35. Protokoll der 254. Sitzung des Bundestags-Ausschusses für Rechtswesen und Verfassungsrecht am 4.5.1953, BAK, B141/618, cited in Goschler, *Wiedergutmachung,* 316. On the absence of reliable data on the total number of those who received compensation, see Karl Hessdörfer, "Die Entschädigungspraxis im Spannungsfeld von Gesetz, Justiz und NS-Opfern," in Herbst and Goschler (eds.), *Wiedergutmachung,* 246.

36. On this process, see the important recent work of Saul Friedländer, *Nazi Germany and the Jews,* vol. 1: *The Years of Persecution* (New York: Harper Collins, 1997); and Marion A. Kaplan, *Between Dignity and Despair: Jewish Life in Nazi Germany* (New York: Oxford University Press, 1998); also David Bankier, *The Germans and the Final Solution: Public Opinion under Nazism* (Oxford: Blackwell, 1992).

37. Goschler, *Wiedergutmachung,* makes this point convincingly.

38. Regina Hennig, *Entschädigung und Interessenvertretung der NS-Verfolgten in Niedersachsen, 1945–1949* (Bielefeld: Verlag für Regionalgeschichte, 1991), 26–31, 45–48, 66, 70–74, 79–86; Wolf-Dietrich Schmidt, "'Wir sind die Verfolgten geblieben': Zur Geschichte der Vereinigung der Verfolgten des Naziregimes (VVN) in Hamburg, 1945–1951," in *Das andere Hamburg: Freiheitliche Bestrebungen in der Hansestadt seit dem Spätmittelalter,* ed. Jörg Berlin (Cologne: Pahl-Rugenstein, 1981), 329–56; and on divisions among victim representatives, Goschler, *Wiedergutmachung,* 194–96.

39. Goschler, *Wiedergutmachung,* esp. 201–2.

40. Hans-Peter Schwarz, *Die Ära Adenauer: Gründerjahre der Republik* (Stuttgart: Deutsche Verlags-Anstalt, 1986), 181–84.

41. Eugen Gerstenmaier (CDU), *VDB,* (1.) Deutscher Bundestag, 254. Sitzung, 18 Mar. 1953, 12276; and Walther Hasemann (FDP), ibid., 12278 ("darkest chapter"). See also Bodemann, *Gedächtnistheater,* 134–35.

42. See Werner Bergmann, "Die Reaktion auf den Holocaust in Westdeutschland von 1945 bis 1989," *Geschichte in Wissenschaft und Unterricht* 43 (1992): 331–32; also the discussion in Josef Foschepoth, *Im Schatten der Vergangenheit: Die Anfänge der Gesellschaften für christlich-jüdische Zusammenarbeit* (Göttingen: Vandenhoeck & Ruprecht, 1993), 21.

43. Marlis G. Steinert, *Hitler's War and the Germans: Public Mood and Attitude during the Second World War*, ed. and trans. Thomas E. J. de Witt (Athens: Ohio State University Press, 1977), 287; Wolfram Wette, "Das Russlandbild in der NS-Propaganda: Ein Problemaufriss," in *Das Russlandbild im Dritten Reich*, ed. Hans-Erich Volkmann (Cologne: Böhlau, 1994), 75; also Bianka Bietrow-Ennker, "Die Sowjetunion in der Propaganda des Dritten Reiches: Das Beispiel der Wochenschau," *Militärgeschichtliche Mitteilungen* 46 (1989): 79–120; and Atina Grossmann, "A Question of Silence: The Rape of German Women by Occupation Soldiers," in Moeller (ed.), *West Germany Under Construction*, 39.

44. Hans-Christoph Seebohm to Franz Böhm, 21 May 1952, BAK, B136/1127, quoted in Goschler, *Wiedergutmachung*, 203.

45. Thomas Dehler in an address to a meeting of Jewish jurists, 17 December 1951, quoted ibid., 202–3.

46. Richard Reitzner (SPD), *VDB*, (1.) Deutscher Bundestag, 254. Sitzung, 18 Mar. 1953, 12236. Reitzner had been active in the Czech Social Democratic Party until his emigration to England in 1938.

47. "Gebt die Kriegsgefangenen frei!" *Stuttgarter Zeitung*, 11 Nov. 1949; see also "Verbrechen gegen die Menschlichkeit," *Bremer Nachrichten*, 28 Jan. 1950; copies of both in the clippings collection of the Presse- und Informationsamt der Bundesregierung [hereafter cited as PIB] in Bonn, Mikrofilm (MF) 1566.

48. Margarete Hütter (FDP), *VDB*, (1.) Deutscher Bundestag, 271. Sitzung, 12 June 1953, 13430.

49. Ibid., 252. Sitzung, 4 Mar. 1953, 12084–90; ibid., 254. Sitzung, 18 Mar. 1953, 12236–51, 12274–83.

50. Konrad Wittmann (CSU), ibid., 115. Sitzung, 31 Jan. 1951, 4374. Wittmann had been expelled from the Sudetenland after the war. The numbers for POWs come from Böhme, *Die deutschen Kriegsgefangenen in sowjetischer Hand*, 151.

51. Hans Lukaschek, *VDB*, (1.) Deutscher Bundestag, 250. Sitzung, 25 Feb. 1953, 11971.

52. Hans Merten (SPD), ibid., 233. Sitzung, 9 Oct. 1952, 10681.

53. Adenauer, *VDB*, (1.) Deutscher Bundestag, 252. Sitzung, 4 Mar. 1953, 12093.

54. The quotation is from Hans-Christoph Seebohm (DP), the minister of transportation and an expellee from the Sudetenland; cited in Wolfssohn, "Globalentschädigung," 177–78; see also Rudolf Huhn, "Die Wiedergutmachungsverhandlungen in Wassenaar," in Herbst and Goschler (eds.), *Wiedergutmachung*, 147; and Jena, "Versöhnung mit Israel?" 462–63. In its most extreme form, the alleged inadequacy of legislation to meet the needs of expellees became the justification for rejecting ratification of the treaty with Israel; see Hans-Joachim von Merkatz (DP), *VDB*, (1.) Deutscher Bundestag, 254. Sitzung, 18 Mar. 1953, 12279; and the written statements of Wilfried Keller (no party affiliation) and Günter Goetzendorff (no party affiliation), ibid., 12287, 12289.

55. See, e.g., Alexander von Plato, "Fremde Heimat: Zur Integration von Flüchtlingen und Einheimischen in die Neue Zeit," in Niethammer and Plato (eds.), *"Wir kriegen jetzt andere Zeiten,"* 172–219; and Rainer Schulze, "Growing Discontent: Relations between Native and Refugee Populations in a Rural

District in Western Germany after the Second World War," in Moeller (ed.), *West Germany Under Construction,* 53–72.

56. The Zentralverband der vertriebenen Deutschen, a national umbrella organization, claimed a membership of 1,753,687 in 1952. The *Landsmannschaften* for East Prussia, Pomerania, Silesia, Upper Silesia, the Sudetenland, and Danzig, the largest regional organizations, reported a total of slightly more than one million members in 1955. See Manfred Max Wambach, *Verbändestaat und Parteienoligopol: Macht und Ohnmacht der Vertriebenenverbände* (Stuttgart: Ferdinand Enke, 1971), 43, 47. See also the important recent work of Ahonen, "Domestic Constraints" and "Expellee Organizations"; and Hughes, *Shouldering the Burdens.* See also Karl O. Kurth, "Presse, Film und Rundfunk," in *Die Vertriebenen in Westdeutschland: Ihre Eingliederung und ihr Einfluss auf Gesellschaft, Wirtschaft, Politik und Geistesleben,* 3 vols., ed. Eugen Lemberg and Friedrich Edding (Kiel: Ferdinand Hirt, 1959), 3:402–34. This massive study of the integration of expellees was financed by the federal government; see the materials in BAK, B150/4591 and B150/4592/Heft 1.

57. Lothar Wieland, *Das Bundesministerium für Vertriebene, Flüchtlinge und Kriegsgeschädigte* (Frankfurt am Main: Athenäum, 1968).

58. In addition to Wambach, *Verbändestaat und Parteienoligopol,* see Hildo M. Jolles, *Zur Soziologie der Heimatvertriebenen und Flüchtlinge* (Cologne: Kiepenheuer & Witsch, 1965), 276, 285; Max Hildebert Boehm, "Gruppenbildung und Organisationswesen," in Lemberg and Edding (eds.), *Die Vertriebenen,* 1:521–605; Karl Heinz Gehrmann, "Kulturpflege und Kulturpolitik," ibid., 3:171–72, 189; and the excellent discussion in Ahonen, "Expellee Organizations," 73–114.

59. See, e.g., Verband der Landsmannschaften, Pressereferat, 13 Oct. 1953, greeting the new government after the 1953 elections, Politisches Archiv des Auswärtigen Amts [hereafter cited as PAAA], Abt. 3/767.

60. On the creation of "Sudeten German" as an identity in Czechoslovakia after 1918, see Nancy Wingfield, *Minority Politics in a Multinational State: The German Social Democrats in Czechoslovakia, 1918–1938* (Boulder: East European Monographs, 1989), xiv–xv.

61. Dieter Bingen, "Westverschiebung Polens und Revisionsanspruch der Bundesrepublik Deutschland: Die polnische Westgrenze als Stein des Anstosses in den polnisch-deutschen Beziehungen," in *Unfertige Nachbarschaften: Die Staaten Osteuropas und die Bundesrepublik Deutschland,* ed. Othmar Nikola Haberl and Hans Hecker (Essen: Reimar Hobbing, 1989), 157–59; Ahonen, "Expellee Organizations," esp. chap. 4; Hans W. Schoenberg, *Germans from the East: A Study of Their Migration, Resettlement, and Subsequent Group History since 1945* (The Hague: Martinus Nijhoff, 1970), 187–207; Elizabeth Wiskemann, *Germany's Eastern Neighbours: Problems Relating to the Oder-Neisse Line and the Czech Frontier Regions* (London: Oxford University Press, 1956); and Hans Georg Lehmann, "Der analytische Bezugsrahmen eines internationalen und intergesellschaftlichen Konflikts am Beispiel der Genesis des Oder-Neisse-Konflikts," in *Das deutsch-polnische Konfliktverhältnis seit dem Zweiten Weltkrieg: Multidisziplinäre Studien über konfliktfördernde und konfliktmindernde Faktoren in den internationalen Beziehungen,* ed. Carl Christoph

Schweitzer and Hubert Feger (Boppard am Rhein: Harald Boldt, 1975), 25–91; and idem, *Der Oder-Neisse-Konflikt* (Munich: C. H. Beck, 1979), 171. On SPD support, see Frank M. Buscher, "Kurt Schumacher, German Social Democracy, and the Punishment of Nazi Crimes," *Holocaust and Genocide Studies* 5 (1990): 263.

62. H. Lehmann, *Oder-Neisse-Konflikt,* provides a useful review of changing British and American attitudes and West German responses on the issue of revising the Oder-Neisse border.

63. McCloy to W. H. Wilbur, 1 Feb. 1952, NA, RG466, Records of the U.S. High Commission for Germany (US HICOG), Classified General Records, 1949–52, 1952, box 36, doc. 309.

64. See, e.g., US HICOG to Secretary of State, 8 Aug. 1950, RG466, Records of the US HICOM, John J. McCloy, Classified General Records, 1949–52, box 17; John Davies, Jr., Deputy Director, HICOG to Secretary of State, 24 July 1952, NA, RG59, Department of State, box 5245, 862A.411/7–2452; and H[ans] C[hristian] Sonne to John J. McCloy, U.S. High Commissioner, 18 Nov. 1950, NA, RG466, Records of the US HICOG, John J. McCloy, Classified Records, 1949–1952, box 21. Sonne was head of a commission that investigated the expellee problem and encouraged McCloy to advocate reducing West German defense spending or making direct payments to the Federal Republic to assist with integration of the expellees. See the commission's report, Bundesministerium für Vertriebene, ed., *Die Eingliederung der Flüchtlinge in die deutsche Gemeinschaft: Bericht der ECA Technical Assistance Commission für die Eingliederung der Flüchtlinge in die deutsche Bundesrepublik, dem Bundeskanzler am 21. März 1951 überreicht* (Bonn: Bonner Universitäts-Buchdruckerei Gebr. Scheur, 1951); also memo from Guy Swope, HICOG Frankfurt, to Department of State, 2 Feb. 1951, describing a press conference held by Sonne, NA, RG59, Department of State, Decimal Files, box 5244, 862A.411/2–251.

65. See, in particular, the excellent analysis of Ahonen in "Expellee Organizations" and "Domestic Constraints"; also H. Lehmann, *Der Oder-Neisse-Konflikt,* 175; Axel Frohn, "Adenauer und die deutschen Ostgebiete in den fünfziger Jahren," *Vierteljahrshefte für Zeitgeschichte* 44 (1996): 485–525; Josef Foschepoth, "Potsdam und danach: Die Westmächte, Adenauer und die Vertriebenen," in *Die Vertreibung der Deutschen aus dem Osten: Ursachen, Ereignisse, Folgen,* ed. Wolfgang Benz (Frankfurt am Main: Fischer Taschenbuch Verlag, 1985), 70–91; and Hans Georg Lehmann, "Oder-Neisse-Linie und Heimatverlust—Interdependenzen zwischen Flucht/Vertreibung und Revisionismus," in Schulze, Brelie-Lewien, and Grebing (eds.), *Flüchtlinge und Vertriebene,* 109; Timothy Garton Ash, *In Europe's Name: Germany and the Divided Continent* (New York: Random House, 1993), 225; and in general, Hansjakob Stehle, "Adenauer, Polen und die deutsche Frage," in *Adenauer und die deutsche Frage,* ed. Josef Foschepoth (Göttingen: Vandenhoeck & Ruprecht, 1988), 80–98.

66. "Adenauer: Schlesien wird eines Tages wieder deutsch," *Welt am Sonntag,* 15 Oct. 1950, copy in PIB, MF 1536; quotation from Franz Thedieck, Staatssekretär im Bundesministerium für gesamtdeutsche Fragen to the annual meeting of the Sudeten Germans, 31 May 1952, reported in *Bulletin des Presse- und Informationsamtes der Bundesregierung,* 6 June 1952, copy in PIB, MF 2672.

See also "Hessischer Ministerpräsident appelliert vor 60 000 Heimatvertriebenen an die Westmächte," *Frankfurter Rundschau,* 11 June 1951; and "Schlesier erwarten klare Entscheidung des Westens: Noch haben die Alliierten keine bindende Zusicherung hinsichtlich der deutschen Ostgrenze abgegeben," *Süddeutsche Zeitung,* 15 Sept. 1951, copies in PIB, MF 1536. See also "Tag der Heimat im Westen: 'Zieht Potsdam-Unterschrift zurück!'" *Der Sudetendeutsche,* 5 Aug. 1950; "Ungerechter Verteidigungsbeitrag," ibid., 23 Mar. 1952; and "Endlose Katastrophenpolitik: Vom Versailler Diktat bis zu Deutschlands Verteidigungsbeitrag," ibid., 14 Apr. 1951. The annual meetings of expellees grew steadily in size. For example, the Sudeten German meeting in May 1953 reportedly attracted 300,000 ("Das grösste Heimattreffen seit dem Kriegsende," *Die Welt,* 26 May 1953); the *Kölner Stadt-Anzeiger* of 27 July 1953 carried a report of a meeting of over 350,000 Silesians in Cologne that same year; and a year later, the annual Sudeten German meeting in Munich claimed an attendance of half a million ("Bayern, Schirmherr der Sudetendeutschen," *Münchener Merkur,* 8 June 1954); copies in PIB, MF 2672.

67. "Lüge oder Idee? Akute Gefahr für den deutschen Osten: Siegen Morgenthau und Baruch?" *Der Sudetendeutsche,* 16 Dec. 1950.

68. On this topic, see Ahonen, "Domestic Consequences" and "Expellee Organizations."

69. Manfred Teschner, "Entwicklung eines Interessenverbandes: Ein empirischer Beitrag zum Problem der Verselbständigung von Massenorganisationen" (Ph.D. diss., Johann Wolfgang Goethe–Universität, Frankfurt, 1961), 6. According to Teschner (42), by 1955, 500,000 returned POWs were members of the organization. My thanks to James Diehl for making this source available to me. See also the important work of Biess, "Protracted War."

70. "Aus einer Rede von Bundeskanzler Dr. Konrad Adenauer auf dem 1. Bundesparteitag der CDU in Goslar vom 20.–22.10.1950," in *Misstrauische Nachbarn: Deutsche Ostpolitik 1919/1970: Dokumentation und Analyse,* ed. Hans-Adolf Jacobsen with assistance of Wilfried von Bredow (Düsseldorf: Droste, 1970), 237.

71. "Regierung protestiert scharf gegen Zurückhaltung der Kriegsgefangenen," *Die Welt,* 28 Jan. 1950, PIB, MF 1566; see also Adenauer's remarks to the Bundestag, *VDB,* (1.) Deutscher Bundestag, 94. Sitzung, 26 Oct. 1950, 3495–96; and "Adenauers Appell an die Welt," *General-Anzeiger für Bonn und Umgegend,* 22 Jan. 1950, PIB, MF 1566. For Schmid, see "Zum Gedenktag für die Kriegsgefangenen," *Stuttgarter Zeitung,* 26 Oct. 1950, PIB, MF 1566; and in general on the SPD's position, see Buscher, "Schumacher," 268–69.

72. Martin Lang, *Stalins Strafjustiz gegen deutsche Soldaten: Die Massenprozesse gegen deutsche Kriegsgefangene in den Jahren 1949 und 1950 in historischer Sicht* (Herford: E. S. Mittler & Sohn, 1981), 52. See also Reinhart Maurach, *Die Kriegsverbrecherprozesse gegen deutsche Gefangene in der Sowjetunion* (Hamburg: Arbeitsgemeinschaft vom Roten Kreuz in Deutschland, Britische Zone, Rechtsschutzstelle für Kriegsgefangene und Zivilarbeiter im Ausland, 1950); and Günther Wagenlehner, ed., *Stalins Willkürjustiz gegen die deutschen Kriegsgefangenen: Dokumentation und Analyse* (Bonn: Verlag der Heimkehrer, 1993).

73. *VDB* (1.) Wahlperiode, 32. Sitzung, 27 Jan. 1950, 1013. The Red Cross

and other church-related organizations also coordinated their efforts to try to generate numbers of those missing on the eastern front and POWs still in the Soviet Union. See, e.g., "Nachweisbare Zahl und Gewahrsamsorte der deutschen Kriegsgefangenen im Gewahrsamsbereich der UdSSR, April 1950," BAK, B150/151, Heft 2. Counting efforts were also coordinated by the Bundesministerium für Vertriebene, Flüchtlinge und Kriegsgeschädigte (hereafter BVFK), which sent out questionnaires to returnees who were asked to report on the whereabouts of any comrades still in the Soviet Union. On efforts to coordinate registration of those missing, see, e.g., memo prepared for the cabinet, 23 Oct. 1951, BAK, B136/6611; and for examples of the form letters used and the information collected see BAK, B150/293 and B150/288.

74. *VDB*, (1.) Wahlperiode, 62. Sitzung, 5 May 1950, 2281–82. In general, see Böhme, *Die deutschen Kriegsgefangenen in sowjetischer Hand*, 127–51; also "Stellungnahme der Regierung der Bundesrepublik Deutschland zur Frage der Zurückhaltung deutscher Kriegsgefangener durch die Union der sozialistischen Sowjetrepubliken," issued by the Presse- und Informationsamt der Bundesregierung, 5 Dec. 1950, in PIB, MF 2190.

75. See the interesting comparative perspective offered by H. Bruce Franklin, *M.I.A., or Mythmaking in America* (Brooklyn, N.Y.: Lawrence Hill Books, 1992).

76. "Hunderttausende von Kriegsgefangenen fehlen," *Tagesspiegel*, 6 Jan. 1949; also "400 000 deutsche Sklaven," *Bonner Rundschau*, 18 Jan. 1950; and "Aussenminister-Appell für Kriegsgefangene," *Die Welt*, 13 May 1950, copies in PIB, MF 1566. See also estimates of the Allied High Commission, 12 June 1950, NA, RG466, Records of the US HICOM, John J. McCloy, Classified General Records, 1949–52, box 15.

77. See Ernest R. May, "The American Commitment to Germany, 1949–55," *Diplomatic History* 13 (1989): 444–45.

78. Quoted in Abenheim, *Reforging the Iron Cross*, 70.

79. Quoted ibid., 70. See also Large, *Germans to the Front*, 114–17; and Brochhagen, *Nach Nürnberg*, 197; Wettig, *Entmilitarisierung*, 400–401. On the background, see Roland G. Foerster, "Innenpolitische Aspekte der Sicherheit Westdeutschlands (1947–1950)," in Foerster et al., *Von der Kapitulation bis zum Pleven-Plan*, 403; Georg Meyer, "Zur Situation der deutschen militärischen Führungsschicht im Vorfeld des westdeutschen Verteidigungsbeitrages, 1945–1950/51," ibid., 652–55; and Hans-Jürgen Rautenberg, "Zur Standortbestimmung für künftige deutsche Streitkräfte," ibid., 803.

80. Thomas Alan Schwartz, "John J. McCloy and the Landsberg Cases," in *American Policy and the Reconstruction of West Germany, 1945–1955*, ed. Jeffry M. Diefendorf, Axel Frohn, and Hermann-Josef Rupieper (New York: Cambridge University Press, 1993), 450; also idem, *America's Germany*, 157–75; and Brochhagen, *Nach Nürnberg*, 44–51.

81. "Statement by the Honorable Edith S. Sampson, U.S. Representative in Committee Three, on the Question of Prisoners of War," 5 Dec. 1950, PAAA, Abt. 2/2073; and on continued negotiations of Americans and West Germans on UN protests, see memo from [Heinz von] Trützschler, 8 Jan. 1952, PAAA, Abt. 2/2074; and notes on a meeting on the issue in the Foreign Office, 17 January 1952, ibid.

82. Outgoing message to U.S. Secretary of State, 21 Sept. 1950, NA, RG466, Records of the US HICOM, John J. McCloy, Classified General Records, 1949–52, box 19. The American insistence on immediate release of all German prisoners came at the same time that the U.S. was demanding "nonforcible repatriation" of Chinese and North Koreans taken captive during the Korean conflict and held in abysmal conditions in UN camps. See Rosemary Foot, *A Substitute for Victory: The Politics of Peacemaking at the Korean Armistice Talks* (Ithaca, N.Y.: Cornell University Press, 1990), 108–10.

83. "Stellungnahme der Regierung der Bundesrepublik Deutschland zur Frage der Zurückhaltung deutscher Kriegsgefangener durch die Union der sozialistischen Sowjetrepubliken," 5 Dec. 1950, PIB, MF 2190; and Kurt W. Böhme, "Hilfen für die deutschen Kriegsgefangenen 1939–1956," in *Die deutschen Kriegsgefangenen des Zweiten Weltkriegs: Eine Zusammenfassung,* ed. Erich Maschke (Bielefeld: Ernst & Werner Gieseking, 1974), 415–16. The 100,000 figure, announced by Heinz von Trützschler, a West German Foreign Ministry representative at the UN in Geneva, is reported in "Über 100 000 Gefangene in der UdSSR," *Frankfurter Rundschau,* 12 Sept. 1953. See also "Die Wahrheit über die Kriegsgefangenenzahlen," *Stuttgarter Zeitung,* 24 Oct. 1953, PIB, MF 2190; and "Kriegsgefangene-Frage kommt vor die UN," *Bulletin des Presse- und Informationsamtes der Bundesregierung,* 18 Sept. 1953, 1485–86; also "Die Tragödie der Kriegsgefangenen und Verschleppten: Namen von 99 856 Kriegsgefangenen und 1 320 966 Vermissten wurden in Genf vorgelegt: Mindestens 750 000 Zivilpersonen nach Sowjetrussland verbracht," ibid., 3 Sept. 1952, 1177–78. Other reported estimates were much lower; see "Es geht um 9297 Deutsche," *Revue,* no. 14 (1954), PIB, MF 2190; and "Die Zahlen sinken," *Spiegel,* 27 May 1953, 5–6. And for reports on the continued efforts to get accurate data as part of preparation for negotiations for the release of all remaining prisoners in 1955, see memo of 4 April 1955 reporting that reliable information existed for some 8,900 POWs, PAAA, Abt. 2/1988; memo prepared by Hergt, 12 Aug. 1955, PAAA, Büro Staatssekretär 15; Grewe to Oberländer, BVFK, 4 Aug. 1955, PAAA, Abt. 2/1992; and notes of Brückner, 2 Sept. 1955, PAAA, Büro Staatssekretär 14.

84. See, e.g., R. Weinmann, "Russland, wie ich es gesehen habe," *Frankfurter Allgemeine Zeitung,* 8 Mar. 1952; Josef Schmidt, "Nachricht aus den Lagern des Schweigens: Im Lager Friedland trafen 193 Spätheimkehrer ein," *Süddeutsche Zeitung,* 21 June 1952; "Der Hölle entronnen," *Berliner Morgenpost,* 27 Sept. 1953; the maps in *Die Welt,* 26 June 1952; and "Hier warten immer noch Kriegsgefangene und Internierte auf ihre Heimkehr," *Münchener Merkur,* 3 Oct. 1953; copies in PIB, MF 2190. See also "Armee hinter Stacheldraht," *Stern,* 12 Feb. 1950. General treatments were also soon available; see, e.g., Helmut Bohn, *Die Heimkehrer aus russischer Kriegsgefangenschaft* (Frankfurt am Main: Wolfgang Metzner, 1951).

85. "Zehn Jahre für Löwenzahnsalat," *Bremer Nachrichten,* 6 Feb. 1953; "'Es war ein richtiger Vorbeimarsch': 72 Kriegsgefangene an einem Tage veurteilt—Bericht eines Heimkehrers," *Tagesspiegel,* 27 Sept. 1953; "Gründe für Schreckensurteile," *Kölnische Rundschau,* 6 Oct. 1953; copies in PIB, MF 2190.

86. Beate Ihme-Tuchel, "Die Entlassung der deutschen Kriegsgefangenen im

Herbst 1955 im Spiegel der Diskussion zwischen SED und KPdSU," *Militär-geschichtliche Mitteilungen* 53 (1994): 450; also idem, "Zwischen Tabu und Propaganda: Hintergründe und Probleme der ostdeutsch-sowjetischen Heimkehrerverhandlungen," in Kaminsky (ed.), *Heimkehr,* 47. On the 1953 release, see "Parole Heimat," *Stern,* 11 Oct. 1953; "Heimkehr zwischen Hoffnung und Trauer," *Hannoversche Allgemeine Zeitung,* 3–4 Oct. 1953; Josef Schmidt, "Was sie daheim und draussen erlebten," *Stuttgarter Nachrichten,* 3 Oct. 1953; copies in PIB, MF 2190.

87. "'Alles in Sowjetrussland ist Lug und Trug,'" *General-Anzeiger für Bonn und Umgegend,* 6 May 1953, PIB, MF 2190.

88. "'Urteile mit Bleistift und ohne Stempel,'" *Kasseler Zeitung,* 8 Oct. 1953, PIB, MF 2190.

89. "Die Welt hinter dem Stacheldraht: Heimkehrer eröffnen die Ausstellung 'Kriegsgefangene mahnen,'" *Neue Zeitung,* 18 Apr. 1953; and "Eine Ausstellung—die jeden angeht," *Bonner Rundschau,* 9 May 1953; clippings in BAK, B150/8076.

90. See the discussions of the stamp within the BVFK, BAK, 150/4450; and *Der Heimkehrer,* May 1953. The association long antedated the stamp; see, e.g., "Verschollen, aber nicht vergessen!" *Süddeutsche Zeitung,* 16 Nov. 1950, PIB, MF 1566; or the illustration accompanying "Arbeiten-verrecken-verscharrt werden," *Stern,* 26 Nov. 1950, in which the POW is depicted with a bald head and deeply sunken eyes. The local office of the League of Returning POWs in Fürth-Stadt used the symbol on its letterhead with the caption "Do Not Forget Us"; see letter dated 5 December 1953, to Bundeskanzleramt, BAK, B136/2726. Nor did this symbol disappear; see, e.g., the graphic on the front page of *Der Heimkehrer,* 5 Jan. 1955, depicting two POWs in striped uniforms, framed by barbed wire with a guard tower in the background; and the draft of the poster for the day of commemoration in 1955, depicting two eyes staring out from behind barbed wire, ibid., 5 Mar. 1955. Stern, *Whitewashing,* 91, traces this association back to the immediate postwar period.

91. *VdH-Pressedienst,* no. 1, 4 Oct. 1954, Archiv des Verbands der Heimkehrer, Kriegsgefangenen und Vermisstenangehörigen (hereafter VdH Archiv), "Tag der Treue 1954." These annual days of remembrance began in October 1950 and were planned in consultation with officials of the federal government. See the materials in BAK, B150/4448, Heft 2; the memo of 26 Oct. 1952 to all member organzations from the Verband der Heimkehrer, outlining activities for that year, in PIB, MF 1566; and "Die Heimat gedachte der Gefangenen," *Der Heimkehrer,* Nov. 1953.

92. Verband der Heimkehrer, Kriegsgefangenen und Vermissten-Angehörigen Deutschlands e.V., Hauptgeschäftsstelle, Rundschreiben Nr. 22/53, "Gedenkwoche 1953," VdH Archiv.

93. Josef Arndgen (CDU), *VDB,* (1.) Deutscher Bundestag, 48. Sitzung, 17 Mar. 1950, 1646.

94. Quotations from Franz Josef Strauss (CSU), ibid., 1644; and Anton Besold (BP), ibid., 1648. See also Heinrich Höfler (CDU), ibid., 58. Sitzung, 26 Apr. 1950, 2136–38; and Margarete Hütter (FDP), ibid., 233. Sitzung, 9 Oct. 1952, 10674, 10683.

95. Hans Merten (SPD), ibid., 271. Sitzung, 12 June 1953, 13427. And for

almost the same formulation, see Maria Probst (CSU), ibid., 13431. This was also a constant theme of local branches of the League of Returning POWs; see the collection of petitions to the federal government from 1953, BAK, B136/2726.

96. Quoted in Teschner, "Entwicklung eines Interessenverbandes," 23. See also Arthur L. Smith, *Heimkehr aus dem Zweiten Weltkrieg: Die Entlassung der deutschen Kriegsgefangenen* (Stuttgart: Deutsche Verlags-Anstalt, 1985), 142–44; and, in general, Albrecht Lehmann, *Gefangenschaft und Heimkehr: Deutsche Kriegsgefangene in der Sowjetunion* (Munich: C. H. Beck, 1986), 134.

97. Speaking of POWs and quoting the West German President Theodor Heuss, Margarete Hütter (FDP), *VDB*, (1.) Deutscher Bundestag, 233. Sitzung, 9 Oct. 1952, 10674.

98. Kurt Pohle (SPD), speaking specifically of POWs, ibid. See also the comments of Theodor Heuss, President of the Federal Republic, during the week of commemoration for POWs in 1953, *Der Heimkehrer,* Nov. 1953.

99. Helmut Bazille (SPD), *VDB*, (1.) Deutscher Bundestag, 236. Sitzung, 30 Oct. 1952, 10883.

100. Kurt Pohle (SPD), ibid., 48. Sitzung, 17 Mar. 1950, 1646.

101. Lukaschek, ibid., 136. Sitzung, 19 Apr. 1951, 5365; also ibid., 52. Sitzung, 27 Mar. 1950, 1887.

102. Bernard Reissmann (Zentrum), ibid., 53. Sitzung, 28 Mar. 1950, 1958.

103. Herbert Kriedemann (SPD), ibid., 48. Sitzung, 17 Mar. 1950, 1665.

104. Erich Mende (FDP), ibid., 58. Sitzung, 26 Apr. 1950, 2147.

105. In general, on the ways in which opposition to Allied occupation provided a basis for unity that spanned the political spectrum, see Barbara Marshall, "German Attitudes to British Military Government, 1945–1947," *Journal of Contemporary History* 15 (1980): 655–84; and Foschepoth, "German Reaction"; also Christa Schick, "Die Internierungslager," in Broszat, Henke, and Woller (eds.), *Von Stalingrad zur Währungsreform,* 318–19. And on the background and consequences of the Potsdam agreement, see H. Lehmann, *Der Oder-Neisse-Konflikt,* 59–63; and Klaus-Dietmar Henke, "Der Weg nach Potsdam: Die Alliierten und die Vertreibung," in Benz (ed.), *Vertreibung der Deutschen aus dem Osten,* 46–69. For a good overview of the policies of U.S. occupation forces, see John Gimbel, *The American Occupation of Germany: Politics and the Military, 1945–1949* (Stanford: Stanford University Press, 1968).

106. Quotation from Eugen Gerstenmaier (CDU), *VDB*, (1.) Deutscher Bundestag, 48. Sitzung, 17 Mar. 1950, 1657. Allied responsibility for the Potsdam agreement was also a frequent theme in the interest group press; see, e.g., "Potsdams Drachensaat ging auf: 15 Millionen Deutsche klagen an—Westen begriff zu spät den Sieg des Ostens," *Der Sudetendeutsche,* 2 Aug. 1952. This analysis became a staple of scholarship on the integration of the expellees; see, e.g., Eugen Lemberg and Friedrich Edding, "Eingliederung und Gesellschaftswandel," in Lemberg and Edding (eds.), *Die Vertriebenen,* 1:157–58. The tendency to blame the Allies for the expulsion dated back to the immediate postwar period; see "German Attitudes toward the Expulsion of German Nationals from Neighboring Countries," Surveys Branch, Information Control Division, 8 July 1946, NA, RG260, OMGUS, Civil Affairs Division, Records Relating to Expellees in the U.S. Zone of Occupation, 1945–49, box 187.

107. Hans Merten (SPD), *VDB*, (1.) Deutscher Bundestag, 233. Sitzung, 9 Oct. 1952, 10680.

108. "'Soziale Atombombe' entschärfen: Bundesminister Seebohm: Flüchtlingsproblem geht über die Kräfte Deutschlands," *General-Anzeiger für Bonn und Umgegend*, 4 Sept. 1950, PIB, MF 1536.

109. *VDB*, (1.) Deutscher Bundestag, 94. Sitzung, 26 Oct. 1950, 3495–96.

110. See Werner Middlemann, "Entstehung und Aufgaben der Flüchtlingsverwaltung," in Lemberg and Edding (eds.), *Die Vertriebenen*, 1:276–99; Georg Müller and Heinz Simon, "Aufnahme und Unterbringung," ibid., 1:300–446; Hartmut Rudolph, *Evangelische Kirche und Vertriebene, 1945 bis 1972*, vol. 1 (Göttingen: Vandenhoeck & Ruprecht, 1984), 1–175; and Diehl, *Thanks of the Fatherland*, 101–7.

111. Hans Günter Hockerts, "Integration der Gesellschaft: Gründungskrise und Sozialpolitik in der frühen Bundesrepublik," *Zeitschrift für Sozialreform* 32 (1986): 25–41. On the law to "equalize burdens," see Hughes, *Shouldering the Burdens;* and Reinhold Schillinger, *Der Entscheidungsprozess beim Lastenausgleich, 1945–1952* (St. Katharinen: Scripta Mercaturae, 1985). On the early provisions for POWs, see Kurt Draeger, *Heimkehrergesetz: Kommentar und sonstiges Heimkehrerrecht*, 2d ed. (Berlin: Franz Vahlen, 1953).

112. Willi Albers, "Die Eingliederung in volkswirtschaftlicher Sicht," in Lemberg and Edding (eds.), *Die Vertriebenen*, 2:424.

113. Karner, *Im Archipel GUPVI*, 219–20; and Biess, "Protracted War."

114. Gerd Bucerius, "Rechnung für Hitlers Krieg," *Die Zeit*, 13 Apr. 1979, in Christoph Klessmann, *Die doppelte Staatsgründung: Deutsche Geschichte, 1945–1955* (Göttingen: Vandenhoeck & Ruprecht, 1982), 492.

115. The most detailed studies of the *Lastenausgleichsgesetz* are offered by Schillinger, *Entscheidungsprozess;* and Hughes, *Shouldering the Burdens*. See also Lutz Wiegand, "Kriegsfolgengesetzgebung in der Bundesrepublik Deutschland," *Archiv für Sozialgeschichte* 35 (1995): 77–90; Werner Abelshauser, "Der Lastenausgleich und die Eingliederung der Vertriebenen und Flüchtlinge: Eine Skizze," in Schulze, Brelie-Lewien, and Grebing (eds.), *Flüchtlinge und Vertriebene*, 229–38; and on measures for veterans, Diehl, *Thanks of the Fatherland*, 239–42.

116. See, e.g., Bundesministerium der Finanzen, *Flüchtlingslasten und Verteidigungsbeitrag: Zwei sich ergänzende und begrenzende Belastungen* (n.p., 1951); Fritz Schäffer's comments, *VDB*, (1.) Deutscher Bundestag, 115. Sitzung, 31 Jan. 1951, 4340; also Hughes, *Shouldering the Burdens*.

117. The position of the West German KPD thus echoed the position of the East German ruling party, the Socialist Unity Party (SED). In general, see Ther, "Integration of Expellees," 792–96; idem, *Deutsche und polnische Vertriebene;* Plato and Meinicke, *Alte Heimat—neue Zeit;* and Wille, Hoffmann, and Meinicke (eds.), *Sie hatten alles verloren*.

118. Heinz Renner (KPD), *VDB*, (1.) Deutscher Bundestag, 58. Sitzung, 26 Apr. 1950, 2156.

119. On POWs, Heinrich Höfler (CDU), ibid., 2136; and in response to KPD critiques, see, e.g., Wilhelm Mellies (SPD), ibid., 250. Sitzung, 25 Feb. 1953, 11983; and Erich Mende (FDP), ibid., 2146.

120. Richard Reitzner (SPD), ibid., 136. Sitzung, 19 Apr. 1951, 5348; also Herbert Kriedemann (SPD), ibid., 115. Sitzung, 31 Jan. 1951, 4352.

121. Erwin Welke (SPD), ibid., 51. Sitzung, 24 Mar. 1950, 1824.

122. Hans-Joachim von Merkatz (DP), ibid., 254. Sitzung, 18 Mar. 1953, 12279.

123. On POWs, in general see Teschner, "Entwicklung eines Interessenverbandes."

124. Schillinger, *Entscheidungsprozess,* 57, 178; Wiskemann, *Germany's Eastern Neighbours,* 192–93; Ahonen, "Expellee Organizations," 90–96. In general, see Franz Neumann, *Der Block der Heimatvertriebenen und Entrechteten, 1950–1960: Ein Beitrag zur Geschichte und Struktur einer politischen Interessenpartei* (Meisenheim am Glan: Anton Hain, 1968); Schoenberg, *Germans from the East;* Michael Imhof, "Die Vertriebenenverbände in der Bundesrepublik Deutschland: Geschichte, Organisation und gesellschaftliche Bedeutung" (Ph.D. diss., Philipps-Universität Marburg, 1975); Everhard Holtmann, "Flüchtlinge in den 50er Jahren: Aspekte ihrer gesellschaftlichen und politischen Integration," in *Modernisierung im Wiederaufbau: Die westdeutsche Gesellschaft der 50er Jahre,* ed. Axel Schildt and Arnold Sywottek (Bonn: J. H. W. Dietz Nachf., 1993), 349–61; also "Das Wahlergebnis und die Vertriebenen," *Bulletin des Presse- und Informationsamtes der Bundesregierung,* 17 Sept. 1953. In *Shouldering the Burdens,* Hughes illuminates the history of the BHE and also offers important insights into the treatment of the "war-damaged" after the two world wars.

125. Ian Connor, "The Refugees and the Currency Reform," in *Reconstruction in Post-War Germany: British Occupation Policy and the Western Zones, 1945–55,* ed. Ian Turner (Oxford: Berg, 1989), 301–24. On the significance of the economic recovery, see Wolfgang Abelshauser, *Die langen fünfziger Jahre: Wirtschaft und Gesellschaft der Bundesrepublik Deutschland, 1949–1966* (Düsseldorf: Pädagogischer Verlag Schwann-Bagel, 1987), 33–42.

126. Paul Lüttinger, with the assistance of Rita Rossmann, *Integration der Vertriebenen: Eine empirische Analyse* (Frankfurt am Main: Campus, 1989). See also Gerold Ambrosius, "Flüchtlinge und Vertriebene in der westdeutschen Wirtschaftsgeschichte: Methodische Überlegungen und forschungsrelevante Probleme," in Schulze, Brelie-Lewien, and Grebing (eds.), *Flüchtlinge und Vertriebene,* 216–28; and Abelshauser, "Lastenausgleich und Eingliederung."

127. Again, I believe that Diehl's comments on veterans can be extended generally to the "war-damaged," including expellees. On the rapid decline in importance of the BHE, see Holtmann, "Flüchtlinge in den 50er Jahren," 358–59.

128. See the insightful comments of Bartov, "Defining Enemies," 788–90. Herf is correct to argue that West German democracy was based on "justice delayed" when it came to prosecuting Nazi criminals, but the choice was not, as he states, "between memory and justice." Memories of German victimization—articulated, encouraged, embraced—were an essential part of West German self-definition in the early 1950s. See Herf, *Divided Memory,* 7, and the review of Herf by Frank Biess in *German Politics and Society* 17 (1999): 144–51.

129. Kurt Bielig (SPD), *VDB,* (1.) Deutscher Bundestag, 27. Sitzung, 18 Jan. 1950, 842–43. On POWs in particular, see Biess, "Protracted War."

130. Linus Kather (CDU), *VDB* (1.) Deutscher Bundestag, 115. Sitzung, 31 Jan. 1951, 4357.

131. This is also one of the most important conclusions of Hughes, *Shouldering the Burdens.*

132. See, e.g., comments of Margot Kalinke (DP), *VDB* (1.) Deutscher Bundestag, 58. Sitzung, 26 Apr. 1950, 2149.

133. Kurt Pohle (SPD), ibid., 233. Sitzung, 9 Oct. 1952, 10673.

Chapter Three

1. John Murray, *Atlas of Central Europe* (London: John Murray, 1963), 105, the British edition of an atlas prepared by the Kartographisches Institut Bertelsmann in Gütersloh.

2. "Erlebnisbericht der Schneiderin Anna Schwartz aus Schönberg, Kreis Karthaus i. Westpr. . . . 5. Januar 1952," in *Dokumentation der Vertreibung der Deutschen aus Ost-Mitteleuropa,* ed. Bundesministerium für Vertriebene, vol. 1, pt. 2: *Die Vertreibung der deutschen Bevölkerung aus den Gebieten östlich der Oder-Neisse* (Munich: Deutscher Taschenbuch Verlag, [1954] 1984), 90–103. In accord with the express wishes of the BVFK, the first volume appeared in 1953 before the parliamentary elections. See Matthias Beer, "Der 'Neuanfang' der Zeitgeschichte nach 1945: Zum Verhältnis von nationalsozialistischer Umsiedlungs- und Vernichtungspolitik und der Vertreibung der Deutschen aus Ostmitteleuropa," in *Deutsche Historiker im Nationalsozialismus,* ed. Winfried Schulze and Otto Gerhard Oexle with the assistance of Gerd Helm and Thomas Ott (Frankfurt am Main: Fischer Taschenbuch Verlag, 1999), 283. A third part of vol. 1, *Polnische Gesetze und Verordnungen, 1944–1955* (Munich: Deutscher Taschenbuch Verlag, [1960] 1984), appeared seven years later. In all subsequent references to individual testimonies in the documentation, I cite the author's name and original residence and, where available, the date the testimony was recorded.

3. See, e.g., Arbeitsgemeinschaft zur Wahrung sudetendeutscher Interessen, ed., *Dokumente zur Austreibung der Sudetendeutschen* (Munich: Arbeitsgemeinschaft zur Wahrung sudetendeutscher Interessen, 1951). Extensive listings of the massive contemporary literature can be found in Karl O. Kurth, *Handbuch der Presse der Heimatvertriebenen* (Kitzingen-Main: Holzner, 1953). For examples, see Martin Bojanowski and Erich Bosdorf, *Striegau: Schicksale einer schlesischen Stadt* (Schöppenstedt [Braunschweig]: Selbstverlag E. Bosdorf, [1951]); Johannes Kaps, ed., *Die Tragödie Schlesiens 1945/49 in Dokumenten unter besonderer Berücksichtigung des Erzbistums Breslau* (Neuötting am Inn: Verlag "Christ unterwegs," 1952–53); Jürgen Thorwald, *Es begann an der Weichsel* (Stuttgart: Steingrüben, 1950) (the third printing, at which time 30,000 copies were in circulation); idem, *Das Ende an der Elbe,* 3d printing (Stuttgart: Steingrüben, 1950); and, in general, Helbig, *Ungeheuerer Verlust,* 15–17.

4. See the general outlines in Marrus, *Unwanted,* 325–31; Kulischer, *Europe on the Move,* 272–73, 282–92; and Ther, *Deutsche und polnische Vertriebene,* 50–66.

5. Elisabeth Pfeil, *Der Flüchtling: Gestalt einer Zeitenwende* (Hamburg: Hans von Hugo, 1948), 110.

6. Ibid., 145. See also the influential study by Helmut Schelsky, *Wandlungen der deutschen Familie in der Gegenwart: Dartstellung und Deutung einer empirisch-soziologischen Tatbestandsaufnahme*, 4th ed. (Stuttgart: Ferdinand Enke, 1960). Schelsky argued that the expellee family was representative of all German families in the postwar period.

7. Bernhard Pfister, "Geleitwort des Herausgebers," in Helmut Arndt, *Die volkswirtschaftliche Eingliederung eines Bevölkerungszustromes: Wirtschaftstheoretische Einführung in das Vertriebenen- und Flüchtlingsproblem* (Berlin: Duncker & Humblot, 1954), 8–9. Individual studies appeared as part of vols. 6–7 of the *Schriften des Vereins für Sozialpolitik.*

8. Eugen Lemberg, ed., with the assistance of Lothar Krecker, *Die Entstehung eines neuen Volkes aus Binnendeutschen und Ostvertriebenen* (Marburg: N. G. Elwert, 1950); and, in general, Lemberg and Edding (eds.), *Die Vertriebenen.* Lemberg and Edding also drew explicit analogies between Jews and victimized Germans, all members of a "community of fate" (*Schicksalsgemeinschaft*) created by the national enmities unleashed by the Second World War. See Lemberg and Edding, "Einführung," ibid., 1:7. See also Gotthold Rhode, "Phasen und Formen der Massenzwangswanderung," ibid., 1:25–26. For a comprehensive discussion of other contemporary accounts that emphasized the Federal Republic's successful integration of the expellees, see Doris von der Brelie-Lewien, "Zur Rolle der Flüchtlinge und Vertriebenen in der westdeutschen Nachkriegsgeschichte: Ein Forschungsbericht," in Schulze, Brelie-Lewien, and Grebing (eds.), *Flüchtlinge und Vertriebene*, 24–45. For useful general overviews of the literature, see Jolles, *Zur Soziologie der Heimatvertriebenen*, 18–29; Wolfrum, "Zwischen Geschichtsschreibung und Geschichtspolitik"; Peter Waldmann, "Die Eingliederung der ostdeutschen Vertriebenen in die westdeutsche Gesellschaft," in *Vorgeschichte der Bundesrepublik Deutschland: Zwischen Kapitulation und Grundgesetz*, ed. Josef Becker, Theo Stammen, and Peter Waldmann (Munich: Wilhelm Fink, 1979), 163–64; and Johannes-Dieter Steinert, *Flüchtlinge, Vertriebene und Aussiedler in Niedersachsen: Eine annotierte Bibliographie* (Osnabrück: Kommissionsverlag H. Th. Wenner, 1986).

9. For a detailed introduction to the background of the project, the recruitment of the editorial staff, and the negotiations between the Ministry of Expellees and Schieder over the final form of the documentation, see Matthias Beer, "Im Spannungsfeld von Politik und Zeitgeschichte: Das Grossforschungsprojekt 'Dokumentation der Vertreibung der Deutschen aus Ost-Mitteleuropa,'" *Vierteljahrshefte für Zeitgeschichte* 49 (1998): 345–89; idem, "Die Dokumentation der Vertreibung der Deutschen aus Ost-Mitteleuropa: Hintergründe—Entstehung—Wirkung," *Geschichte in Wissenschaft und Unterricht* 50 (1999): 99–117; idem, "'Neuanfang.'" Beer's analysis does not include a consideration of the content of the reports, the primary focus of this chapter. On Schieder and the intellectual milieu from which he emerged, see also Jörn Rüsen, "Continuity, Innovation, and Self-Reflection in Late Historicism: Theodor Schieder (1908–1984)," in *Paths of Continuity: Central European Historiography from the 1930s to the 1950s*, ed. Hartmut Lehmann and James van Horn Melton (Cambridge: Cam-

bridge University Press, 1994), 353–88; Hans-Ulrich Wehler, "Nachruf auf Theodor Schieder, 11. April 1908–8. Oktober 1984," *Geschichte und Gesellschaft* 11 (1985): 143–53; Werner Conze, "Die Königsberger Jahre," in *Vom Beruf des Historikers in einer Zeit beschleunigten Wandels: Akademische Gedenkfeier für Theodor Schieder am 8. Februar 1985 an der Universität Köln*, ed. Andreas Hillgruber (Munich: R. Oldenbourg, 1985), 23–31; Wolfgang J. Mommsen, "Vom Beruf des Historikers in einer Zeit beschleunigten Wandels: Theodor Schieders historiographisches Werk," ibid., 48–50; and Ingo Haar, "'Revisionistische' Historiker und Jugendbewegung: Das Königsberger Beispiel," in *Geschichtsschreibung als Legitimationswissenschaft, 1918–1945*, ed. Peter Schöttler (Frankfurt am Main: Suhrkamp, 1997), 52–103. And for useful general treatments of the historical profession under the Nazis, see Willi Oberkrome, *Volksgeschichte: Methodische und völkische Ideologisierung in der deutschen Geschichtswissenschaft, 1918–1945* (Göttingen: Vandenhoeck & Ruprecht, 1993); idem, "Historiker im 'Dritten Reich': Zum Stellenwert volkshistorischer Ansätze zwischen klassischer Politik- und neuerer Sozialgeschichte," *Geschichte in Wissenschaft und Unterricht* 50 (1999): 74–98; and Karen Schönwälder, *Historiker und Politik: Geschichtswissenschaft im Nationalsozialismus* (Frankfurt am Main: Campus, 1992).

10. Murray, *Atlas of Central Europe*, 112.

11. Schieder's Nazi past has triggered considerable controversy in recent years, with assessments of his activities under the Nazis diverging dramatically. According to one variant, he is seen as contributing to plans for the "racial cleansing" of Poland. See, e.g., Angelika Ebbinghaus and Karl Heinz Roth, "Vorläufer des 'Generalplans Ost': Eine Dokumentation über Theodor Schieders Polendenkschrift vom 7. Oktober 1939," *1999: Zeitschrift für Sozialgeschichte des 20. und 21. Jahrhunderts* 1 (1992): 62–94; also Götz Aly, *Macht-Geist-Wahn: Kontinuität deutschen Denkens* (Berlin: Argon, 1997), 153–83; and idem, *"Endlösung": Völkerverschiebung und der Mord an den europäischen Juden* (Frankfurt am Main: S. Fischer, 1995), 16. Aly equates Schieder's endorsement of the transfer of Poles, including many Polish Jews, from occupied Poland and their replacement with ethnic Germans with the "preliminary stages of physical destruction." See Aly, "Theodor Schieder, Werner Conze, oder die Vorstufen der physischen Vernichtung," in Schulze and Oxele (eds.), *Deutsche Historiker im Nationalsozialismus*, 163–83. I am convinced by those who counter that it is a mistake to trace a straight line from Schieder's rabid, aggressive, racially charged nationalism to the "final solution." See, e.g., Christof Dipper, "Auschwitz erklären," *Aschkenas* 5 (1995): 204; the exchange in the *Frankfurter Allgemeine Zeitung* between Hans-Ulrich Wehler, "In den Fussstapfen der kämpfenden Wissenschaft," 4 Jan. 1999, and Götz Aly, "Stakkato der Vertreibung, Pizzikato der Entlastung," 3 Feb. 1999; Wolfgang Mommsen, "Vom 'Volkstumskampf' zur nationalsozialistischen Vernichtungspolitik in Osteuropa: Zur Rolle der deutschen Historiker unter dem Nationalsozialismus," in Schulze and Oexle (eds.), *Deutsche Historiker im Nationalsozialismus*, 183–214; Ingo Haar, "'Kämpfende Wissenschaft': Entstehung und Niedergang der völkischen Geschichtswissenschaft im Wechsel der Systeme," ibid., 218–19; and Hans-Ulrich Wehler, "Nationalsozialismus und Historiker," ibid., 306–39. The controversy surrounding the re-

lationship of Schieder and Werner Conze to National Socialism and *Ostforschung* was the subject of a special session at the German historical professional association meetings (*Historikertag*) in 1998, the papers from which appear in Schulze and Oexle (eds.), *Deutsche Historiker im Nationalsozialismus*. See the introduction to this volume by Winfried Schulze, Gerd Helm, and Thomas Ott, "Deutsche Historiker im Nationalsozialismus: Beobachtungen und Überlegungen zu einer Debatte," ibid., 11–48. See also "Dienstbare Geister," *Der Spiegel*, 21 Sept. 1998, 102–3, 107; Franziska Augstein, "Schlangen in der Grube," *Frankfurter Allgemeine Zeitung*, 14 Sept. 1998; and Volker Ullrich, "Späte Reue der Zunft: Endlich arbeiten die deutschen Historiker die braune Vergangenheit ihres Faches auf," *Die Zeit*, 17 Sept. 1998. My thanks to Josef Mooser for providing me with these newspaper references.

12. Hans-Ulrich Wehler, "Vorwort," in *Sozialgeschichte Heute: Festschrift für Hans Rosenberg zum 70. Geburtstag*, ed. Hans-Ulrich Wehler (Göttingen: Vandenhoeck & Ruprecht, 1974), 16.

13. Schieder had become his successor, assuming Rothfels's Königsberg chair in 1942. See Lothar Gall, "Theodor Schieder, 1908–1984," *Historische Zeitschrift* 241 (1985): 7.

14. Klemens von Klemperer, "Hans Rothfels (1891–1976)," in Lehmann and Melton (eds.), *Paths of Continuity*, 127–32; Douglas A. Unfug, "Comment: Hans Rothfels," ibid., 140; Hans Mommsen, "Hans Rothfels," in *Deutsche Historiker*, ed. Hans-Ulrich Wehler (Göttingen: Vandenhoeck & Ruprecht, 1982), 9:136; Haar, "'Revisionistische' Historiker," 52–53, 70–81; and Beer, "Im Spannungsfeld von Politik," 365.

15. Oberkrome, *Volksgeschichte*, 15–16, 137–40, 160–61, 196–97, 212, 222–23; Wolfgang Schieder, "Sozialgeschichte zwischen Soziologie und Geschichte: Das wissenschaftliche Lebenswerk Werner Conzes," *Geschichte und Gesellschaft* 13 (1987): 251; Reinhart Koselleck, "Werner Conze: Tradition und Innovation," *Historische Zeitschrift* 245 (1987): 529; and, on Conze's postwar influence, Irmline Veit-Brause, "Werner Conze (1910–1986): The Measure of History and the Historian's Measures," in Lehmann and Melton (eds.), *Paths of Continuity*, 299–43; and Peter Reill, "Comment: Werner Conze," ibid., 345–51. Conze was not among the editors of the first volume published by the project. On the recent controversy over Conze's Nazi past, see Aly, "Theodor Schieder, Werner Conze"; and Wehler, "Nationalsozialismus und Historiker."

16. For reviews of postwar West German historiography, see James van Horn Melton, "Introduction: Continuities in German Historical Scholarship, 1930–1960," in Lehmann and Melton (eds.), *Paths of Continuity*, 1–18; and Winfried Schulze, "German Historiography from the 1930s to the 1950s," ibid., 19–42. Hans-Ulrich Wehler subsequently drew heavily on the Yugoslavia volume in his study of the effect of the Second World War on the German minority in that country. See Wehler, *Nationalitätenpolitik in Jugoslawien: Die deutsche Minderheit, 1918–1978* (Göttingen: Vandenhoeck & Ruprecht, 1980), esp. 83–92, 103.

17. The series is BVFK, ed., *Dokumentation der Vertreibung der Deutschen aus Ost-Mitteleuropa*, and the volumes in it appeared between 1953 and 1961. The editorial board, headed by Theodor Schieder, included Adolf Diestelkamp

(for vol. 1 only), Rudolf Laun, Peter Rassow (vols. 1–4), and Hans Rothfels. Werner Conze joined this group beginning with volume 2. The individual volumes, each prepared by a different team of project members but all appearing under the general editorship of Theodor Schieder, include: vol. 1, *Die Vertreibung der deutschen Bevölkerung aus den Gebieten östlich der Oder-Neisse;* vol. 2, *Das Schicksal der Deutschen in Ungarn* (Munich: Deutscher Taschenbuch Verlag, [1956] 1984); vol. 3, *Das Schicksal der Deutschen in Rumänien* (Munich: Deutscher Taschenbuch Verlag, [1957] 1984); vol. 4, *Die Vertreibung der deutschen Bevölkerung aus der Tschechoslowakei* (Augsburg: Weltbild Verlag, [1957] 1994); vol. 5, *Das Schicksal der Deutschen in Jugoslawien* (Munich: Deutscher Taschenbuch Verlag, [1961] 1984); and in addition, Käthe von Normann, *Ein Tagebuch aus Pommern, 1945–1946* (Gross-Denkte/Wolfenbüttel: Grenzland-Druckerei, 1955); Margarete Schell, *Ein Tagebuch aus Prag, 1945–46* (Kassel-Wilh.: Herbert M. Nuhr, 1957); and Hans Graf von Lehndorff, *Ein Bericht aus Ost- und Westpreussen, 1945–1947* (Düsseldorf: Oskar-Leiner-Druck, 1960). On the background of the project, see Josef Henke, "Exodus aus Ostpreussen und Schlesien: Vier Erlebnisberichte," in Benz (ed.), *Vertreibung der Deutschen,* 91; Beer, "Im Spannungsfeld von Politik"; idem, "Die Dokumentation der Vertreibung der Deutschen aus Ost-Mitteleuropa: Hintergründe—Entstehung—Ergebnis—Wirkung," *Geschichte in Wissenschaft und Unterricht* 50 (1999): 99–117; and Kulturstiftung der deutschen Vertriebenen, ed., *Vertreibung und Vertreibungsverbrechen 1945–1948: Bericht des Bundesarchivs vom 28. Mai 1974* (Meckenheim: DCM Druck, 1989), 17–22.

18. Beer, "Im Spannungsfeld von Politik," 366–67.

19. My thanks to Axel Schmidt of the Bundesarchiv (Koblenz), conversation of 4 July 1995, for an enlightening introduction to the collection.

20. Hans Rothfels, "Zeitgeschichte als Aufgabe," *Vierteljahrshefte für Zeitgeschichte* 1 (1953): 5–6. See also the discussion of the concept of *Zeitgeschichte* in Hans Günter Hockerts, "Zeitgeschichte in Deutschland: Begriff, Methoden, Themenfelder," *Historisches Jahrbuch* 6 (1993): 98–127.

21. Martin Broszat, "Massendokumentation als Methode zeitgeschichtlicher Forschung," *Vierteljahrshefte für Zeitgeschichte* 2 (1954): 203. See also Theodor Schieder, "Die Vertreibung der Deutschen aus dem Osten als wissenschaftliches Problem," *Vierteljahrshefte für Zeitgeschichte* 8 (1960): 1–16.

22. See Broszat, "Massendokumentation," 203; and in general, Oberkrome, *Volksgeschichte,* 222–23. For examples of how the documentation was immediately used to write the "contemporary history" of the postwar period, see Friedrich Zipfel, "Vernichtung und Austreibung der Deutschen aus den Gebieten östlich der Oder-Neisse-Linie," *Jahrbuch für die Geschichte Mittel- und Ostdeutschlands* 3 (1954): 145–79; and idem, "Schicksal und Vertreibung der Deutschen aus Ungarn, Rumänien und der Tschechoslowakei," *Jahrbuch für die Geschichte Mittel- und Ostdeutschlands* 7 (1958): 379–93. More recently, Alfred M. de Zayas, in *Nemesis at Potsdam: The Expulsion of Germans from the East* (Lincoln: University of Nebraska, 1989), a book that first appeared in 1977, unabashedly and uncritically reproduces the postwar West German attacks on Allied policies and horrifying accounts of mistreatment of Germans; see also Josef Henke, "Flucht und Vertreibung der Deutschen aus ihrer Heimat im Osten und

Südosten, 1944–1947," *Aus Politik und Zeitgeschichte: Beilage zur Wochenzeitung "Das Parlament,"* B23 (1985), 15–34; Zeidler, *Kriegsende,* 143–52; and
Rudolf von Thadden, "Die Gebiete östlich der Oder-Neisse in den Übergangsjahren 1945–1949: Eine Vorstudie," in Schulze, Brelie-Lewien, and Grebing (eds.),
Flüchtlinge und Vertriebene, 117. Thadden recommends the Schieder volumes
as "the starting point for all scholarly work" on the expulsion.

23. Beer, "Im Spannungsfeld von Politik," largely endorses this view, emphasizing the project's influence as a model for social historical documentation.

24. Rothfels, "Zeitgeschichte als Aufgabe," 4.

25. On his practical efforts in support of the project, see Schieder to Wilpert,
BVFK, 7 Nov. 1951, BAK, B106/27733.

26. See Schieder's "Zur Methode der kritischen Dokumentenbearbeitung," an
appendix to his "Bericht über die Dokumentation der Vertreibung," 1 Apr. 1952,
BAK, B150/4173. See also Schieder, "Arbeitsplan für die Authentifizierung des
Materials zur Vertreibung von Deutschen aus den Ostgebieten," 25 Oct. 1951,
BAK, B150/4171/Heft 1. My unsystematic review of some of the original documents, housed in the Bundesarchiv, revealed that staff applied these criteria un-
evenly. Assessments appended to some documents suggest reviewers were keen to
exclude exaggeration or accounts that focused exclusively on acts of destruction
but also favored reports that provided graphic details, if they were presented in
a sober tone. See, e.g., reports attached to the documents from BAK, Ost-Dok
2/313, Kreis Prag; ibid. /68, Kreis Elbing; ibid. /69, Kreis Marienburg; ibid. /45,
Kreis Danzig; ibid. /58, Kreis Neustadt (Westpreussen); ibid. /73, Kreis Altburg-
land; ibid. /56, Kreis Kulm; ibid. /21, Königsberg/Stadt; ibid. /72, Kreis Stuhm;
ibid. /44, Danzig Stadt. Schieder's involvement in all aspects of the project is amply documented by Beer, "Dokumentation der Vertreibung."

27. *Oder-Neisse,* 1/1:iii–iv.

28. Ibid., quotations from vii, i.

29. Broszat, "Massendokumentation," 204. Broszat provides a thorough review of the methodological approach of the project. See also the useful critical
reflections of Albrecht Lehmann, *Im Fremden ungewollt zuhaus: Flüchtlinge und
Vertriebene in Westdeutschland, 1945–1990* (Munich: C. H. Beck, 1991), 189,
191, 193.

30. Quotations are respectively from "Dokumente des Grauens," *Stuttgarter
Zeitung,* 2 Sept. 1954; and "Katastrophen der Deutschen-Vertreibung aus dem
Osten in Dokumenten," *Westdeutsche Allgemeine Zeitung,* 6 May 1954; copies
of both in BAK, B150/5641. This enthusiastic tone characterized most reviews.
See, e.g., O. E. H. Becker, "Das Schicksal der Rumänien-Deutschen," *Tagesspiegel,* 25 Mar. 1958; and "Zeitgeschichte in Dokumenten," *Westfälische Allgemeine Zeitung,* 5 Sept. 1958; copies in BAK, B150/5643.

31. Theodor Schieder, "Gutachten über eine Dokumentation der Vertreibung
der Deutschen aus den Ostgebieten für das Bundesministerium für die Angele-
genheiten der Vertriebenen," 1 Oct. 1951, BAK, B150/4171/Heft 1.

32. Ibid.

33. Adolf Diestelkamp, "Denkschrift zur Dokumentation der Vertreibung der
Deutschen aus dem Osten," 22 May 1951, ibid. Diestelkamp was the board's
Bundesarchiv representative.

34. The English-language versions are *The Expulsion of the German Population from the Territories East of the Oder-Neisse-Line* (Leer [Ostfriesland]: Gerhard Rautenberg, n.d.); *The Fate of the Germans in Hungary* (Göttingen: Schwartz & Co., 1961); *The Fate of the Germans in Rumania* (Göttingen: Schwartz & Co., 1961); and *The Expulsion of the German Population from Czechoslovakia* (Leer [Ostfriesland]: Gerhard Rautenberg, 1960). All were published under the auspices of the BVFK. On the usefulness of the documentation in this international context, see Schieder, "Gutachten über eine Dokumentation," 1 Oct. 1951, BAK, B150/4171/Heft 1; "Aufzeichnung über die Besprechung über die Fortführung der Dokumentation im Bundesministerium für Vertriebene am 13.7.51," ibid.

35. Memo from v. Wilpert, 20 Apr. 1951, ibid. See also Diestelkamp, "Denkschrift zur 'Dokumentation der Vertreibung der Deutschen aus den Ostgebieten,'" 22 May 1951, ibid.

36. Memo from v. Wilpert, 20 Apr. 1951, ibid.

37. T. Schieder, "Die Vertreibung als wissenschaftliches Problem," 15. For the critique of East German historians, see F.-H. Gentzen, J. Kalisch, G. Voigt, and E. Wolfgramm, "Die 'Ostforschung': Ein Stosstrupp des deutschen Imperialismus," *Zeitschrift für Geschichtswissenschaft* 6 (1958): 1214; and in general, Michael Burleigh, *Germany Turns Eastwards: A Study of Ostforschung in the Third Reich* (Cambridge: Cambridge University Press, 1988), 308. And on the complaints of eastern European regional interest groups in the Federal Republic, see, e.g., Josef Trischler, Rat der Südostdeutschen, to Theodor Oberländer, BVFK, 12 Aug. 1956, BAK, B150/4194/Heft 1; Heinrich Reitinger, national spokesman for the Landsmannschaft of the Germans from Hungary to BVFK, 31 Oct. 1957, BAK, B150/4194/Heft 2; and Schieder to Kleberg in BVFK, 13 May 1958, BAK, B150/5642. The negative reaction of the Sudetendeutsche Landsmannschaft to the publication of Schell's diary was particularly severe. See the notes of Schlicker of BVFK, 30 June and 10 July 1958, BAK, B150/5630; also correspondence and newspaper clippings in BAK, B150/5644.

38. "Erlebnisbericht des Gutsbesitzers Franz Adalbert Frhr. von Rosenberg aus Kloetzen, Kreis Marienwerder in Westpr. . . . April 1951," *Oder-Neisse*, 1/1:155. See also Beer, "Im Spannungsfeld von Politik," 376. The best source on German population transfers and resettlement after 1939 is Lumans, *Himmler's Auxiliaries*.

39. "Erlebnisbericht des Dr. med. Karl Grimm aus Brüx . . . 4. Dezember 1950," *Tschechoslowakei*, 4/2: 465–66.

40. "Bericht des Fleischermeisters O. G. aus Regenwalde i. Pom. . . . 19. Oktober 1952," *Oder-Neisse*, 1/1:233.

41. Lehndorff, *Bericht*, 59; also "Erlebnisbericht des A. S. aus Schlagenthin, Kreis Arnswalde i. Pom. . . . 12. Juli 1952," *Oder-Neisse*, 1/1:201.

42. *Oder-Neisse*, 1/1:64E; and "Erlebnisbericht des Gutsbeamten A. B. aus Eichmedien, Kreis Sensburg i. Ostpr. . . . Mai 1950," ibid., 1/2:178.

43. "Bericht des ehemaligen Bezirksbürgermeisters H. aus Breslau . . . (1946)," *Oder-Neisse*, 1/2:328. The "notarized copy" of his report was delivered after his departure from the east.

44. "Bericht (Brief) der H. T. aus Hermannstadt (Sibiu) in Süd-Siebenbürgen . . . 23 November 1956," *Rumänien*, 3:401.

45. *Oder-Neisse*, 1/1:60E–63E.

46. On this topic in general, see Naimark, *Russians in Germany,* 69–140; Grossmann, "Question of Silence," 33–52; and Marlene Epp, "The Memory of Violence: Soviet and East European Mennonite Refugees and Rape in the Second World War," *Journal of Women's History* 9 (1997): 58–87.

47. "Erlebnisbericht der Hausfrau A. F. aus Königsberg i. Ostpr. . . . 25. November 1952," *Oder-Neisse,* 1/1:131–2.

48. "Bericht der Frau H. H. aus Nakel, Kreis Wirsitz i. Westpr.," n.d., ibid., 181.

49. "Erlebnisbericht von Frau G. F. aus Kanth, Landkreis Breslau . . . 10. Dezember 1951," ibid., 453.

50. See, e.g., "Erlebnisbericht des R. G. aus Gross-Schamm (Jamul-Mare), Plasa Deta, Judeţ Timiţ-Torontal im Banat . . . 1. April 1956," *Rumänien,* 3:355; "Erlebnisbericht des Dr.-Ing. Kurt Schmidt aus Brünn . . . Frühjahr 1957," *Tschechoslowakei,* 4/2: 159, 163; "Erlebnisbericht der Bauersfrau Elisabeth Peschke aus Seifersdorf, Kreis Jägerndorf . . . 17. April 1947," ibid., 223; "Protokollarische Aussage der Bäuerin A. S. aus M., Judeţ Câmpulung (Kimpolung) in der Bukowina . . . 1. Februar 1951," *Rumänien,* 3:331–32; "Erlebnisbericht der Frau Berta Ludwig aus Temeschburg (Timişoara), Judeţ Timiş-Torontal im Banat . . . 15. Juni 1956," ibid., 182; "Erlebnisbericht des Landwirts H. B. aus Sartscha (Sarča), Bezirk Alibunar im Banat . . . 15. April 1958," *Jugoslawien,* 5:207; "Erlebnisbericht eines Lehrers aus Ödenburg (Sopron) . . . 14. April 1955," *Ungarn,* 2:38; and "Erlebnisbericht des Géza Becker aus Majs, Bezirk Mohács im Komitat Baranya," n.d., ibid., 145.

51. See Zeidler, *Kriegsende,* 150.

52. "Erlebnisbericht des A. S.," *Oder-Neisse,* 1/1:199, 201.

53. "Erlebnisbericht der Frau Anitta Graeser aus dem Bezirk Modern, Pressburger Sprachinsel . . . 12. Januar 1954," *Tschechoslowakei,* 4/2:793.

54. "Erlebnisbericht der Kaufmannsfrau Charlotte Hedrich aus Rospitz, Kreis Marienwerder i. Westpr. . . . 27. Januar 1952," *Oder-Neisse,* 1/1:277.

55. *Oder-Neisse,* 1/1:60E–61E; also *Tschechoslowakei,* 4/1:30.

56. Quoted in Niethammer, "Privat-Wirtschaft," 31. And see, in general, Heineman, "Hour of the Woman," 380–86.

57. See the useful comments of Heineman, "Hour of the Woman," 364–65.

58. "Bericht der Bäuerin I. K. aus Eichfier, Kreis Deutsch Krone i. Pom. . . . 21. Juni 1950," *Oder-Neisse,* 1/1:193–4.

59. "Erlebnisbericht des Gutsbesitzers und ehemaligen Mitglieds des tschechoslowakischen Parlaments Friedrich Graf Stolberg aus Kiowitz, Kreis Wagstadt . . . 21. Febaruar [*sic*] 1947," *Tschechoslowakei,* 4/2:13.

60. "Erlebnisbericht der Frau A. L., ehemals Nachrichtenhelferin in Prag . . . 17. April 1952," ibid., 139.

61. "Erlebnisbericht der Buchhalterin Adele Scholtz aus Leibitz bei Käsmark, Oberzips . . . 22. August 1954," ibid., 752.

62. "Erlebnisbericht von Frau A. K. aus Gerdauen i. Ostpr. . . . 18. März 1951," *Oder-Neisse,* 1/2:17.

63. Lehndorff, *Bericht,* 57.

64. "Erlebnisbericht der Schneiderin Anna Schwartz," *Oder-Neisse,* 1/2:95.

65. "Erlebnisbericht der Frau Ruth Dorsch aus Rössel i. Ostpr. . . . 10. No-

vember 1952," ibid., 176; and "Erlebnisbericht des ehemaligen Bürgermeisters Franz Hickl aus Mahrisch Trübau . . . Ende 1954," *Tschechoslowakei*, 4/2:42.

66. "Erlebnisbericht eines Tierarztes aus dem Ungarischen Banat," n.d., *Ungarn*, 2:47.

67. "'Oder' or 'Siberia'": quoted in Normann, *Tagebuch*, 122.

68. "Erlebnisbericht von Annemarie Kniep aus Loschkeim, Kreis Bartenstein i. Ostpr. . . . Februar 1946," *Oder-Neisse*, 1/1:102–3.

69. "Erlebnisbericht der Hausfrau Hermine Mückusch aus Jägerndorf . . . August 1947," *Tschechoslowakei*, 4/2:368.

70. "Erlebnisbericht von Frau Charlotte Dölling aus Bütow i. Pom. . . . 10. Januar 1953," *Oder-Neisse*, 1/1:247.

71. "Bericht des B. S. aus Bistritz (Bistriţa), Judeţ Năsăud (Nassod) in Nord-Siebenbürgen . . . 24. Februar 1956," *Rumänien*, 3:121.

72. "Erlebnisbericht der Hausfrau Hermine Mückusch," *Tschechoslowakei*, 4/2:366.

73. "Erlebnisbericht der Frau Maria Zatschek aus Brünn," n.d., ibid., 449.

74. "Erlebnisbericht der Lehrerin Mathilde Maurer aus Sächsisch-Sankt Georgen (Sângeorzul-Nou), Plasa Şieu (Grossschogen), Judeţ Năsăud (Nassod) in Nord Siebenbürgen . . . 22. Mai 1956," *Rumänien*, 3:345.

75. Normann, *Tagebuch*, 125.

76. "Erlebnisbericht der Pastorenfrau Annemarie Glück aus Filehne, Kreis Czarniskau i. Posen . . . Februar 1949," *Oder-Neisse*, 1/1:372, 374.

77. "Bericht von Frau Dr. I. R. aus Schreiberhau, Kreis Hirschberg/Riesengebirge i. Niederschles. . . . September 1946," ibid., 1/2:362.

78. "Bericht des Oberst a. D. Eberhard Schöpffer aus Elbing i. Westpr. . . . 22. März 1952," ibid., 1/1:317.

79. "Befragungsbericht nach Aussagen des Angestellten Stefan Blum aus Beremend, Bezirk Siklós im Komitat Baranya . . . 25. Juli 1952," *Ungarn*, 2:83; and "Erlebnisbericht des Dipl.-Ing. Otto Hölter aus Mährisch Ostrau . . . 2. April 1955," *Tschechoslowakei*, 4/2:137.

80. "Bericht des ehemaligen Bezirksbürgermeisters H. aus Breslau," *Oder-Neisse*, 1/2:327.

81. *Ungarn*, 2:31E, 43E, 46E.

82. *Tschechoslowakei*, 4/1:62.

83. "Erlebnisbericht einer Bauersfrau aus Budaörs, Bezirk Köspont im Komitat Pest," n.d., *Ungarn*, 2:175; and "Erlebnisbericht des Kaufmanns Matthias Kaiser aus Hetin, Bezirk Modosch (Jaša Tomić) im Banat . . . 1946/47," *Jugoslawien*, 5: 226. See also Herbert, "'Die guten und die schlechten Zeiten,'" 67–96.

84. "Erlebnisbericht des Tischlermeisters Franz Meditz aus Büchel (Hrib) in der Gottschee . . . 23. März 1958," *Jugoslawien*, 5:167.

85. "Erlebnisbericht des Landwirts Johann Brendel aus Krummöls, Kreis Löwenberg i. Niederschles. . . . 12. Januar 1953," *Oder-Neisse*, 1/2:700.

86. "Erlebnisbericht des Kaufmanns Matthias Kaiser aus Hetin," *Jugoslawien*, 5:222.

87. "Bericht des Kaplan Paul Pfuhl aus Filipovo, Bezirk Hodschag (Odžaci) in der Batschka . . . 19. Oktober 1956," ibid., 262. See the introduction to Lem-

berg and Edding (eds.), *Die Vertriebenen,* 1:4; and Jolles, *Zur Soziologie der Heimatvertriebenen,* 265.

88. "Erlebnisbericht des Grosskaufmanns Dr. August Kurt Lassmann aus Troppau," n.d., *Tschechoslowakei,* 4/2:46.

89. See the summary of this procedure in *Findbuch Ost-Dokumentation 2: Erlebnisbericht zur Dokumentation der Vertreibung der Deutschen aus Ost-Mitteleuropa, Sudetenland und Südosteuropa (Personenschicksale),* prepared by Tiebel [1962], in BAK; also Schieder's "Arbeitsplan für die Authentizierung des Materials zur Vertreibung von Deutschen aus den Ostgebieten," 25 Oct. 1951, BAK, B150/4171/Heft 1.

90. On the plan for an "Ergebnisband," see the detailed discussion in Beer, "Im Spannungsfeld von Politik," 378–85; idem, "Dokumentation der Vertreibung," 109–12; and idem, "'Neuanfang,'" 281–90; also, Schieder to Theodor Oberländer, BVFK, 18 Mar. 1957, with an outline of the proposed volume, BAK, B150/4173. In his 1960 article "Die Vertreibung der Deutschen aus dem Osten als wissenschaftliches Problem," Schieder also suggests this larger framework. In the work of Martin Broszat and the Institut für Zeitgeschichte, at least some of this agenda was ultimately realized; see, e.g., Martin Broszat, *National-sozialistische Polenpolitik, 1939–1945* (Frankfurt am Main: Fischer, [1961] 1965); and Hans Mommsen, "Zeitgeschichte als 'kritische Aufklärungsarbeit': Zur Erinnerung an Martin Broszat (1926–1989)," *Geschichte und Gesellschaft* 17 (1991): 142. It is, however, worth noting that in neither Schieder's proposals nor the work of the Institut were there any plans for collecting eyewitness accounts of the victims of Germans, which would have served as a counterpoint to the voices gathered in the volumes on the expulsion.

91. See Anthony Komajathy and Rebecca Stockwell, *German Minorities and the Third Reich: Ethnic Germans of East Central Europe between the Wars* (New York: Holmes & Meier, 1980); Lumans, *Himmler's Auxiliaries;* idem, "Ethnic German Minority"; Rolf-Dieter Müller, *Hitlers Ostkrieg und die deutsche Sied-lungspolitik: Die Zusammenarbeit von Wehrmacht, Wirtschaft und SS* (Frankfurt am Main: Fischer, 1991); Martin Broszat, "Faschismus und Kollaboration in Ostmitteleuropa zwischen den Weltkriegen," *Vierteljahrshefte für Zeitge-schichte* 14 (1966): 225–51; and Wiskemann, *Germany's Eastern Neighbours,* 114–15. On the extensive use of forced slave labor, see Herbert, *Fremdarbeiter;* idem, "Labour and Extermination: Economic Interest and the Primacy of Weltan-schauung in National Socialism," *Past and Present,* no. 138 (1993): 144–95; and Lüdtke, "Appeal of Exterminating 'Others,'" S63–S65.

92. "Erlebnisbericht der Angestellten Eva Kuckuk aus Königsberg i. Ostpr. . . . 2. Oktober 1952," *Oder-Neisse,* 1/1:84.

93. "Bericht des ehemaligen Kreisbauernführers G. Fieguth aus Tiegenhof, Kreis Gr. Werder i. Westpr. . . . 12. September 1952," ibid., 292.

94. "Erlebnisbericht des Gutsbeamten A. B. aus Eichmedien," ibid., 1/2:185.

95. "Erlebnisbericht des Reg.-Inspektors E. Wollmann aus Friedland (Is-ergebirge) . . . 27. April 1953," *Tschechoslowakei,* 4/2:386; also Lehndorff, *Bericht,* 73.

96. "Gold birds": "Erlebnisbericht der Frau Wilhelmine von Hoffmann aus Reichenberg . . . Winter 1956/57," *Tschechoslowakei,* 4/2:680.

97. "Erlebnisbericht des A. S. aus Leba, Kreis Lauenburg i. Pom. . . . 9. August 1950," *Oder-Neisse,* 1/1:270.

98. "Bericht des Journalisten Friedrich v. Wilpert aus Danzig, ehemals Rittmeister und Ordonnanzoffizier des Befehlshabers im Raum Danzig-Gdingen . . . Februar 1953," ibid., 284. On resistance to recruitment in the Waffen-SS, see in particular a series of reports in *Jugoslawien,* 5:65–87.

99. T. Schieder, "Die Vertreibung als Wissenschaftliches Problem," 13.

100. "Erlebnisbericht des Pfarrers Peter Fischer aus Dalj, Bezirk Esseg (Osijek) in Slawonien . . . 23. Mai 1958," *Jugoslawien,* 5:538.

101. "Bericht des ehemaligen Bezirksbürgermeisters H. aus Breslau," *Oder-Neisse,* 1/2:333.

102. "Erlebnisbericht des ehemaligen Landrats des Kreises Samland, v.d. Gröben . . . September 1952," ibid., 1/1:136.

103. "Erlebnisbericht von Berginspektor a. D. Karl Wasner aus Friedenshütte, Kreis Königshütte i. Oberschles. . . . August 1952," *Oder-Neisse,* 1/1:406.

104. "Erlebnisbericht des ehemaligen Direktors des Jakob-Bleyer-Gymnasiums Dr. Johannes Weidlein aus Budapest . . . 27. August 1952," *Ungarn,* 2:15.

105. "Bericht des Majors i. G., a. D. Udo Ritgen aus Gr. Falkenau, Kreis Rosenberg i. Westpr. . . . 12. November 1952," *Oder-Neisse,* 1/1:322.

106. "Erlebnisbericht der M. W. aus Landeshut i. Niederschles. . . . 24. Oktober 1951," ibid., 1/2:439–40; and for references to similar cases, 441n.1.

107. "Erlebnisbericht der Lehrerin Mathilde Maurer," *Rumänien,* 3:350; "Befragungsbericht nach Aussagen des Angestellten Stefan Blum aus Beremend," *Ungarn,* 2:83.

108. "Bericht des Bibliotheksdirektors i. R. Hans Kreal aus Iglau . . . 5. Mai 1955," *Tschechoslowakei,* 4/2:182.

109. "Erlebnisbericht eines Bauern aus dem Bezirk Központ im Komitat Pest . . . 3. Mai 1955," *Ungarn,* 2:91.

110. "Befragungsbericht nach Aussagen von Frau R. A. aus Dunabogdány, Bezirk Pomáz im Komitat Pest . . . 15. April 1951," ibid., 95.

111. "Erlebnisbericht des F. J. aus Waier, Kreis Bischofteinitz . . . 1955," *Tschechoslowakei,* 4/2:83.

112. "Erlebnisbericht der Frau Wilhelmine von Hoffmann aus Reichenberg," ibid., 681.

113. "Erlebnisbericht des Ingenieurs Gustav Grüner aus Asch," n.d., ibid., 467.

114. "Erlebnisbericht des Maklers B. F. aus Breslau . . . Januar 1953," *Oder-Neisse,* 1/2:342.

115. "Bericht des Dipl.-Ing. H. F. aus Pressburg, ehemals Kulturreferent in den volksdeutschen Organisationen der Slowakei . . . 23. Mai 1952," *Tschechoslowakei,* 4/2:733.

116. "Erlebnisbericht der E. L. aus Posen . . . 17. April 1951," *Oder-Neisse,* 1/2:572.

117. Lehndorff, *Bericht,* 66.

118. "Erlebnisbericht der Frau Maria Zatschek aus Brünn," *Tschechoslowakei,* 4/2:439.

119. "Erlebnisbericht des Dozenten Dr. Korkisch aus Prag . . . 2. März 1947," ibid., 144.

120. "Protokollierte Aussage der Ch. Sch. aus Sombor in der Batschka . . . April 1955," *Jugoslawien*, 5: 177.

121. "Erlebnisbericht (Brief) des Kaufmanns und ehemaligen Stadtrats Hubert Schütz sen. aus Jägerndorf . . . 4. Januar 1947," *Tschechoslowakei*, 4/2: 216.

122. See the highly suggestive comments of Utz Jeggle, "Sage und Verbrechen," in Schulze, Brelie-Lewien, and Grebing (eds.), *Flüchtlinge und Vertriebene*, 201–6; also A. Lehmann, *Im Fremden ungewollt zuhaus*, 240–41; and Plato, "Fremde Heimat," 198–99.

123. "Erlebnisbericht des Pfarrers Pöss aus Glaserhau im Hauerland . . . 22. September 1951," *Tschechoslowakei*, 4/2:769–70. See also, e.g., "Protokollierte Aussage der Margarethe Themare aus Deutsch-Zerne (Nemačka Crnja), Bezirk Modosch (Jaša Tomić) im Banat . . . 5. Juli 1946," *Jugoslawien*, 5:219 and the editorial note, 219–20.

124. "Protokollierte Aussage der Katharina Haller aus Neu-Schowe (Nove Šove), Bezirk Neusatz (Novi Sad) in der Batschka . . . 20. Januar 1952," *Jugoslawien*, 5:402–3.

125. "Erlebnisbericht der Hausfrau Maria Spiegl aus Mies . . . März 1947," *Tschechoslowakei*, 4/2:331.

126. "Erlebnisbericht der Hilda Kautzner aus Karlsdorf (Banatski Karlovac), Bezirk Weisskirchen (Bela Crkva) im Banat . . . 17. März 1958," *Jugoslawien*, 5:298.

127. "Brief des Handelsvertreters Berthold Anders aus Lodz . . . 14. Juli 1946," *Oder-Neisse*, 1/2:56.

128. "Erlebnisbericht der Lehrerin Mathilde Maurer," *Rumänien*, 3:341.

129. "Erlebnisbericht des Superintendenten W. L. aus Schivelbein, Kreis Belgard i. Pom. . . . 31. Januar 1952," *Oder-Neisse*, 1/2:759.

130. "Erlebnisbericht des Photographen Josef Buhl (gest. 11. November 1947) aus Klodebach, Kreis Grottkau i. Oberschles. . . . 1946/47," ibid., 792. Cf. Claudia Koonz, *Mothers in the Fatherland: Women, the Family, and Nazi Politics* (New York: St. Martin's Press, 1987), 405.

131. "Erlebnisbericht des F. K. aus Burgkampen (Jentkutkampen), Kreis Ebenrode (Stallupönen) i. Ostpr. . . . November 1951," *Oder-Neisse*, 1/2:12.

132. "Erlebnisbericht des Bauern Peter Koy aus Tolkemit, Kreis Elbing i. Westpr. . . . 21. Dezember 1952," ibid., 26. See also, e.g., charges that Germans feared the Poles' "passion for gold," which led them to rip "gold teeth . . . out of your mouth," in "Bericht von Frau Dr. I. R. aus Schreiberhau," ibid., 356.

133. See "Erlebnisbericht des Gabriel Lang aus Ragendorf (Rajka) im Komitat Moson (Wieselburg) . . . April 1955," *Ungarn*, 2:40; "Erlebnisbericht eines Tierarztes aus dem Ungarischen Banat," ibid., 47; and "Erlebnisbericht eines Bauern aus dem Bezirk Központ im Komitat Pest," ibid., 33.

134. On the use of the press in the U.S. zone to communicate details of Nazi atrocities, particularly the practices of the concentration camps, see Elisabeth Matz, *Die Zeitungen der US-Armee für die deutsche Bevölkerung (1944–1946)* (Münster [Westf.]: C. J. Fahle, 1969), 52–56; Chamberlin, "Todesmühlen," 420–36; and in general, on the "collective guilt" thesis, pushed particularly aggressively by the U.S. and British forces of occupation immediately after the war's end, Barbro Eberan, *Luther? Friedrich "der Grosse"? Wagner? Nietzsche? . . . ?*

. . . ? *Wer war an Hitler schuld? Die Debatte um die Schuldfrage, 1945–1949* (Munich: Minerva, 1983), esp. 21–25.

135. "Erlebnisbericht von Irene Kahl aus Königsbach (Bukowiec), Kreis Lodz i. Polen . . . 13. Juli 1952," *Oder-Neisse,* 1/1:348.

136. *Tschechoslowakei,* 4/1:81; see also *Oder-Neisse,* 1/1:111E.

137. "Bericht des Kaufmanns E. M. aus Saaz . . . November 1945," *Tschechoslowakei,* 4/2:313, and ibid., n.2.

138. Quotations from Inge Kellerman to the British Military Government in Berlin, 1 June 1946, copy forwarded by the Sudeten German interest group organization, BAK, Ost-Dok 2/312, 349; and report of a Sudeten German, BAK, Ost-Dok 2/260, 417.

139. *Oder-Neisse,* 1/1:112E.

140. "Bericht des Kaplan Paul Pfuhl aus Filipovo," *Jugoslawien,* 5:261.

141. "Bericht des Organisationssekretärs Roman Wirkner aus Tetschen . . . 1957," *Tschechoslowakei,* 4/2:527.

142. Normann, *Tagebuch,* 33. See also Göttinger Arbeitskreis, ed., *Dokumente der Menschlichkeit aus der Zeit der Massenaustreibungen,* 2d ed. (Würzburg: Holzner, 1960). This collection was first published in 1950, and an English-language edition followed in 1954.

143. "Erlebnisbericht des A. S. aus Schlagenthin," *Oder-Neisse,* 1/1:199–200; and "Bericht der Frau E. K. aus Gr. Küdde, Kreis Neustettin i. Pom. . . . 4. Januar 1952," ibid., 205–6.

144. "Erlebnisbericht des Bauern Hans Hanel aus Freihermersdorf, Kreis Freudenthal . . . 19. Februar 1953," *Tschechoslowakei,* 4/2:261, 263.

145. Alfred Karasek-Langer, "Volkstum im Umbruch," in Lemberg and Edding (eds.), *Die Vertriebenen,* 1:654; also Lemberg, "Völkerpsychologische und weltgeschichtliche Aspekte," ibid., 3:587–90; and Pfeil, *Flüchtling,* 145, 206.

146. Some of the reports from Yugoslavia were gathered as late as 1959 (see BAK, Ost-Dok 2/410, Batschka, Bezirk Sombor), and the published reports include examples from 1958 and 1959.

147. See Gottfried Niedhardt and Normen Altmann, "Zwischen Beurteilung und Verurteilung: Die Sowjetunion im Urteil Konrad Adenauers," in Foschepoth (ed.), *Adenauer und die deutsche Frage,* 99–117.

148. Quoted in *Tschechoslowakei,* 4/2:195–96n.3.

149. *Oder-Neisse,* 1/1:60E.

150. Beer, "Dokumentation der Vertreibung," 116.

151. For contemporary reviews of Lehndorff's diary, see Josef Müller-Marein, "'Bittet, dass eure Flucht nicht im Winter geschehe': Die Niederschriften des Chirurgen Dr. Graf Lehndorff und das Schicksal der Deutschen," *Die Zeit,* 19 May 1961, copy in BAK, B150/5644. The book also was included in the top-pick list for September 1961 (see "Unser Seller-Teller September 1961," *Die Zeit,* 6 Oct. 1961); it was in ninth place in the end-of-year review ("Unser Seller-Teller Dezember 1961," ibid., 5 Jan. 1962); and it topped the list the following March ("Unser Seller-Teller März 1962," ibid., 6 Apr. 1962; copies in BAK, B150/5644). Gaining an even broader circulation, the book also appeared in serialized form in the *Bonner Rundschau* in September 1961 and in the tabloid *Bild-Zeitung* from December 1961 to January 1962. On the abiding impact of the individual

diaries, see Helbig, *Der ungeheuere Verlust,* 69. In a German bookstore in the summer of 1997, I purchased a copy of the latest edition of Lehndorff's diary published by Deutscher Taschenbuch Verlag; this was the twenty-second edition, and 171,000 copies of the DTV edition were in circulation.

152. On the importance of this recognition, denied other groups of victims, see William G. Niederland, "Die verkannten Opfer: Späte Entschädigung für seelische Schäden," in Herbst and Goschler (eds.), *Wiedergutmachung,* 359; and Herbert, "Nicht entschädigungsfähig?" ibid., 302.

153. *Oder-Neisse,* 1/1:442.

154. Quotations are respectively from "Dokumente des Grauens," *Stuttgarter Zeitung,* 2 Sept. 1954; and "Katastrophen der Deutschen-Vertreibung aus dem Osten in Dokumenten," *Westdeutsche Allgemeine Zeitung,* 6 May 1954.

155. Kogon, *Der NS-Staat;* Hans Guenter Adler, *Theresienstadt, 1941–1945: Das Antlitz einer Zwangsgemeinschaft* (Tübingen: J. C. B. Mohr [Paul Siebeck], 1955); and idem, *Die verheimlichte Wahrheit: Theresienstädter Dokumente* (Tübingen: J. C. B. Mohr [Paul Siebeck], 1958).

156. Otto D. Kulka, "Major Trends and Tendencies in German Historiography on National Socialism and the 'Jewish Question' (1924–1984)," *Yearbook of the Leo Baeck Institute* 30 (1985): 222. See also the useful reflections of Dan Diner, "Zwischen Bundesrepublik und Deutschland: Ein Vortrag," in *Von der Gnade der geschenkten Nation,* ed. Hajo Funke (Berlin: Rotbuch, 1988), 194–95.

157. Helmut Peitsch, *"Deutschlands Gedächtnis an seine dunkelste Zeit": Zur Funktion der Autobiographik in den Westzonen Deutschlands und den Westsektoren von Berlin, 1945 bis 1949* (Berlin: Edition Sigma, 1990), 55–60, 101–2. See also Grossmann, "Trauma, Memory, and Motherhood," 215–39.

158. Alvin H. Rosenfeld, "Popularization and Memory: The Case of Anne Frank," in *Lessons and Legacies: The Meaning of the Holocaust in a Changing World,* ed. Peter Hayes (Evanston, Ill.: Northwestern University Press, 1991), 251, 259, 264, 266, 268, 270; Anat Feinberg, *Wiedergutmachung im Programm: Jüdisches Schicksal im deutschen Nachkriegsdrama* (Cologne: Prometh, 1988), 17–18; and Adorno, "What Does Coming to Terms with the Past Mean?" 127.

159. Alfred Karasek-Langer, "Volkskundliche Erkenntnisse aus der Vertreibung und Eingliederung der Ostdeutschen," *Jahrbuch für Volkskunde der Heimatvertriebenen* 1 (1955): 24. See also Lehmann, *Im Fremden ungewollt zuhaus,* 229; and Jeggle, "Sage und Verbrechen," 201–6.

160. The quotations are respectively from "Erlebnisbericht von Annemarie Kniep aus Koschkeim," *Oder-Neisse,* 1:1/102; and "Erlebnisbericht des Pfarrers i.R. Prof. Friedrich Krauss aus Bistritz (Bistriţa), Judeţ Năsăud (Nassod) in Nord-Siebenbürgen . . . 6. September 1956," *Rumänien,* 3:151.

161. See the useful comments of Arno J. Mayer, "Memory and History: On the Poverty of Remembering and Forgetting the Judeocide," *Radical History Review,* no. 54 (1993): 13.

162. "Dokumente," *Deutsche Zeitung und Wirtschafts-Zeitung,* 24 Mar. 1954, copy in BAK, B150/5641.

Chapter Four

1. Falk Bente, "Heidelberg grüsst seine Heimkehrer," *Rhein-Neckar-Zeitung,* 12 Oct. 1955.

2. Elizabeth Heineman, in "Hour of the Woman," argues that in the immediate postwar period, women's stories became Germany's stories, but a decade later, when POWs returned from the Soviet Union, it was the "hour of the man."

3. Jan Molitor, "Die letzten Soldaten des grossen Krieges," *Die Zeit,* 13 Oct. 1955. See also Otto Mark, "Die letzten Soldaten," *Münchener Merkur,* 11 Oct. 1955, PIB MF 2191.

4. The phrase is from Rudolf Augstein, publisher of *Der Spiegel,* quoted in H.-P. Schwarz, *Ära Adenauer,* 365.

5. Letter to Adenauer, 5 Aug. 1955, PAAA, Abt. 2/1994.

6. Hans Schuster, "In Bonn gehen die Uhren anders als in Weimar"; Gerda Bödefeld, "Aus Hungerrationen wurden Riesenportionen"; and Walter Slotosch, "Der Weg vom Hunger zur Hochkonjunktur"; all in *Süddeutsche Zeitung,* 8–9 Oct. 1955.

7. "Wooly mammoths": Erich Kuby, "Mit dem Blick auf Friedland," *Süddeutsche Zeitung,* 11 Oct. 1955.

8. On the relationship of the print media to the construction of public memory, see Naumann, "Im Sog des Endes," 176. Also useful is the discussion in Peter Fritzsche, *Reading Berlin 1900* (Cambridge, Mass.: Harvard University Press, 1996), 25–26.

9. In general, see Josef Foschepoth, "Westintegration statt Wiedervereinigung: Adenauers Deutschlandpolitik, 1949–1955," in Foschepoth (ed.), *Adenauer und die deutsche Frage,* 29–60.

10. See Boris Meissner, ed., *Moskau-Bonn: Die Beziehungen zwischen der Sowjetunion und der Bundesrepublik Deutschland, 1955–1973, Dokumentation* (Cologne: Wissenschaft und Politik, 1975), 14; Bruno Thoss, "Der Beitritt der Bundesrepublik zur WEU und NATO im Spannungsfeld von Blockbildung und Entspannung (1954–1956)," in Hans Ehlert, Christian Greiner, Georg Meyer, and Bruno Thoss, *Anfänge westdeutscher Sicherheitspolitik 1945–1956,* vol. 3 of *Die NATO-Option,* ed. Militärgeschichtliches Forschungsamt (Munich: R. Oldenbourg, 1993), 154–77; and, in general, Josef Foschepoth, "Adenauers Moskaureise 1955," *Aus Politik und Zeitgeschichte: Beilage zur Wochenzeitung "Das Parlament,"* B22 (1986): 30–46; Max Schulze-Vorberg, "Die Moskaureise, 1955," in *Konrad Adenauer und seine Zeit: Politik und Persönlichkeit des ersten Bundeskanzlers,* vol. 1: *Beiträge von Weg- und Zeitgenossen,* ed. Dieter Blumenwitz et al. (Stuttgart: Deutsche Verlags-Anstalt, 1976), 651–64; and Ludolf Herbst, "Stil und Handlungsspielräume westdeutscher Integrationspolitik," in *Vom Marshallplan zur EWG: Die Eingliederung der Bundesrepublik Deutschland in die westliche Welt,* ed. Ludolf Herbst, Werner Bührer, and Hanno Sowade (Munich: R. Oldenbourg, 1990), 5–17.

11. In addition to Meissner, *Moskau-Bonn,* see Christoph Klessmann, "Adenauers Deutschland- und Ostpolitik 1955–1963," in Foschepoth (ed.), *Adenauer und die deutsche Frage,* 62–64; Foschepoth, "Adenauers Moskaureise 1955"; Rainer Salzmann, "Adenauers Moskaureise in sowjetischer Sicht," in Blumen-

witz et al. (eds.), *Konrad Adenauer und seine Zeit,* vol. 2: *Beiträge der Wissenschaft* (Stuttgart: Deutsche Verlags-Anstalt, 1976), 131–59; and Adolf M. Birke, *Nation ohne Haus: Deutschland, 1945–1961* (Berlin: Wolf Jobst Siedler Verlag, 1989), 447–53.

12. The newspapers I consulted include: *Der Abend* (Berlin); *abz Illustrierte* (Düsseldorf); *Allgemeine Wochenzeitung der Juden in Deutschland; Bunte Illustrierte; Frankfurter Allgemeine Zeitung; Frankfurter Rundschau; Hamburger Abendblatt; Kölnische Rundschau; Quick; Revue; Rhein-Neckar-Zeitung; Rheinischer Merkur; Der Stern; Stuttgarter Nachrichten; Süddeutsche Zeitung; Der Tagesspiegel; Der Telegraf* (Berlin); *Die Welt; Westdeutsche Allgemeine Zeitung; Westfälische Rundschau;* and *Die Zeit.* In addition, I made extensive use of the excellent press clippings collection of the Presse- und Informationsamt der Bundesregierung in Bonn. Articles that are not from the newspapers listed above come from that collection. My thanks to Harold Marcuse for making me aware of this invaluable collection. My approach in this chapter has been influenced by the work of Susan Jeffords, *The Remasculinization of America: Gender and the Vietnam War* (Bloomington: Indiana University Press, 1989). See also Emily S. Rosenberg, "Walking the Borders," *Diplomatic History* 14 (1990): 565–73; and idem, "'Foreign Affairs' after World War II: Connecting Sexual and International Politics," *Diplomatic History* 18 (1994): 59–70.

13. Georg Schröder, "Adenauer und Bulganin bekräftigen den Willen zu guten Beziehungen," *Die Welt,* 10 Sept. 1955. See also "Diktatoren von heute," *Spiegel,* 14 Sept. 1955; and Hilmar Pabel, "Mit der Kamera nach Moskau," *Quick,* 10 Sept. 1955. On the history of Friedland, see Bundesministerium für Vertriebene, Flüchtlinge und Kriegsgeschädigte, ed., *20 Jahre Lager Friedland* (n.p., n.d. [Bonn, 1965]).

14. Norbert Frei, "Die Presse," in *Die Geschichte der Bundesrepublik Deutschland,* vol. 4: *Kultur,* ed. Wolfgang Benz (Frankfurt am Main: Fischer Taschenbuch Verlag, 1989), 393; Axel Schildt, *Moderne Zeiten: Freizeit, Massenmedien und "Zeitgeist" in der Bundesrepublik der 50er Jahre* (Hamburg: Hans Christians, 1995), 268; and idem, "From Reconstruction to 'Leisure Society': Free Time, Recreational Behaviour, and the Discourse on Leisure Time in West German Recovery Society of the 1950s," *Contemporary European History* 5 (1996): 203.

15. Hans Zehrer, "Volk ohne Heimkehr," *Die Welt,* 15 Oct. 1955.

16. Paul Weymar, *Konrad Adenauer: Die autorisierte Biographie* (Munich: Kindler, 1955), 348. The biography was serialized in the illustrated weekly *Revue,* and also appeared in serialized installments in the *Kölnische Rundschau* in the fall of 1955. See also Henning Köhler, *Adenauer: Eine politische Biographie* (Frankfurt am Main: Propyläen, 1994), 447.

17. Ian Kershaw, *The "Hitler Myth": Image and Reality in the Third Reich* (Oxford: Oxford University Press, 1987), 59, 72, 79; and Koonz, *Mothers in the Fatherland,* 67.

18. Letters to Adenauer, 19 and 9 Aug. 1955, PAAA, Abt. 2/1993 and 2/2026. I have provided no identifying information about letter writers in order to preserve their privacy.

19. Letter to Adenauer, 17 July 1955, from 124 men and women in Essen,

including members of the League of Returning Veterans (Verband der Heimkehrer), PAAA, Abt. 2/2000.

20. Liesel Hartmann to Adenauer, 19 Aug. 1955, PAAA, Abt. 2/1993. Hartmann would ultimately not only be able to embrace her son, but she could also read about him in the paper. Steadfastly resisting all Communist entreaties to fly for the "Soviet zone" in return for release, he would return in October to West Germany, where his "accomplishment will remain a part of the history of flying." See "Zwölf Jahre nach Schatalowka," *Die Welt,* 19 Oct. 1955; also Manfred Lütgenhorst, "'Ich pfeife auf das Ehrenwort eines russischen Offiziers,'" *Münchener Merkur,* 17 Oct. 1955. Because she was identified in these other sources, I have named Hartmann as the author of the letter.

21. Letter to Adenauer, 24 Apr. 1955, PAAA, Abt. 2/1989.

22. Letters to Adenauer, 28, 22, and 19 Aug. 1955, PAAA, Abt. 2/1994 and 2/1993.

23. Letter to Adenauer, 3 Sept. 1955, PAAA, Abt. 2/1998.

24. Letter to Adenauer, 30 Aug. 1955, PAAA, Abt. 2/1994.

25. Letter to Adenauer, 2 Aug. 1955, PAAA, Abt. 2/1999.

26. Letter to Adenauer, 23 Aug. 1955, signed by nine children from the Protestant Volksschule in Kisselbach, PAAA, Abt. 2/1996.

27. Letter to Adenauer, 31 Aug. 1955, PAAA, Abt. 2/1994.

28. Letter to Hallstein, 6 May 1955, PAAA, Abt. 2/1989.

29. Letter to Adenauer, 6 May 1955, PAAA, Abt. 2/1989.

30. Letter to Adenauer, 16 Aug. 1955, PAAA, Abt. 2/1992. See also "Mehr Aktion notwending," *Tagesspiegel,* 23 Oct. 1954; "SPD: Bundesregierung war nicht aktiv genug," *General-Anzeiger für Bonn und Umgegend,* 30 July 1955; and "Streit um die Gefangenenfrage," *Frankfurter Allgemeine Zeitung,* 1 Aug. 1955. See also Karl-Heinz Janssen, "Heimkehr—fünf Jahre zu spät," *Die Zeit,* 8 Jan. 1993.

31. See a copy of this form letter from the chancellor's staff (Bundeskanzleramt) dated September 1955, PAAA, Abt. 2/1995.

32. Foschepoth, "Adenauers Moskaureise 1955," 32–33, quoting *Jahrbuch der öffentlichen Meinung,* 1957, 209.

33. Erich Dombrowski, "Nicht nur Kriegsgefangene," *Frankfurter Allgemeine Zeitung,* 9 Sept. 1955. See also Hergt memo in preparation for Moscow trip, 11 Aug. 1955, PAAA, Abt. 2/1992; and for an interesting set of reflections on the domestic importance of the issue from the U.S. perspective, see Conant to Department of State, 13 Jan. 1955, NA, RG 59, Central Files, 661.6224/1–1355.

34. On the rehabilitation of the national carrier, see "Lufthansa: Die Tabellen-Piloten," *Spiegel,* 25 May 1955, 32–40.

35. Picture caption in *Stern,* 25 Sept. 1955.

36. One estimate put the price tag for the trip at around 1 million DM; see the memo prepared by Haenlein in the Bundeskanzleramt, 3 Aug. 1955, BAK, B136/2053. See also Konrad Adenauer, *Erinnerungen, 1953–1955* (Stuttgart: Deutsche Verlags-Anstalt, 1966), 497.

37. See Arno Scholz, "Die Stadt der Gegensätze," *Telegraf,* 11 Sept. 1955;

Guido Zöller, "Die Eroberung von Moskau," *Rheinischer Merkur,* 16 Sept. 1955; and the photo essay in *Stern,* 18 Sept. 1955.

38. "Will to consume": Ludwig Erhard, "Einen Kühlschrank in jeden Haushalt," *Welt der Arbeit,* 16 June 1953, republished in idem, *Deutsche Wirtschaftspolitik: Der Weg der sozialen Marktwirtschaft* (Düsseldorf: Econ, 1962), 221. See also idem, *Wohlstand für alle* (Düsseldorf: Econ, [1957] 1960), 234, 239, 241.

39. Zöller, "Eroberung von Moskau," *Rheinischer Merkur,* 16 Sept. 1955. See also picture captions, attributed to Ernst Grossar, in *Stern,* 18 Sept. 1955; and "Sonderangebote der Fleischer," *Hamburger Abendblatt,* 8 Sept. 1955.

40. Zöller, "Eroberung von Moskau," *Rheinischer Merkur,* 16 Sept. 1955. See also "Reise in eine andere Welt," *Westfälische Nachrichten,* 10 Sept. 1955; and Immanuel Birnbaum, "Begegnung zweier Welten," *Süddeutsche Zeitung,* 10 Sept. 1955.

41. See *Stern,* 30 Oct. 1955. This photo essay stressed that "Der seidene Vorhang trennt im Land der Mode die Welt des Ostens und des Westens ebenso, wie der eiserne Vorhang die politischen Welten trennt" (In the land of fashion, the silk curtain divides the world of East and West in the same way the iron curtain divides the political worlds).

42. Zöller, "Eroberung von Moskau," *Rheinischer Merkur,* 16 Sept. 1955.

43. Arno Scholz, "Die Stadt der Gegensätze," *Telegraf,* 11 Sept. 1955. See also Heinz Meske, "Stadt ohne Erotik," *Abend,* 21 Sept. 1955; and the picture in *Stern,* 18 Sept. 1955, captioned "Überall in Moskau arbeiten Frauen." In addition, see Wilhelm Backhaus, *Begegnung im Kreml: So wurden die Gefangenen befreit* (Berlin: Ullstein, 1955), 26.

44. See Adenauer's comments before the CDU Bundestag caucus on 30 September 1955 in Günter Buchstab, ed., *Adenauer—"Wir haben wirklich etwas geschaffen": Die Protokolle des CDU-Bundesvorstandes, 1953–1957* (Düsseldorf: Droste, 1990), 596; and Adenauer, *Erinnerungen,* 531; also Niedhardt and Altmann, "Zwischen Beurteilung und Verurteilung," 105.

45. Quotation in "Impressionen am Rande der Moskauer Konferenz," *Stuttgarter Zeitung,* 12 Sept. 1955. In general, see Moeller, *Protecting Motherhood;* also Erica Carter, "Alice in Consumer Wonderland: West German Case Studies in Gender and Consumer Culture," in Moeller (ed.), *West Germany Under Construction,* 347–71; idem, *How German Is She? Postwar West German Reconstruction and the Consuming Woman* (Ann Arbor: University of Michigan Press, 1997); and the half-page ad in *Die Welt,* 10 Oct. 1955, showing a smiling economics minister, Ludwig Erhard, with an address "An alle Hausfrauen!"

46. Clifton Daniel, "Bulganin Rejects Prisoner Issue in German Talks," *New York Times,* 11 Sept. 1955; idem, "Germans to Raise Prisoner Issue Again in Moscow," ibid., 12 Sept. 1955.

47. Adenauer's opening statement, 9 September 1955, in Meissner, *Moskau-Bonn,* 85.

48. Bulganin's declaration of 10 September 1955, ibid., 89–91. See also Backhaus, *Begegnung im Kreml,* 41.

49. Adenauer, statement of 10 September 1955, in Meissner (ed.), *Moskau-Bonn*, 92–94.

50. Khrushchev, statement of 10 September 1955, ibid., 96–97; and Molotov, statement of 10 September 1955, ibid., 99.

51. Indeed, in his memoirs Adenauer recalls stating this explicitly, directly posing to Molotov the rhetorical question, "Who actually concluded the agreement with Hitler, you or I?" See Adenauer, *Erinnerungen*, 515.

52. Paul Wilhelm Wenger, "Was nun?" *Rheinischer Merkur*, 23 Sept. 1955. See also "Die Gipfel-Taktik" and "200 Jahre deutsch-russische Beziehungen," *Spiegel*, 7 Sept. 1955.

53. Adenauer, statement of 10 September 1955, in Meissner (ed.), *Moskau-Bonn*, 103.

54. Herbert von Borch, "Wer hat gesiegt?" *Frankfurter Allgemeine Zeitung*, 15 Sept. 1955.

55. Quotations in "Offene Aussprache," *Hamburger Abendblatt*, 12 Sept. 1955; and "Protest," *Frankfurter Allgemeine Zeitung*, 12 Sept. 1955. In general, see Heineman, "Hour of the Woman," 370–74; A. Grossmann, "Question of Silence"; and Naimark, *Russians in Germany*, 69–140.

56. Werner Friedmann, "Die kalte Dusche," *Süddeutsche Zeitung*, 12 Sept. 1955.

57. "Die Erpressung," *Rheinischer Merkur*, 16 Sept. 1955.

58. Heinz Winkler, "Die Last der Vergangenheit," *Rhein-Neckar-Zeitung*, 12 Sept. 1955; von Borch, "Wer hat gesiegt?" *Frankfurter Allgemeine Zeitung*, 15 Sept. 1955.

59. Khrushchev, statement of 10 September 1955, in Meissner (ed.), *Moskau-Bonn*, 106.

60. Friedmann, "Kalte Dusche," *Süddeutsche Zeitung*, 12 Sept. 1955. See also Grewe's account in telegram from Moscow to Bonn, 11 Sept. 1955, PAAA, Büro Staatssekretär 16.

61. Henri Nannen and Ernst Grossar, "In Moskau siegte die Vernunft," *Stern*, 25 Sept. 1955.

62. See, e.g., Köhler, *Adenauer*, 880; Adenauer, *Erinnerungen*, 530; Wilhelm G. Grewe, *Rückblenden, 1976–1951* (Frankfurt am Main: Propyläen, 1979), 243; and Herbert Blankenhorn, *Verständnis und Verständigung: Blätter eines politischen Tagebuchs, 1949 bis 1979* (Frankfurt am Main: Propyläen, 1980), 227. For newspaper accounts, see, from 13 September 1955: "Stadtrundfahrt in der Verhandlungspause," *Frankfurter Allgemeine Zeitung*; Walter Henkels, "Globke trank aus Chrustschews Glas," *Düsseldorfer Nachrichten*; Karl Lerch, "Carlo Schmid imponiert durch Wodkafestigkeit," *Reutlinger Nachrichten*; and from 14 September: Walter Henkels, "Adenauer trinkt sechs Glas Wodka," *Neuer Mainzer Anzeiger*; Heinrich Schlegel, "In und um Moskau," *Stuttgarter Zeitung*; and "Chruschtschow gab Carlo Schmid einen Spitznamen," *Freie Presse Bielefeld*.

63. Georg Schröder, "Der dramatische Tag in Moskau," *Die Welt*, 12 Sept. 1955; "Geste der 'feindlichen Brüder,'" *Neue Rhein-Zeitung*, 12 Sept. 1955; Walter Henkels, "Verblüffte Diplomaten," *Trierischer Volksfreund*, 13 Sept. 1955.

64. E. M. Lang, "Das russische Bajonett-Wunder," *Süddeutsche Zeitung* 10–11 Sept. 1955.

65. Martin Saller, "Hohe Kunst im Bolschoi-Theater," *Schwarzwälder Bote*, 13 Sept. 1955; and "Heilige Messe in Moskau," *Christ und Welt*, 14 Sept. 1955. See also Adenauer, *Erinnerungen*, 531.

66. See, e.g., H.-P. Schwarz, *Ära Adenauer*, 277.

67. Adenauer, *Erinnerungen*, 544. See also the account of Adenauer's press conference on his return to Bonn, 16 September 1955, in Meissner (ed.), *Moskau-Bonn*, 130; and his comments before the CDU Bundestag caucus on 30 September 1955, in Buchstab (ed.), *Adenauer*, 595.

68. Grewe, *Rückblenden*, 233.

69. Zöller, "Eroberung von Moskau," *Rheinischer Merkur*, 16 Sept. 1955. See also the picture caption of the "unermüdliche[r] 79jährige[r] Staatsgast" in *Stern*, 25 Sept. 1955.

70. See Ihme-Tuchel, "Entlassung der deutschen Kriegsgefangenen," 449–65; and idem, "Zwischen Tabu und Propaganda," 49–53. Some contemporaries were aware that the Soviets were beginning to prepare for release of German POWs; see "Im August Heimkehrer aus Russland zu erwarten," *Hamburger Abendblatt*, 8 Aug. 1955; and "Entlassungsvorbereitungen seit März," *Frankfurter Rundschau*, 9 Aug. 1955.

71. Ernst Hess, "'Was sagen Sie zu den Moskauer Entscheidungen?'" *Süddeutsche Zeitung*, 17–18 Sept. 1955; see also Junius, "Adenauers grosser Entschluss," ibid., 15 Sept. 1955.

72. "Ernüchterung in Bonn" and "Staatsverträge DDR-UdSSR vorgeschlagen," *Neues Deutschland*, 18 Sept. 1955.

73. Telegram from U.S. embassy in Moscow to Department of State, 14 Sept. 1955, *Foreign Relations of the United States, 1955–57*, vol. 5: *Austrian State Treaty; Summit and Foreign Ministries Meetings, 1955*, 583. See also Conant, ambassador to Bonn, to State Department, 15 Sept. 1955, ibid., 584–85; telegram from U.S. embassy in Moscow to Department of State, 13 Sept. 1955, ibid., 579–81; Secretary of State John Foster Dulles's words of support for Adenauer, letter of 3 Oct. 1955, ibid., 611. For an assessment of domestic political criticism, see Conant to Secretary of State, 29 Sept. 1955, NA, RG 59, Central Files, 661.62A/9-2455; and Elim O'Shaughnessy to Department of State, 11 Oct. 1955, ibid., 10-1155. For press accounts, see "Zwiespältige Betrachtung der Ergebnisse," *Frankfurter Allgemeine Zeitung*, 16 Sept. 1955; Annamarie Doherr, "Ost-Berlin spricht von Anerkennung des Status quo," *Frankfurter Rundschau*, 15 Sept. 1955; "Die Regierungen der Westmächte stellen sich hinter Adenauer: Geteiltes Echo auf deutsch-russische Vereinbarung," *Die Welt*, 15 Sept. 1955; Hans Henrich, "Mit dem Gesicht im Wind," *Frankfurter Rundschau*, 15 Sept. 1955; and Friedrich Stampfer, "Die Vergessenen," *Hamburger Echo*, 13 Sept. 1955. Also see Charles E. Bohlen, *Witness to History, 1929–1969* (New York: Norton, 1973), 387; Brochagen, *Nach Nürnberg*, 241, 246–47; and in general, Foschepoth, "Adenauers Moskaureise"; and Hans-Peter Schwarz, *Konrad Adenauer: A German Politician and Statesman in a Period of War, Revolution, and Reconstruction*, vol. 2: *The Statesman: 1952–1967* (Providence, R.I.: Berghahn Books, 1997), 171–74.

74. Marion Gräfin Döhnhoff, "Das Moskauer Ja-Wort," *Die Zeit*, 22 Sept.

1955. See also idem, "Ein harter Kampf in Moskau: Am Konferenztisch eiskalt, beim Bankett eng umschlungen," ibid., 15 Sept. 1955; G. von Uexküll, "Einig— aber worüber?" *Die Zeit,* 29 Sept. 1955; the critical response of the SPD, "Zwischen Moskau und Genf," *Vorwärts,* 23 Sept. 1955; the largely critical assessment in "Lesen Sie Karl Marx," *Spiegel,* 21 Sept. 1955; Jens Daniel, "Die Quittung," ibid.; and in response to Adenauer's presentation of the outcome of the Moscow negotiations to the Bundestag, Erich Ollenhauer, for the SPD, *VDB,* 2. Deutscher Bundestag, 102. Sitzung, 23 Sept. 1955, 5653–59. Adenauer's comments to the Bundestag are republished in Meissner (ed.), *Moskau-Bonn,* 135–41.

75. "Das grosse Risiko," *Hamburger Abendblatt,* 23 Sept. 1955. See also "Der Draht nach Moskau," *Tagesspiegel,* 15 Sept. 1955; and "Dank," *Die Welt,* 15 Sept. 1955. Much the same tone is repeated in historical accounts; see, e.g., H.-P. Schwarz, *Ära Adenauer,* 277; and Köhler, *Adenauer,* 886. On Adenauer's attitude toward the Soviet Union, see Niedhardt and Altmann, "Zwischen Beurteilung und Verurteilung," 100–105.

76. J.M.-M., "Ganz der Alte," *Die Zeit,* 15 Sept. 1955; and Gräfin Marion Dönhoff, "Ein harter Kampf in Moskau," ibid.

77. Von Borch, "Wer hat gesiegt?" *Frankfurter Allgemeine Zeitung,* 15 Sept. 1955.

78. "Dank," *Die Welt,* 15 Sept. 1955.

79. Quotation from Richard Adelt, "Die Schlacht von Moskau," *Main-Post,* 15 Sept. 1955. See also Hans Baumgarten, "Arbeit mit zwei freien Händen!" *Frankfurter Allgemeine Zeitung,* 17 Sept. 1955; and "Warnung," *Die Welt,* 23 Sept. 1955.

80. A public opinion poll conducted by the weekly magazine *Der Spiegel,* published on 4 January 1956 on the occasion of Adenauer's eightieth birthday, showed that he topped the list of men "whom you find the most amazing," outdistancing Churchill, Eisenhower, Albert Schweitzer, and Pope Pius XII. Forty-five out of every 100 people interviewed named Adenauer as the "living man they most admired." Five years before, only one in ten named Adenauer.

81. Quotations from "Flugplatzarbeiter riefen: 'Vielen Dank, Conny,'" *General-Anzeiger für Bonn und Umgegend,* 15 Sept. 1955; and "Tage des Dankes," *Kölnische Rundschau,* 16 Sept. 1955. See also Max Karl Feiden, "Arnold: Die Reise hat sich wirklich gelohnt," *Ruhr Nachrichten,* 15 Sept. 1955; Horst Schubert, "Die Reisenden aus Moskau wurden dicht umlagert," *Neue Rhein-Zeitung,* 12 Sept. 1955; "Adenauer wieder in Bonn," *Rheinische Post,* 15 Sept. 1955; Bruno Lenz, "Heimkehrer," *Hannoversche Allgemeine Zeitung,* 15 Sept. 1955; and "Sie war es, die dem Bundeskanzler dankte: Frau Margarete Schumacher brachte auf dem Flugplatz Wahn die Empfindungen vieler Mütter zum Ausdruck," *Kölnische Rundschau,* 17 Sept. 1955. The picture is reproduced in Brochhagen, *Nach Nürnberg,* 247. Newsreel footage from the *Wochenschau* is reproduced in Guido Knopp, ed., *Damals 1955: Das Jahr der Anerkennung* (Stuttgart: ZDF/DVA, 1995), a video produced by the Zweites Deutsches Fernsehen. My thanks to Heide Fehrenbach for helping me to obtain this source.

82. "Sie war es, die dem Bundeskanzler dankte," *Kölnische Rundschau,* 17 Sept. 1955.

83. "In Friedland läutete die Freiheitsglocke," *Kölnische Rundschau,* 10 Oct. 1955; and BVFK, *20 Jahre Lager Friedland,* 60.

84. "An den Strassen der Heimkehr: Diskussion um ein zeitnahes Bild," *Kölnische Rundschau,* 19 Oct. 1955. See also Manfred Ph. Obst and Egon E. Vogt, "Deutschlands Herz schlägt in Friedland," *Hessische Nachrichten,* 10 Oct. 1955; and Werner Peschke, "Friedland—Kreuzweg der Hoffnungen," *Westdeutsche Rundschau,* 21 Oct. 1955.

85. "Nun kommen sie heim!" *Kölnische Rundschau,* 17 Sept. 1955.

86. "Wir grüssen uns wieder," *Kölnische Rundschau,* 15 Sept. 1955; "Willkommen!" ibid., 10 Oct. 1955; "Rundschau-Leser diskutieren: An den Strassen der Heimkehr," ibid., 22 Oct. 1955.

87. Erik Verg, "Heimkehr ohne Illusion," ibid., 10 Sept. 1955.

88. Barbara Groneweg, "Das erste—Ein Telegramm nach Hause," *Frankfurter Rundschau,* 11 Oct. 1955; "Rundschau-Leser diskutieren: An den Strassen der Heimkehr," *Kölnische Rundschau,* 22 Oct. 1955.

89. See the interesting comparisons with Sara Fishman, "Waiting for the Captive Sons of France: Prisoners of War Wives, 1940–1945," in *Behind the Lines: Gender and the Two World Wars,* ed. Margaret Randolph Higgonet et al. (New Haven: Yale University Press, 1987), 191.

90. Falk Bente, "Nach zehn Jahren: Heidelberger kehren heim," *Rhein-Neckar-Zeitung,* 10 Oct. 1955.

91. "Freudentränen in Friedland," *Hamburger Echo,* 10 Oct. 1955; see also the transcript of the speech, Nordwestdeutscher Rundfunk (NWDR), 10 Oct. 1955, PIB, MF 2191.

92. Falk Bente, "Heidelberg grüsst seine Heimkehrer," *Rhein-Neckar-Zeitung,* 12 Oct. 1955.

93. In general, see Moeller, *Protecting Motherhood.*

94. Marianne Morawe, "Das Herz in Friedland," *Frankfurter Allgemeine Zeitung,* 17 Oct. 1955.

95. "Weit ist der Weg zurück," *Frankfurter Rundschau,* 24 Dec. 1955. See also "Heimkehr mit Wermutstropfen," *Hamburger Echo,* 11 Oct. 1955; and Ingeborg Glupp, "Endlich zu Hause—aber verzweifelt," *Berliner Morgenpost,* 19 Oct. 1955.

96. Heinz-Arndt Brüggemann, "'Es wäre schön, wenn er blond wäre,'" *Westdeutsche Allgemeine Zeitung,* 11 Oct. 1955. See M. von Conta, "Um 10 Uhr 58 begann ihr neues Leben," *Süddeutsche Zeitung,* 12 Oct. 1955.

97. Heineman, "Hour of the Woman," 381–84; Fehrenbach, *Cinema in Democratizing Germany,* 98–99. On conceptions of gender in the immediate postwar period, see also Mariatte C. Denman, "Staging the Nation: Representations of Nationhood and Gender in Plays, Images, and Films in Postwar West Germany (1945–1949)" (Ph.D. diss., University of California, Davis, 1997).

98. Heinz-Arndt Brüggemann, "'Es wäre schön, wenn er blond wäre,'" *Westdeutsche Allgemeine Zeitung,* 11 Oct. 1955. On "women standing alone," see Heineman, *What Difference Does a Husband Make?*

99. "Der erste Bummel seines Lebens," *Telegraf,* 14 Oct. 1955.

100. Günter Arendt, "Der erste Tag im alten Hause," ibid., 11 Oct. 1955; and "'Ich bringe ein kleines Frühstück,'" ibid., 12 Oct. 1955.

101. Hans Malten, "Heimkehrer," *Medizinische Klinik* 41 (1946): 598, quoted in Biess, "Protracted War"; see also Gauger, "Die Dystrophie als Gesamterkrankung," in *Extreme Lebensverhältnisse und ihre Folgen: Handbuch der ärztlichen Erfahrungen aus der Gefangenschaft,* ed. E. G. Schenck and W. von Nathusius (n.p.: Schriftenreihe des Ärztlich-wissenschaftlichen Beirates des Verbandes der Heimkehrer Deutschlands e.V., 1959), 7:12–21.

102. H. Kilian, "Das Wiedereinleben des Heimkehrers in Familie, Ehe und Beruf," in *Die Sexualität des Heimkehrers: Vorträge gehalten auf dem 4. Kongress der Deutschen Gesellschaft für Sexualforschung in Erlangen 1956* (Stuttgart: Ferdinand Enke, 1957), 34. See also Lehmann, *Gefangenschaft und Heimkehr,* 89, 149–50; and the excellent discussion in Biess, "Protracted War." On the public discussion of homosexuality in the 1950s, see Moeller, "Homosexual Man, Homosexual Woman."

103. Gabriele Müller, "Wenn die Lager-Kameradschaft zerflattert ist—Der schwere Weg zurück: Mit Heimkehrern auf dem Kurfürstendamm," *Tagesspiegel,* 30 Oct. 1955; also published as "Nylonstrümpfe—wie sie der Russland-Heimkehrer sieht," *Süddeutsche Zeitung,* 31 Oct. 1955.

104. Karl Heinz Christiansen, "Krawall um Louis Armstrong," *Die Welt,* 18 Oct. 1955; and Karl-Heinz Krüger, "Satchmo," *Der Abend,* 28 Oct. 1955. In general on the reception of jazz and its centrality for discussions of "Americanization" in postwar West Germany, see Poiger, *Jazz, Rock, and Rebels.*

105. Herbert L. Schrader, "Der Tumult der Jazz-Anhänger," *Hamburger Abendblatt,* 19 Oct. 1955. See also "Sturm um den Jazzkönig," ibid., 18 Oct. 1955.

106. See the review of "Die Saat der Gewalt," *Der Abend,* 3 Nov. 1955; also Hans Steinitz, "Amerikas 'Krankheit der Jugend': Eine Folge von Wohlleben und Bequemlichkeit?" *Die Welt,* 3 Nov. 1955; and the ad for the movie *Die Saat der Gewalt,* which located the film "in the crossfire of protest and enthusiasm," *Die Welt,* 18 Nov. 1955. In general, see Poiger, "Rebels with a Cause?"; idem, "Rock 'n' Roll," 373–410; idem, "A New, 'Western' Hero? Reconstructing German Masculinity in the 1950s," *Signs* 24 (1998): 147–62; and Carter, "Alice in Consumer Wonderland."

107. Joachim Besser, "Handkuss an der Bahnhofsrampe," *Die Welt,* 15 Oct. 1955.

108. I have been unable to locate an exact count of returning women. Press coverage of transports that included women ends in mid-October, and one report concludes, "In drei Transporten auch 400 Frauen nach Friedland," *Hamburger Abendblatt,* 15–16 Oct. 1955.

109. Thea Splicke, "Zwei Frauen kamen aus Workuta," *Der Abend,* 12 Oct. 1955.

110. "Ihre Kinder sprechen nur Russisch," *Berliner Morgenpost,* 12 Oct. 1955. See also "Müttern wurden ihre Kinder weggenommen: Heimkehrerinnen berichten über ihr schweres Schicksal—Erster Wunsch: ein Bad," *Westdeutsche Allgemeine Zeitung,* 12 Oct. 1955; and "Frauen und Kinder kamen aus Russland," *Kölnische Rundschau,* 12 Oct. 1955.

111. Quotations respectively from Lothar K. Wiedemann, "Fellmützen,

Russenstiefel und etwas Lippenstift," *Mittag,* 12 Oct. 1955; Ingeborg Glupp, "Wir kamen in den Himmel," *Berliner Morgenpost,* 6 Nov. 1955; and photo caption for a picture of a woman holding a mirror in front of her face, *Hamburger Abendblatt,* 13 Oct. 1955.

112. Dietrich Koch, "Kommen sie wirklich mit leeren Händen?" *Die Welt,* 15 Oct. 1955; also "In der Heimat," *Frankfurter Allgemeine Zeitung,* 11 Oct. 1955. See also "Die grosse Passion deutscher Frauen in sibirischen Lagern," *Echo der Zeit,* 30 Oct. 1955.

113. Julius Hermann, "Die Heimkehrer erleben eine völlig neue Welt," *Hamburger Abendblatt,* 5–6 Nov. 1955; Werner Tamms, "Lasst ihnen Zeit . . . ," *Westdeutsche Allgemeine Zeitung,* 22 Oct. 1955; Müller, "Wenn die Lager-Kameradschaft zerflattert ist," *Tagesspiegel,* 30 Oct. 1955.

114. Eberhard Stammler, "Busstag," *Westdeutsche Allgemeine Zeitung,* 16 Nov. 1955. See also "Verwandelte Welt," *Rheinische Post,* 19 Oct. 1955; and K. Ludwig, "Heimkehrer als soziologisches Problem," in *Sexualität des Heimkehrers,* 74.

115. "'Habt ihr auch eine Idee?'" *Volkswirt,* nos. 51–52 (1955). See also Ursula von Kardorff, "Was denkt der Heimkehrer heute?" *Die Welt,* 21 Apr. 1956; and idem, "Ihnen erging es wie dem Mönch von Heisterbach," *Süddeutsche Zeitung,* 29 Mar. 1956; also "'Wir haben Köln nicht wiedererkannt,'" *Kölnische Rundschau,* 9 Nov. 1955.

116. Alex Schmalfuss, "Zum Kriegsgefangenen-Gedenktag 1955," *Tagesspiegel,* 26 Nov. 1955. See also Eberhard von Wiese, "Elf Jahre war Vater nicht daheim," *Hamburger Abendblatt,* 25 Dec. 1955; and "Das Erlebnis der Heimkehr," *Rhein-Neckar-Zeitung,* 10 Oct. 1955.

117. "Freudentränen in Friedland," *Hamburger Echo,* 10 Oct. 1955.

118. Ingeborg Glupp, "Das Erlebnis der Freiheit," *Berliner Morgenpost,* 23 Oct. 1955. See also Walter Vitton, "'Ich kann es jetzt noch nicht fassen!'" *Rheinische Post,* 22 Oct. 1955; Renate Marbach, "In der Ecke steht noch der Holzkoffer," *Der Tag,* 16 Oct. 1955; Gabriele Müller, "Der Weg zurück: Heimkehrer—vier Wochen danach," *Rheinische Post,* 5 Nov. 1955; Armin Koblitz, "Die Heimkehr ist erst ein Anfang: Wiedereingliederung der Heimkehrer ist ein soziales Problem," *Der Mittag,* 26 Nov. 1955; Hans Joachim Ehlers, "Nach Friedland begann ihre Not," *Kasseler Post,* 26 Nov. 1955; and "Der Freiheit entwöhnt: Heimkehrer brauchen zur Umstellung viel Zeit und Geduld," *Deutsche Zeitung und Wirtschafts-Zeitung,* 17 Dec. 1955; Josef Schmidt, "'In Workuta sah die Heimat anders aus,'" *Stuttgarter Nachrichten,* 23 Mar. 1956; B[arbara] Groneweg, "Sechs Monate nach der Rückkehr," *Stuttgarter Zeitung,* 27 Mar. 1956; and Ursula von Kardorff, "Ihnen erging es wie dem Mönch von Heisterbach," *Süddeutsche Zeitung,* 29 Mar. 1956; Werner Tamms, "Lasst ihnen Zeit . . . ," *Westdeutsche Allgemeine Zeitung,* 22 Oct. 1955; Rudolf Walter Leonhardt, "Viele sagen: Heimkehren ist schwerer als Weggehen," *Die Zeit,* 15 Dec. 1955; "Zurück aus 'Golgatha,'" *abz Illustrierte,* 16 Oct. 1955; and Hermann Pörzgen, "'Weit ist der Weg': Was für die Heimkehrer noch getan werden muss," *Frankfurter Allgemeine Zeitung,* 28 Jan. 1956, reviewing a film produced by the Verband der Heimkehrer and directed by Gerhard Kluh. The Bundesarchiv has

a copy of the film, which reviews the history of the integration of the POWs, climaxing with the 1955 "homecoming."

119. "Erlebnis der Heimkehr," *Rhein-Neckar-Zeitung,* 10 Oct. 1955.

120. Dietrich Schwarzkopf, "'Jetzt bist du ein freier deutscher Bürger,'" *Tagesspiegel,* 15 Oct. 1955. See also Dietrich Koch, "Kommen sie wirklich mit leeren Händen?" *Die Welt,* 15 Oct. 1955; and idem, "'Ihr habt alle keine Zeit,'" ibid., 16 Nov. 1955.

121. Quotation from Schwarzkopf, "'Jetzt bist du ein freier deutscher Bürger,'" *Tagesspiegel,* 15 Oct. 1955; other examples are drawn from "Heimkehr über stille Wege: Erster Grosstransport von Nicht-Amnestierten traf in der Bundesrepublik ein," *Hamburger Abendblatt,* 16 Jan. 1956; and "Alle nichtamnestierten Gefangenen jetzt zurück?" *Frankfurter Allgemeine Zeitung,* 16 Jan. 1955.

122. "Hunderte von Heimkehrern beschwören ihre Unschuld," *Hamburger Echo,* 14 Dec. 1955. See also "Heimkehrertransporte rollen wieder," *Rhein-Neckar-Zeitung,* 14 Dec. 1955; and "'Wir kommen mit reinen Händen und Herzen,'" *Hessische Nachrichten,* 12 Oct. 1955.

123. Hans Henrich, "Gegen die Kollektiv-Unschuld," *Frankfurter Rundschau,* 17 Jan. 1956. See also Werner Friedmann, "Wasser im deutschen Wein," *Süddeutsche Zeitung,* 29 Oct. 1955.

124. "Heimkehrerzug mit verriegelten Türen," *Stuttgarter Nachrichten,* 18 Jan. 1955. See also "Schlaglichter von Heimkehrer-Schicksalen in Friedland," *Stuttgarter Nachrichten,* 22 Oct. 1955; Alfred Schulze, "Bonner Korridorgespräche," *Allgemeine Wochenzeitung der Juden in Deutschland,* 28 Oct. 1955; Peter Maslowski, "Der Fall liegt tiefer," *Vorwärts,* 11 Nov. 1955; and "Entlassung Claubergs ein Test-Fall?" *Westfälische Rundschau,* 21 Dec. 1955. On Clauberg's background, see Ernst Klee, *Auschwitz, die NS-Medizin und ihre Opfer* (Frankfurt am Main: S. Fischer, 1997), 436–41. Sorge ultimately did stand trial, but his guilty verdict and life sentence were not issued until February 1959, and even then, this outcome was exceptional. See Brochhagen, *Nach Nürnberg,* 250, and the discussion below in the Epilogue.

125. Quotation from "Heimkehrer ohne Namen," *General-Anzeiger für Bonn und Umgegend,* 16 Jan. 1956. See also Hans Ulrich Kersten, "Heimkehr ins Gefängnis: SED-Propaganda auf Hochtouren—Sühne ohne Schuldbeweis," *Bremer Nachrichten,* 21 Dec. 1955; "Pankow erkennt Moskaus Urteile an," *Frankfurter Rundschau,* 18 Jan. 1955; "Die Heimkehrer und die Schuldigen: Auch von den wahren Kriegsverbrechern muss einmal gesprochen werden," *Welt der Arbeit,* 30 Dec. 1955; Heinz Kall, "Glocken von Herleshausen läuteten nicht zum Empfang," *Neue Rhein-Zeitung,* 16 Jan. 1956; "Heimkehrer in Zuchthäusern," *Die Welt,* 21 Dec. 1955; and Annamarie Doherr, "'Jeder Rückkehrer muss kontrolliert werden!'" *Frankfurter Rundschau,* 29 Oct. 1955. According to a U.S. State Department report, the Soviets did not produce evidence of the guilt of the 469 nonamnestied prisoners released in January 1956; see Elim O'Shaughnessy to Department of State, 21 Mar. 1956, NA, RG 59, Central Files, 661.6224/3–2156. On the reception in the East, see Biess, "Protracted War."

126. "Frauen und Kinder unter den Heimkehrern," *Frankfurter Allgemeine*

Zeitung, 12 Oct. 1955. See also Walter Fischer, "'. . . bis ihr mich aufnehmt,'" *Westfalenpost,* 13 Oct. 1955; and "Das gerettete Transparent," *Rhein-Neckar-Zeitung,* 12 Oct. 1955

127. Quotations in Seff Schmidt, "'Wir sind zutiefst erschüttert,'" *Westdeutsche Allgemeine Zeitung,* 16 Oct. 1955; and Josef Schmidt, "'Gehirnwäsche' an 305 Heimkehrern," *Süddeutsche Zeitung,* 12 Oct. 1955. See also "Eine einzige Blamage für die Partei," *Westfälische Nachrichten,* 4 Nov. 1955.

128. Heide Fehrenbach, "*Die Sünderin,* or Who Killed the German Male: Early Postwar Cinema and the Betrayal of the Fatherland," in *Gender and German Cinema: Feminist Interventions,* vol. 2: *German Film History/German History on Film,* ed. Sandra Frieden et al. (Providence, R.I.: Berg, 1993), 138–40; and Barnouw, *Germany 1945,* 173–84.

129. "Freudentränen in Friedland," *Hamburger Echo,* 10 Oct. 1955.

130. "Heimkehr 55: Zehn Jahre nach dem Kriege kamen die Letzten," *Stern,* 23 Oct. 1955; also "Fragen, die an uns gerichtet sind," *Stuttgarter Zeitung,* 28 Jan. 1956.

131. Morawe, "Herz in Friedland," *Frankfurter Allgemeine Zeitung,* 17 Oct. 1955.

132. Karl-Heinz Frieser, *Krieg hinter Stacheldraht: Die deutschen Kriegsgefangenen in der Sowjetunion und das Nationalkomitee "Freies Deutschland"* (Mainz: v. Hase & Koehler Verlag, 1981); Bodo Scheurig, *Free Germany: The National Committee and the League of German Officers,* trans. Herbert Arnold (Middletown, Conn.: Wesleyan University Press, 1969); and Gerd R. Ueberschär, ed., *Das Nationalkomitee "Freies Deutschland" und der Bund Deutscher Offiziere* (Frankfurt am Main: Fischer Taschenbuch Verlag, 1995). Seydlitz's wife and daughters had also appealed directly to Adenauer to obtain his release on the eve of the chancellor's trip to Moscow; see Brückner to Grewe, Foreign Ministry, 6 Sept. 1955, PAAA, Abt. 2/1995.

133. H. J. Wiessner, "Die Heimkehrer aus Iwanowo erzählen," *Tagesspiegel,* 8 Oct. 1955.

134. "Moskaus dreissig Silberlinge," *Frankfurter Allgemeine Zeitung,* 13 Feb. 1956.

135. Quotations from Wiessner, "Heimkehrer aus Iwanowo," *Tagesspiegel,* 8 Oct. 1955. See also Joachim Besser, "Ich sprach mit den Generalen [*sic*]," *Die Welt,* 8 Oct. 1955; Josef Schmidt, "Als erste kamen die Generäle . . . ," *Süddeutsche Zeitung,* 8–9 Oct. 1955; H[ans] Z[ehrer], "Rückkehr," *Die Welt,* 8 Oct. 1955; "Das erste Gespräch in der Heimat: Was sagte Seydlitz?" ibid., 8 Oct. 1955; "Zwischenfall mit Ex-General Seydlitz," *Hamburger Echo,* 7 Oct. 1955; and "Der General, den die anderen meiden," *abz Illustrierte,* 23 Oct. 1955; and the far more sympathetic account in "Seydlitz: Widerstandskämpfer oder Landesverräter?" *Süddeutsche Zeitung,* 10 Oct. 1955.

136. Wiessner, "Heimkehrer aus Iwanowo," *Tagesspiegel,* 8 Oct. 1955. See also "Heimkehr 1955," *Telegraf,* 9 Oct. 1955.

137. Seff Schmidt, "'Auf gut Glück fuhr ich nach Friedland,'" *Westdeutsche Allgemeine Zeitung,* 8 Oct. 1955. See also "Die ersten Stunden in der Heimat," *Hamburger Abendblatt,* 8–9 Oct. 1955; and "Gefangenen-Heimkehr," *Tagesspiegel,* 8 Oct. 1955.

138. Erich Kuby, "Mit dem Blick auf Friedland," *Süddeutsche Zeitung,* 11 Oct. 1955; and responses, ibid., 15–16 Oct. 1955.

139. "Heuss begrüsste 599 Heimkehrer," *Tagesspiegel,* 19 Oct. 1955.

140. Account of an exchange between a major in the Bundesgrenzschutz and a POW in Friedland in Josef Schmidt, "Zwanzig Güterwagen mit Heimkehrern," *Süddeutsche Zeitung,* 10 Oct. 1955.

141. "Friedland: Deutsche Geschichte im Zeitraffer," *Westdeutsche Allgemeine Zeitung,* 15 Oct. 1955.

142. Schwartz, *America's Germany,* 169.

143. J. Schmidt, "Zwanzig Güterwagen," *Süddeutsche Zeitung,* 10 Oct. 1955; Karl Sabel, "Harald von Bohlens grösster Wunsch: Ein Zimmer für sich allein," *Westdeutsche Allgemeine Zeitung,* 10 Oct. 1955; also Max Karl Feiden, "Bohlenkamp, Büter, Borowski—Wir haben alle losgeheult, als am Sonntagmorgen in Herleshausen die Heimkehrer kamen," *Ruhr-Nachrichten,* 10 Oct. 1955.

144. J. Schmidt, "Zwanzig Güterwagen," *Süddeutsche Zeitung,* 10 Oct. 1955.

145. "Legende und Wahrheit," *Telegraf,* 11 Oct. 1955. See also Wilhelm Ingesand, "Kaviar oder Salzhering," *Freie Presse,* 15 Oct. 1955.

146. Schelsky elaborated on the thesis in *Wandlungen der deutschen Familie in der Gegenwart;* see also Hans Braun, "Helmut Schelskys Konzept der 'nivellierten Mittelstandsgesellschaft' und die Bundesrepublik der 50er Jahre," *Archiv für Sozialgeschichte* 29 (1985): 199–223.

147. "Das erste—ein Telegramm nach Hause," *Frankfurter Rundschau,* 11 Oct. 1955. At least some information on individual returnees is available in a report dated 25 January 1956 prepared by the U.S. Mission in Berlin for the Department of State, using materials from the Berlin Document Center. Of 858 returnees traced in the report, 320 returned to parts of the Federal Republic that had been their home before the war; the rest were former residents of the "Soviet Zone of Germany," East Prussia, Poland, Czechoslovakia, or Austria. See NA, RG 59, Central Files, 661.6224/1–2556.

148. Morawe, "Herz in Friedland," *Frankfurter Allgemeine Zeitung,* 17 Oct. 1955. See also Dietrich Koch, "Heimkehrer 1954 empfängt einen Spätheimkehrer 1955," *Die Welt,* 13 Oct. 1955.

149. "In Friedland sind die Tore der Heimat weit geöffnet," *Hamburger Abendblatt,* 10 Oct. 1955; "In Friedland läutete die Freiheitsglocke," *Kölnische Rundschau,* 10 Oct. 1955; Joachim Besser, "Sonntag, 6 Uhr: Eine grosse Stunde unseres Volkes," *Die Welt,* 10 Oct. 1955; and a transcript of the speech, broadcast by the NWDR on 9 November 1955, PIB, MF 2101.

150. Part of a front-page cover story in *Bunte Illustrierte,* no. 22 (1955). See also Anton Müller Engstfeld, "'Ich sah nie soviele Tränen,'" *Neue Rhein-Zeitung,* 10 Oct. 1955; and Armin Koblitz, "Tränen im Lager der tausend Hoffnungen," *Der Mittag,* 10 Oct. 1955. For another perspective on the postwar construction of new German conceptions of fatherhood, see Heide Fehrenbach, "Rehabilitating Father*land*: Race and German Remasculinization," *Signs* 24 (1998): 107–27.

151. See the interesting discussion in Thomas Kühne, "Kameradschaft—'das

Beste im Leben des Mannes': Die deutschen Soldaten des Zweiten Weltkriegs
in erfahrungs- und geschlechtergeschichtlicher Perspektive,'' *Geschichte und
Gesellschaft* 22 (1996): 504–29; and idem, '' . . . aus diesem Krieg werden nicht
nur harte Männer heimkehren': Kriegskameradschaft und Männlichkeit im 20.
Jahrhundert,'' in *Männergeschichte—Geschlechtergeschichte: Männlichkeit im
Wandel der Moderne,* ed. Thomas Kühne (Frankfurt am Main: Campus, 1996),
174–92.

152. Hans Gerlach, "Die Heimat empfängt ihre Söhne," *Wiesbadener Kurier,*
10 Oct. 1955.

153. The quotations are from "Das echte Deutschland," *Hamburger Anzeiger,*
11 Oct. 1955; and "Ein einzig' Volk," *Aachener Volkszeitung,* 11 Oct. 1955. See
also, e.g., Egon E. Vogt and Manfred Ph. Obst, "Deutschlands Herz schlägt in
Friedland," *Hessische Nachrichten,* 10 Oct. 1955.

154. "Nun danket alle Gott," *Westfälische Nachrichten,* 15 Oct. 1955. See
also Robert B. Lebeck, "Nun danket alle Gott," *Revue,* 22 Oct. 1955. The newsreel footage from Friedland also featured the returnees intoning this familiar
hymn. On the importance of the churches in integrating returning POWs, see the
insightful treatment of Biess, "Protracted War."

155. Erik Verg, "Heimkehr ohne Illusion," *Kölnische Rundschau,* 10 Sept.
1955.

156. Morawe, "Herz in Friedland," *Frankfurter Allgemeine Zeitung,* 17 Oct.
1955.

157. "Die Glocke von Friedland grüsste die Heimkehrer," *Hamburger Abendblatt,* 7 Oct. 1955. For comparisons with the post–World War I era, see, in addition to Kühne, "'Kameradschaft,'" and "' . . . aus diesem Krieg,'" Diehl,
Thanks of the Fatherland, 231; Mosse, *Fallen Soldiers,* 210–11, 217; Omer Bartov, *Murder in Our Midst: The Holocaust, Industrial Killing, and Representation* (New York: Oxford University Press, 1996), 15–32; and Klaus Theweleit,
Male Fantasies, 2 vols., trans. Erica Carter, Stephen Conway, and Chris Turner
(Minneapolis: University of Minnesota Press, 1987–89).

158. Alexander Mitscherlich, "Der geteilte Vater: Generationskonflikte in der
modernen Welt," *Tagesspiegel,* 13 Nov. 1955. Mitscherlich developed these arguments at length in "Der unsichtbare Vater: Ein Problem für Psychoanalyse und
Soziologie," *Kölner Zeitschrift für Soziologie und Sozialpsychologie* 7 (1955):
188–201; and *Auf dem Wege zur vaterlosen Gesellschaft: Ideen zur Sozialpsychologie* (Munich: Piper, [1963] 1973), published in English as *Society without
the Father: A Contribution to Social Psychology,* trans. Eric Mosbacher (New
York: Harcourt, Brace & World, 1969).

159. "Heimkehrer streichelte blondes Kinderhaar," *Kasseler Zeitung,* 10 Oct.
1955.

160. "Bundestag prüft Soldatengesetz," *Kölnische Rundschau,* 13 Oct. 1955;
and "Die ersten Generale [*sic*] können ernannt werden," *Die Welt,* 15 Oct. 1955.
See also Joachim Besser, "Wohin kommen die Soldaten?" ibid., 18 Oct. 1955,
one in a series of articles about the organization and training procedures for the
new army; "Die ersten 101 Soldaten der neuen deutschen Armee sind ernannt,"
ibid., 14 Nov. 1955; and Hellmuth Brenneck, "Die ersten Baracken sind bereit
für die neuen Soldaten," ibid., 14 Oct. 1955.

161. *Westdeutsche Allgemeine Zeitung,* 15 Oct. 1955.

162. Abenheim, *Reforging the Iron Cross,* 102–3. On rearmament in general, see Large, *Germans to the Front;* and Detlef Bald, *Militär und Gesellschaft, 1945–1990: Die Bundeswehr der Bonner Republik* (Baden-Baden: Nomos Gesellschaft, 1994); idem, "'Bürger in Uniform': Tradition und Neuanfang des Militärs in Westdeutschland," in Schildt und Sywottek (eds.), *Modernisierung im Wiederaufbau,* 392–402; Rautenberg, "Zur Standortbestimmung," 747, 872, 879; Hans-Adolf Jacobsen, "Zur Rolle der öffentlichen Meinung bei der Debatte um die Wiederbewaffnung 1950–1955," in *Aspekte der deutschen Wiederbewaffnung bis 1955,* ed. Militärgeschichtliches Forschungsamt (Boppard am Rhein: Harald Boldt, 1975), 70–89; Georg Meyer, "Innenpolitische Voraussetzungen der westdeutschen Wiederbewaffnung," in *Wiederbewaffnung in Deutschland nach 1945,* ed. Alexander Fischer (Berlin: Duncker & Humblot, 1986), 31–44.

163. "An den Strassen der Heimkehr . . . ," *Kölnische Rundschau,* 15 Oct. 1955.

164. "Legende und Wahrheit," *Telegraf,* 11 Oct. 1955.

165. Elisabeth Noelle-Neumann, "Die Verklärung: Adenauer und die öffentliche Meinung 1946 bis 1976," in Blumenwitz (ed.), *Beiträge der Wissenschaft,* 552. See also Elim O'Shaughnessy to Department of State, 11 Oct. 1955, NA, RG 59, Central Files, 661.62A/10–1155; H.-P. Schwarz, *Ära Adenauer,* 279; and Foschepoth, "Adenauers Moskaureise."

166. Hanns Jürgen Küsters, ed., *Adenauer: Teegespräche, 1955–1958* (Berlin: Wolf Jobst Siedler, 1986), 7.

167. Weymar, *Adenauer,* 11.

168. Hans Zehrer, "Brückenschlag über den Abgrund," *Die Welt,* 4 Jan. 1956. See also Georg Schröder, "Konrad Adenauer," ibid., 5 Jan. 1956.

169. Bente, "Heidelberg grüsst seine Heimkehrer," *Rhein-Neckar-Zeitung,* 12 Oct. 1955; and "Freudentränen in Friedland," *Hamburger Echo,* 10 Oct. 1955.

170. See, e.g., "Heimkehrer-Debatte im Stadtrat," *Münchener Stadtanzeiger,* supplement to *Süddeutsche Zeitung,* 28 Oct. 1955; "Streitgespräch über die Heimkehrer," *Süddeutsche Zeitung,* 26 Oct. 1955; "Schlaglichter von Heimkehrer-Schicksalen in Friedland," *Stuttgarter Nachrichten,* 22 Oct. 1955; H. G. van Dam, "Seltsame Kontraste: Heimkehrerhilfe und Wiedergutmachung," *Allgemeine Wochenzeitung der Juden in Deutschland,* 7 Oct. 1955; "Friedland ohne Frieden," ibid., 23 Dec. 1955; "Der Abtransport badischer Juden," *Rhein-Neckar-Zeitung,* 22–23 Oct. 1955; resolution of the Kreisvereinigung der Vereinigten der Verfolgten des Naziregimes, Arzberg, 8 Oct. 1955, PAAA, Abt. 2/1997; and Stern, *Whitewashing of the Yellow Badge,* for postwar West German anti-Semitism in general.

171. The position of the West German Communist Party echoed the critical comments of the official East German news organ, *Neues Deutschland.* See, e.g., "Zweierlei Empfang," *Neues Deutschland,* 9 Oct. 1955; "Humanität und Missbrauch," ibid., 11 Oct. 1955; "Mit dem Blick auf die Rückkehr," ibid., 12 Oct. 1955; and "Ehemalige Kriegsverurteilte gegen die Bonner Hetze," ibid., 13 Dec. 1955. The Communist Party in West Germany was officially outlawed by the Federal Constitutional Court in 1956.

172. Elisabeth Domansky, "Militarization and Reproduction in World War I Germany," in *Society, Culture, and the State in Germany, 1870–1930*, ed. Geoff Eley (Ann Arbor: University of Michigan Press, 1996), 437.

173. Gisela Bock, "Antinatalism, Maternity, and Paternity in National Socialist Racism," in *Maternity and Gender Policies: Women and the Rise of the European Welfare States, 1880s–1950s*, ed. Gisela Bock and Pat Thane (London: Routledge, 1991), 243; Domansky, "Militarization and Reproduction," 437.

174. Friedrich Sieburg, "Der schönste Mann im Staate," *Die Zeit*, 28 July 1955. See also "Was steht ihrer Meinung nach einem Mann besser—ein Zivilanzug oder eine Uniform?" *Spiegel*, 5 Oct. 1955, a public opinion poll that revealed that 77 percent of men and 76 percent of women preferred to see men in civilian clothing; and Joachim Besser, "Nicht alle tragen Uniform . . . ," *Die Welt*, 20 Oct. 1955.

175. Hans Baumgarten, "Die Armee der Demokratie," *Frankfurter Allgemeine Zeitung*, 15 Oct. 1955. See also Georg Herda, "Der Schlussstrich," *Frankfurter Rundschau*, 10 Oct. 1955; and "Der Schlussstrich," *Hamburger Echo*, 30 Sept. 1955.

176. Josef Reding, "Friedland wird zu deutscher Geschichte," *Echo der Zeit*, 16 Oct. 1955.

177. Stammler, "Busstag," *Westdeutsche Allgemeine Zeitung*, 16 Nov. 1955.

Chapter Five

1. In this chapter, unless otherwise indicated, translations from dialogue in the film are my own.

2. Fehrenbach, *Cinema in Democratizing Germany*. The quotation is the subtitle of Fehrenbach's book.

3. For a useful survey, see Claudius Seidl, *Der deutsche Film der fünfziger Jahre* (Munich: Wilhelm Heyne, 1987); also Fritz Göttler, "Westdeutscher Nachkriegsfilm: Land der Väter," in *Geschichte des deutschen Films*, ed. Wolfgang Jacobsen, Anton Kaes, and Hans Helmut Prinzler (Stuttgart: J. B. Metzler, 1993), 171–210; Klaus Kreimeier, *Kino und Filmindustrie in der BRD: Ideologieproduktion und Klassenwirklichkeit nach 1945* (Kronberg/Taunus: Scriptor, 1973); idem, "Der westdeutsche Film in den fünfziger Jahren," in *Die fünfziger Jahre: Beiträge zu Politik und Kultur*, ed. Dieter Baensch (Tübingen: Gunter Narr, 1985), 283–305; and Friedrich P. Kahlenberg, "Der Film der Ära Adenauer," in *Trümmer und Träume: Nachkriegszeit und fünfziger Jahre auf Zelluloid*, ed. Ursula Bessen (Bochum: Studienverlag Dr. N. Brockmeyer, 1989), 236–47.

4. See Peter Pleyer, *Deutscher Nachkriegsfilm, 1946–1948* (Münster: C. J. Fahle, 1965); Thomas Brandlmeier, "Von Hitler zu Adenauer: Deutsche Trümmerfilme," in *Zwischen Gestern und Morgen: Westdeutscher Nachkriegsfilm, 1946–1962*, ed. Hilmar Hoffmann and Walter Schobert (Frankfurt am Main: Deutsches Filmmuseum, 1989), 32–59; Klaus Jaeger and Helmut Regel, eds., *Deutschland in Trümmern: Filmdokumente der Jahre 1945–1949* (Oberhausen:

Karl Maria Laufen, 1976); and the insightful discussion of Staudte in Denman, "Staging the Nation," 205–34.

5. "Überholte Filme," *Wirtschaftszeitung*, 16 July 1949. With the exception of reviews in *Der Heimkehrer*, unless otherwise indicated, all reviews of the movies discussed here are in the remarkable collection of the Deutsches Filminstitut (formerly Deutsches Institut für Filmkunde; hereafter DFI).

6. Fehrenbach, *Cinema in Democratizing Germany*, 153; also Wolfgang Becker and Norbert Schöll, *In jenen Tagen . . . : Wie der deutsche Nachkriegsfilm die Vergangenheit bewältigte* (Opladen: Leske & Budrich, 1995).

7. A study that exhaustively explored how West German filmmakers illuminated the history of the Second World War and its aftermath in popular movies of the 1950s would constitute a very different project, key parts of which have already been accomplished by Fehrenbach. In this chapter, I attempt no such broad sweep. The movies I discuss, listed with information on the director (D), screenplay writer (S), and production company (P), include: *Ännchen von Tharau* (1954; D, Wolfgang Schleif; S, Otto-Heinz Jahn; P, Apollo-Film; b&w); *Der Arzt von Stalingrad* (1958; D, Geza von Radvanyi; S, Werner P. Zibaso; P, Divina-Film; b&w); *Grün ist die Heide* (1951; D, Hans Deppe; S, B. E. Luethge; P, Berolina-Film; color); *Suchkind 312* (1955; D, Gustav Machaty; S, Machaty and W. P. Zibaso; P, Unicorn-Produktion; b&w); *Taiga* (1958; D, Wolfgang Liebeneiner; S, Herbert Reinecker; P, Bavaria-Filmkunst; b&w); *Der Teufel spielte Balalaika* (1961; D, Leopold Lahola; S, Heinrich Déchamps, Johannes Kai, and Leopold Lahola; P, Peter Bamberger; b&w); and *Waldwinter: Glocken der Heimat* (1956; D, Wolfgang Liebeneiner; S, Werner P. Zibaso and Frank Dimen, based on a novel by Paul Keller; P, Apollo-Film; color).

8. Gertrud Koch et al., "Die fünfizger Jahre: Heide und Silberwald," in *Der deutsche Heimatfilm: Bildwelten und Weltbilder*, ed. Dieter Bahlinger et al. (Tübingen: Tübinger Chronik, 1989), 88. See also Wolfgang Kaschuba, "Bildwelten als Weltbilder," ibid., 7–13; Margit Szöllösi-Janze, "'Aussuchen und abschiessen': Der Heimatfilm der fünfziger Jahre als historische Quelle," *Geschichte in Wissenschaft und Unterricht* 44 (1993): 308–21; and Klaus Sigl, Werner Schneider, and Ingo Tornow, *Jede Menge Kohle? Kunst und Kommerz auf dem deutschen Filmmarkt der Nachkriegszeit, Filmpreise und Kassenerfolge, 1949–1985* (Munich: Filmland Presse, 1986), 125.

9. Hans-Ulrich Horster [Eduard Rudolf Rhein], *Suchkind 312* (Frankfurt am Main: Ullstein, 1995). See also Eduard Rhein, *Der Jahrhundert Mann: Hans-Ulrich Horster erzählt die Geschichte seines Lebens und seiner Zeit* (Vienna: Paul Neff, 1990), 419.

10. Alexander U. Martens, *Heinz G. Konsalik: Portrait eines Bestseller-Autors* (Munich: Wilhelm Heyne, 1991).

11. On Bartok, see "Talent ist nicht alles," *Spiegel*, 21 July 1954. See also Curt Riess, *Das gibt's nur einmal: Das Buch des deutschen Films nach 1945* (Hamburg: Henri Nannen, 1958), 335–38.

12. Herbert Reinecker, *Pimpfenwelt*, new ed. (Berlin: W. Limpert, 1940).

13. "Favoriten in der Publikumsgunst," *Der neue Film*, 28 Jan. 1960; and Riess, *Das gibt's nur einmal*, 330–35.

14. For example, *Menschen in Gottes Hand* (1948; D, Rolf Meyer) features

the conflict between a father, driven from his East Prussian home, and his son, who has settled in western Germany; *Der Weg zu Dir* (1951; D, Harald Röbbeling) depicts the trials of a minister assigned to care for expellees, whose confrontation with the misery of the postwar world challenges his belief in God, but the love of a good woman and the generosity of a working-class family restore his faith; *Die Mühle vom Schwarzwäldertal* (1953; D, Hermann Kugelstadt) portrays an expellee who finds a home with two brothers, one good, one evil, and chooses between them; *Die Herrin von Sölderhof* (1955; D, Jürgen von Alten) and *Die grosse Versuchung* (1952; D, Rolf Hansen) both address the problems of reintegrating POWs into the alienating economic prosperity of the early 1950s; *Gefangene der Liebe* (1954; D, Rudolf Jugert) presents a woman who returns from Siberia with a child born in captivity, a development to which her husband adjusts only with difficulty; *Der Förster vom Silberwald* (1954; D, Alfons Stummer) depicts an honest, industrious protector of fauna and flora, an outsider from the east who has found his way west; *Der Schmied von St. Bartholomä* (1955; D, Max Michel) focuses on an embittered returning POW who, assisted by a good woman, finds the way back to normalcy by rediscovering his love for his son; *Heimat, deine Lieder* (1959; D, Paul May) tells the story of a woman who becomes the ersatz mother for an endlessly adorable group of homeless children, the charges of a social welfare institution located in an idyllic rural landscape, and makes explicit the analogy between displaced children from broken homes and displaced expellees from a broken Germany (in a scene where the children's choir performs for a local meeting of the *Landsmannschaft*, the regional interest group); *Rose Bernd* (1957; D, Wolfgang Staudte), a movie version of a Gerhart Hauptmann play, tells the story of a Silesian maid transferred at war's end to an unusually inhospitable West German countryside; and *Nacht fiel über Gotenhafen* (1960; D, Frank Wisbar) tells the story of the *Wilhelm Gutsloff,* a Nazi "Strength through Joy" ship converted to transport expellees from East Prussia in January 1945 and sunk by a submarine. The Federal Ministry of Expellees also became involved in soliciting scripts for potential movies about the expulsion, but I have found no evidence that any of the scripts submitted were actually produced. For samples of the scripts submitted, see BAK, B150/6989/Hefte 1 and 2, B150/6990/Hefte 1 and 2, B150/6991, Hefte 1 and 2. See also the discussion in Kurth, "Presse, Film und Rundfunk," 416–23; Barbara Bongartz, *Von Caligari zu Hitler—von Hitler zu Dr. Mabuse? Eine "psychologische" Geschichte des deutschen Films von 1946 bis 1960* (Münster: MAkS Publikationen, 1992), 45–46; Gerd Albrecht, "Fern der Wirklichkeit: Deutsche Spielfilme der Nachkriegszeit zum Thema Kriegsgefangenschaft und Heimkehr," in Haus der Geschichte der Bundesrepublik (ed.), *Kriegsgefangene-Voennoplennye,* 100–105.

15. In approaching these movies, I have found useful the comments on melodrama offered by Jackie Byars, *All That Hollywood Allows: Re-reading Gender in 1950s Melodrama* (Chapel Hill: University of North Carolina Press, 1991), 11; and, in general, Peter Brooks, *The Melodramatic Imagination: Balzac, Henry James, Melodrama, and the Mode of Excess* (New Haven: Yale Univerity Press, [1976] 1995), 14–15. Linda Schulte-Sasse, in *Entertaining the Third Reich: Illusions of Wholeness in Nazi Cinema* (Durham: Duke University Press, 1996),

31, writes of Nazi historical films that they "assume a foreknowledge on the part of the . . . viewer, and their pleasure generally derives less from teaching new material than in affirming the audience's foreknowledge, allowing it to savor what it already 'knows.'" Much the same could be said of the movies discussed here.

16. Kahlenberg, "Film der Ära Adenauer," 369; Anton Kaes, *From Hitler to Heimat: The Return of History as Film* (Cambridge, Mass.: Harvard University Press, 1989), 14; Bärbel Westermann, *Nationale Identität im Spielfilm der fünfziger Jahre* (Frankfurt am Main: Peter Lang, 1990), 157–75; Seidl, *Der deutsche Film,* 68; Gerhard Bliersbach, *So grün war die Heide: Der Nachkriegsfilm in neuer Sicht* (Weinheim: Beltz, 1985); and in general, Willi Höfig, *Der deutsche Heimatfilm, 1947–1960* (Stuttgart: Ferdinand Enke, 1973).

17. Celia Applegate, *A Nation of Provincials: The German Idea of Heimat* (Berkeley: University of California Press, 1990), 242 (quotation), see also 229, 243–44.

18. Alon Confino, "The Nation as a Local Metaphor: Heimat, National Memory, and the German Empire, 1871–1918," *History and Theory* 5 (1993): 54; and in general, idem, *Nation as Local Metaphor.* See also the useful comments of Erich Rentschler, *The Ministry of Illusion: Nazi Cinema and Its Afterlife* (Cambridge, Mass.: Harvard University Press, 1996), 74.

19. See Arnd Bauerkämper, "Landwirtschaft und ländliche Gesellschaft in der Bundesrepublik in den 50er Jahren," in Schildt and Sywottek (eds.), *Modernisierung im Wiederaufbau,* 188–200; Herbert Kötter, "Die Landwirtschaft," in *Sozialgeschichte der Bundesrepublik Deutschland: Beiträge zum Kontinuitätsproblem,* ed. Werner Conze and M. Rainer Lepsius (Stuttgart: Klett-Cotta, 1983), 115–42; Schildt, *Moderne Zeiten,* 48–63; Krause, *Flucht vor dem Bombenkrieg;* G. Schroeder, *Long Road Home;* and Dietrich Hilger, "Die mobilisierte Gesellschaft," in *Die zweite Republik: 25 Jahre Bundesrepublik Deutschland—eine Bilanz,* ed. Richard Löwenthal and Hans-Peter Schwarz (Stuttgart: Seewald, 1974), 95–122.

20. See the useful comments of Georg Seesslen, "Durch die Heimat und so weiter: Heimatfilme, Schlagerfilme und Ferienfilme der fünfziger Jahre," in Hoffmann and Schobert (eds.), *Zwischen Gestern und Morgen,* 139–41.

21. See Fehrenbach's discussion of this film in *Cinema in Democratizing Germany,* 158–61; also Kreimeier, *Kino und Filmindustrie in der BRD,* 103; Westermann, *Nationale Identität,* 189–203; and Cornelia Fleer, *Vom Kaiser-Panorama zum Heimatfilm: Kinogeschichten aus Bielefeld und der Provinz Westfalen* (Marburg: Jonas, 1996), 160.

22. "Das Geheimnis der 'Grünen Heide,'" *Süderländer Tageblatt,* 21 Mar. 1952.

23. Summary from Berolina, the distributor of the film, in DFI.

24. The quotation is taken from Fehrenbach, *Cinema in Democratizing Germany,* 153.

25. "Das Hohelied der Heimat in einem Farbfilm gesungen," *Selber Tagblatt,* 22 Mar. 1952.

26. Review in *Neue Tagespost,* 24 Nov. 1951.

27. Review in *Abend-Zeitung* (Munich), 21 Dec. 1951.

28. Fehrenbach, *Cinema in Democratizing Germany,* 153–54.

29. See, e.g., R. Schulze, "Growing Discontent."

30. "Sentimentaler Heimatfilm," *nacht-depesche*, 22 Dec. 1951.

31. Review in *Selber Tagblatt*, 22 Mar. 1952.

32. Review in *Trierischer Volksfreund*, 14 Jan. 1952.

33. Review in *Selber Tagblatt*, 22 Mar. 1952. See also "Sentimentaler Heimatfilm," *nacht-depesche*, 22 Dec. 1951; review in *Weinheimer Nachrichten*, 22 Dec. 1951; and "Das Geheimnis der 'Grünen Heide,'" *Süderländer Tageblatt*, 21 Mar. 1952.

34. In general, see Large, *Germans to the Front*.

35. See Garner, "Public Service Personnel," 135–95; also Ingo Müller, *Hitler's Justice: The Courts of the Third Reich*, trans. Deborah Lucas Schneider (Cambridge, Mass.: Harvard University Press, 1991), 204–7.

36. "Das Geheimnis der 'Grünen Heide,'" *Süderländer Tageblatt*, 21 Mar. 1952.

37. Klaus Kreimeier, *The Ufa Story: A History of Germany's Greatest Film Company, 1918–1945*, trans. Robert Kimber and Rita Kimber (New York: Hill & Wang, 1996), 275, 345–46; and on the continuities in directors and screenwriters from the Third Reich to the Bonn Republic in general, see Hans-Peter Kochenrath, "Kontinuität im deutschen Film," in *Film und Gesellschaft in Deutschland: Dokumente und Materialien*, ed. Wilfried von Bredow and Rolf Zurek (Hamburg: Hoffmann & Campe, 1975), 286–92.

38. Götz Aly, "Medicine against the Useless," in *Cleansing the Fatherland: Nazi Medicine and Racial Hygiene*, ed. Götz Aly, Peter Chroust, and Christian Pross, trans. Belinda Cooper (Baltimore: Johns Hopkins University Press, 1994), 27.

39. Quotations are from Hans-Christoph Blumenberg, *Das Leben geht weiter: Der letzte Film des Dritten Reichs* (Berlin: Rowohlt, 1993), 43. The book provides extensive background material on Liebeneiner's career in the Third Reich. On the background of the movie, see also Karl Ludwig Rost, "'Ich klage an'—ein historischer Film?" in *Medizin im Spielfilm des Nationalsozialismus*, ed. Udo Benzenhöfer and Wolfgang U. Eckart (Tecklenburg: Burg, 1990), 34–51; and David Welch, *Propaganda and the German Cinema, 1933–1945* (Oxford: Clarendon Press, 1983), 121–32. In general, on the Nazi euthanasia campaign, see Michael Burleigh, *Death and Deliverance: "Euthanasia" in Germany c. 1900–1945* (Cambridge: Cambridge University Press, 1994); and Henry Friedlander, *The Origins of Nazi Genocide: From Euthanasia to the Final Solution* (Chapel Hill: University of North Carolina Press, 1995).

40. Wolfgang Liebeneiner, "Was ist ein 'Heimatfilm'?" included in publicity materials from the film's distributor, copy in DFI.

41. Review in *Aachener Volkszeitung*, 31 Mar. 1956. See also reviews in *Freie Presse Bielefeld*, 1 Apr. 1956; and in *Trierische Landeszeitung*, 1 Apr. 1956.

42. Review in *Rhein-Neckar-Zeitung*, 22 June 1956. For a useful historical account of this part of the story, see Sebastian Siebel-Achenbach, *Lower Silesia from Nazi Germany to Communist Poland, 1942–49* (New York: St. Martin's Press, 1994), 117–48.

43. Review in *Westfalen-Blatt*, 29 Mar. 1956.

44. Szöllösi-Janze, "'Aussuchen und abschiessen,'" 319.

45. On the background of this mix between sentimentality and modernity, see Confino, *Nation as a Local Metaphor*, 112–14.

46. This theme generally echoed sociological accounts of the successful integration of expellees and newspaper stories that emphasized the economic contributions of expellees to the expanding West German economy. See, e.g., "Vertriebene Unternehmer bauen auf," *Frankfurter Allgemeine Zeitung,* 12 Dec. 1950, PIB, MF 1535; Gustav Stein, "Bisher fast eine Million neuer Arbeitsplätze für Vertriebene," *Die Zeit,* 3 Jan. 1952, PIB, MF 1536; "Geigenbauer und Glasbläser: Industrie und Handwerk aus dem Osten bauen in Bayern wieder auf," *Parlament,* 12 Mar. 1952, PIB, MF 1536.

47. Among those works that emphasize that the "economic miracle" began to bring marked improvement in the lives of most West Germans only in the last third of the 1950s, see Josef Mooser, *Arbeiterleben in Deutschland 1900–1970: Klassenlagen, Kultur und Politik* (Frankfurt am Main: Suhrkamp, 1984); Schildt, *Moderne Zeiten;* and Axel Schildt and Arnold Sywottek, "'Reconstruction' and 'Modernization': West German Social History during the 1950s," in Moeller (ed.), *West Germany Under Construction,* 413–43.

48. "Nicht verweht vom Winde," *Landshuter Zeitung,* 30 Mar. 1956.

49. Szöllösi-Janze, "'Aussuchen und abschiessen,'" 316.

50. Mitscherlich and Mitscherlich, *Unfähigkeit zu trauern,* 19.

51. "Film mit fränkischer Kulisse," *Volksblatt,* 7 Aug. 1954.

52. The materials are in DFI.

53. Review in *Film Echo,* 7 Aug. 1954.

54. See the discussion in Moeller, *Protecting Motherhood,* esp. 180–209; also Fehrenbach, "Rehabilitating Father*land.*"

55. See Hansjörg Kalcyk and Hans-Joachim Westholt, *Suchdienst-Kartei: Millionen Schicksale in der Nachkriegszeit* (Bonn: Stiftung Haus der Geschichte, n.d.).

56. The popularity of the program guide is discussed in Schildt, "From Reconstruction to 'Leisure Society,'" 202.

57. These materials on *Suchkind 312* are in the archive of the Stiftung Deutsche Kinemathek.

58. "Kinder suchen ihre Eltern . . . ," *Wilhelmshavener Zeitung,* 1 Dec. 1955.

59. Lothar Papke, "Scheingefecht mit der Aktualität," *Frankfurter Allgemeine Zeitung,* 18 Nov. 1955; also "Gegenwartsprobleme als Kolportage," *Kölner Stadt-Anzeiger,* 12 Nov. 1955.

60. "Kinder suchen ihre Eltern . . . ," *Wilhelmshavener Zeitung,* 1 Dec. 1955. See also review in *Trierischer Volksfreund,* 26 Mar. 1956.

61. Moeller, *Protecting Motherhood,* 171; quotation is from a 1954 case of a secretary employed in a federal ministry office in Bonn.

62. See the useful discussion of some of the war movies in Becker and Schöll, *In jenen Tagen;* also Reinold E. Thiel, "Acht Typen des Kriegsfilms," *Filmkritik,* no. 11 (1961): 514–19. For comparative perspectives on the genre elsewhere in the 1950s, see John Ramsden, "Refocusing 'The People's War': British War Films in the 1950s," *Journal of Contemporary History* 33 (1998): 35–63; Denise J. Youngblood, "*Ivan's Childhood* (USSR, 1962) and *Come and See* (USSR, 1985): Post-Stalinist Cinema and the Myth of World War II," in *World War II, Film, and History,* ed. John Whiteclay Chambers II and David Culbert (New York: Oxford University Press, 1996), 85–96; and Jeanine Basinger, *The World War*

II Combat Film: Anatomy of a Genre (New York: Columbia University Press, 1986).

63. "Kritikerpreis für Adorno und Wisbar," *Abendzeitung,* 17 Aug. 1959. See also the discussion of the movie in Westermann, *Nationale Identität,* 67–84.

64. Quotations from "So hart wie der Titel?" *Telegraf,* 1 Feb. 1959; "Ein deutsches Requiem," *Telegraf,* 7 May 1959; and *Frankfurter Nachtausgabe,* 23 Apr. 1959. See also Hans Hellmut Kirst, "Filmunternehmen Stalingrad," *Münchener Merkur,* 14 May 1959; "Keine Zeit für Heldentum," *Westfälische Rundschau,* 19 Mar. 1959; and Wilhelm Mogge, "Gipfel der deutschen Tragödie," *Kölnische Rundschau,* 11 April 1959.

65. Gunter Groll, "Frauen ohne Namen," *Süddeutsche Zeitung,* 27 Oct. 1951; "Irgendwo in Europa: Ein Filmdokument aus unseren Tagen," *Frankfurter Allgemeine Zeitung,* 4 Mar. 1952; and Klaus Bertram, "'Der Arzt von Stalingrad': Ein 'besessener' Regisseur: Geza von Radvani [*sic*] und ein ausgesuchtes Team profilierter Darsteller," *Ludwigsburger Kreiszeitung,* 12 Dec. 1958.

66. Quotation from Karena Nichoff, "Film ist Kompromiss," *Tagesspiegel,* 29 Jan. 1955. See also Irmgard Gödde, "Fernsehen ist an allem Schuld," *Westfalenpost,* 9 Dec. 1954; and "Die Staffelei des Filmregisseurs," *Frankfurter Rundschau,* 27 July 1954.

67. Heinz G. Konsalik, *Der Arzt von Stalingrad* (Munich: Wilhelm Heyne Verlag, 1997) (the thirty-ninth reprinting of the novel by this publisher).

68. "'Der Arzt von Stalingrad': Ehrgeiziger Gloriafilm im Atelier," *Stuttgarter Zeitung,* 10 Jan. 1958.

69. On *Canaris,* directed by Alfred Widemann, see Rudolf Lange, "Canaris—Verräter oder Held?" *Die Welt,* 31 Jan. 1955.

70. Hans Hellmut Kirst, *Zero Eight Fifteen: The Strange Mutiny of Gunner Asch,* trans. Robert Kee (London: Weidenfeld & Nicolson, 1955); idem, *Gunner Asch Goes to War: Zero Eight Fifteen II,* trans. Robert Kee (London: Weidenfeld & Nicolson, 1956); and idem, *The Return of Gunner Asch: Zero Eight Fifteen III,* trans. Robert Kee (London: Weidenfeld & Nicolson, 1957). On the second installment of the movie version that followed Asch to the war in Russia, see Friedrich A. Wagner, "Null-acht-fuffzehn im russischen Winter," *Frankfurter Allgemeine Zeitung,* 20 Aug. 1955; and Herbert Hohenemser, " . . . übrig bleibt brüllendes Vergnügen," *Münchener Merkur,* 28 Aug. 1955.

71. Hans-Jürgen Winkler, "Stacheldraht, Schlamm und heisere Schreie 'Dawai, Plenny!'" *Abendpost,* 23 Dec. 1957.

72. "Liebe lässt sich nicht verbieten," *Star-Revue,* no. 4 (1958).

73. On the participation of the German medical profession in crimes against humanity and the enforcement of racialist codes at home, see Alexander Mitscherlich and Fried Mielke, *Doctors of Infamy: The Story of the Nazi Medical Crimes* (New York: Schuman, 1949). See also idem, eds., *Medizin ohne Menschlichkeit: Dokumente des Nürnberger Ärzteprozesses* (Frankfurt am Main: Fischer, 1995); Robert Jay Lifton, *The Nazi Doctors: Medical Killing and the Psychology of Genocide* (New York: Basic Books, 1986); Aly, Chroust, and Pross (eds.), *Cleansing the Fatherland;* and Gabriele Czarnowski, *Das kontrollierte Paar: Ehe- und Sexualpolitik im Nationalsozialismus* (Weinheim: Deutscher Studien Verlag, 1991). On the proliferation of doctor movies in the 1950s in general, see

Udo Benzenhöfer, ed., *Medizin im Spielfilm der fünfziger Jahre* (Pfaffenweiler: Centaurus, 1993).

74. Discussions of the Hauptausschuss der freiwilligen Selbstkontrolle der Filmwirtschaft, meetings of 7 and 15 Feb. 1958, Stiftung Deutsche Kinemathek. On the background of this organization, see Fehrenbach, *Cinema in Democratizing Germany,* 83–84.

75. "Eine knappe Filmreise nach München: Besuch beim 'Arzt von Stalingrad' in Baldham—und einige andere Neuigkeiten," *Fränkische Tagespost,* 30 Nov. 1957.

76. Michael Lentz, "Samariter hinter Stacheldraht: 'Der Arzt von Stalingrad'— ein guter deutscher Film," *Westdeutsche Allgemeine Zeitung,* 22 Feb. 1958.

77. Karl Horn, "Heroische Sentimentalität, ein Filmlaster," *Frankfurter Allgemeine Zeitung,* 28 Feb. 1958; and Sabine Winter, "Der Illustriertenstil im Film: Schluss mit der kommerziellen Auswertung des Elends!" *Duisburger General-Anzeiger,* 5 Mar. 1958.

78. Klaus Bresser, "Stalingrad als Vorwand," *Kölner Stadtanzeiger,* 22 Feb. 1958.

79. Horn, "Heroische Sentimentalität," *Frankfurter Allgemeine Zeitung,* 28 Feb. 1958. See also Winter, "Illustriertenstil im Film," *Duisburger General-Anzeiger,* 5 Mar. 1958; and Alfred Happ, "Von Stalingrad ist kaum die Rede," *Die Welt,* 22 Feb. 1958.

80. "War es wirklich so? 'Der Arzt von Stalingrad' im Capitol," *Kölnische Rundschau,* 22 Feb. 1958.

81. The phrase "das ewig Weibliche" is employed in a critical review of the movie by Karena Niehoff, "Gefangenenschicksale," *Tagesspiegel,* 7 Sept. 1958.

82. See the nuanced discussion in Johannes von Moltke, "Trapped in America: The Americanization of the *Trapp-Familie,* or 'Papas Kino' Revisited," *German Studies Review* 19 (1996): 455–78; also Westermann, *Nationale Identität,* 130–42.

83. "Engel von Sibirien," *Star-Revue,* no. 13 (1958).

84. Review in *Wiesbadener Kurier,* 20 August 1959.

85. Joachim Reifenrath, "Plennis haben das Wort," *Kölner Stadtanzeiger,* 4 Oct. 1958.

86. Quotations from letter of Werner Kiessling to Utz Utermann, producer of the film, 29 Aug. 1958; see also the letter of Rabe, Verband der Heimkehrer, Kulturabteilung, to Herbert Reinecker, 11 Feb. 1958; and Werner Kiessling, business director of the Verband, to Utz Utermann–Produktion, 9 Apr. 1958; all in VdH Archiv, Kulturarbeit, Kgf.-Film Taiga, no. 58. See also the highly favorable review "Es geschah in der Taiga," *Heimkehrer,* 16 July 1958; also the review in *Spiegel,* 27 Aug. 1958; "Es geschah in der Taiga: Das Schicksal der Kriegsgefangenen in Film," *Wiesbadener Tageblatt,* 30–31 Aug. 1958; Heinz Koch, "Mehr als Leben sind Hoffnung und Glaube," *Göttinger Tageblatt,* 4 Oct. 1958; and "Film und Wirklichkeit: Heimkehrer diskutieren über neuen Kriegsgefangenenfilm," *Stuttgarter Zeitung,* 1 Aug. 1958. The figures on membership come from Teschner, "Entwicklung eines Interessenverbandes," 43.

87. "Ansprache des 1. Vorsitzenden des VdH, KV Pforzheim bei der festlichen Pforzheimer Aufführung des Filmes 'Taiga' 2.10.58"; and Ruth Leuwerik to

Werner Kiessling, 10 Dec. 1958; both in VdH Archiv, Kulturarbeit, Kgf.-Film Taiga, no. 58.

88. *Frankfurter Allgemeine Zeitung,* 10 Jan. 1962. See also "Der echteste Kriegsgefangenfilm," *Heimkehrer,* 25 Jan. 1962.

89. Ruth Leuwerik, "Ein Film, der notwendig ist . . . ," interview distributed by the film production company, copy in DFI; published as "Ein Film, der notwendig ist," *Frankfurter Neue Presse,* 1 Sept. 1958.

90. On this "new woman," see Atina Grossmann, *Reforming Sex: The German Movement for Birth Control and Abortion Reform, 1920–1950* (New York: Oxford University Press, 1995).

91. Heinz Koch, "Mehr als Leben sind Hoffnung und Glaube," *Göttinger Tageblatt,* 4 Oct. 1958.

92. Review by Hans Bender, *Deutsche Zeitung,* 25 Feb. 1961. See also the favorable review by Günter Dahl, "Ist der Teufel musikalisch?" *Die Zeit,* 3 Mar. 1961; "Zwei Methoden, Gefangene zu behandeln," *Stuttgarter Zeitung,* 24 Feb. 1961; reviews in *Die andere Zeitung,* 1 Mar. 1961; and review in *Film-Dienst,* 8 Mar. 1961.

93. Rosenfeld, "Popularization and Memory," 258.

94. Quotes from Friedrich A. Wagner, "Die Plennys von Sibirien," *Frankfurter Allgemeine Zeitung,* 22 July 1961. See also review by Hans Bender, *Deutsche Zeitung,* 25 Feb. 1961; Günter Dahl, "Ist der Teufel musikalisch?" *Die Zeit,* 3 Mar. 1961; "Zwei Methoden, Gefangene zu behandeln," *Stuttgarter Nachrichten,* 24 Feb. 1961; "Ein Film, der uns alle angeht," *Hannoversche Allgemeine,* 22 Feb. 1961; and review in *Rhein-Neckar-Zeitung,* 3 Mar. 1961.

95. Herms Senator, "Im Räderwerk der Diktatur," *Westdeutsche Allgemeine Zeitung,* 31 Dec. 1960; and, on the Soviet response, "Mut fehlt den deutschen Produzenten," *Weser Kurier,* 12 Aug. 1961.

96. Angela Stent, *From Embargo to Ostpolitik: The Political Economy of West German-Soviet Relations, 1955–1980* (Cambridge: Cambridge University Press, 1981), 79.

97. Friedrich A. Wagner, "Die Plennys von Sibirien," *Frankfurter Allgemeine Zeitung,* 27 July 1961.

98. See, e.g., the assessments of *Der Arzt von Stalingrad* from the Filmbewertungsstelle (Film Rating Office) Wiesbaden to Divina-Film, 10 May 1958; and Filmbewertungsstelle der Länder der Bundesrepublik Deutschland to Divina-Film, 20 Feb. 1958; and of *Taiga,* Filmbewertungsstelle Wiesbaden to Bavaria-Filmkunst, 9 June 1958; all in VdH Archiv, Kulturarbeit, Kgf.-Film Taiga, No. 58.

99. Wilfried von Bredow, "Filmpropaganda für Wehrbereitschaft: Kriegsfilme in der Bundesrepublik," in Bredow and Zurek (eds.), *Film und Gesellschaft in Deutschland,* 316–26; Westermann, *Nationale Identität,* 30–95; Seidl, *Der deutsche Film,* 34, 36–37.

100. Erich Kuby, *Mein ärgerliches Vaterland* (Munich: Carl Hanser, 1989), 210.

101. On Germans' increased geographic mobility, see Schildt and Sywottek, "'Reconstruction' and 'Modernization,'" 423–24.

102. "Waldwinter: Ein Farbfilm frei nach dem Roman des schlesischen Heimatdichters Paul Keller," distributed by Deutsche London Film, copy in DFI.

103. Interview in *Film-Telegramm*, 17 Jan. 1961. See also Bamberger's comments in "Mut fehlt den deutschen Produzenten," *Weser Kurier*, 12 Aug. 1961. Although I do not discuss television in this book, it is worth noting that two years earlier West Germans could see other tales of POWs in Soviet hands on the small screen, in Fritz Umgelter's version of Josef M. Bauer's novel *Soweit die Füsse tragen*, a six-part epic drama of a German POW's escape from a Siberian camp and his long journey home. It was a production of the Arbeitsgemeinschaften der Rundfunkanstalten Deutschlands, broadcast on the Westdeutscher Rundfunk. See Knut Hickethier, with the assistance of Peter Hoff, *Geschichte des deutschen Fernsehens* (Stuttgart: J. B. Metzler, 1998), 155. My thanks to Axel Schildt for this reference. The novel on which the miniseries was based is still avaiable in at least two inexpensive paperback editions, and in the summer of 1997 I was able to purchase a copy of the video through a German mail-order house.

104. Fehrenbach, *Cinema in Democratizing Germany*, 211–13.

105. Irmgard Wilharm, "Krieg in deutschen Nachkriegsspielfilmen," in *Lernen aus dem Krieg? Deutsche Nachkriegszeiten 1918 und 1945*, ed. Gottfried Niedhart and Dieter Riesenberger (Munich: C. H. Beck, 1992), 295–96; and Ludwig Gatter, "Die schlesische Magd Maria Schell," *Kölnische Rundschau*, 17 Apr. 1957. Another example is *Die Brücke* (D, Berhard Wicki; S, Michael Mansfeld and Karl-Wilhelm Vivier; P, Deutsche Film Hansa), a 1959 film that followed the end of the war in the west, not the east. It told the story of deluded German youths, mustered at the last minute to fight to the end. See Hans-Dieter Roos, "Bernhard Wickis Film von der 'Brücke,'" *Süddeutsche Zeitung*, 25 Oct. 1959; and Hans Schwab-Fehlisch, "Opfergang der Siebzehnjährigen," *Frankfurter Allgemeine Zeitung*, 24 Oct. 1959.

106. Review in *Süddeutsche Zeitung*, 16 Mar. 1961.

107. Heinz Ungureit, "Verwischte Konturen im sibirischen Lager," *Frankfurter Rundschau*, 24 July 1961.

108. Joe Hembus, *Der deutsche Film kann gar nicht besser sein: Ein Pamphlet von gestern, eine Abrechnung von heute* (Munich: Rogner & Bernhard, 1981).

Epilogue

1. The following discussion draws heavily on Hans Rothfels, "Zehn Jahre danach," *Vierteljahrshefte für Zeitgeschichte* 3 (1955); quotations are from 227–28, 232, 234–35, 237–38. Rothfels's sentiments were widely echoed in contemporary press accounts commemorating the tenth anniversary of the end of the war. See, e.g., "Vor zehn Jahren: Zusammenbruch," *Frankfurter Allgemeine Zeitung*, 6 May 1955; and C. H. Zodel, "Die grosse Zeremonie des Friedens steht noch aus," *Stuttgarter Nachrichten*, 5 May 1955.

2. This point is made by Elisabeth Domansky, "A Lost War: World War II in Postwar German Memory," in *Thinking about the Holocaust after Half a Century*, ed. Alvin H. Rosenfeld (Bloomington: Indiana University Press, 1997), 233–72; see also Geyer, "Place of the Second World War," 5–40. For some suggestive attempts to begin to record this other, "private" history of the war, see

Hans Joachim Schröder, "Die Vergegenwärtigung des Zweiten Weltkriegs in biographischen Interviewerzählungen," *Militärgeschichtliche Mitteilungen* 49
(1991): 9–37; idem, *Die gestohlenen Jahre: Erzählgeschichten und Geschichtserzählung im Interview: Der Zweite Weltkrieg aus der Sicht ehemaliger
Mannschaftssoldaten* (Tübingen: Max Niemeyer, 1992); A. Lehmann, *Im Fremden ungewollt zuhaus;* idem, *Gefangenschaft und Heimkehr;* and Rosenthal,
"Vom Krieg erzählen," 651–63. Specifically on the expellees, see Plato, "Fremde
Heimat." For a suggestive comparison of officers' memoirs from the 1950s and
1980s, see Friedrich Gerstenberger, "Strategische Erinnerungen: Die Memoiren
deutscher Offiziere," in Heer and Naumann (eds.), *Vernichtungskrieg,* 620–29.
Pathbreaking in its approach to a generational history of Germany from 1930
to 1960 is the work of Lutz Niethammer, especially "Heimat und Front: Versuch, zehn Kriegserinnerungen aus der Arbeiterklasse des Ruhrgebietes zu verstehen," in Niethammer (ed.), *"Die Jahre weiss man nicht,"* 162–232; and "Privat-
Wirtschaft." The same intention—to tell another story of the war and German
loss—was apparent in different forms in Alexander Kluge's 1979 film *Die Patriotin* and Helke Sanders's *BeFreier und Befreite* (discussed below). All attempts
to open what Domansky calls the "black boxes of memory filled with mementos wrapped in silence," I would emphasize, must be sensitive to the ways in which
private memories articulated many years after the war were filtered and shaped
by public memories that emerged in the first postwar decade and that have en-
joyed extraordinary longevity. See the comments of Michael Geyer, "The Politics of Memory in Contemporary Germany," in *Radical Evil,* ed. Joan Copjec
(London: Verso, 1996), 186; also, on the use and abuse of *Alltagsgeschichte,* see
Mary Nolan, "The *Historikerstreit* and Social History," in Baldwin (ed.), *Reworking the Past,* 224–48. For attempts to capture other memories in the 1950s,
see the fascinating study by the Institut für Sozialforschung, *Zum politischen Bewusstsein ehemaliger Kriegsgefangener: Eine soziologische Untersuchung im Verband der Heimkehrer—Forschungsbericht* (Frankfurt am Main, 1957). Also offering a more critical perspective on the attitudes of expellees is another work
done under the auspices of the Institut für Sozialforschung: Friedrich Pollock,
Gruppenexperiment: Ein Studienbericht (Frankfurt am Main: Europäische Verlagsanstalt, 1955).

3. For a good introduction to the historiography on National Socialism, see
Ian Kershaw, *The Nazi Dictatorship: Problems and Perspectives of Interpretation,* 3d ed. (London: Edward Arnold, 1993); Bernd Faulenbach, "Emanzipation von der deutschen Tradition? Geschichtsbewusstsein in den sechziger
Jahren," in *Politische Kultur und deutsche Frage: Materialien zum Staats- und
Nationalbewusstsein in der Bundesrepublik Deutschland,* ed. Werner Weidenfeld (Cologne: Wissenschaft & Politik, 1989), 73–92; and Omer Bartov, "Wem
gehört die Geschichte? Wehrmacht und Geschichtswissenschaft," in Heer and
Naumann (eds.), *Vernichtungskrieg,* 601–19. I have also benefited enormously
from the superb essay by Jane Caplan, "The Historiography of National Socialism," in *Companion to Historiography,* ed. Michael Bentley (London: Routledge, 1997), 545–90.

4. H. G. van Dam and Ralph Giordano, eds., *KZ-Verbrechen vor deutschen
Gerichten: Dokumente aus den Prozesssen gegen Sommer (KZ Buchenwald),*

Sorge, Schubert (*KZ Sachsenhausen*), *Unkelbach* (*Ghetto in Czenstochau*) (Frankfurt am Main: Europäische Verlagsanstalt, 1962), 152–510; also Brochhagen, *Nach Nürnberg*, 250. In general on changing attitudes in the 1960s, see Harold Marcuse, "The Revival of Holocaust Awareness in West Germany, Israel, and the United States," in *1968: The World Transformed*, ed. Carole Fink, Philipp Gassert, and Detlef Junker (Cambridge: Cambridge University Press, 1998), 421–38.

5. Twenty-two were originally charged, but two left the proceedings because of illness. See Gerhard Werle and Thomas Wandres, *Auschwitz vor Gericht: Völkermord und bundesdeutsche Strafjustiz* (Munich: C. H. Beck, 1995); and Hermann Langbein, *Der Auschwitz-Prozess: Eine Dokumentation*, 2 vols. (Frankfurt am Main: Neue Kritik, [1965] 1995).

6. In general, see Dubiel, *Niemand ist frei*, 103–10; Adalbert Rückerl, *NS-Verbrechen vor Gericht: Versuch einer Vergangenheitsbewältigung* (Heidelberg: C. F. Müller, 1982); Alfred Streim, "Saubere Wehrmacht? Die Verfolgung von Kriegs- und NS-Verbrechen in der Bundesrepublik und in der DDR," in Heer and Naumann (eds.), *Vernichtungskrieg*, 575–87; Jürgen Weber and Peter Steinbach, eds., *Vergangenheitsbewältigung durch Strafverfahren? NS-Prozesse in der Bundesrepublik Deutschland* (Munich: G. Olzog, 1984); and Christoph Klessmann, *Zwei Staaten, eine Nation: Deutsche Geschichte, 1955–1970* (Göttingen: Vandenhoeck & Ruprecht, 1988), 180. Particularly illuminating is Marcuse, *Legacies of Dachau*.

7. The literature on *Ostpolitik* is vast. For an introduction, see Ash, *In Europe's Name*.

8. On the history of the project in general, see Rolf Steininger, "Some Reflections on the Maschke Commission," in Bischof and Ambrose (eds.), *Eisenhower and the German POWs*, 170–80; and Maschke (ed.), *Die deutschen Kriegsgefangenen*, 3–37; see also the discussion of the project in BVFK, 27 Mar. 1957, BAK, B150/4376/Heft 3.

9. Schönwälder, *Historiker und Politik*, 104, 148, and 153 (quotations), also 126, 143, 260. On Maschke's background, including his service in the educational and political work of the Nazi Party, see Burleigh, *Germany Turns Eastwards*, 137.

10. Quoted in Schönwälder, *Historiker und Politik*, 242.

11. W. Schulze, "German Historiography," 36.

12. In general, see Smith, *Heimkehr*, 151–69; and Steininger, "Reflections," 177, who, writing in 1992, called the series "the authoritative study of the German POWS" and predicted that it would continue to hold that status "for some time to come." Here, I refer only to the volumes on eastern Europe and the Soviet Union.

13. Quoted in letter from Stoeppel of the legal office of the Verband der Heimkehrer to members of the *Präsidium* of the organization, 2 Mar. 1959, VdH Archiv, 15/12, Dokumentation, Wissenschaftliche Kommission.

14. Erich Maschke, "Das Schicksal der deutschen Kriegsgefangenen des Zweiten Weltkrieges als Aufgabe zeitgeschichtlicher Forschung," in Kurt W. Böhme, *Die deutschen Kriegsgefangenen in Jugoslawien*, vol. 1: *1944–1949* (Bielefeld: Ernst & Werner Gieseking, 1962), pt. 1, x; also idem, "Deutsche

Kriegsgefangenengeschichte: Der Gang der Forschung," in Maschke (ed.), *Die deutschen Kriegsgefangenen*, 3–7.

15. Maschke, "Deutsche Kriegsgefangenengeschichte," 18.

16. Carl Schuster, "Kriegsgefangene schreiben ihre Geschichte,"*Aachener Volkszeitung,* 19 Apr. 1961; also Overmans, "German Historiography," 138.

17. Maschke, "Deutsche Kriegsgefangenengeschichte," 22–23.

18. See Johann Gottschick, *Psychiatrie der Kriegsgefangenschaft dargestellt auf Grund von Beobachtungen in den USA an deutschen Kriegsgefangenen aus dem letzten Weltkrieg* (Stuttgart: Gustav Fischer, 1963), 3; also K. H. Flothmann, "Typische Gefangenschaftskrankheiten und ihre somatischen und psychischen Entstehungsfaktoren," in *Extreme Lebensverhältnisse und ihre Folgen: Handbuch der ärztlichen Erfahrungen aus der Gefangenschaft,* ed. E. G. Schenck and W. von Nathusius, vol. 1. (n.p.: Schriftenreihe des ärztlich-wissenschaftlichen Beirates des Verbandes der Heimkehrer Deutschlands e.V., 1958), 53. For refugees, the counterpart to "barbed-wire sickness" was the "refugee neurosis"; see Alfred Karasek-Langer, "Volkstum im Umbruch," in Lemberg and Edding (ed.), *Die Vertriebenen,* 1:638.

19. See speech by Maschke to the 72. Diskussionswoche in Mehlem, 24 Jan. 1962, an event sponsored by the League of Returning Prisoners of War, Bundesarchiv-Militärarchiv (Freiburg) [hereafter BAMF], B205/1125.

20. Maschke, "Sinn und Aufgabe der Kriegsgefangenendokumentation," speech given at 6. Verbandstag des Verbandes der Heimkehrer Deutschlands, 2 Sept. 1960, BAMF, B205/1d.

21. See, e.g., Maschke's notes on meeting with Foreign Ministry officials, 30 July 1963, BAMF, B205/694; Maschke's notes, 1 Aug. 1963, ibid.; and "Kriegsgefangenen-Dokumentation auf Eis?" *Heimkehrer,* 10 Sept. 1963. See also memo prepared by Peter Paul Nahm, 30 July 1963, BAK, B106/33889.

22. Heiko Wegener, "Kriegsgefangenen-Buch soll Geheimnis bleiben," *Westfalen-Blatt,* 18 Apr. 1969; "CSU-Organ beschuldigt Brandt," *Frankfurter Rundschau,* 8 May 1969; and Karl Friedrich Grosse, "Wer klagt die Wahrheit an?" *Bayern-Kurier,* 17 Aug. 1974; copies in BAMF, B205/5.

23. "Wieder ein Geheimdokument in Quick: Diesmal geht es um den grausamen Tod von 1,5 Millionen deutschen Soldaten," *Quick,* 2 Mar. 1972. The series continued through 17 July 1972. See also Lothar Labusch, "'Noch mal satt werden und dann Schluss': Dokumentation unter Verschluss," *Kölner Stadt-Anzeiger,* 31 Mar.–1 Apr. 1973, copy in BAMF, B205/5; and Maschke's account of the political reasons for the delay of release of all volumes in "Deutsche Kriegsgefangenengeschichte," 27–37.

24. Published as *Ostpreussisches Tagebuch: Aufzeichnungen eines Arztes aus den Jahren 1945–1947* (Munich: Biederstein, 1966). Käthe von Normann's *Tagebuch aus Pommern 1945/46,* another of the diaries published in the expellee project, also appeared in an inexpensive paperback edition, published by Deutscher Taschenbuch Verlag in Munich in 1962.

25. See, e.g., Hans Edgar Jahn, *Pommersche Passion* (Preetz/Holstein: Ernst Gerdes, 1964); Rolf O. Becker, *Niederschlesien 1945: Die Flucht—Die Besetzung* (Bad Nauheim: Podzun, 1965); and Wolfgang Schwarz, *Die Flucht und Vertreibung: Oberschlesien 1945/46* (Bad Nauheim: Podzun, 1965). These vol-

umes, though providing no specific citations, claimed to be based "on documents of the Bundesministerium für Vertriebene, Flüchtlinge und Kriegsgeschädigte" and "documents from the Bundesarchiv in Koblenz." See also, e.g., Karl Friedrich Grau, *Schlesisches Inferno: Kriegsverbrechen der Roten Armee beim Einbruch in Schlesien 1945* (Stuttgart: Seewald, 1966); Egbert Kieser, *Danziger Bucht 1945: Dokumentation einer Katastrophe* (Esslingen am Neckar: Bechtle, 1978); Fritz Brustat-Naval, *Unternehmen Rettung: Letztes Schiff nach Westen* (Herford: Koehler, 1970); Günter Böddeker, *Die Flüchtlinge: Die Vertreibung der Deutschen im Osten* (Munich: F. A. Herbig, 1980); and Donauschwäbische Kulturstiftung, ed., *Leidensweg der Deutschen im kommunistischen Jugoslawien,* vol. 1: *Ortsberichte über die Verbrechen an den Deutschen durch das Tito-Regime in der Zeit von 1944–1948,* and vol. 2: *Erlebnisberichte über die Verbrechen an den Deutschen durch das Tito-Regime in der Zeit von 1944–1948* (Munich: Donauschwäbische Kulturstiftung, 1992–93). For a detailed review of novels, see Helbig, *Der ungeheuere Verlust.* The American author Alfred-Maurice de Zayas also contributed to this steady stream, publishing in both English and German; see, most recently, *A Terrible Revenge: The Ethnic Cleansing of the East European Germans, 1944–1950* (New York: St. Martin's Press, 1994).

26. See, e.g., Bundesministerium für Vertriebene, Flüchtlinge und Kriegsgeschädigte, ed., *Dokumente deutscher Kriegsschäden: Evakuierte, Kriegssachgeschädigte, Währungsgeschädigte,* vols. 1–2 (Düsseldorf: Triltsch-Druck, 1958–60); and idem, ed., *Die Lastenausgleichsgesetze: Dokumente zur Entwicklung des Gedankens, der Gesetzgebung und der Durchführung,* vol. 1/1: *Soforthilfe und Festellungsgesetz* (Bielefeld-Bethel: Ernst Gieseking, 1962); and vol. 2/1: *Die Änderungsgesetzgebung zum LAG von der ersten bis zur achten Novelle* (Stuttgart: Ackermann & Honold, 1962).

27. In the 1950s, these institutes were often filled with historians who were themselves expellees and whose scholarly careers under the Nazis included "scientific" justification of the Nazis' expansionist policies. See Christoph Klessmann, "Geschichtsbewusstsein nach 1945: Ein neuer Anfang?" in *Geschichtsbewusstsein der Deutschen: Materialien zur Spurensuche einer Nation,* ed. Werner Weidenfeld (Cologne: Wissenschaft & Politik, 1987), 118–19; Burleigh, *Germany Turns Eastward,* 306, 313–14; and Eduard Mühle, "'Ostforschung': Beobachtungen zu Aufstieg und Niedergang eines geschichtswissenschaftlichen Paradigmas," *Zeitschrift für Ost-Mitteleuropaforschung* 46 (1997): 336–46.

28. See, e.g., Bingen, "Westverschiebung Polens," 155–76; Werner Jakobsmeier, "Das Münchner Abkommen: Unüberbrückbarer Graben zwischen Bonn und Prag?" in Haberl and Hecker (eds.), *Unfertige Nachbarschaften,* 177–203; and Ahonen, "Expellee Organizations."

29. Dieter von König, "Auch Deutsche mussten leiden," *Rhein-Neckar-Zeitung,* 31 July 1974, copy in BAMF, B205/6.

30. See, in particular, Ahonen, "Expellee Organizations."

31. Ivo Frenzel and Peter Märthesheimer, eds., *Im Kreuzfeuer: Der Fernsehfilm "Holocaust"* (Frankfurt am Main: Fischer Taschenbuch Verlag, 1979); Jeffrey Herf, "The 'Holocaust' Reception in West Germany: Right, Center and Left," *New German Critique,* no. 19 (1980): 30–52.

32. Rudolf Mühlfenzl, "Warum erst jetzt?" in *Geflohen und vertrieben: Augenzeugen berichten,* ed. Rudolf Mühlfenzl (Königstein/Taunus: Athenäum, 1981), 8; and the enthusiastic reception in "Persönliches Leid, kollektives Schicksal," *Süddeutsche Zeitung,* 29 Jan. 1981. See also "Die alten Wunden: Zur Dokumentation der Vertreibung im Fernsehen," *Frankfurter Allgemeine Zeitung,* 29 Jan. 1981; "Wahrheit ist keine Rache," *Die Welt,* 7 Feb. 1981; and Klaus Naumann, "'Flucht und Vertreibung': Aktuelle und historische Aspekte eines bundesdeutschen Syndroms," *Blätter für deutsche und internationale Politik,* no. 8 (1981): 981–95, a critical assessment that places the series in the longer-term perspective of the West German preoccupation with the expulsion.

33. Mühlfenzl, "Warum erst jetzt?" 8. See also the large-format, richly illustrated book by Frank Grube and Gerhard Richter, *Flucht und Vertreibung: Deutschland zwischen 1944 und 1947* (Hamburg: Hoffmann & Campe, 1980).

34. Arno Surminski, *Jokehnen: oder, Wie lange fährt man von Ostpreussen nach Deutschland?* (Stuttgart: Werner Gebühr, 1974). The three-part miniseries was directed by Michael Lahn and was produced in 1987.

35. Gotthold Rhode, "Das Leid der Vertreibung: Zum Neudruck einer Dokumentation," *Frankfurter Allgemeine Zeitung,* 14 May 1985. See also Henke, "Flucht und Vertreibung."

36. A good overview of this work is provided in Schulze, Brelie-Lewien, and Grebing (eds.), *Flüchtlinge und Vertriebene;* also Wolfrum, "Zwischen Geschichtsschreibung und Geschichtspolitik," 500–522.

37. See, e.g., Eva Berthold, *Kriegsgefangene im Osten: Bilder, Briefe, Berichte* (Königstein/Taunus:Athenäum, 1981), 8–9; also Paul Carell and Günter Böddeker, *Die Gefangenen: Leben und Überleben deutscher Soldaten hinter Stacheldraht* (Frankfurt am Main: Ullstein, 1980); also Steininger, "Some Reflections," 177n.16.

38. Detlev J. K. Peukert, "Alltag und Barbarei: Zur Normalität des Dritten Reiches," in *Ist der Nationalsozialismus Geschichte? Zu Historisierung und Historikerstreit,* ed. Dan Diner (Frankfurt am Main: Fischer Taschenbuch Verlag, 1987), 56. See also the important essay by Herbert, "'Die guten und die schlechten Zeiten,'" 67–96; and Kaplan, *Between Dignity and Despair,* 8–9.

39. See, e.g., Berthold, *Kriegsgefangene im Osten;* also Lehmann, *Im Fremden ungewollt zuhaus* and *Gefangenschaft und Heimkehr.*

40. My thought on these subjects is particularly influenced by Kaes, *From Hitler to Heimat.*

41. See ibid., 150; Barbara Kosta, *Recasting Autobiography: Women's Counterfictions in Contemporary German Literature and Film* (Ithaca, N.Y.: Cornell University Press, 1994), 144; Richard W. McCormick, "Confronting German History: Melodrama, Distantiation, and Women's Discourse in *Germany, Pale Mother,*" in *Gender and German Cinema: Feminist Interventions,* vol. 2: *German Film History/German History on Film,* ed. Sandra Frieden et al. (Providence: Berg, 1993), 201; the insightful review of the film by Jane Caplan, *American Historical Review* 96 (1991): 1126–28; and Helma Sanders-Brahms, *Deutschland, bleiche Mutter: Film Erzählung* (Reinbek bei Hamburg: Rowohlt, 1980), 71–80.

42. Mühlfenzl (ed.), *Geflohen,* 159.

43. Alexander Kluge, *Die Patriotin: Texte/Bilder 1–6* (Frankfurt am Main: Zweitausendeins, 1979), 59.

44. Ibid., 54–58. See also "Herrlicher Quatsch," *Spiegel,* 17 Dec. 1979; Volker Bauer, "Das Knie und die Weltgeschichte," *Tagesspiegel,* 21 Dec. 1979; Wolfram Schütte, "Lichte Tiefen auf Bohrgelände," *Frankfurter Rundschau,* 9 Dec. 1979; and H. G. Pflaum, "Das Knie des Obergefreiten Wieland," *Süddeutsche Zeitung,* 15 Dec. 1979; copies in DFI.

45. Wolfgang Borchert, *The Man Outside: Prose Works of Wolfgang Borchert,* trans. David Porter, intro. Stephen Spender (Norfolk, Conn.: New Directions, 1952), 77–78. A paperback edition of *Draussen vor der Tür und ausgewählte Erzählungen* was published by the German publisher Rowohlt in 1956. By 1957 it was in a third printing and 100,000 copies were in circulation; by 1970 the number was 878,000.

46. Kaes, *From Hitler to Heimat,* 133. On the reception of *Night and Fog* in late 1950s West Germany, see Marcuse, "Revival of Holocaust Awareness," 422. On Kluge, see Bartov, *Murder,* 139–52; and the otherwise highly favorable reflections of Stefanie Carp, "Schlachtbeschreibungen: Ein Blick auf Walter Kempowski und Alexander Kluge," in Herr and Naumann (eds.), *Vernichtungskrieg,* 677. Kluge's fascination with the battle of Stalingrad long predated the film; see Alexander Kluge, *The Battle,* trans. Leila Vennewitz (New York: McGraw Hill, 1967).

47. Alon Confino, "Edgar Reitz's *Heimat* and German Nationhood: Film, Memory, and Understandings of the Past," *German History* 16 (1998): 204–5.

48. See Kenneth Barkin's review of the miniseries in *American Historical Review* 96 (1991): 1124; and Santner, *Stranded Objects,* 60.

49. Karsten Witte, "Of the Greatness of the Small People: The Rehabilitation of a Genre," *New German Critique,* no. 36 (1985): 8. See also Gertrud Koch, "How Much Naiveté Can We Afford? The New *Heimat* Feeling," ibid., 13–16; Kenneth D. Barkin, "Modern Germany: A Twisted Vision," *Dissent* 34 (1987): 252–55; and, in general, the thoughtful treatment of Kaes, *From Hitler to Heimat,* 163–92.

50. "Address by Chancellor Helmut Kohl to German and American Soldiers and Their Families at Bitburg, May 5, 1985," in Hartman (ed.), *Bitburg in Moral and Political Perspective,* 256. Hartman's collection is an excellent source for key documents on the controversy surrounding Reagan's trip.

51. "Remarks of President Ronald Reagan to Regional Editors, White House, April 18, 1985," ibid., 240.

52. "Speech by Richard von Weizsäcker, President of the Federal Republic of Germany, in the Bundestag during the Ceremony Commemorating the 40th Anniversary of the End of the War in Europe and of National Socialist Tyranny, May 8, 1985," ibid., 263. In general, see Dubiel, *Niemand ist frei,* 200–215.

53. Timothy Garton Ash, "Germany after Bitburg," *New Republic,* 15 and 22 July 1985, 15–17, reprinted in Hartman (ed.), *Bitburg,* 199–203.

54. "Schindluder mit der Friedenspolitik," *Spiegel,* 4 Feb. 1985, 93. See also "'Die Polen sind Teil des Abendlandes': Der Vorsitzende der CDU/CSU-Fraktion, Alfred Dregger, über Ostpolitik und Vertriebene," ibid., 95.

55. Among the most important are Geoff Eley, "Nazism, Politics and Public Memory: Thoughts on the West German *Historikerstreit,* 1986–1987," *Past and*

Present, no. 121 (1988): 171–208; Charles S. Maier, *The Unmasterable Past: History, Holocaust, and German National Identity* (Cambridge, Mass.: Harvard University Press, 1988); Richard J. Evans, *In Hitler's Shadow: West German Historians and the Attempt to Escape from the Nazi Past* (New York: Pantheon, 1989); the essays collected in Baldwin (ed.), *Reworking the Past;* and Saul Friedlander, ed., *Probing the Limits of Representation: Nazism and the "Final Solution"* (Cambridge, Mass.: Harvard University Press, 1992).

56. Andreas Hillgruber, *Zweierlei Untergang: Die Zerschlagung des Deutschen Reiches und das Ende des europäischen Judentums* (Berlin: Siedler, 1986).

57. Kulka, "Major Tendencies," 228. See in particular Andreas Hillgruber, "Die 'Endlösung' und das deutsche Ostimperium als Kernstück des rassenideologischen Programms des Nationalsozialismus," *Vierteljahrshefte für Zeitgeschichte* 20 (1982): 133–53; and the discussion in Maier, *Unmasterable Past,* 19.

58. Perry Anderson, "On Emplotment: Two Kinds of Ruin," in Friedlander (ed.), *Probing the Limits of Representation,* 58; also Günter Wollstein, "Andreas Hillgruber: Historiker der Grossmacht Deutsches Reich," *Militärgeschichtliche Mitteilungen* 46 (1989): 9–19; Hillgruber's comments in Hillgruber (ed.), *Vom Beruf des Historikers,* 9–10; the insightful analysis of Bartov, *Murder,* 71–89; and Hans-Ulrich Wehler, *Entsorgung der Vergangenheit? Ein polemischer Essay zum "Historikerstreit"* (Munich: C. H. Beck, 1988), 20–23, 47.

59. Hillgruber, *Zweierlei Untergang,* 24–25.

60. Maier, *Unmasterable Past,* 23.

61. Hillgruber, *Zweierlei Untergang,* 24. See also idem, "Jürgen Habermas, Karl-Heinz Janssen und die Aufkärung Anno 1986," in *"Historikerstreit": Die Dokumentation der Kontroverse um die Einzigartigkeit der nationalsozialistischen Judenvernichtung* (Munich: Piper, 1987), 331–51. The texts are available in English translation in *Forever in the Shadow of Hitler? Original Documents of the Historikerstreit, the Controversy Concerning the Singularity of the Holocaust,* trans. James Knowlton and Truett Cates (Atlantic Highlands, N.J.: Humanities Press, 1993). Critical commentaries can be found in Evans, *In Hitler's Shadow,* 54; Jörg Friedrich, "Die Schlacht bei Auschwitz: Zur Entstehung der KZ-Prozesse," in *Von der Gnade der geschenkten Nation: Zur politischen Moral der Bonner Republik,* ed. Hajo Funke (Berlin: Rotbuch Verlag, 1988), 173; and Wehler, *Entsorgung der Vergangenheit,* 164–65.

62. Andreas Hillgruber, "Für die Forschung gibt es kein Frageverbot," in *"Historikerstreit,"* 239; also Maier, *Unmasterable Past,* 23–25.

63. Kulka, "Major Tendencies," 227.

64. Wehler, *Entsorgung der Vergangenheit,* 13.

65. Ernst Nolte, *Der Faschismus in seiner Epoche,* 2d ed. (Munich, 1965), 436, quoted in Hillgruber, "'Endlösung,'" 138.

66. On Nolte and the atrocities of Stalinism, see Wehler, *Entsorgung der Vergangenheit,* 15.

67. Ernst Nolte, "Vergangenheit, die nicht vergehen will: Eine Rede, die geschrieben, aber nicht gehalten werden konnte," in *"Historikerstreit,"* 45. The article appeared originally in the 6 June 1986 issue of the *Frankfurter Allgemeine Zeitung.*

68. Bartov, *Murder,* 120, also 86–88.

69. Saul Friedlander, *A Conflict of Memories? The New German Debates about the "Final Solution"* (New York: Leo Baeck Institute, 1987), 14.

70. Rothfels, "Zehn Jahre danach," 232.

71. On anti-Asian racism in Nazi propaganda, see Evans, *In Hitler's Shadow,* 138.

72. See, e.g., Otto Dov Kulka, "Singularity and Its Relativization: Changing Views in the German Historiography on National Socialism and the 'Final Solution,'" in Baldwin (ed.), *Reworking the Past,* 146–70; and the lucid treatment of Ian Kershaw, "'Normality' and Genocide: The Problem of 'Historicization,'" in *Reevaluating the Third Reich,* ed. Thomas Childers and Jane Caplan (New York: Holmes & Meier, 1993), 20–41.

73. Rothfels, "Zehn Jahre danach," 252.

74. Michael Stürmer, "Kein Eigentum der Deutschen: Die deutsche Frage," in *Die Identität der Deutschen,* ed. Werner Weidenfeld (Munich: Carl Hanser, 1983), 84.

75. Joachim Fest, "Die geschuldete Erinnerung: Zur Kontroverse über die Unvergleichbarkeit der nationalsozialistischen Massenverbrechen," in *"Historikerstreit,"* 100.

76. Martin Broszat, "A Plea for the Historicization of National Socialism," in Baldwin (ed.), *Reworking the Past,* 77–87. See also Saul Friedländer, "Some Reflections on the Historicization of National Socialism," ibid., 88–101; Martin Broszat and Saul Friedländer, "A Controversy about the Historicization of National Socialism," ibid., 102–34; and Dan Diner, "Between Aporia and Apology: On the Limits of Historicizing National Socialism," ibid., 135–45. On Hillgruber's familiarity with the Schieder documentation project, see his review of the volumes on Hungary and Romania in *Neue politische Literatur* 2 (1957): 969–74.

77. There are interesting parallels with postwar French history, as described by Henry Rousso in *The Vichy Syndrome: History and Memory in France since 1944,* trans. Arthur Goldhammer (Cambridge, Mass.: Harvard University Press, 1991). However, the "repressed" that returned in 1970s France was the repressed history of collaboration and French anti-Semitism. Another potential point of reference is the Japanese case, where memories of Japanese aggression and terror were far more completely submerged. See Carol Gluck, "The Past in the Present," in *Postwar Japan as History,* ed. Andrew Gordon (Berkeley and Los Angeles: University of California Press, 1993), 64–95; Dower, "Triumphal and Tragic Narratives," 1130–31; the thoughtful reflections of Norma Field, *In the Realm of a Dying Emperor: Japan at Century's End* (New York: Vintage Books, 1993); and John W. Dower, "The Bombed: Hiroshimas and Nagasakis in Japanese Memory," *Diplomatic History* 19 (1995): 275–95. For a bibliographic overview of postwar historiography in general, see R. J. B. Bosworth, *Explaining Auschwitz and Hiroshima: History Writing and the Second World War, 1945–1990* (London: Routledge, 1993); and Buruma, *Wages of Guilt.*

78. Peter Schneider, "Hitler's Shadow: On Being a Self-Conscious German," *Harper's,* Sept. 1987, 50; also Bartov, *Murder,* 120; and Dower, "Triumphal and Tragic Narratives," 1124.

79. Michael Stürmer, "Weder verdrängen noch bewältigen: Geschichte und Gegenwartsbewusstsein der Deutschen," *Schweizer Monatshefte* 66 (1986): 690.

80. Jürgen Habermas, "A Kind of Settlement of Damages (Apologetic Tendencies)," *New German Critique*, no. 44 (1988): 26.

81. Eugen Kogon, "Über die Situation," *Frankfurter Hefte* 2, no. 1 (Jan. 1947): 17–37, quotation on 34.

82. See the suggestive comments of Claudia Koonz, "Between Memory and Oblivion: Concentration Camps in German Memory," in *Commemorations: The Politics of National Identity,* ed. John R. Gillis (Princeton: Princeton University Press, 1994), 258–80; idem, "Germany's Buchenwald," 111–19; and Michael Geyer and Miriam Hansen, "German-Jewish Memory and National Consciousness," in *Holocaust Remembrance: The Shapes of Memory,* ed. Geoffrey H. Hartman (Cambridge, Mass.: Harvard University Press, 1994), 175–90.

83. Young, *Texture of Memory,* 25.

84. Stephen Kinzer, "The War Memorial: To Embrace the Guilty, Too?" *New York Times,* 15 Nov. 1993; Daniela Büchten and Anja Frey, eds., *Im Irrgarten deutscher Geschichte: Die neue Wache, 1818 bis 1993* (Berlin: Movimento Druck, 1993); Reichel, *Politik mit der Erinnerung,* 231–46; and Mariatte C. Denman, "Visualizing the Nation: Madonnas and Mourning Mothers in Postwar Germany," in *Gender and Germanness: Cultural Production of Nation,* ed. Patricia Herminghouse and Magda Mueller (Providence, R.I.: Berghahn Books, 1997), 189–201.

85. In a personal communication of 18 September 1998, Hans-Joachim Westholt, the curator of the exhibition, confirmed that the film is a compilation of different clips from the winter of 1944–45. He writes that the "film contains different materials cut together. The scene 'Flight across Fields of Ice' can definitively be dated for winter 1944/45. The exact location cannot be identified, although it is probably the so-called 'Frisches Haff,' part of the Baltic Sea." In general on the museum, see Reichel, *Politik mit der Erinnerung,* 249–52.

86. Helke Sander and Barbara Johr, eds., *BeFreier und Befreite: Krieg, Vergewaltigungen, Kinder* (Munich: Antje Kunstmann, 1992). See interview with Sanders, "Dokumentation eines grauenhaften Tabus," *Süddeutsche Zeitung,* 8 Dec. 1992; "Trophäen für die Sieger," *Spiegel,* 1 June 1992; Anke Sterneborg, "Das Schweigen brechen," *Tagesspiegel,* 26 Feb. 1992; the critical assessment of Gertrud Koch, "Kurzschluss der Perspektiven," *Frankfurter Rundschau,* 17–18 Nov. 1992; and Sanders's response, "'Du machst es Dir viel zu einfach,'" ibid., 26 Nov. 1992; copies in DFI. See also Grossmann, "Question of Silence" (originally published as part of a special issue of the journal *October,* no. 72 [1995]); Heineman, "Hour of the Woman," 365–74; Barbara Kosta, "Rape, Nation and Remembering History: Helke Sander's *Liberators Take Liberties,*" in Herminghouse and Mueller (eds.), *Gender and Germanness,* 217–31; and the insightful reflections of Marcia Klotz, "New German Documentary: The Impossible Struggle for a Fascism Vérité," *Arachnē* 3 (1996): 13–17.

87. Gabriele Riedle, "Die Deutschen, ein Volk von Frauen," *Tagesspiegel,* 10 Oct. 1992, copy in DFI.

88. Andreas Kilb, "Warten, bis Spielberg kommt," *Die Zeit,* 28 Jan. 1994. On the continuing difficulties of balancing German and Soviet losses, see Timothy W. Ryback, "Stalingrad: Letters from the Dead," *New Yorker,* 1 Feb. 1983, 58–71.

89. The quotation is from Marcia Klotz's thoughtful discussion of the movie in "New German Documentary," 17.

90. Ibid., 18–27, esp. 21. See also the review of the movie by Omer Bartov in *American Historical Review* 97 (1992): 1155–57.

91. "Speech by Richard von Weizsäcker," in Hartman (ed.), *Bitburg,* 272.

92. Elie Wiesel, "Ein Volk auslöschen," *Die Zeit,* 21 Apr. 1995, 16.

93. Peter Glotz, "Die Krankheit Nationalismus," *Die Zeit,* 24 Mar. 1995, 16. The same issue carried a long account titled "The Fight for East Prussia," referring to the spring of 1945; see Heinz Werner Hübner, "Noch siebzig Tage bis Pillau," ibid., 6–8.

94. See also Helmut Kohl, "Jedem einzelnen Schicksal schulden wir Achtung," *Frankfurter Allgemeine Zeitung,* 6 May 1995. It is also worth noting that in 1994 Weltbild Verlag in Augsburg commenced another reprinting of the original Schieder project's documentation on the expulsion.

95. Theo Sommer, "Jetzt erst ist der Krieg zu Ende," *Die Zeit,* 9 Sept. 1994.

96. Maier, *Unmasterable Past,* 23.

97. See, e.g., "'Alles so trostlos': SPIEGEL-Redakteur Hans-Ulrich Stoldt über die Hoffnung der tschechischen Nazi-Opfer auf Entschädigung aus Bonn," *Spiegel,* 8 May 1995; Berthold Kohler, "Havels Heimkehr," *Frankfurter Allgemeine Zeitung,* 20 Feb. 1995; "Europa, das bedeutet vor allem die Freiheit der Person: Auszüge aus der Rede des polnischen Aussenministers Bartoszewski vor dem Deutschen Bundestag," ibid., 29 Apr. 1995; "Klaus bedauert Verbrechen bei der Vertreibung," ibid., 8 May 1995; Alan Cowell, "Memories of Wartime Brutalities Revive Czech-German Animosity," *New York Times,* 9 Feb. 1996; Herbert Ammon, "Politisch-psychologisch brisant: Beim Thema Vertreibung weist die deutsche Zeitgeschichtsschreibung grosse Defizite auf," *Frankfurter Allgemeine Zeitung,* 24 Aug. 1998, and Dubiel, *Niemand ist frei,* 264–67.

98. Plaschka et al. (eds.), *Nationale Frage und Vertreibung;* and Klaus Bachmann and Jerzy Kranz, eds., *Verlorene Heimat: Die Vertreibungsdebatte in Polen* (Bonn: Bouvier, 1998); Brandes and Kural (eds.), *Weg in die Katastrophe.* See also the insightful comments of Timothy W. Ryback, "The First Draft: Writing History for the General Public," in Denham, Kacandes, and Petropoulos (eds.), *User's Guide,* 372–75; idem, "Dateline Sudetenland: Hostages to History," *Foreign Policy,* no. 105 (1996): 162–78; and Jaroslav Kučera, "Zwischen Geschichte und Politik: Die aktuelle Diskussion über die Vertreibung der Deutschen in der tschechischen Gesellschaft und Politik," in Streibel (ed.), *Flucht und Vertreibung,* 174–87. The expulsion remains highly relevant in Austrian politics. In February 2000, the right-wing Austrian political leader Jörg Haider proposed that Germans expelled from Czechoslovakia at the war's end should be "entitled to the same compensation as Austrian Jews persecuted by the Nazis." See Roger Cohen, "Haider Opens Old Wound over Germans Czechs Ousted," *New York Times,* 7 Feb. 2000.

99. See Wolfgang Zank, *Wirtschaft und Arbeit in Ostdeutschland, 1945–1949: Probleme des Wiederaufbaus in der sowjetischen Besatzungszone*

Deutschlands (Munich: R. Oldenbourg, 1987), 142–52; the excellent framework offered by Naimark, *Russians in Germany;* Claudia Koonz, "Germany's Buchenwald: Whose Shrine? Whose Memory?" in *The Art of Memory: Holocaust Memorials in History,* ed. James E. Young (New York: Prestel, 1994), 111–19; and, for recent research on expellees, Ther, "Integration of Expellees," 792–96; idem, *Deutsche und polnische Vertriebene;* M. Schwarz, "Vertreibung und Vergangenheitspolitik"; Plato and Meinicke, *Alte Heimat—neue Zeit;* Wille, Hoffmann, and Meinicke, *Sie hatten alles verloren;* and, on POWs, Biess, "Protracted War."

100. Hamburger Institut für Sozialforschung, ed., *Vernichtungskrieg: Verbrechen der Wehrmacht, 1941 bis 1944. Ausstellungskatalog* (Hamburg: Hamburger Edition, 1996); Heer and Naumann, *Vernichtungskrieg;* Theo Sommer, ed., *Gehorsam bis zum Mord? Der verschwiegene Krieg der deutschen Wehrmacht—Fakten, Analysen, Debatte* (Gütersloh: Mohndruck, n.d.), a collection of articles that appeared in the weekly newspaper *Die Zeit;* "Am Abgrund der Erinnerung," *Die Zeit,* 27 May 1999; Heribert Prantl, ed., *Wehrmachtsverbrechen: Eine deutsche Kontroverse* (Hamburg: Hoffmann & Campe, 1997); and, most recently, Bogdan Musial, "Bilder einer Ausstellung: Kritische Anmerkungen zur Wanderausstellung 'Vernichtungskrieg: Verbrechen der Wehrmacht 1941 bis 1944,'" *Vierteljahrshefte für Zeitgeschichte* 47 (1999): 563–91. The controversy sparked by charges that some of the photographs were incorrectly identified led to the decision to postpone a planned visit of the exhibition to the United States in December 1999. See, e.g., Uwe Schmitt, "'Antideutsche Gefühle werden nicht geweckt': Der Zeitgeschichtler Omer Bartow [*sic*] bereitet die Wehrmachtausstellung in den USA vor," *Die Welt,* 29 Oct. 1999; Volker Ullrich, "Von Bildern und Legenden: Der neue Streit um die Wehrmachtausstellung zeigt, wie sorgfältig mit Fotodokumenten gearbeitet werden muss," *Die Zeit,* 28 Oct. 1999; and "Atina Grossmann über die 'Wehrmachtausstellung': Anstössiger Anstoss," *Basler Zeitung,* 30 Dec. 1999. My thanks to Omer Bartov and Josef Mooser for making these newspaper articles available to me.

Bibliography

Archival Sources

POLITISCHES ARCHIV DES AUSWÄRTIGEN AMTS (BONN)

Politische Abteilung 2

Politische Abteilung 3

Politische Abteilung 7

Büro Staatssekretär

ARCHIV DES VERBANDS DER HEIMKEHRER (BONN)

PRESSE- UND INFORMATIONSAMT DER BUNDESREGIERUNG (BONN)

Press clippings collection, 1949–56

NATIONAL ARCHIVES

RG 59, Department of State, Central Files, US-German Relations

RG 466, US HICOG, John J. McCloy Papers 1949–1952 RG 260,
OMGUS (Records of the Office of Military Government, United States)

BUNDESARCHIV-FILMARCHIV

BUNDESARCHIV (KOBLENZ) [BAK]

B106 Bundesministerium des Innern

B126 Bundesfinanzministerium

B136 Bundeskanzleramt

B150 Bundesministerium für Vertriebene, Flüchtlinge und Kriegsgeschädigte

Ost-Dokumentation

Nachlass Hans Rothfels

BUNDESARCHIV-MILITÄRARCHIV

B205, Sammlung zur Geschichte der deutschen Kriegsgefangenen des Zweiten Weltkrieges

Msg200gen, Sammlung Kriegsgefangenenwesen

DEUTSCHES FILMINSTITUT

STIFTUNG DEUTSCHE KINEMATHEK

Published Sources

Abelshauser, Werner. "Der Lastenausgleich und die Eingliederung der Vertriebenen und Flüchtlinge—eine Skizze." In *Flüchtlinge und Vertriebene in der westdeutschen Nachkriegsgeschichte: Bilanzierung der Forschung und Perspektiven für die künftige Forschungsarbeit,* edited by Rainer Schulze, Doris von der Brelie-Lewien, and Helga Grebing, 229–38. Hildesheim: August Lax, 1987.
———. *Die langen fünfziger Jahre: Wirtschaft und Gesellschaft der Bundesrepublik Deutschland, 1949–1966.* Düsseldorf: Pädagogischer Verlag Schwann-Bagel, 1987.
Abenheim, Donald. *Reforging the Iron Cross: The Search for Tradition in the West German Armed Forces.* Princeton: Princeton University Press, 1988.
Abzug, Robert H. *Inside the Vicious Heart: Americans and the Liberation of Nazi Concentration Camps.* New York: Oxford University Press, 1985.
Adenauer, Konrad. *Erinnerungen, 1953–1955.* Stuttgart: Deutsche Verlags-Anstalt, 1966.
Adler, Hans Guenter. *Theresienstadt, 1941–1945: Das Antlitz einer Zwangsgemeinschaft.* Tübingen: J. C. B. Mohr [Paul Siebeck], 1955.
———. *Die verheimlichte Wahrheit: Theresienstädter Dokumente.* Tübingen: J. C. B. Mohr [Paul Siebeck], 1958.
Adorno, Theodor W. "What Does Coming to Terms with the Past Mean?" In *Bitburg in Moral and Political Perspective,* edited by Geoffrey H. Hartman, 114–29. Bloomington: Indiana University Press, 1986.
Ahonen, Pertti [Tapio]. "Domestic Constraints on West German Ostpolitik: The Role of the Expellee Organizations in the Adenauer Era." *Central European History* 31 (1998): 31–63.
———. "The Expellee Organizations and West German Ostpolitik, 1949–1969." Ph.D. diss., Yale University, 1999.

Albers, Willi. "Die Eingliederung in volkswirtschaftlicher Sicht." In *Die Vertriebenen in Westdeutschland: Ihre Eingliederung und ihr Einfluss auf Gesellschaft, Wirtschaft, Politik und Geistesleben,* edited by Eugen Lemberg and Friedrich Edding, 2:418–557. Kiel: Ferdinand Hirt, 1959.

Albrecht, Gerd. "Fern der Wirklichkeit: Deutsche Spielfilme der Nachkriegszeit zum Thema Kriegsgefangenschaft und Heimkehr." In *Kriegsgefangene-Voennoeplennye: Sowjetische Kriegsgefangene in Deutschland, Deutsche Kriegsgefangene in der Sowjetunion,* edited by Haus der Geschichte der Bundesrepublik, 100–105. Düsseldorf: Droste, 1995.

Albrecht, Willy. *Kurt Schumacher: Ein Leben für den demokratischen Sozialismus.* Bonn: Neue Gesellschaft, 1985.

Aly, Götz. *"Endlösung": Völkerverschiebung und der Mord an den europäischen Juden.* Frankfurt am Main: S. Fischer, 1995.

———. *Macht-Geist-Wahn: Kontinuität deutschen Denkens.* Berlin: Argon, 1997.

———. "Medicine against the Useless." In *Cleansing the Fatherland: Nazi Medicine and Racial Hygiene,* edited by Götz Aly, Peter Chroust, and Christian Pross, translated by Belinda Cooper, 22–98. Baltimore: Johns Hopkins University Press, 1994.

———. "Theodor Schieder, Werner Conze, oder die Vorstufen der physischen Vernichtung." In *Deutsche Historiker im Nationalsozialismus,* edited by Winfried Schulze and Otto Gerhard Oexle with the assistance of Gerd Helm and Thomas Ott, 163–82. Frankfurt am Main: Fischer Taschenbuch Verlag, 1999.

Aly, Götz, Peter Chroust, and Christian Pross, eds. *Cleansing the Fatherland: Nazi Medicine and Racial Hygiene.* Translated by Belinda Cooper. Baltimore: Johns Hopkins University Press, 1994.

Ambrosius, Gerold. "Flüchtlinge und Vertriebene in der westdeutschen Wirtschaftsgeschichte: Methodische Überlegungen und forschungsrelevante Probleme." In *Flüchtlinge und Vertriebene in der westdeutschen Nachkriegsgeschichte: Bilanzierung der Forschung und Perspektiven für die künftige Forschungsarbeit,* edited by Rainer Schulze, Doris von der Brelie-Lewien, and Helga Grebing, 216–28. Hildesheim: August Lax, 1987.

Anderson, Benedict. *Imagined Communities: Reflections on the Origin and Spread of Nationalism.* Rev. ed. London: Verso, 1991.

Anderson, Perry. "On Emplotment: Two Kinds of Ruin." In *Probing the Limits of Representation: Nazism and the "Final Solution,"* edited by Saul Friedlander, 54–65. Cambridge, Mass.: Harvard University Press, 1992.

Applegate, Celia. *A Nation of Provincials: The German Idea of Heimat.* Berkeley: University of California Press, 1990.

Arbeitsgemeinschaft zur Wahrung sudetendeutscher Interessen, ed. *Dokumente zur Austreibung der Sudetendeutschen.* Munich: Arbeitsgemeinschaft zur Wahrung sudetendeutscher Interessen, 1951.

Arendt, Hannah. "The Aftermath of Nazi Rule: Report from Germany." *Commentary* 10 (1950): 342–53.

Ash, Timothy Garton. *In Europe's Name: Germany and the Divided Continent.* New York: Random House, 1993.

Ayass, Wolfgang. *"Asoziale" im Nationalsozialismus*. Stuttgart: Klett-Cotta, 1995.

Bachmann, Klaus, and Jerzy Kranz, eds. *Verlorene Heimat: Die Vertreibungs-debatte in Polen*. Bonn: Bouvier, 1998.

Backhaus, Wilhelm. *Begegnung im Kreml: So wurden die Gefangenen befreit*. Berlin: Ullstein, 1955.

Balabkins, Nicholas. *West German Reparations to Israel*. New Brunswick, N.J.: Rutgers University Press, 1971.

Bald, Detlef. "'Bürger in Uniform': Tradition und Neuanfang des Militärs in West-deutschland." In *Modernisierung im Wiederaufbau: Die westdeutsche Gesellschaft der 50er Jahre*, edited by Axel Schildt and Arnold Sywottek, 392–402. Bonn: J. H. W. Dietz Nachf., 1993.

———. *Militär und Gesellschaft, 1945–1990: Die Bundeswehr der Bonner Republik*. Baden-Baden: Nomos Gesellschaft, 1994.

Baldwin, Peter, ed. *Reworking the Past: Hitler, the Holocaust, and the Historians' Debate*. Boston: Beacon Press, 1990.

Bankier, David. *The Germans and the Final Solution: Public Opinion under Nazism*. Oxford: Blackwell, 1992.

Barber, John, and Mark Harrison. *The Soviet Home Front, 1941–1945: A Social and Economic History of the USSR in World War II*. London: Longman, 1991.

Baring, Arnulf. *Aussenpolitik in Adenauers Kanzlerdemokratie: Bonns Beitrag zur europäischen Verteidigungsgemeinschaft*. Munich: R. Oldenbourg, 1969.

Barkin, Kenneth D. "Modern Germany: A Twisted Vision." *Dissent* 34 (1987): 252–55.

———. Review of television miniseries *Heimat*. *American Historical Review* 96 (1991): 1124–26.

Barnouw, Dagmar. *Germany 1945: Views of War and Violence*. Bloomington: Indiana University Press, 1996.

Bartov, Omer. "The Conduct of War: Soldiers and the Barbarization of Warfare." *Journal of Modern History* 64 suppl. (1992): S32–S45.

———. "Defining Enemies, Making Victims: Germans, Jews, and the Holocaust." *American Historical Review* 103 (1998): 771–816.

———. *The Eastern Front, 1941–45: German Troops and the Barbarisation of Warfare*. Houndmills, Basingstoke, Hampshire: Macmillan Press, 1985.

———. *Hitler's Army: Soldiers, Nazis, and War in the Third Reich*. New York: Oxford University Press, 1992.

———. *Mirrors of Destruction: War, Genocide, and Modern Identity*. New York: Oxford University Press, 2000.

———. *Murder in Our Midst: The Holocaust, Industrial Killing, and Representation*. New York: Oxford University Press, 1996.

———. "'Seit die Juden weg sind . . .': Germany, History, and Representations of Absence." In *A User's Guide to German Cultural Studies*, edited by Scott Denham, Irene Kacandes, and Jonathan Petropoulos, 209–26. Ann Arbor: University of Michigan Press, 1997.

———. "Wem gehört die Geschichte? Wehrmacht und Geschichtswissenschaft." In *Vernichtungskrieg: Verbrechen der Wehrmacht, 1941–1944*, edited by Hannes Heer and Klaus Naumann, 601–19. Hamburg: Hamburger Edition, 1995.

Basinger, Jeanine. *The World War II Combat Film: Anatomy of a Genre*. New York: Columbia University Press, 1986.

Bauerkämper, Arnd. "Landwirtschaft und ländliche Gesellschaft in der Bundesrepublik in den 50er Jahren." In *Modernisierung im Wiederaufbau: Die westdeutsche Gesellschaft der 50er Jahre*, edited by Axel Schildt and Arnold Sywottek, 188–200. Bonn: J. H. W. Dietz Nachf., 1993.

Becker, Rolf O. *Niederschlesien, 1945: Die Flucht—Die Besetzung*. Bad Nauheim: Podzun, 1965.

Becker, Wolfgang, and Norbert Schöll. *In jenen Tagen . . . : Wie der deutsche Nachkriegsfilm die Vergangenheit bewältigte*. Opladen: Leske & Budrich, 1995.

Beer, Matthias. "Die Dokumentation der Vertreibung der Deutschen aus Ost-Mitteleuropa: Hintergründe—Entstehung—Wirkung." *Geschichte in Wissenschaft und Unterricht* 50 (1999): 99–117.

———. "Im Spannungsfeld von Politik und Zeitgeschichte: Das Grossforschungsprojekt 'Dokumentation der Vertreibung der Deutschen aus Ost-Mitteleuropa.'" *Vierteljahrshefte für Zeitgeschichte* 49 (1998): 345–89.

———. "Der 'Neuanfang' der Zeitgeschichte nach 1945: Zum Verhältnis von nationalsozialistischer Umsiedlungs- und Vernichtungspolitik und der Vertreibung der Deutschen aus Ostmitteleuropa." In *Deutsche Historiker im Nationalsozialismus,* edited by Winfried Schulze and Otto Gerhard Oexle with the assistance of Gerd Helm and Thomas Ott, 274–301. Frankfurt am Main: Fisher Taschenbuch Verlag, 1999.

Benz, Wolfgang. "Postwar Society and National Socialism: Remembrance, Amnesia, Rejection." *Tel Aviver Jahrbuch für deutsche Geschichte* 19 (1990): 1–12.

Benz, Wolfgang, and Angelika Schardt, eds. *Deutsche Kriegsgefangene im Zweiten Weltkrieg: Erinnerungen*. Frankfurt am Main: Fischer Taschenbuch Verlag, 1995.

Benzenhöfer, Udo, ed. *Medizin im Spielfilm der fünfziger Jahre*. Pfaffenweiler: Centaurus, 1993.

Berenbaum, Michael, ed. *A Mosaic of Victims: Non-Jews Persecuted and Murdered by the Nazis*. New York: New York University Press, 1990.

Bergen, Doris L. "The Nazi Concept of 'Volksdeutsche' and the Exacerbation of Anti-Semitism in Eastern Europe, 1939–45." *Journal of Contemporary History* 29 (1994): 569–82.

Berghoff, Hartmut. "Zwischen Verdrängung und Aufarbeitung." *Geschichte in Wissenschaft und Unterricht* 49 (1998): 96–114.

Bergmann, Werner. "Die Reaktion auf den Holocaust in Westdeutschland von 1945 bis 1989." *Geschichte in Wissenschaft und Unterricht* 43 (1992): 327–50.

Bergmann, Werner, and Rainer Erb. *Anti-Semitism in Germany: The Post-Nazi Epoch since 1945*. Translated by Belinda Cooper and Allison Brown. New Brunswick, N.J.: Transaction Publishers, 1997.

Bergmann, Werner, Rainer Erb, and Albert Lichtblau, eds. *Schwieriges Erbe: Der Umgang mit dem Nationalsozialismus und Antisemitismus in Österreich, der DDR und der Bundesrepublik Deutschland*. Frankfurt am Main: Campus, 1995.

Berthold, Eva. *Kriegsgefangene im Osten: Bilder, Briefe, Berichte.* Königstein/
Taunus: Athenäum, 1981.

Biess, Frank P. "'Pioneers of a New Germany': Returning POWs from the Soviet
Union and the Making of East German Citizens, 1945–1950." *Central European History* 32 (1999): 143–80.

———. "The Protracted War: Returning POWs and the Making of East and West
German Citizens, 1945–1955." Ph.D. diss., Brown University, 2000.

———. "Survivors of Totalitarianism: Returning POWs and the Reconstruction
of Masculine Citizenship in West Germany, 1945–1955." In *The Miracle Years
Revisited: A Cultural History of West Germany,* edited by Hanna Schissler.
Princeton: Princeton University Press, 2000.

Bietrow-Ennker, Bianka. "Die Sowjetunion in der Propaganda des Dritten Reiches: Das Beispiel der Wochenschau." *Militärgeschichtliche Mitteilungen* 46
(1989): 79–120.

Bingen, Dieter. "Westverschiebung Polens und Revisionsanspruch der Bundesrepublik Deutschland: Die polnische Westgrenze als Stein des Anstosses
in den polnisch-deutschen Beziehungen." In *Unfertige Nachbarschaften: Die
Staaten Osteuropas und die Bundesrepublik Deutschland,* edited by Othmar
Nikola Haberl and Hans Hecker, 155–76. Essen: Reimar Hobbing, 1989.

Bird, Kai, and Lawrence Lifschultz, eds. *Hiroshima's Shadow.* Stony Creek,
Conn.: Pamphleteer's Press, 1998.

Birke, Adolf M. *Nation ohne Haus: Deutschland, 1945–1961.* Berlin: Wolf Jobst
Siedler, 1989.

Blankenhorn, Herbert. *Verständnis und Verständigung: Blätter eines politischen
Tagebuchs, 1949 bis 1979.* Frankfurt am Main: Propyläen, 1980.

Bliersbach, Gerhard. *So grün war die Heide: Der Nachkriegsfilm in neuer Sicht.*
Weinheim: Beltz, 1985.

Blumenberg, Hans-Christoph. *Das Leben geht weiter: Der letzte Film des Dritten Reichs.* Berlin: Rowohlt, 1993.

Bock, Gisela. "Antinatalism, Maternity, and Paternity in National Socialist
Racism." In *Maternity and Gender Policies: Women and the Rise of the European Welfare States, 1880s–1950s,* edited by Gisela Bock and Pat Thane,
233–55. London: Routledge, 1991.

Böddeker, Günter. *Die Flüchtlinge: Die Vertreibung der Deutschen im Osten.* Munich: F. A. Herbig, 1980.

Bodemann, Y. Michael, with a contribution by Jael Geis. *Gedächtnistheater: Die
jüdische Gemeinschaft und ihre deutsche Erfindung.* Hamburg: Rotbuch,
1996.

Boehm, Max Hildebert. "Gruppenbildung und Organisationswesen." In *Die
Vertriebenen in Westdeutschland: Ihre Eingliederung und ihr Einfluss auf
Gesellschaft, Wirtschaft, Politik und Geistesleben,* edited by Eugen Lemberg
and Friedrich Edding, 1:521–605. Kiel: Ferdinand Hirt, 1959.

Bohlen, Charles E. *Witness to History, 1929–1969.* New York: Norton, 1973.

Böhme, Kurt W. *Die deutschen Kriegsgefangenen in Jugoslawien.* Vol. 1/1:
1944–1949. Bielefeld: Ernst & Werner Gieseking, 1962.

———. *Die deutschen Kriegsgefangenen in sowjetischer Hand: Eine Bilanz.* Bielefeld: Ernst & Werner Gieseking, 1966.

————. "Hilfen für die deutschen Kriegsgefangenen, 1939–1956." In *Die deutschen Kriegsgefangenen des Zweiten Weltkriegs: Eine Zusammenfassung,* edited by Erich Maschke, 374–446. Bielefeld: Ernst & Werner Gieseking, 1974.

Bohn, Helmut. *Die Heimkehrer aus russischer Kriegsgefangenschaft.* Frankfurt am Main: Wolfgang Metzner, 1951.

Bojanowski, Martin, and Erich Bosdorf. *Striegau: Schicksale einer schlesischen Stadt.* Schöppenstedt: Selbstverlag E. Bosdorf, [1951].

Bongartz, Barbara. *Von Caligari zu Hitler—von Hitler zu Dr. Mabuse? Eine "psychologische" Geschichte des deutschen Films von 1946 bis 1960.* Münster: MAkS Publikationen, 1992.

Boog, Horst, et al. *Der Angriff auf die Sowjetunion.* Frankfurt am Main: Fischer Taschenbuch Verlag, 1991.

Borchert, Wolfgang. *"Draussen vor der Tür" und ausgewählte Erzählungen.* Hamburg: Rowohlt, [1956] 1970. Published in English as *The Man Outside: The Prose Works of Wolfgang Borchert.* Translated by David Porter. Norfolk, Conn.: New Directions, 1952.

Bosworth, R. J. B. *Explaining Auschwitz and Hiroshima: History Writing and the Second World War, 1945–1990.* London: Routledge, 1993.

Bourke, Joanna. *Dismembering the Male: Men's Bodies, Britain, and the Great War.* London: Reaktion Books, 1996.

Brandes, Detlef. *Die Tschechen unter deutschem Protektorat.* Part 1: *Besatzungspolitik, Kollaboration und Widerstand im Protektorat Böhmen und Mähren bis Heydrichs Tod (1939–1942).* Munich: R. Oldenbourg, 1969.

————. *Die Tschechen unter deutschem Protektorat.* Part 2: *Besatzungspolitik, Kollaboration und Widerstand im Protektorat Böhmen und Mähren von Heydrichs Tod bis zum Prager Aufstand (1942–1945).* Munich: R. Oldenbourg, 1975.

Brandes, Detlef, and Václav Kural, eds. *Der Weg in die Katastrophe: Deutschtschechoslowakische Beziehungen, 1938–1947.* Essen: Klartext, 1994.

Brandlmeier, Thomas. "Von Hitler zu Adenauer: Deutsche Trümmerfilme." In *Zwischen Gestern und Morgen: Westdeutscher Nachkriegsfilm, 1946–1962,* edited by Hilmar Hoffmann and Walter Schobert, 32–59. Frankfurt: Deutsches Filmmuseum, 1989.

Braun, Hans. "Helmut Schelskys Konzept der 'nivellierten Mittelstandsgesellschaft' und die Bundesrepublik der 50er Jahre." *Archiv für Sozialgeschichte* 29 (1985): 199–223.

Bredow, Wilfried von. "Filmpropaganda für Wehrbereitschaft: Kriegsfilme in der Bundesrepublik." In *Film und Gesellschaft in Deutschland: Dokumente und Materialien,* edited by Wilfried von Bredow and Rolf Zurek, 316–26. Hamburg: Hoffmann & Campe, 1975.

Brelie-Lewien, Doris von der. "Zur Rolle der Flüchtlinge und Vertriebenen in der westdeutschen Nachkriegsgeschichte: Ein Forschungsbericht." In *Flüchtlinge und Vertriebene in der Nachkriegsgeschichte: Bilanzierung der Forschung und Perspektiven für die künftige Forschungsarbeit,* edited by Rainer Schulze, Doris von der Brelie-Lewien, and Helga Grebing, 24–45. Hildesheim: August Lax, 1987.

Brenner, Michael. *Nach dem Holocaust: Juden in Deutschland, 1945–1950.* Munich: C. H. Beck, 1995.

Brink, Cornelia. *Ikonen der Vernichtung: Öffentlicher Gebrauch von Fotografien aus nationalsozialistischen Konzentrationslagern nach 1945.* Berlin: Akademie, 1998.

Brochhagen, Ulrich. *Nach Nürnberg: Vergangenheitsbewältigung und Westintegration in der Ära Adenauer.* Hamburg: Junius, 1994.

Brooks, Peter. *The Melodramatic Imagination: Balzac, Henry James, Melodrama, and the Mode of Excess.* New Haven: Yale Univerity Press, [1976] 1995.

Broszat, Martin. "Faschismus und Kollaboration in Ostmitteleuropa zwischen den Weltkriegen." *Vierteljahrshefte für Zeitgeschichte* 14 (1966): 225–51.

———. "Massendokumentation als Methode zeitgeschichtlicher Forschung." *Vierteljahrshefte für Zeitgeschichte* 2 (1954): 202–13.

———. *Nationalsozialistische Polenpolitik, 1939–1945.* Frankfurt am Main: Fischer Bücherei, [1961] 1965.

———. "A Plea for the Historicization of National Socialism." In *Reworking the Past: Hitler, the Holocaust, and the Historians' Debate,* edited by Peter Baldwin, 77–87. Boston: Beacon Press, 1990.

Broszat, Martin, and Saul Friedländer. "A Controversy about the Historicization of National Socialism." In *Reworking the Past: Hitler, the Holocaust, and the Historians' Debate,* edited by Peter Baldwin, 102–34. Boston: Beacon Press, 1990.

Broszat, Martin, Klaus-Dietmar Henke, and Hans Woller, eds. *Von Stalingrad zur Währungsreform: Zur Sozialgeschichte des Umbruchs in Deutschland.* Munich: R. Oldenbourg, 1988.

Brüdigam, Heinz. *Der Schoss ist fruchtbar noch . . . : Neonazistische, militaristische, nationalistische Literatur und Publizistik in der Bundesrepublik.* 2d ed. Frankfurt am Main: Röderberg, 1965.

Brustat-Naval, Fritz. *Unternehmen Rettung: Letztes Schiff nach Westen.* Herford: Koehler, 1970.

Buchstab, Günter, ed. *Adenauer—"Wir haben wirklich etwas geschaffen": Die Protokolle des CDU-Bundesvorstandes, 1953–1957.* Düsseldorf: Droste, 1990.

Büchten, Daniela, and Anja Frey, eds. *Im Irrgarten deutscher Geschichte: Die neue Wache, 1818 bis 1993.* Berlin: Movimento Druck, 1993.

Bundesministerium der Finanzen. *Flüchtlingslasten und Verteidigungsbeitrag: Zwei sich ergänzende und begrenzende Belastungen.* N.p., 1951.

Bundesministerium für Vertriebene, ed. *Dokumentation der Vertreibung der Deutschen aus Ost-Mitteleuropa.* Vol. 1: *Die Vertreibung der deutschen Bevölkerung aus den Gebieten östlich der Oder-Neisse.* 3 parts. Munich: Deutscher Taschenbuch Verlag, [1954 (pts. 1–2), 1960 (pt. 3)] 1984. Excerpts published in English as *The Expulsion of the German Population from the Territories East of the Oder-Neisse-Line.* Leer [Ostfriesland]: Gerhard Rautenberg, n.d.

———, ed. *Dokumentation der Vertreibung der Deutschen aus Ost-Mitteleuropa.* Vol. 2: *Das Schicksal der Deutschen in Ungarn.* Munich: Deutscher Taschenbuch Verlag, [1956] 1984. Excerpts published in English as *The Fate of the Germans in Hungary.* Göttingen: Schwartz & Co., 1961.

————, ed. *Dokumentation der Vertreibung der Deutschen aus Ost-Mitteleuropa.* Vol. 3: *Das Schicksal der Deutschen in Rumänien.* Munich: Deutscher Taschenbuch Verlag, [1957] 1984. Excerpts published in English as *The Fate of the Germans in Rumania.* Göttingen: Schwartz & Co., 1961.

————, ed. *Dokumentation der Vertreibung der Deutschen aus Ost-Mitteleuropa.* Vol. 4: *Die Vertreibung der deutschen Bevölkerung aus der Tschechoslowakei.* 2 parts. Augsburg: Weltbild Verlag, [1957] 1994. Excerpts published in English as *The Expulsion of the German Population from Czechoslovakia.* Leer [Ostfriesland]: Gerhard Rautenberg, 1960.

————, ed. *Dokumentation der Vertreibung der Deutschen aus Ost-Mitteleuropa.* Vol. 5: *Das Schicksal der Deutschen in Jugoslawien.* Munich: Deutscher Taschenbuch Verlag, [1961] 1984.

————, ed. *Dokumentation der Vertreibung der Deutschen aus Ost-Mitteleuropa.* 1. Beiheft. Käthe von Normann. *Ein Tagebuch aus Pommern, 1945–1946.* Gross-Denkte/Wolfenbüttel: Grenzland-Druckerei, 1955.

————, ed. *Dokumentation der Vertreibung der Deutschen aus Ost-Mitteleuropa.* 2. Beiheft. Margerete Schell. *Ein Tagebuch aus Prag, 1945–46.* Kassel-Wilh.: Herbert M. Nuhr, 1957.

————, ed. *Dokumentation der Vertreibung der Deutschen aus Ost-Mitteleuropa.* 3. Beiheft. Hans Graf von Lehndorff. *Ein Bericht aus Ost- und Westpreussen, 1945–1947.* Düsseldorf: Oskar-Leiner-Druck, 1960.

————. *Die Eingliederung der Flüchtlinge in die deutsche Gemeinschaft: Bericht der ECA Technical Assistance Commission für die Eingliederung der Flüchtlinge in die deutsche Bundesrepublik, dem Bundeskanzler am 21. März 1951 überreicht.* Bonn: Bonner Universitäts-Buchdruckerei Gebr. Scheur, 1951.

Bundesministerium für Vertriebene, Flüchtlinge und Kriegsgeschädigte, ed. *Dokumente deutscher Kriegsschäden: Evakuierte, Kriegssachgeschädigte, Währungsgeschädigte.* Vols. 1–2. Düsseldorf: Triltsch-Druck, 1958–60.

————, ed. *Die Lastenausgleichsgesetze: Dokumente zur Entwicklung des Gedankens, der Gesetzgebung und der Durchführung.* Vol. 1/1: *Soforthilfe und Feststellungsgesetz.* Bielefeld-Bethel: Ernst Gieseking, 1962.

————, ed. *Die Lastenausgleichsgesetze: Dokumente zur Entwicklung des Gedankens, der Gesetzgebung und der Durchführung.* Vol. 2/1: *Die Änderungsgesetzgebung zum LAG von der ersten bis zur achten Novelle.* Stuttgart: Ackermann & Honold, 1962.

————, ed. *20 Jahre Lager Friedland.* N.p., n.d. [Bonn, 1965].

Burleigh, Michael. *Death and Deliverance: "Euthanasia" in Germany c. 1900–1945.* Cambridge: Cambridge University Press, 1994.

————. *Germany Turns Eastwards: A Study of Ostforschung in the Third Reich.* Cambridge: Cambridge University Press, 1988.

Burleigh, Michael, and Wolfgang Wippermann. *The Racial State: Germany, 1933–1945.* Cambridge: Cambridge University Press, 1991.

Buruma, Ian. *The Wages of Guilt: Memories of War in Germany and Japan.* New York: Penguin Books, 1994.

Buscher, Frank M. "Kurt Schumacher, German Social Democracy, and the Punishment of Nazi Crimes." *Holocaust and Genocide Studies* 5 (1990): 261–73.

Byars, Jackie. *All That Hollywood Allows: Re-reading Gender in 1950s Melo-drama.* Chapel Hill: University of North Carolina Press, 1991.

Caplan, Jane. "The Historiography of National Socialism." In *Companion to Historiography,* edited by Michael Bentley, 545–90. London: Routledge, 1997.

———. Review of the film *Deutschland, bleiche Mutter. American Historical Review* 96 (1991): 1126–28.

Carell, Paul, and Günter Böddeker. *Die Gefangenen: Leben und Überleben deutscher Soldaten hinter Stacheldraht.* Frankfurt am Main: Ullstein, 1980.

Carp, Stefanie. "Schlachtbeschreibungen: Ein Blick auf Walter Kempowski und Alexander Kluge." In *Vernichtungskrieg: Verbrechen der Wehrmacht, 1941–1944,* edited by Hannes Heer and Klaus Naumann, 664–79. Hamburg: Hamburger Edition, 1995.

Carter, Erica. "Alice in Consumer Wonderland: West German Case Studies in Gender and Consumer Culture." In *West Germany Under Construction: Politics, Society, and Culture in the Adenauer Era,* edited by Robert G. Moeller, 347–71. Ann Arbor: University of Michigan Press, 1997.

———. *How German Is She? Postwar West German Reconstruction and the Consuming Woman.* Ann Arbor: University of Michigan Press, 1997.

Cary, Noel D. *The Path to Christian Democracy: German Catholics and the Party System from Windthorst to Adenauer.* Cambridge, Mass.: Harvard University Press, 1996.

Chalmers, Douglas A. *The Social Democratic Party of Germany: From Working-Class Movement to Modern Political Party.* New Haven: Yale University Press, 1964.

Chamberlin, Brewster S. "Todesmühlen: Ein früher Versuch zur Massen-'Umerziehung' im besetzten Deutschland, 1945–1946." *Vierteljahrshefte für Zeitgeschichte* 29 (1981): 420–36.

Chorkow, Anatolij. "Zur Organisation des Kriegsgefangenenwesens in der UdSSR." In *Deutsch-russische Zeitenwende: Krieg und Frieden, 1941–1995,* edited by Hans-Adolf Jacobsen et al., 455–63. Baden-Baden: Nomos, 1995.

Confino, Alon. "Collective Memory and Cultural History: Problems of Method." *American Historical Review* 102 (1997): 1386–1403.

———. "Edgar Reitz's *Heimat* and German Nationhood: Film, Memory, and Understandings of the Past." *German History* 16 (1998): 185–208.

———. "The Nation as a Local Metaphor: Heimat, National Memory, and the German Empire, 1871–1918." *History and Memory* 5 (1993): 42–86.

———. *The Nation as a Local Metaphor: Württemberg, Imperial Germany, and National Memory, 1871–1918.* Chapel Hill: University of North Carolina Press, 1997.

Connelly, John. "Nazis and Slavs: From Racial Theory to Racist Practice." *Central European History* 32 (1999): 1–33.

Connor, Ian. "The Refugees and the Currency Reform." In *Reconstruction in Post-War Germany: British Occupation Policy and the Western Zones, 1945–55,* edited by Ian Turner, 301–24. Oxford: Berg, 1989.

Conze, Werner. "Die Königsberger Jahre." In *Vom Beruf des Historikers in einer Zeit beschleunigten Wandels: Akademische Gedenkfeier für Theodor Schieder am 8. Februar 1985 an der Universität zu Köln,* edited by Andreas Hillgruber, 23–31. Munich: R. Oldenbourg, 1985.

Crane, Susan A. "Writing the Individual Back into Collective Memory." *American Historical Review* 102 (1997): 1372–85.

Croix, Ernst Féaux de la, and Helmut Rumpf, eds. *Der Werdegang des Entschädigungsrechts unter national- und völkerrechtlichem und politologischem Aspekt.* Munich: C. H. Beck, 1985. (= Vol. 3 of *Die Wiedergutmachung nationalsozialistischen Unrechts durch die Bundesrepublik Deutschland,* edited by the Bundesministerium der Finanzen.)

Culbert, David. "American Film Policy in the Re-Education of Germany after 1945." In *The Political Re-Education of Germany and Her Allies after World War II,* edited by Nicholas Pronay and Keith Wilson, 173–202. London: Croom Helm, 1985.

Czarnowski, Gabriele. *Das kontrollierte Paar: Ehe- und Sexualpolitik im Nationalsozialismus.* Weinheim: Deutscher Studien Verlag, 1991.

Dam, H. G. van, and Ralph Giordano, eds. *KZ-Verbrechen vor deutschen Gerichten: Dokumente aus den Prozessen gegen Sommer (KZ Buchenwald), Sorge, Schubert (KZ Sachsenhausen), Unkelbach (Ghetto in Czenstochau).* Frankfurt am Main: Europäische Verlagsanstalt, 1962.

Danyel, Jürgen. "Die beiden deutschen Staaten und ihre nationalsozialistische Vergangenheit: Elitenwechsel und Vergangenheitspolitik." In *Deutsche Vergangenheiten—eine gemeinsame Herausforderung: Der schwierige Umgang mit der doppelten Nachkriegsgeschichte,* edited by Christoph Klessmann, Hans Misselwitz, and Günter Wichert, 128–38. Berlin: Ch. Links, 1999.

———. "Die geteilte Vergangenheit: Gesellschaftliche Ausgangslagen und politische Dispositionen für den Umgang mit Nationalsozialismus und Widerstand in beiden deutschen Staaten nach 1949." In *Historische DDR-Forschung: Aufsätze und Studien,* edited by Jürgen Kocka, 129–47. Berlin: Akademie, 1993.

———, ed. *Die geteilte Vergangenheit: Zum Umgang mit Nationalsozialismus und Widerstand in beiden deutschen Staaten.* Berlin: Akademie, 1995.

Danyel, Jürgen, Olaf Groehler, and Mario Kessler. "Antifaschismus und Verdrängung: Zum Umgang mit der NS-Vergangenheit in der DDR." In *Die DDR als Geschichte: Fragen—Hypothesen—Perspektiven,* edited by Jürgen Kocka and Martin Sabrow, 148–52. Berlin: Akademie, 1994.

Denman, Mariatte C. "Staging the Nation: Representations of Nationhood and Gender in Plays, Images, and Films in Postwar West Germany (1945–1949)." Ph.D. diss., University of California, Davis, 1997.

———. "Visualizing the Nation: Madonnas and Mourning Mothers in Postwar Germany." In *Gender and Germanness: Cultural Production of Nation,* edited by Patricia Herminghouse and Magda Mueller, 189–201. Providence, R.I.: Berghahn Books, 1997.

Deutsch, Karl W., and Lewis J. Edinger. *Germany Rejoins the Powers: Mass Opinion, Interest Groups, and Elites in Contemporary German Foreign Policy.* Stanford: Stanford University Press, 1959.

Diehl, James M. *The Thanks of the Fatherland: German Veterans after the Second World War.* Chapel Hill: University of North Carolina Press, 1993.

Diner, Dan. "Between Aporia and Apology: On the Limits of Historicizing National Socialism." In *Reworking the Past: Hitler, the Holocaust, and the Historians' Debate*, edited by Peter Baldwin, 135–45. Boston: Beacon Press, 1990.

———. "Zwischen Bundesrepublik und Deutschland: Ein Vortrag." In *Von der Gnade der geschenkten Nation*, edited by Hajo Funke, 188–99. Berlin: Rotbuch, 1988.

Dipper, Christof. "Auschwitz erklären." *Aschkenas* 5 (1995): 199–204.

Dobroszycki, Lucjan, ed. *The Chronicle of the Łódź Ghetto, 1941–1944.* Translated by Richard Lourie et al. New Haven: Yale University Press, 1984.

Domansky, Elisabeth. "A Lost War: World War II in Postwar German Memory." In *Thinking about the Holocaust after Half a Century*, edited by Alvin H. Rosenfeld, 233–72. Bloomington: Indiana University Press, 1997.

———. "Militarization and Reproduction in World War I Germany." In *Society, Culture, and the State in Germany, 1870–1930*, edited by Geoff Eley, 427–63. Ann Arbor: University of Michigan Press, 1996.

Donauschwäbische Kulturstiftung, ed. *Leidensweg der Deutschen im kommunistischen Jugoslawien.* Vol. 1: *Ortsberichte über die Verbrechen an den Deutschen durch das Tito-Regime in der Zeit von 1944–1948.* Munich: Donauschwäbische Kulturstiftung, 1992.

———, ed. *Leidensweg der Deutschen im kommunistischen Jugoslawien.* Vol. 2: *Erlebnisberichte über die Verbrechen an den Deutschen durch das Tito-Regime in der Zeit von 1944–1948.* Munich: Donauschwäbische Kulturstiftung, 1993.

Dower, John W. "The Bombed: Hiroshimas and Nagasakis in Japanese Memory." *Diplomatic History* 19 (1995): 275–95.

———. *Embracing Defeat: Japan in the Wake of World War II.* New York: Norton, 1999.

———. "Triumphal and Tragic Narratives of the War in Asia." *Journal of American History* 82 (1995): 1124–35.

Draeger, Kurt. *Heimkehrergesetz: Kommentar und sonstiges Heimkehrerrecht.* 2d ed. Berlin: Franz Vahlen, 1953.

Dubiel, Helmut. *Niemand ist frei von der Geschichte: Die nationalsozialistische Herrschaft in den Debatten des Deutschen Bundestages.* Munich: Carl Hanser, 1999.

Duff, Sheila Grant. *A German Protectorate: The Czechs under Nazi Rule.* London: Frank Cass, 1970.

Ebbinghaus, Angelika, and Karl Heinz Roth, ed. "Vorläufer des 'Generalplans Ost': Theodor Schieders Polendenkschrift vom 7. Oktober 1939." *1999: Zeitschrift für Sozialgeschichte des 20. und 21. Jahrhunderts* 1 (1992): 62–94.

Eberan, Barbro. *Luther? Friedrich "der Grosse"? Wagner? Nietzsche? . . . ? . . . ? Wer war an Hitler schuld? Die Debatte um die Schuldfrage, 1945–1949.* Munich: Minerva, 1983.

Eley, Geoff. "Nazism, Politics, and Public Memory: Thoughts on the West German *Historikerstreit*, 1986–1987." *Past and Present*, no. 121 (1988): 171–208.

Epp, Marlene. "The Memory of Violence: Soviet and East European Mennonite Refugees and Rape in the Second World War." *Journal of Women's History* 9 (1997): 58–87.

Erb, Rainer. "Die Rückerstattung: Ein Kristallisationspunkt für den Antisemitismus." In *Antisemitismus in der politischen Kultur nach 1945*, edited by Werner Bergmann and Rainer Erb, 238–52. Opladen: Westdeutscher Verlag, 1990.

Erhard, Ludwig. *Deutsche Wirtschaftspolitik: Der Weg der sozialen Marktwirtschaft*. Düsseldorf: Econ, 1962.

———. *Wohlstand für alle*. Düsseldorf: Econ, [1957] 1960.

Evans, Richard J. *In Hitler's Shadow: West German Historians and the Attempt to Escape from the Nazi Past*. New York: Pantheon, 1989.

Faulenbach, Bernd. "Emanzipation von der deutschen Tradition? Geschichtsbewusstsein in den sechziger Jahren." In *Politische Kultur und deutsche Frage: Materialien zum Staats- und Nationalbewusstsein in der Bundesrepublik Deutschland*, edited by Werner Weidenfeld, 73–92. Cologne: Wissenschaft & Politik, 1989.

Fehrenbach, Heide. *Cinema in Democratizing Germany: Reconstructing National Identity after Hitler*. Chapel Hill: University of North Carolina Press, 1995.

———. "*Die Sünderin*, or Who Killed the German Male: Early Postwar Cinema and the Betrayal of the Fatherland." In *Gender and German Cinema: Feminist Interventions*, vol. 2: *German Film History/German History on Film*, edited by Sandra Frieden et al., 135–60. Providence, R.I.: Berg, 1993.

———. "Rehabilitating Father*land*: Race and Remasculinization." *Signs* 24 (1998): 107–27.

Feinberg, Anat. *Wiedergutmachung im Programm: Jüdisches Schicksal im deutschen Nachkriegsdrama*. Cologne: Prometh, 1988.

Feldman, Lily Gardner. *The Special Relationship between West Germany and Israel*. Boston: George Allen & Unwin, 1984.

Fest, Joachim. "Die geschuldete Erinnerung: Zur Kontroverse über die Unvergleichbarkeit der nationalsozialistischen Massenverbrechen." In *"Historikerstreit": Die Dokumentation der Kontroverse um die Einzigartigkeit der nationalsozialistischen Judenvernichtung*, 100–112. Munich: Piper, 1987.

Field, Norma. *In the Realm of a Dying Emperor: Japan at Century's End*. New York: Vintage Books, 1993.

Fischer-Hübner, Helga, and Hermann Fischer-Hübner. *Die Kehrseite der "Wiedergutmachung": Das Leiden von NS-Verfolgten in den Entschädigungsverfahren*. Gerlingen: Bleicher, 1990.

Fishman, Sara. "Waiting for the Captive Sons of France: Prisoners of War Wives, 1940–1945." In *Behind the Lines: Gender and the Two World Wars*, edited by Margaret R. Higgonet et al., 182–93. New Haven: Yale University Press, 1987.

Fleer, Cornelia. *Vom Kaiser-Panorama zum Heimatfilm: Kinogeschichten aus Bielefeld und der Provinz Westfalen*. Marburg: Jonas Verlag, 1996.

Flothmann, K. H. "Typische Gefangenschaftskrankheiten und ihre somatischen und psychischen Entstehungsfaktoren." In *Extreme Lebensverhältnisse und ihre Folgen: Handbuch der ärztlichen Erfahrungen aus der Gefangenschaft*, edited by E. G. Schenck and W. von Nathusius, 1:35–53. N.p.: Schriftenreihe des ärztlich-wissenschaftlichen Beirates des Verbandes der Heimkehrer Deutschlands e.V., 1958.

Foerster, Roland G. "Innenpolitische Aspekte der Sicherheit Westdeutschlands

(1947–1950)." In *Von der Kapitulation bis zum Pleven-Plan,* by Roland G. Foerster et al., vol. 1 of *Anfänge westdeutscher Sicherheitspolitik, 1945–1956,* edited by Militärgeschichtliches Forschungsamt, 403–575. Munich: R. Oldenbourg, 1982.

———. Christian Greiner, Georg Meyer, Hans-Jürgen Rautenberg, and Norbert Wiggershaus. *Von der Kapitulation bis zum Pleven-Plan.* Vol. 1 of *Anfänge westdeutscher Sicherheitspolitik, 1945–1956,* edited by Militärgeschichtliches Forschungsamt. Munich: R. Oldenbourg, 1982.

Foot, Rosemary. *A Substitute for Victory: The Politics of Peacemaking at the Korean Armistice Talks.* Ithaca, N.Y.: Cornell University Press, 1990.

Foreign Relations of the United States, 1950. Vol. 4: *Central and Eastern Europe; The Soviet Union.* Washington, D.C.: U.S. Government Printing Office, 1980.

Foreign Relations of the United States, 1955–57. Vol. 5: *Austrian State Treaty; Summit and Foreign Ministries Meetings, 1955.* Washington, D.C.: U.S. Government Printing Office, 1988.

Foreign Relations of the United States, 1952–54. Vol. 7: *Germany and Austria (in Two Parts),* Part 1. Washington, D.C.: U.S. Government Printing Office, 1986.

Foreign Relations of the United States, 1955–57. Vol. 26: *Central and Southeastern Europe.* Washington, D.C.: U.S. Government Printing Office, 1992.

Förster, Jürgen. "The German Army and the Ideological War against the Soviet Union." In *The Policies of Genocide: Jews and Soviet Prisoners of War in Nazi Germany,* edited by Gerhard Hirschfeld, 15–29. London: Allen & Unwin, 1986.

———. "The Relation between Operation Barbarossa as an Ideological War of Extermination and the Final Solution." In *The Final Solution: Origins and Implementation,* edited by David Cesarani, 58–102. London: Routledge, 1994.

Foschepoth, Josef. "Adenauers Moskaureise, 1955." *Aus Politik und Zeitgeschichte: Beilage zur Wochenzeitung "Das Parlament,"* B22 (1986): 30–46.

———. "German Reaction to Defeat and Occupation." In *West Germany Under Construction: Politics, Society, and Culture in the Adenauer Era,* edited by Robert G. Moeller, 73–89. Ann Arbor: University of Michigan Press, 1997.

———. *Im Schatten der Vergangenheit: Die Anfänge der Gesellschaften für christlich-jüdische Zusammenarbeit.* Göttingen: Vandenhoeck & Ruprecht, 1993.

———. "Potsdam und danach: Die Westmächte, Adenauer und die Vertriebenen." In *Die Vertreibung der Deutschen aus dem Osten: Ursachen, Ereignisse, Folgen,* edited by Wolfgang Benz, 70–90. Frankfurt am Main: Fischer Taschenbuch Verlag, 1985.

———. "Westintegration statt Wiedervereinigung: Adenauers Deutschlandpolitik, 1949–1955." In *Adenauer und die deutsche Frage,* edited by Josef Foschepoth, 29–60. Göttingen: Vandenhoeck & Ruprecht, 1988.

Franklin, H. Bruce. *M.I.A., or Mythmaking in America.* Brooklyn, N.Y.: Lawrence Hill Books, 1992.

Frei, Norbert. "Die deutsche Wiedergutmachungspolitik gegenüber Israel im

Urteil der öffentlichen Meinung der USA." In *Wiedergutmachung in der Bundesrepublik Deutschland,* edited by Ludolf Herbst and Constantin Goschler, 215–30. Munich: R. Oldenbourg, 1989.

———. "Erinnerungskampf: Zur Legitimationsproblematik des 20. Juli 1944 im Nachkriegsdeutschland." In *Von der Aufgabe der Freiheit: Politische Verant-wortwortung und bürgerliche Gesellschaft im 19. und 20. Jahrhundert,* edited by Christian Jansen, Lutz Niethammer, and Bern Weisbrod, 493–504. Berlin: Akademie, 1995.

———. "NS-Vergangenheit unter Ulbricht und Adenauer: Gesichtspunkte einer 'vergleichenden Bewältigungsforschung.'" In *Die geteilte Vergangenheit: Zum Umgang mit Nationalsozialismus und Widerstand in beiden deutschen Staaten,* edited by Jürgen Danyel, 125–32. Berlin: Akademie, 1995.

———. "Die Presse." In *Die Geschichte der Bundesrepublik Deutschland,* vol. 4: *Kultur,* edited by Wolfgang Benz, 370–416. Frankfurt am Main: Fischer Taschenbuch Verlag, 1989.

———. *Vergangenheitspolitik: Die Anfänge der Bundesrepublik und die NS-Vergangenheit.* Munich: C. H. Beck, 1996.

———. "Von deutscher Erfindungskraft, oder: Die Kollektivschuldthese in der Nachkriegszeit." *Rechtshistorisches Journal* 17 (1997): 621–34.

———. "'Wir waren blind, ungläubig und langsam': Buchenwald, Dachau und die amerikanischen Medien im Frühjahr 1945." *Vierteljahrshefte für Zeitgeschichte* 35 (1987): 385–401.

Frenzel, Ivo, and Peter Märthesheimer, eds. *Im Kreuzfeuer: Der Fernsehfilm "Holocaust."* Frankfurt am Main: Fischer Taschenbuch Verlag, 1979.

Frevert, Ute. "Das Militär als 'Schule der Männlichkeit': Erwartungen, Angebote, Erfahrungen im 19. Jahrhundert." In *Militär und Gesellschaft im 19. und 20. Jahrhundert,* edited by Ute Frevert, 145–73. Stuttgart: Klett-Cotta, 1997.

———. "Soldaten, Staatsbürger: Überlegungen zur historischen Konstruktion von Männlichkeit." In *Männergeschichte—Geschlechtergeschichte: Männlichkeit im Wandel der Moderne,* edited by Thomas Kühne, 69–87. Frankfurt am Main: Campus, 1996.

———. "Die Sprache des Volkes und die Rhetorik der Nation: Identitätssplitter in der deutschen Nachkriegszeit." In *Doppelte Zeitgeschichte: Deutsch-deutsche Beziehungen, 1945–1990,* edited by Arnd Bauerkämper, Martin Sabrow, and Bernd Stöver, 18–31. Bonn: J. H. W. Dietz Nachf., 1998.

Friedlander, Henry. *The Origins of Nazi Genocide: From Euthanasia to the Final Solution.* Chapel Hill: University of North Carolina Press, 1995.

Friedlander [Friedländer], Saul. *A Conflict of Memories? The New German Debates about the "Final Solution."* New York: Leo Baeck Institute, 1987.

———. *Nazi Germany and the Jews.* Vol. 1: *The Years of Persecution.* New York: HarperCollins, 1997.

———. "Some Reflections on the Historicization of National Socialism." In *Reworking the Past: Hitler, the Holocaust, and the Historians' Debate,* edited by Peter Baldwin, 88–101. Boston: Beacon Press, 1990.

———, ed. *Probing the Limits of Representation: Nazism and the "Final Solution."* Cambridge, Mass.: Harvard University Press, 1992.

Friedrich, Jörg. "Die Schlacht bei Auschwitz: Zur Entstehung der KZ-Prozesse."

In *Von der Gnade der geschenkten Nation: Zur politischen Moral der Bonner Republik,* edited by Hajo Funke, 161–73. Berlin: Rotbuch, 1988.

Frieser, Karl-Heinz. *Krieg hinter Stacheldraht: Die deutschen Kriegsgefangenen in der Sowjetunion und das Nationalkomitee "Freies Deutschland."* Mainz: von Hase & Koehler, 1981.

Fritzsche, Peter. *Reading Berlin 1900.* Cambridge, Mass.: Harvard University Press, 1996.

Frohn, Axel. "Adenauer und die deutschen Ostgebiete in den fünfziger Jarhen." *Vierteljahrshefte für Zeitgeschichte* 44 (1996): 485–525.

———, ed. *Holocaust and Shilumim: The Policy of Wiedergutmachung in the Early 1950s.* Washington, D.C.: German Historical Institute, 1991.

Gall, Lothar. "Theodor Schieder, 1908–1984." *Historische Zeitschrift* 241 (1985): 1–25.

Garner, Curt. "Public Service Personnel in West Germany in the 1950s: Controversial Policy Decisions and Their Effects on Social Composition, Gender Structure, and the Role of Former Nazis." In *West Germany Under Construction: Politics, Society, and Culture in the Adenauer Era,* edited by Robert G. Moeller, 135–95. Ann Arbor: University of Michigan Press, 1997.

———. "Schlussfolgerungen aus der Vergangenheit? Die Auseinandersetzungen um die Zukunft des deutschen Berufsbeamtentums nach dem Ende des Zweiten Weltkrieges." In *Ende des Dritten Reiches—Ende des Zweiten Weltkrieges: Eine perspektivistische Rückschau,* edited by Hans-Ulrich Volkmann, 607–74. Munich: Piper, 1995.

Gauger. "Die Dystrophie als Gesamterkrankung." In *Extreme Lebensverhältnisse und ihre Folgen: Handbuch der ärztlichen Erfahrungen aus der Gefangenschaft,* edited by E. G. Schenck and W. von Nathusius, 7:12–21. N.p.: Schriftenreihe des ärztlich-wissenschaftlichen Beirates des Verbandes der Heimkehrer Deutschlands e.V., 1959.

Gehrmann, Karl Heinz. "Kulturpflege und Kulturpolitik." In *Die Vertriebenen in Westdeutschland: Ihre Eingliederung und ihr Einfluss auf Gesellschaft, Wirtschaft, Politik und Geistesleben,* edited by Eugen Lemberg and Friedrich Edding, 3:159–203. Kiel: Ferdinand Hirt, 1959.

Gentzen, F.-H., J. Kalisch, G. Voigt, and E. Wolfgramm. "Die 'Ostforschung': Ein Stosstrupp des deutschen Imperialismus." *Zeitschrift für Geschichtswissenschaft* 6 (1958): 1181–1220.

Gerstenberger, Friedrich. "Strategische Erinnerungen: Die Memoiren deutscher Offiziere." In *Vernichtungskrieg: Verbrechen der Wehrmacht, 1941–1944,* edited by Hannes Heer and Klaus Naumann, 620–29. Hamburg: Hamburger Edition, 1995.

Geyer, Michael. "The Place of the Second World War in German Memory and History." *New German Critique,* no. 71 (1997): 5–40.

———. "The Politics of Memory in Contemporary Germany." In *Radical Evil,* edited by Joan Copjec, 169–200. London: Verso, 1996.

Geyer, Michael, and Miriam Hansen. "German-Jewish Memory and National Consciousness." In *Holocaust Remembrance: The Shapes of Memory,* edited by Geoffrey H. Hartman, 175–90. Cambridge, Mass.: Blackwell, 1994.

Giessler, Hans. "Die Grundsatzbestimmungen des Entschädigungsrechts." In *Das*

Bundesentschädigungsgesetz: Erster Teil (§§1 bis 50 BEG), by Walter Brunn et al., 1–114. Munich: C. H. Beck, 1981. (= Vol. 4 of *Die Wiedergutmachung nationalsozialistischen Unrechts durch die Bundesrepublik Deutschland*, edited by the Bundesministerium der Finanzen.)

Gillis, John R., ed. *Commemorations: The Politics of National Identity*. Princeton: Princeton University Press, 1994.

Gimbel, John. *The American Occupation of Germany: Politics and the Military, 1945–1949*. Stanford: Stanford University Press, 1968.

Gluck, Carol. "The Past in the Present." In *Postwar Japan as History*, edited by Andrew Gordon, 64–95. Berkeley: University of California Press, 1993.

Goschler, Constantin. "The Attitude towards Jews in Bavaria after the Second World War." In *West Germany Under Construction: Politics, Society and Culture in the Adenauer Era*, edited by Robert G. Moeller, 231–49. Ann Arbor: University of Michigan Press, 1997.

———. *Wiedergutmachung: Westdeutschland und die Verfolgten des Nationalsozialismus (1950–1954)*. Munich: R. Oldenbourg, 1992.

Göttinger Arbeitskreis, ed. *Dokumente der Menschlichkeit aus der Zeit der Massenaustreibungen*. 2d ed. Würzburg: Holzner, 1960.

Göttler, Fritz. "Westdeutscher Nachkriegsfilm: Land der Väter." In *Geschichte des deutschen Films*, edited by Wolfgang Jacobsen, Anton Kaes, and Hans Helmut Prinzler, 171–210. Stuttgart: J. B. Metzler, 1993.

Gottschick, Johann. *Psychiatrie der Kriegsgefangenschaft: Dargestellt auf Grund von Beobachtungen in den USA an deutschen Kriegsgefangenen aus dem letzten Weltkrieg*. Stuttgart: Gustav Fischer, 1963.

Graml, Hermann. "Die verdrängte Auseinandersetzung mit dem Nationalsozialismus." In *Zäsuren nach 1945: Essays zur Periodisierung der deutschen Nachkriegsgeschichte*, edited by Martin Broszat, 169–83. Munich: R. Oldenbourg, 1990.

Grau, Karl Friedrich. *Schlesisches Inferno: Kriegsverbrechen der Roten Armee beim Einbruch in Schlesien, 1945*. Stuttgart: Seewald, 1966.

Grewe, Wilhelm Georg. *Rückblenden, 1976–1951*. Frankfurt am Main: Propyläen, 1979.

Grossmann, Atina. "A Question of Silence: The Rape of German Women by Occupation Soldiers." In *West Germany Under Construction: Politics, Society, and Culture in the Adenauer Era*, edited by Robert G. Moeller, 33–52. Ann Arbor: University of Michigan Press, 1997.

———. *Reforming Sex: The German Movement for Birth Control and Abortion Reform, 1920–1950*. New York: Oxford University Press, 1995.

———. "Trauma, Memory, and Motherhood: Germans and Jewish Displaced Persons in Post-Nazi Germany, 1945–1949." *Archiv für Sozialgeschichte* 38 (1998): 215–39.

Grossmann, Kurt R. *Die Ehrenschuld: Kurzgeschichte der Wiedergutmachung*. Frankfurt am Main: Ullstein, 1967.

Grube, Frank, and Gerhard Richter. *Flucht und Vertreibung: Deutschland zwischen 1944 und 1947*. Hamburg: Hoffmann & Campe, 1980.

Gutman, Israel [Yisrael]. *The Jews of Warsaw, 1939–1943: Ghetto, Underground, Revolt*. Bloomington: Indiana University Press, 1982.

————. *Resistance: The Warsaw Ghetto Uprising.* Boston: Houghton Mifflin, 1994.

Gutscher, Jörg Michael. *Die Entwicklung der FDP von ihren Anfängen bis 1961.* Meisenheim am Glan: Anton Hain, 1967.

Haar, Ingo. "'Kämpfende Wissenschaft': Entstehung und Niedergang der völkischen Geschichtswissenschaft im Wechsel der Systeme." In *Deutsche Historiker im Nationalsozialismus,* edited by Winfried Schulze and Otto Gerhard Oexle with the assistance of Gerd Helm and Thomas Ott, 215–40. Frankfurt am Main: Fischer Taschenbuch Verlag, 1999.

————. "'Revisionistische' Historiker und Jugendbewegung: Das Königsberger Beispiel." In *Geschichtsschreibung als Legitimationswissenschaft, 1918– 1945,* edited by Peter Schöttler, 52–103. Frankfurt am Main: Suhrkamp, 1997.

Habermas, Jürgen. "A Kind of Settlement of Damages (Apologetic Tendencies)." *New German Critique,* no. 44 (1988): 25–39.

Halbwachs, Maurice. *On Collective Memory.* Translated by Lewis A. Coser. Chicago: University of Chicago Press, 1992.

Hamburger Institut für Sozialforschung, ed. *Vernichtungskrieg: Verbrechen der Wehrmacht, 1941 bis 1944. Ausstellungskatalog.* Hamburg: Hamburger Edition, 1996.

Hartman, Geoffrey H., ed. *Bitburg in Moral and Political Perspective.* Bloomington: Indiana University Press, 1986.

Heer, Hannes, and Klaus Naumann, eds. *Vernichtungskrieg: Verbrechen der Wehrmacht, 1941–1944.* Hamburg: Hamburger Edition, 1995.

Heimann, Siegfried. "Die Sozialdemokratische Partei Deutschlands." In *Parteien-Handbuch: Die Parteien der Bundesrepublik Deutschland, 1945–1980,* edited by Richard Stöss, 2:2025–2216. Opladen: Westdeutscher Verlag, 1984.

Hein, Dieter. *Zwischen liberaler Milieupartei und nationaler Sammlungsbewegung: Gründung, Entwicklung und Struktur der Freien Demokratischen Partei, 1945–1949.* Düsseldorf: Droste, 1985.

Heineman, Elizabeth. "Complete Families, Half Families, No Families at All: Female-Headed Households and the Reconstruction of the Family in the Early Federal Republic." *Central European History* 29 (1996): 29–60.

————. "The Hour of the Woman: Memories of Germany's 'Crisis Years' and West German National Identity." *American Historical Review* 101 (1996): 354–95.

————. *What Difference Does a Husband Make? Marital Status in Germany, 1933–1961.* Berkeley: University of California Press, 1999.

Helbig, Louis Ferdinand. *Der ungeheure Verlust: Flucht und Vertreibung in der deutschsprachigen Belletristik der Nachkriegszeit.* Wiesbaden: Otto Harrassowitz, 1988.

Hembus, Joe. *Der deutsche Film kann gar nicht besser sein: Ein Pamphlet von gestern, eine Abrechnung von heute.* Munich: Rogner & Bernhard, 1981.

Henke, Josef. "Exodus aus Ostpreussen und Schlesien: Vier Erlebnisberichte." In *Die Vertreibung der Deutschen aus dem Osten: Ursachen, Ereignisse, Folgen,* edited by Wolfgang Benz, 91–104. Frankfurt am Main: Fischer, 1985.

————. "Flucht und Vertreibung der Deutschen aus ihrer Heimat im Osten und

Südosten, 1944–1947." *Aus Politik und Zeitgeschichte: Beilage zur Wochen-zeitung "Das Parlament,"* B23 (1985): 15–34.

Henke, Klaus-Dietmar. "Der Weg nach Potsdam: Die Alliierten und die Vertrei-bung." In *Die Vertreibung der Deutschen aus dem Osten: Ursachen, Ereignisse, Folgen,* edited by Wolfgang Benz, 49–69. Frankfurt am Main: Fischer, 1985.

Hennig, Regina. *Entschädigung und Interessenvertretung der NS-Verfolgten in Niedersachsen, 1945–1949.* Bielefeld: Verlag für Regionalgeschichte, 1991.

Herbert, Ulrich. *Fremdarbeiter: Politik und Praxis des "Ausländer-Einsatzes" in der Kriegswirtschaft des Dritten Reiches.* Bonn: J. H. W. Dietz Nachf., 1985.

———. "'Die guten und die schlechten Zeiten': Überlegungen zur diachronen Analyse lebensgeschichtlicher Interviews." In *"Die Jahre weiss man nicht, wo man die heute hinsetzen soll": Faschismus-Erfahrungen im Ruhrgebiet,* edited by Lutz Niethammer, 67–96. Bonn: J. H. W. Dietz Nachf., 1983.

———. "Labour and Extermination: Economic Interest and the Primacy of *Weltanschauung* in National Socialism." *Past and Present,* no. 138 (1993): 144–95.

———. "Nicht entschädigungsfähig? Die Wiedergutmachungsansprüche der Aus-länder." In *Wiedergutmachung in der Bundesrepublik Deutschland,* edited by Ludolf Herbst and Constantin Goschler, 273–302. Munich: R. Oldenbourg, 1989.

Herbst, Ludolf. "Stil und Handlungsspielräume westdeutscher Integrations-politik." In *Vom Marshallplan zur EWG: Die Eingliederung der Bundes-republik Deutschland in die westliche Welt,* edited by Ludolf Herbst, Werner Bührer, and Hanno Sowade, 3–18. Munich: R. Oldenbourg, 1990.

Herbst, Ludolf, and Constantin Goschler, eds. *Wiedergutmachung in der Bun-desrepublik Deutschland.* Munich: R. Oldenbourg, 1989.

Herf, Jeffrey. *Divided Memory: The Nazi Past in the Two Germanys.* Cambridge, Mass.: Harvard University Press, 1997.

———. "The 'Holocaust' Reception in West Germany: Right, Center, and Left." *New German Critique,* no. 19 (1980): 30–52.

Hessdörfer, Karl. "Die Entschädigungspraxis im Spannungsfeld von Gesetz, Justiz und NS-Opfern." In *Wiedergutmachung in der Bundesrepublik Deutschland,* edited by Ludolf Herbst and Constantin Goschler, 231–48. Munich: R. Oldenbourg, 1989.

Hettling, Manfred. "Täter und Opfer? Die deutschen Soldaten in Stalingrad." *Archiv für Sozialgeschichte* 35 (1995): 515–31.

Hickethier, Knut, with the assistance of Peter Hoff. *Geschichte des deutschen Fernsehens.* Stuttgart: J. B. Metzler, 1998.

Hilger, Dietrich. "Die mobilisierte Gesellschaft." In *Die zweite Republik: 25 Jahre Bundesrepublik Deutschland—eine Bilanz,* edited by Richard Löwenthal and Hans-Peter Schwarz, 95–122. Stuttgart: Seewald, 1974.

Hillgruber, Andreas. "Die 'Endlösung' und das deutsche Ostimperium als Kern-stück des rassenideologischen Programms des Nationalsozialismus." *Viertel-jahrshefte für Zeitgeschichte* 20 (1982): 133–53.

———. "Jürgen Habermas, Karl-Heinz Janssen und die Aufklärung Anno

1986." In *"Historikerstreit"*: *Die Dokumentation der Kontroverse um die Einzigartigkeit der nationalsozialistischen Judenvernichtung,* 331–51. Munich: Piper, 1987.

———. *Zweierlei Untergang: Die Zerschlagung des deutschen Reiches und das Ende des europäischen Judentums.* Berlin: Siedler, 1986.

———, ed. *Vom Beruf des Historikers in einer Zeit beschleunigten Wandels: Akademische Gedenkfeier für Theodor Schieder am 8. Februar 1985 in der Universität zu Köln.* Munich: R. Oldenbourg, 1985.

"Historikerstreit": Die Dokumentation der Kontroverse um die Einzigartigkeit der nationalsozialistischen Judenvernichtung. Munich: Piper, 1987. Published in English as *Forever in the Shadow of Hitler? Original Documents of the Historikerstreit, the Controversy concerning the Singularity of the Holocaust.* Translated by James Knowlton and Truett Cates. Atlantic Highlands, N.J.: Humanities Press, 1993.

Hockerts, Hans Günter. "Integration der Gesellschaft: Gründungskrise und Sozialpolitik in der frühen Bundesrepublik." *Zeitschrift für Sozialreform* 32 (1986): 25–41.

———. "Zeitgeschichte in Deutschland: Begriff, Methoden, Themenfelder." *Historisches Jahrbuch* 6 (1993): 98–127.

Hoenisch, Michael. "Film as an Instrument of the U.S. Reeducation Program in Germany after 1945 and the Example of *Todesmühlen.*" In *The Role of the United States in the Reconstruction of Italy and West Germany, 1943–1949,* edited by Ekkehart Krippendorff, 127–57. Berlin: Zentrale Universitätsdruckerei der Freien Universität, 1981.

Hoensch, Jörg K. *A History of Modern Hungary, 1867–1986.* Translated by Kim Traynor. London: Longman, 1988.

———. "The Slovak Republic, 1939–1945." In *A History of the Czechoslovak Republic, 1918–1948,* edited by Victor S. Mamatey and Radomír Luža, 271–95. Princeton: Princeton University Press, 1973.

Höfig, Willi. *Der deutsche Heimatfilm, 1947–1960.* Stuttgart: Ferdinand Enke, 1973.

Hoffmann, Christa. *Stunden Null? Vergangenheitsbewältigung in Deutschland, 1945 bis 1989.* Bonn: Bouvier, 1992.

Hogan, Michael J., ed. *Hiroshima in History and Memory.* New York: Cambridge University Press, 1996.

Holtmann, Everhard. "Flüchtlinge in den 50er Jahren: Aspekte ihrer gesellschaftlichen und politischen Integration." In *Modernisierung im Wiederaufbau: Die westdeutsche Gesellschaft der 50er Jahre,* edited by Axel Schildt and Arnold Sywottek, 349–61. Bonn: J. H. W. Dietz Nachf., 1993.

Horster, Hans-Ulrich [Eduard Rudolf Rhein]. *Suchkind 312.* Frankfurt am Main: Ullstein, 1995.

Hughes, Michael L. *Shouldering the Burdens of Defeat: West Germany and the Reconstruction of Social Justice.* Chapel Hill: University of North Carolina Press, 1999.

Huhn, Rudolf. "Die Wiedergutmachungsverhandlungen in Wassenaar." In *Wiedergutmachung in der Bundesrepublik Deutschland,* edited by Ludolf Herbst and Constantin Goschler, 139–60. Munich: R. Oldenbourg, 1989.

Ihme-Tuchel, Beate. "Die Entlassung der deutschen Kriegsgefangenen im Herbst 1955 im Spiegel der Diskussion zwischen SED und KPdSU." *Militärgeschichtliche Mitteilungen* 53 (1994): 449–65.

———. "Zwischen Tabu und Propaganda: Hintergründe und Probleme der ostdeutsch-sowjetischen Heimkehrerverhandlungen." In *Heimkehr 1948*, edited by Annette Kaminsky, 38–54. Munich: C. H. Beck, 1998.

Imhof, Michael. "Die Vertriebenenverbände in der Bundesrepublik Deutschland: Geschichte, Organisation und gesellschaftliche Bedeutung." Ph.D. diss., Philipps-Universität Marburg, 1975.

Institut für Sozialforschung. *Zum politischen Bewusstsein ehemaliger Kriegsgefangener: Eine soziologische Untersuchung im Verband der Heimkehrer— Forschungsbericht.* Frankfurt am Main, 1957.

Irwin-Zarecka, Iwona. *Frames of Remembrance: The Dynamics of Collective Memory.* New Brunswick, N.J.: Transaction Publishers, 1994.

Jacobsen, Hans-Adolf. "Zur Rolle der öffentlichen Meinung bei der Debatte um die Wiederbewaffnung, 1950–1955." In *Aspekte der deutschen Wiederbewaffnung bis 1955*, edited by the Militärgeschichtliches Forschungsamt, 61–98. Boppard am Rhein: Harald Boldt, 1975.

Jacobsen, Hans-Adolf, ed., with the assistance of Wilfried von Bredow. *Misstrauische Nachbarn: Deutsche Ostpolitik 1919/1970. Dokumentation und Analyse.* Düsseldorf: Droste, 1970.

Jaeger, Klaus, and Helmut Regel, eds. *Deutschland in Trümmern: Filmdokumente der Jahre 1945–1949.* Oberhausen: Karl Maria Laufen, 1976.

Jahn, Hans Edgar. *Pommersche Passion.* Preetz/Holstein: Ernst Gerdes, 1964.

Jahn, Peter, and Reinhard Rürup, eds. *Erobern und Vernichten: Der Krieg gegen die Sowjetunion, 1941–1945.* Berlin: Argon, 1991.

Jakobsmeier, Werner. "Das Münchner Abkommen: Unüberbrückbarer Graben zwischen Bonn und Prag?" In *Unfertige Nachbarschaften: Die Staaten Osteuropas und die Bundesrepublik Deutschland,* edited by Othmar Nikola Haberl and Hans Hecker, 177–203. Essen: R. Hobbing, 1989.

Janowitz, Morris. "German Reactions to Nazi Atrocities." *American Journal of Sociology* 52 (1946): 141–46.

Jasper, Gotthard. "Die disqualifizierten Opfer: Der Kalte Krieg und die Entschädigung für Kommunisten." In *Wiedergutmachung in der Bundesrepublik Deutschland,* edited by Ludolf Herbst and Constantin Goschler, 361–84. Munich: R. Oldenbourg, 1989.

Jaspers, Karl. *The Question of German Guilt.* Translated by E. B. Ashton. New York: Capricorn Books, 1961.

Jeffords, Susan. *The Remasculinization of America: Gender and the Vietnam War.* Bloomington: Indiana University Press, 1989.

Jeggle, Utz. "Sage und Verbrechen." In *Flüchtlinge und Vertriebene in der westdeutschen Nachkriegsgeschichte: Bilanzierung der Forschung und Perspektiven für die künftige Forschungsarbeit,* edited by Rainer Schulze, Doris von der Brelie-Lewien, and Helga Grebing, 201–6. Hildesheim: August Lax, 1987.

Jelinek, Yeshayahu A. "Die Krise der Shilumim/Wiedergutmachungs-Verhandlungen im Sommer 1952." *Vierteljahrshefte für Zeitgeschichte* 38 (1990): 113–39.

———. *The Lust for Power: Nationalism, Slovakia, and the Communists,*
1918–1948. Boulder, Colo.: East European Monographs, 1983.

———. "Political Acumen, Altruism, Foreign Pressure, or Moral Debt: Konrad
Adenauer and the 'Shilumim.'" *Tel Aviver Jahrbuch für deutsche Geschichte*
19 (1990): 77–102.

———, ed. *Zwischen Moral and Realpolitik: Deutsch-israelische Beziehungen,*
1945–1965. Gerlingen: Bleicher, 1997.

Jena, Kai von. "Versöhnung mit Israel? Die deutsch-israelischen Verhandlungen
bis zum Wiedergutmachungsabkommen von 1952." *Vierteljahrshefte für Zeit-*
geschichte 34 (1986): 457–80.

Jolles, Hildo M. *Zur Soziologie der Heimatvertriebenen und Flüchtlinge.* Cologne:
Kiepenheuer & Witsch, 1965.

Josko, Anna. "The Slovak Resistance Movement." In *A History of the Czechoslo-*
vak Republic, 1918–1948, edited by Victor S. Mamatey and Radomír Luža,
362–84. Princeton: Princeton University Press, 1973.

Kaes, Anton. *From Hitler to Heimat: The Return of History as Film.* Cambridge,
Mass.: Harvard University Press, 1989.

Kahlenberg, Friedrich P. "Der Film der Ära Adenauer." In *Trümmer und Träume:*
Nachkriegszeit und fünfziger Jahre auf Zelluloid, edited by Ursula Bessen,
236–47. Bochum: Studienverlag Dr. N. Brockmeyer, 1989.

Kalcyk, Hansjörg, and Hans-Joachim Westholt. *Suchdienst-Kartei: Millionen*
Schicksale in der Nackkriegszeit. Bonn: Stiftung Haus der Geschichte, n.d.

Kaminsky, Annette, ed. *Heimkehr 1948.* Munich: C. H. Beck, 1998.

Kaplan, Marion A. *Between Dignity and Despair: Jewish Life in Nazi Germany.*
New York: Oxford University Press, 1998.

Kaps, Johannes, ed. *Die Tragödie Schlesiens 1945/46 in Dokumenten unter beson-*
derer Berücksichtigung des Erzbistums Breslau. Munich: Verlag "Christ unterwegs," 1952–53.

Karasek-Langer, Alfred. "Volkskundliche Erkenntnisse aus der Vertreibung und
Eingliederung der Ostdeutschen." *Jahrbuch für Volkskunde der Heimatver-*
triebenen 1 (1955): 11–65.

———. "Volkstum im Umbruch." In *Die Vertriebenen in Westdeutschland: Ihre*
Eingliederung und ihr Einfluss auf Gesellschaft, Wirtschaft, Politik und Geis-
tesleben, edited by Eugen Lemberg and Friedrich Edding, 1:606–94. Kiel: Ferdinand Hirt, 1959.

Karner, Stefan. "Die sowjetische Hauptverwaltung für Kriegsgefangene und Internierte." *Vierteljahrshefte für Zeitgeschichte* 42 (1994): 447–71.

———. *Im Archipel GUPVI: Kriegsgefangenschaft und Internierung in der Sow-*
jetunion, 1941–1956. Munich: R. Oldenbourg, 1995.

———. "Verlorene Jahre: Deutsche Kriegsgefangene und Internierte im
Archipel GUPWI." In *Kriegsgefangene-Voennoeplennye: Sowjetische Kriegs-*
gefangene in Deutschland, Deutsche Kriegsgefangene in der Sowjetunion,
edited by Haus der Geschichte der Bundesrepublik, 59–65. Düsseldorf:
Droste, 1995.

Kaschuba, Wolfgang. "Bildwelten als Weltbilder." In *Der deutsche Heimatfilm:*
Bildwelten und Weltbilder, edited by Dieter Bahlinger et al., 7–13. Tübingen:
Tübinger Chronik, 1989.

Kershaw, Ian. *The "Hitler Myth": Image and Reality in the Third Reich.* Oxford: Oxford University Press, 1987.

———. *The Nazi Dictatorship: Problems and Perspectives of Interpretation.* 3d ed. London: Edward Arnold, 1993.

———. "'Normality' and Genocide: The Problem of 'Historicization.'" In *Reevaluating the Third Reich,* edited by Thomas Childers and Jane Caplan, 20–41. New York: Holmes & Meier, 1993.

Kieser, Egbert. *Danziger Bucht 1945: Dokumentation einer Katastrophe.* Esslingen am Neckar: Bechtle, 1978.

Kilian, H. "Das Wiedereinleben des Heimkehrers in Familie, Ehe und Beruf." In *Die Sexualität des Heimkehrers: Vorträge gehalten auf dem 4. Kongress der Deutschen Gesellschaft für Sexualforschung in Erlangen, 1956,* 27–38. Stuttgart: Ferdinand Enke, 1957.

Kittel, Manfred. *Die Legende von der "zweiten Schuld": Vergangenheitsbewältigung in der Ära Adenauer.* Frankfurt am Main: Ullstein, 1993.

Klee, Ernst. *Auschwitz, die NS-Medizin und ihre Opfer.* Frankfurt am Main: S. Fischer, 1997.

Klee, Ernst, Willi Dressen, and Volker Riess, eds. *"The Good Old Days": The Holocaust As Seen by Its Perpetrators and Bystanders.* Translated by Deborah Burnstone. New York: Free Press, 1991.

Klemperer, Klemens von. "Hans Rothfels (1891–1976)." In *Paths of Continuity: Central European Historiography from the 1930s to the 1950s,* edited by Hartmut Lehmann and James van Horn Melton, 119–35. Cambridge: Cambridge University Press, 1994.

Klessmann, Christoph. "Adenauers Deutschland- und Ostpolitik, 1955—1963." In *Adenauer und die deutsche Frage,* edited by Josef Foschepoth, 61–79. Göttingen: Vandenhoeck & Ruprecht, 1988.

———. *Die doppelte Staatsgründung: Deutsche Geschichte, 1945–1955.* Göttingen: Vandenhoeck & Ruprecht, 1982.

———. "Geschichtsbewusstsein nach 1945: Ein neuer Anfang?" In *Geschichtsbewusstsein der Deutschen: Materialien zur Spurensuche einer Nation,* edited by Werner Weidenfeld, 111–29. Cologne: Wissenschaft & Politik, 1987.

———. *Zwei Staaten, eine Nation: Deutsche Geschichte, 1955–1970.* Göttingen: Vandenhoeck & Ruprecht, 1988.

Klotz, Marcia. "New German Documentary: The Impossible Struggle for a Fascism Vérité." *Arachnē* 3 (1996): 9–30.

Klotzbach, Kurt. *Der Weg zur Staatspartei: Programmatik, praktische Politik und Organisation der deutschen Sozialdemokratie, 1945 bis 1965.* Bonn: J. H. W. Dietz Nachf., 1982.

Kluge, Alexander. *The Battle.* Translated by Leila Vennewitz. New York: McGraw-Hill, 1967.

———. *Die Patriotin: Texte/Bilder 1–6.* Frankfurt am Main: Zweitausendeins, 1979.

Knopp, Guido, ed. *Damals 1955: Das Jahr der Anerkennung.* Video. Stuttgart: ZDF/DVA, 1995.

Koch, Gertrud. "How Much Naiveté Can We Afford? The New *Heimat* Feeling." *New German Critique,* no. 36 (1985): 13–15.

Koch, Gertrud, Klaus Konz, Wolfgang Oehrle, Gundula Schmidt, and Barbara Wilzcek. "Die fünfizger Jahre: Heide und Silberwald." In *Der deutsche Heimatfilm: Bildwelten und Weltbilder*, edited by Dieter Bahlinger et al., 69–95. Tübingen: Tübinger Chronik, 1989.

Kochenrath, Hans-Peter. "Kontinuität im deutschen Film." In *Film und Gesellschaft in Deutschalnd: Dokumente und Materialien*, edited by Wilfried von Bredow and Rolf Zurek, 286–92. Hamburg: Hoffmann & Campe, 1975.

Koehl, Robert L. *RKFDV: German Resettlement and Population Policy, 1939–1945*. Cambridge, Mass.: Harvard University Press, 1957.

Kogon, Eugen. *Der NS-Staat: Das System der deutschen Konzentrationslager*. Munich: Alber, 1946.

———. "Über die Situation." *Frankfurter Hefte* 2, no. 1 (Jan. 1947): 17–37.

Köhler, Henning. *Adenauer: Eine politische Biographie*. Frankfurt am Main: Propyläen, 1994.

Kohn, Richard H. "History and the Culture Wars: The Case of the Smithsonian Institution's *Enola Gay* Exhibition." *Journal of American History* 82 (1995): 1036–63.

Komjathy, Anthony, and Rebecca Stockwell. *German Minorities and the Third Reich: Ethnic Germans of East Central Europe between the Wars*. New York: Holmes & Meier, 1980.

Koonz, Claudia. "Between Memory and Oblivion: Concentration Camps in German Memory." In *Commemorations: The Politics of National Identity*, edited by John R. Gillis, 258–80. Princeton: Princeton University Press, 1994.

———. "Germany's Buchenwald: Whose Shrine? Whose Memory?" In *The Art of Memory: Holocaust Memorials in History*, edited by James E. Young, 111–19. New York: Prestel, 1994.

———. *Mothers in the Fatherland: Women, the Family, and Nazi Politics*. New York: St. Martin's Press, 1987.

Koselleck, Reinhart. "Werner Conze: Tradition und Innovation." *Historische Zeitschrift* 245 (1987): 529–43.

Koshar, Rudy. *Germany's Transient Pasts: Preservation and National Memory in the Twentieth Century*. Chapel Hill: University of North Carolina Press, 1998.

Kosta, Barbara. "Rape, Nation, and Remembering History: Helke Sander's *Liberators Take Liberties*." In *Gender and Germanness: Cultural Productions of Nation*, edited by Patricia Herminghouse and Magda Mueller, 217–31. Providence, R.I.: Berghahn Books, 1997.

———. *Recasting Autobiography: Women's Counterfictions in Contemporary German Literature and Film*. Ithaca, N.Y.: Cornell University Press, 1994.

Kötter, Herbert. "Die Landwirtschaft." In *Sozialgeschichte der Bundesrepublik Deutschland: Beiträge zum Kontinuitätsproblem*, edited by Werner Conze and M. Rainer Lepsius, 115–42. Stuttgart: Klett-Cotta, 1983.

Krause, Michael. *Flucht vor dem Bombenkrieg: "Umquartierungen" im Zweiten Weltkrieg und die Wiedereingliederung der Evakuierten in Deutschland, 1943–1963*. Düsseldorf: Droste, 1997.

Kreimeier, Klaus. *Kino und Filmindustrie in der BRD: Ideologieproduktion und Klassenwirklichkeit nach 1945*. Kronberg/Taunus: Scriptor, 1973.

———. *The Ufa Story: A History of Germany's Greatest Film Company,*

1918–1945. Translated by Robert Kimber and Rita Kimber. New York: Hill & Wang, 1996.

———. "Der westdeutsche Film in den fünfizger Jahren." In *Die fünfziger Jahre: Beiträge zu Politik und Kultur,* edited by Dieter Baensch, 283–305. Tübingen: Gunter Narr, 1985.

Kuby, Erich. *Mein ärgerliches Vaterland.* Munich: Carl Hanser, 1989.

Kučera, Jaroslav. "Zwischen Geschichte und Politik: Die aktuelle Diskussion über die Vertreibung der Deutschen in der tschechischen Gesellschaft und Politik." In *Flucht und Vertreibung: Zwischen Aufrechnung und Verdrängung,* edited by Robert Streibel, 174–87. Vienna: Picus, 1994.

Kühne, Thomas. "' . . . aus diesem Krieg werden nicht nur harte Männer heimkehren': Kriegskameradschaft und Männlichkeit im 20. Jahrhundert." In *Männergeschichte—Geschlechtergeschichte: Männlichkeit im Wandel der Moderne,* edited by Thomas Kühne, 174–92. Frankfurt am Main: Campus, 1996.

———. "Kameradschaft—'das Beste im Leben des Mannes': Die deutschen Soldaten des Zweiten Weltkriegs in erfahrungs- und geschlechtergeschichtlicher Perspektive." *Geschichte und Gesellschaft* 22 (1996): 504–29.

Kulischer, Eugene M. *Europe on the Move: War and Population Changes, 1917–47.* New York: Columbia University Press, 1948.

Kulka, Otto D. "Major Trends and Tendencies in German Historiography on National Socialism and the 'Jewish Question' (1924–1984)." *Yearbook of the Leo Baeck Institute* 30 (1985): 215–42.

———. "Singularity and Its Relativization: Changing Views in the German Historiography on National Socialism and the 'Final Solution.'" In *Reworking the Past: Hitler, the Holocaust, and the Historians' Debate,* edited by Peter Baldwin, 146–70. Boston: Beacon Press, 1990.

Kulturstiftung der deutschen Vertriebenen, ed. *Vertreibung und Vertreibungsverbrechen, 1945–1948: Bericht des Bundesarchivs vom 28. Mai 1974.* Meckenheim: DCM Druck, 1989.

Kumpfmüller, Michael. *Die Schlacht von Stalingrad: Metamorphosen eines deutschen Mythos.* Munich: Wilhelm Fink, 1995.

Kurth, Karl O. *Handbuch der Presse der Heimatvertriebenen.* Kitzingen-Main: Holzner, 1953.

———. "Presse, Film und Rundfunk." In *Die Vertriebenen in Westdeutschland: Ihre Eingliederung und ihr Einfluss auf Gesellschaft, Wirtschaft, Politik und Geistesleben,* edited by Eugen Lemberg and Friedrich Edding, 3:402–34. Kiel: Ferdinand Hirt, 1959.

Küsters, Hanns Jürgen, ed. *Adenauer: Teegespräche, 1955–1958.* Berlin: Wolf Jobst Siedler, 1986.

Lang, Martin. *Stalins Strafjustiz gegen deutsche Soldaten: Die Massenprozesse gegen deutsche Kriegsgefangene in den Jahren 1949 und 1950 in historischer Sicht.* Herford: E. S. Mittler & Sohn, 1981.

Langbein, Hermann. *Der Auschwitz-Prozess: Eine Dokumentation.* 2 vols. Frankfurt am Main: Neue Kritik, [1965] 1995.

Large, David Clay. *Germans to the Front: West German Rearmament in the Adenauer Era.* Chapel Hill: University of North Carolina Press, 1996.

Lehmann, Albrecht. *Gefangenschaft und Heimkehr: Deutsche Kriegsgefangene in der Sowjetunion.* Munich: C. H. Beck, 1986.

———. *Im Fremden ungewollt zuhaus: Flüchtlinge und Vertriebene in Westdeutschland, 1945–1990.* Munich: C. H. Beck, 1991.

Lehmann, Hans Georg. "Der analytische Bezugsrahmen eines internationalen und intergesellschaftlichen Konflikts am Beispiel der Genesis des Oder-Neisse-Konflikts." In *Das deutsch-polnische Konfliktverhältnis seit dem Zweiten Weltkrieg: Multidisziplinäre Studien über konfliktfördernde und konfliktmindernde Faktoren in den internationalen Beziehungen,* edited by Carl Christoph Schweitzer and Hubert Feger, 25–91. Boppard am Rhein: Harald Boldt, 1975.

———. *Der Oder-Neisse-Konflikt.* Munich: C. H. Beck, 1979.

———. "Oder-Neisse-Linie und Heimatverlust—Interdependenzen zwischen Flucht/Vertreibung und Revisionismus." In *Flüchtlinge und Vertriebene in der westdeutschen Nachkriegsgeschichte: Bilanzierung der Forschung und Perspektiven für die künftige Forschungsarbeit,* edited by Rainer Schulze, Doris von der Brelie-Lewien, and Helga Grebing, 107–17. Hildesheim: August Lax, 1987.

Lehndorff, Hans Graf von. *Ein Bericht aus Ost- und Westpreussen, 1945 – 1947.* Düsseldorf: Oskar-Leiner-Druck, 1960.

———. *Ostpreussisches Tagebuch: Aufzeichnungen eines Arztes aus den Jahren 1945–1947.* Munich: Biederstein, 1966.

Lemberg, Eugen. "Völkerpsychologische und weltgeschichtliche Aspekte." In *Die Vertriebenen in Westdeutschland: Ihre Eingliederung und ihr Einfluss auf Gesellschaft, Wirtschaft, Politik und Geistesleben,* edited by Eugen Lemberg and Friedrich Edding, 3:578–95. Kiel: Ferdinand Hirt, 1959.

Lemberg, Eugen, ed., with the assistance of Lothar Krecker. *Die Entstehung eines neuen Volkes aus Binnendeutschen und Ostvertriebenen.* Marburg: N. G. Elwert, 1950.

Lemberg, Eugen, and Friedrich Edding. "Eingliederung und Gesellschaftswandel." In *Die Vertriebenen in Westdeutschland: Ihre Eingliederung und ihr Einfluss auf Gesellschaft, Wirtschaft, Politik und Geistesleben,* edited by Eugen Lemberg and Friedrich Edding, 1:156–73. Kiel: Ferdinand Hirt, 1959.

———, eds. *Die Vertriebenen in Westdeutschland: Ihre Eingliederung und ihr Einfluss auf Gesellschaft, Wirtschaft, Politik und Geistesleben.* 3 vols. Kiel: Ferdinand Hirt, 1959.

Lifton, Robert Jay. *The Nazi Doctors: Medical Killing and the Psychology of Genocide.* New York: Basic Books, 1986.

Lübbe, Hermann. "Der Nationalsozialismus im politischen Bewusstsein der Gegenwart." In *Deutschlands Weg in die Diktatur: Internationale Konferenz zur nationalsozialistischen Machtübernahme im Reichstagsgebäude zu Berlin,* edited by Martin Broszat et al., 329–49. Berlin: Siedler, 1983.

Lüdtke, Alf. "The Appeal of Exterminating 'Others': German Workers and the Limits of Resistance." *Journal of Modern History* 64 suppl. (1992): S46–S67.

———. "'Coming to Terms with the Past': Illusions of Remembering, Ways of Forgetting Nazism in West Germany." *Journal of Modern History* 65 (1993): 542–72.

————, ed. *Stalingrad: Erinnerung und Identitätssuche*. Special issue of *SOWI* 22, no. 1 (1993).

Ludwig, K. "Heimkehrer als soziologisches Problem." In *Die Sexualität des Heimkehrers: Vorträge gehalten auf dem 4. Kongress der Deutschen Gesellschaft für Sexualforschung in Erlangen, 1956*, 72–76. Stuttgart: Ferdinand Enke, 1957.

Lumans, Valdis O. "The Ethnic German Minority of Slovakia and the Third Reich, 1938–45." *Central European History* 15 (1982): 266–97.

————. *Himmler's Auxiliaries: The Volksdeutsche Mittelstelle and the German National Minorities of Europe, 1933–1945*. Chapel Hill: University of North Carolina Press, 1993.

Lüttinger, Paul, with the assistance of Rita Rossmann. *Integration der Vertriebenen: Eine empirische Analyse*. Frankfurt: Campus, 1989.

Maase, Kaspar. *BRAVO Amerika: Erkundungen zur Jugendkultur der Bundesrepublik in den fünfziger Jahren*. Hamburg: Junius, 1992.

Madajczyk, Czesław. *Die Okkupationspolitik Nazideutschlands in Polen, 1939–1945*. Berlin: Akademie, 1987.

Maier, Charles S. *The Unmasterable Past: History, Holocaust, and German National Identity*. Cambridge, Mass.: Harvard University Press, 1988.

Major, Patrick. *The Death of the KPD: Communism and Anti-Communism in West Germany, 1945–1956*. Oxford: Clarendon Press, 1997.

Marcuse, Harold. "Das ehemalige Konzentrationslager Dachau: Der mühevolle Weg zur Gedenkstätte, 1945–1968." *Dachauer Hefte* 6 (1990): 182–205.

————. *Legacies of Dachau: The Uses and Abuses of a Concentration Camp, 1933–2001*. Cambridge: Cambridge University Press, forthcoming.

————. "The Revival of Holocaust Awareness in West Germany, Israel, and the United States." In *1968: The World Transformed*, ed. Carole Fink, Philipp Gassert, and Detlef Junker, 421–38. Cambridge: Cambridge University Press, 1998.

Margalit, Gilad. "Die deutsche Zigeunerpolitik nach 1945." *Vierteljahrshefte für Zeitgeschichte* 45 (1997): 557–88.

Marrus, Michael R. *The Unwanted: European Refugees in the Twentieth Century*. New York: Oxford University Press, 1985.

Marshall, Barbara. "German Attitudes to British Military Government, 1945–1947." *Journal of Contemporary History* 15 (1980): 655–84.

Martens, Alexander U. *Heinz G. Konsalik: Leben und Werk eines Bestseller-Autors*. Munich: Wilhelm Heyne, 1991.

Maschke, Erich. "Deutsche Kriegsgefangenengeschichte: Der Gang der Forschung." In *Die deutschen Kriegsgefangenen des Zweiten Weltkrieges: Eine Zusammenfassung*, edited by Erich Maschke, 1–37. Bielefeld: Ernst & Werner Gieseking, 1974.

————. "Das Schicksal der deutschen Kriegsgefangenen des Zweiten Weltkrieges als Aufgabe zeitgeschichtlicher Forschung." In *Die deutschen Kriegsgefangenen in Jugoslawien, 1941–1949*, vol. 1, by Kurt W. Böhme, pt. 1, vii–xx. Bielefeld: Ernst & Werner Gieseking, 1962.

————, ed. *Die deutschen Kriegsgefangenen des Zweiten Weltkrieges: Eine Zusammenfassung*. Bielefeld: Ernst & Werner Gieseking, 1974.

Mastny, Vojtech. *The Czechs under Nazi Rule: The Failure of National Resistance, 1939–1942.* New York: Columbia University Press, 1971.

Matz, Elisabeth. *Die Zeitungen der US-Armee für die deutsche Bevölkerung (1944–1946).* Münster [Westf.]: C. J. Fahle, 1969.

Maurach, Reinhart. *Die Kriegsverbrecherprozesse gegen deutsche Gefangene in der Sowjetunion.* Hamburg: Arbeitsgemeinschaft vom Roten Kreuz in Deutschland, Britische Zone, Rechtsschutzstelle für Kriegsgefangene und Zivilarbeiter im Ausland, 1950.

May, Ernest R. "The American Commitment to Germany, 1949–55." *Diplomatic History* 13 (1989): 431–60.

Mayer, Arno J. "Memory and History: On the Poverty of Remembering and Forgetting the Judeocide." *Radical History Review,* no. 56 (1993): 5–20.

McCormick, Richard W. "Confronting German History: Melodrama, Distantiation, and Women's Discourse in *Germany, Pale Mother.*" In *Gender and German Cinema: Feminist Interventions,* vol. 2: *German Film History/German History on Film,* edited by Sandra Frieden et al., 185–206. Providence, R.I.: Berg, 1993.

Meissner, Boris, ed. *Moskau-Bonn: Die Beziehungen zwischen der Sowjetunion und der Bundesrepublik Deutschland, 1955–1973. Dokumentation.* Cologne: Wissenschaft & Politik, 1975.

Melton, James van Horn. "Introduction: Continuities in German Historical Scholarship, 1930–1960." In *Paths of Continuity: Central European Historiography from the 1930s to the 1950s,* edited by Hartmut Lehmann and James van Horn Melton, 1–18. Cambridge: Cambridge University Press, 1994.

Mendelsohn, Ezra. *The Jews of East Central Europe between the World Wars.* Bloomington: Indiana University Press, 1983.

Messerschmidt, Manfred. *Die Wehrmacht im NS-Staat: Zeit der Indoktrination.* Heidelberg: R. v. Decker, 1969.

Meyer, Georg. "Innenpolitische Voraussetzungen der westdeutschen Wiederbewaffnung." In *Wiederbewaffnung in Deutschland nach 1945,* edited by Alexander Fischer, 31–44. Berlin: Duncker & Humblot, 1986.

———. "Zur Situation der deutschen militärischen Führungsschicht im Vorfeld des westdeutschen Verteidigungsbeitrages, 1945–1950/51." In *Von der Kapitulation bis zum Pleven-Plan,* by Roland G. Foerster et al., vol. 1 of *Anfänge westdeutscher Sicherheitspolitik, 1945–1956,* edited by Militärgeschichtliches Forschungsamt, 577–735. Munich: R. Oldenbourg, 1982.

Meyer, Sibylle, and Eva Schulze. *Von Liebe sprach damals keiner: Familienalltag in der Nachkriegszeit.* Munich: C. H. Beck, 1985.

———. *Wie wir das alles geschafft haben: Alleinstehende Frauen berichten über ihr Leben nach 1945.* Munich: C. H. Beck, 1985.

Middlemann, Werner. "Entstehung und Aufgaben der Flüchtlingsverwaltung." In *Die Vertriebenen in Westdeutschland: Ihre Eingliederung und ihr Einfluss auf Gesellschaft, Wirtschaft, Politik und Geistesleben,* edited by Eugen Lemberg and Friedrich Edding, 1:276–99. Kiel: Ferdinand Hirt, 1959.

Mitchell, Maria. "Materialism and Secularism: CDU Politicians and National Socialism, 1945–1949." *Journal of Modern History* 67 (1995): 273–308.

Mitscherlich, Alexander. *Auf dem Wege zur vaterlosen Gesellschaft: Ideen zur Sozialpsychologie*. Munich: Piper, [1963] 1973.

———. "Der unsichtbare Vater: Ein Problem für Psychoanalyse und Soziologie." *Kölner Zeitschrift für Soziologie und Sozialpsychologie* 7 (1955): 188–201.

Mitscherlich, Alexander, and Fried Mielke. *Doctors of Infamy: The Story of the Nazi Medical Crimes*. New York: Schuman, 1949.

———. *Medizin ohne Menschlichkeit: Dokumente des Nürnberger Ärzteprozesses*. Frankfurt am Main: Fischer Taschenbuch Verlag, 1995.

Mitscherlich, Alexander, and Margarete Mitscherlich. *Die Unfähigkeit zu trauern: Grundlagen kollektiven Verhaltens*. Munich: Piper, 1967.

Moeller, Robert G. "The Homosexual Man Is a 'Man,' the Homosexual Woman Is a 'Woman': Sex, Society, and the Law in Postwar West Germany." In *West Germany Under Construction: Politics, Society and Culture in the Adenauer Era*, edited by Robert G. Moeller, 251–84. Ann Arbor: University of Michigan Press, 1997.

———. *Protecting Motherhood: Women and the Family in the Politics of Postwar West Germany*. Berkeley: University of California Press, 1993.

———. "War Stories: The Search for a Usable Past in the Federal Republic of Germany." *American Historical Review* 101 (1996): 1008–48.

Moltke, Johannes von. "Trapped in America: The Americanization of the *Trapp-Familie*, or 'Papas Kino' Revisited." *German Studies Review* 19 (1996): 455–78.

Mommsen, Hans. "Hans Rothfels." In *Deutsche Historiker*, edited by Hans-Ulrich Wehler, 9:127–47. Göttingen: Vandenhoeck & Ruprecht, 1982.

———. "Zeitgeschichte als 'kritische Aufklärungsarbeit': Zur Erinnerung an Martin Broszat (1926–1989)." *Geschichte und Gesellschaft* 17 (1991): 141–57.

Mommsen, Wolfgang J. "Vom Beruf des Historikers in einer Zeit beschleunigten Wandels: Theodor Schieders historiographisches Werk." In *Vom Beruf des Historikers in einer Zeit beschleunigten Wandels: Akademische Gedenkfeier für Theodor Schieder am 8. Februar 1985 an der Universität zu Köln*, edited by Andreas Hillgruber, 33–59. Munich: R. Oldenbourg, 1985.

———. "Vom 'Volkstumskampf' zur nationalsozialistischen Vernichtungspolitik in Osteuropa: Zur Rolle der deutschen Historiker unter dem Nationalsozialismus." In *Deutsche Historiker im Nationalsozialismus*, edited by Winfried Schulze and Otto Gerhard Oexle with the assistance of Gerd Helm and Thomas Ott, 183–214. Frankfurt am Main: Fischer Taschenbuch Verlag, 1999.

Mooser, Josef. *Arbeiterleben in Deutschland, 1900–1970: Klassenlagen, Kultur und Politik*. Frankfurt am Main: Suhrkamp, 1984.

Mosse, George L. *Fallen Soldiers: Reshaping the Memory of the World Wars*. New York: Oxford University Press, 1990.

Mühle, Eduard. "'Ostforschung': Beobachtungen zu Aufstieg und Niedergang eines geschichtswissenschaftlichen Paradigmas." *Zeitschrift für Ost-Mitteleuropaforschung* 46 (1997): 336–46.

Mühlfenzl, Rudolf. "Warum erst jetzt?" In *Geflohen und Vertrieben: Augenzeugen berichten*, edited by Rudolf Mühlfenzl, 3–13. Königstein/Taunus: Athenäum, 1981.

————, ed. *Geflohen und Vertrieben: Augenzeugen berichten.* Königstein/ Taunus: Athenäum, 1981.

Müller, Georg, and Heinz Simon. "Aufnahme und Unterbringung." In *Die Vertriebenen in Westdeutschland: Ihre Eingliederung und ihr Einfluss auf Gesellschaft, Wirtschaft, Politik und Geistesleben,* edited by Eugen Lemberg and Friedrich Edding, 1:300–446. Kiel: Ferdinand Hirt, 1959.

Müller, Ingo. *Hitler's Justice: The Courts of the Third Reich.* Translated by Deborah Lucas Schneider. Cambridge, Mass.: Harvard University Press, 1991.

Müller, Rolf-Dieter. *Hitlers Ostkrieg und die deutsche Siedlungspolitik: Die Zusammenarbeit von Wehrmacht, Wirtschaft und SS.* Frankfurt am Main: Fischer, 1991.

Murray, John. *Atlas of Central Europe.* London: John Murray, 1963.

Musial, Bogdan. "Bilder einer Ausstellung: Kritische Anmerkungen zur Wanderausstellung 'Vernichtungskrieg: Verbrechen der Wehrmacht 1941 bis 1944.'" *Vierteljahrshefte für Zeitgeschichte* 47 (1999): 563–91.

Naimark, Norman M. *The Russians in Germany: A History of the Soviet Zone of Occupation, 1945–1949.* Cambridge, Mass.: Harvard University Press, 1995.

Naumann, Klaus. "'Flucht und Vertreibung': Aktuelle und historische Aspekte eines bundesdeutschen Syndroms." *Blätter für deutsche und internationale Politik,* no. 8 (1981): 981–95.

————. "Im Sog des Endes: Umrisse einer Printmedienanalyse zur deutschen Erinnerungspolitik im Gedenkjahr 1995." *Relation* 3 (1996): 175–96.

————. *Der Krieg als Text: Das Jahr 1945 im kulturellen Gedächtnis der Presse.* Hamburg: Hamburger Edition, 1998.

————. "Die Mutter, das Pferd und die Juden: Flucht und Vertreibung als Themen deutscher Erinnerungspolitik." *Mittelweg 36* 5, no. 4 (1996): 70–83.

————. "Die Rhetorik des Schweigens: Die Lagerbefreiungen im Gedächtnisraum der Presse 1995." *Mittelweg 36* 5, no. 3 (1996): 23–30.

Neumann, Franz. *Der Block der Heimatvertriebenen und Entrechteten 1950–1960: Ein Beitrag zur Geschichte und Struktur einer politischen Interessenpartei.* Meisenheim am Glan: Anton Hain, 1968.

Niederland, William G. "Die verkannten Opfer: Späte Entschädigung für seelische Schäden." In *Wiedergutmachung in der Bundesrepublik Deutschland,* edited by Ludolf Herbst and Constantin Goschler, 351–60. Munich: R. Oldenbourg, 1989.

Niedhardt, Gottfried, and Normen Altmann. "Zwischen Beurteilung und Verurteilung: Die Sowjetunion im Urteil Konrad Adenauers." In *Adenauer und die deutsche Frage,* edited by Josef Foschepoth, 99–117. Göttingen: Vandenhoeck & Ruprecht, 1988.

Niethammer, Lutz. "Heimat und Front: Versuch zehn Kriegserinnerungen aus der Arbeiterklasse des Ruhrgebietes zu verstehen." In *"Die Jahre weiss man nicht, wo man die heute hinsetzen soll": Faschismus-Erfahrungen im Ruhrgebiet,* edited by Lutz Niethammer, 162–232. Bonn: J. H. W. Dietz Nachf., 1983.

————. "Privat-Wirtschaft: Erinnerungsfragmente einer anderen Umerziehung." In *"Hinterher merkt man, dass es richtig war, dass es schiefgegangen ist":*

Nachkriegserfahrungen im Ruhrgebiet, edited by Lutz Niethammer, 17–105. Berlin: J. H. W. Dietz Nachf., 1983.

Noelle-Neumann, Elisabeth. "Die Verklärung: Adenauer und die öffentliche Meinung, 1946 bis 1976." In *Konrad Adenauer und seine Zeit: Politik und Persönlichkeit des ersten Bundeskanzlers,* vol. 2: *Beiträge der Wissenschaft,* edited by Dieter Blumenwitz et al., 523–54. Stuttgart: Deutsche Verlags-Anstalt, 1976.

Nolan, Mary. "The *Historikerstreit* and Social History." In *Reworking the Past: Hitler, the Holocaust, and the Historians' Debate,* edited by Peter Baldwin, 224–48. Boston: Beacon Press, 1990.

Normann, Käthe von. *Tagebuch aus Pommern 1945/46.* Munich: Deutscher Taschenbuch Verlag, 1962.

Oberkrome, Willi. "Historiker im 'Dritten Reich': Zum Stellenwert volkshistorischer Ansätze zwischen klassischer Politik- und neuerer Sozialgeschichte." *Geschichte in Wissenschaft und Unterricht* 50 (1999): 74–98.

———. *Volksgeschichte: Methodische Innovation und völkische Ideologisierung in der deutschen Geschichtswissenschaft, 1918–1945.* Göttingen: Vandenhoeck & Ruprecht, 1993.

Oppen, Beate Ruhm von, ed. *Documents on Germany under Occupation, 1945–1954.* London: Oxford University Press, 1955.

Overmans, Rüdiger. "'Amtlich und wissenschaftlich erarbeiten': Zur Diskussion über die Verluste während Flucht und Vertreibung der Deutschen aus der ČSR." In *Erzwungene Trennung: Vertreibungen und Aussiedlungen in und aus der Tschechoslowakei, 1938–1947, im Vergleich mit Polen, Ungarn und Jugoslawien,* edited by Detlef Brandes, Edita Ivaničková, and Jiří Pešek, 149–77. Essen: Klartext, 1999.

———. *Deutsche militärische Verluste im Zweiten Weltkrieg.* Munich: R. Oldenbourg, 1999.

———. "55 Millionen Opfer des Zweiten Weltkrieges? Zum Stand der Forschung nach mehr als 40 Jahren." *Militärgeschichtliche Mitteilungen* 48 (1990): 103–21.

———. "German Historiography, the War Losses, and the Prisoners of War." In *Eisenhower and the German POWS: Facts against Falsehood,* edited by Günter Bischof and Stephen E. Ambrose, 127–69. Baton Rouge: Louisiana State University Press, 1992.

———. "Personelle Verluste der deutschen Bevölkerung durch Flucht und Vertreibung." *Dzieje najnowsze* 26 (1994): 51–65.

Peitsch, Helmut. *"Deutschlands Gedächtnis an seine dunkelste Zeit": Zur Funktion der Autobiographik in den Westzonen Deutschlands und den Westsektoren von Berlin, 1945 bis 1949.* Berlin: Edition Sigma, 1990.

———. "Towards a History of *Vergangenheitsbewältigung:* East and West German War Novels of the 1950s." *Monatshefte* 87 (1995): 287–308.

Peukert, Detlev J. K. "Alltag und Barbarei: Zur Normalität des Dritten Reiches." In *Ist der Nationalsozialismus Geschichte? Zu Historisierung und Historikerstreit,* edited by Dan Diner, 51–61. Frankfurt am Main: Fischer Taschenbuch Verlag, 1987.

Pfeil, Elisabeth. *Der Flüchtling: Gestalt einer Zeitenwende.* Hamburg: Hans von Hugo, 1948.

Pfister, Bernhard. "Geleitwort des Herausgebers." In *Die volkswirtschaftliche Eingliederung eines Bevölkerungszustromes: Wirtschaftstheoretische Einführung in das Vertriebenen- und Flüchtlingsproblem,* edited by Helmut Arndt, 7–9. Berlin: Duncker & Humblot, 1954.

Piehler, G. Kurt. *Remembering War the American Way.* Washington, D.C.: Smithsonian Institution Press, 1995.

Plaschka, Richard G., Horst Haselsteiner, Arnold Suppan, and Anna M. Drabek, eds. *Nationale Frage und Vertreibung in der Tschechoslowakei und Ungarn, 1938–1948.* Vienna: Verlag der Österreichischen Akademie der Wissenschaften, 1997.

Plato, Alexander von. "Fremde Heimat: Zur Integration von Flüchtlingen und Einheimischen in die Neue Zeit." In *"Wir kriegen jetzt andere Zeiten": Auf der Suche nach der Erfahrung des Volkes in nachfaschistischen Ländern,* edited by Lutz Niethammer and Alexander von Plato, 172–219. Bonn: J. H. W. Dietz Nachf., 1985.

Plato, Alexander von, and Wolfgang Meinicke. *Alte Heimat—neue Zeit: Flüchtlinge, Umgesiedelte, Vertriebene in der Sowjetischen Besatzungszone und in der DDR.* Berlin: Verlags-Anstalt Union, 1991.

Pleyer, Peter. *Deutscher Nachkriegsfilm, 1946–1948.* Münster: C. J. Fahle, 1965.

Poiger, Uta G. *Jazz, Rock, and Rebels: Cold War Politics and American Culture in a Divided Germany.* Berkeley: University of California Press, 2000.

———. "A New, 'Western' Hero? Reconstructing German Masculinity in the 1950s." *Signs* 24 (1998): 147–62.

———. "Rebels with a Cause? American Popular Culture, the 1956 Youth Riots, and New Conceptions of Masculinity in East and West Germany." In *The American Impact on Postwar Germany,* edited by Reiner Pommerin, 93–124. Providence, R.I.: Berghahn Books, 1995.

———. "Rock 'n' Roll, Female Sexuality, and the Cold War Battle over German Identities." In *West Germany Under Construction: Politics, Society, and Culture in the Adenauer Era,* edited by Robert G. Moeller, 373–410. Ann Arbor: University of Michigan Press, 1997.

Pollock, Friedrich. *Gruppenexperiment: Ein Studienbericht.* Frankfurt am Main: Europäische Verlagsanstalt, 1955.

Prantl, Heribert, ed. *Wehrmachtsverbrechen: Eine deutsche Kontroverse.* Hamburg: Hoffmann & Campe, 1997.

Pridham, Geoffrey. *Christian Democracy in Western Germany: The CDU/CSU in Government and Opposition, 1945–1976.* London: Croom Helm, 1977.

Pross, Christian. *Wiedergutmachung: Der Kleinkrieg gegen die Opfer.* Frankfurt am Main: Athenäum, 1988.

Prümm, Karl. "Entwürfe einer zweiten Republik: Zukunftsprogramme in den 'Frankfurter Heften,' 1946–1949." In *Deutschland nach Hitler: Zukunftspläne im Exil und aus der Besatzungszeit, 1939–1949,* edited by Thomas Koebner, Gert Sautermeister, and Sigrid Schneider, 330–43. Opladen: Westdeutscher Verlag, 1987.

Rabinbach, Anson. *In the Shadow of Catastrophe: German Intellectuals between Apocalypse and Enlightenment.* Berkeley: University of California Press, 1997.

———. "The Jewish Question in the German Question." In *Reworking the Past: Hitler, the Holocaust, and the Historians' Debate,* edited by Peter Baldwin, 45–73. Boston: Beacon Press, 1990.

Ramsden, John. "Refocusing 'The People's War': British War Films in the 1950s." *Journal of Contemporary History* 33 (1998): 35–63.

Rautenberg, Hans-Jürgen. "Zur Standortbestimmung für künftige deutsche Streitkräfte." In *Von der Kapitulation bis zum Pleven-Plan,* by Roland G. Foerster et al., vol. 1 of *Anfänge westdeutscher Sicherheitspolitik, 1945–1956,* edited by Militärgeschichtliches Forschungsamt, 737–879. Munich: R. Oldenbourg, 1982.

Reichel, Peter. *Politik mit der Erinnerung: Gedächtnisorte im Streit um die nationalsozialistische Vergangenheit.* Munich: Carl Hanser, 1995.

Reichling, Gerhard. *Die deutschen Vertriebenen in Zahlen.* Part 1: *Umsiedler, Verschleppte, Vertriebene, Aussiedler, 1945–1985.* Bonn: Kulturstiftung der deutschen Vertriebenen, 1986.

———. *Die deutschen Vertriebenen in Zahlen.* Part 2: *40 Jahre Eingliederung in der Bundesrepublik Deutschland.* Bonn: Kulturstiftung der deutschen Vertriebenen, 1989.

———. "Flucht und Vertreibung der Deutschen: Statistische Grundlage und terminologische Probleme." In *Flüchtlinge und Vertriebene in der westdeutschen Nachkriegsgeschichte: Bilanzierung der Forschung und Perspektiven für die künftige Forschungsarbeit,* edited by Rainer Schulze, Doris von der Brelie-Lewien, and Helga Grebing, 46–56. Hildesheim: August Lax, 1987.

Reill, Peter. "Comment: Werner Conze." In *Paths of Continuity: Central European Historiography from the 1930s to the 1950s,* edited by Hartmut Lehmann and James van Horn Melton, 345–51. Cambridge: Cambridge University Press, 1994.

Reinecker, Herbert. *Pimpfenwelt.* New ed. Berlin: W. Limpert, 1940.

Rentschler, Eric. *The Ministry of Illusion: Nazi Cinema and Its Afterlife.* Cambridge, Mass.: Harvard University Press, 1996.

Rhein, Eduard. *Der Jahrhundert Mann: Hans-Ulrich Horster erzählt die Geschichte seines Lebens und seiner Zeit.* Vienna: Paul Neff, 1990.

Rhode, Gotthold. "Phasen und Formen der Massenzwangswanderung." In *Die Vertriebenen in Westdeutschland: Ihre Eingliederung und ihr Einfluss auf Gesellschaft, Wirtschaft, Politik und Geistesleben,* edited by Eugen Lemberg and Friedrich Edding, 1:17–36. Kiel: Ferdinand Hirt, 1959.

———. "The Protectorate of Bohemia and Moravia, 1939–1945." In *A History of the Czechoslovak Republic, 1918–1948,* edited by Victor S. Mamatey and Radomír Luža, 296–321. Princeton: Princeton University Press, 1973.

Riess, Curt. *Das gibt's nur einmal: Das Buch des deutschen Films nach 1945.* Hamburg: Henri Nannen, 1958.

Robin, Ron. *The Barbed-Wire College: Reeducating German POWs in the United States during World War II.* Princeton: Princeton University Press, 1995.

Rohde, Horst. "Hitler's First Blitzkrieg and Its Consequences for North-eastern Europe." In *Germany and the Second World War,* vol 2: *Germany's Initial Conquests of Europe,* edited by the Militärgeschichtliches Forschungsamt, 67–150. Oxford: Clarendon Press, 1991.

Rosenberg, Emily S. "'Foreign Affairs' after World War II: Connecting Sexual and International Politics." *Diplomatic History* 18 (1994): 59–70.
———. "Walking the Borders." *Diplomatic History* 14 (1990): 565–73.
Rosenfeld, Alvin H. "Popularization and Memory: The Case of Anne Frank." In *Lessons and Legacies: The Meaning of the Holocaust in a Changing World*, edited by Peter Hayes, 243–78. Evanston, Ill.: Northwestern University Press, 1991.
Rosenthal, Gabriele. "Vom Krieg erzählen, von den Verbrechen schweigen." In *Vernichtungskrieg: Verbrechen der Wehrmacht, 1941 bis 1944*, edited by Hannes Heer and Klaus Naumann, 651–63. Hamburg: Hamburger Edition, 1995.
Rost, Karl Ludwig. "'Ich klage an'—ein historischer Film?" In *Medizin im Spielfilm des Nationalsozialismus*, edited by Udo Benzenhöfer and Wolfgang U. Eckart, 34–51. Tecklenburg: Burg, 1990.
Rothfels, Hans. "Zehn Jahre danach." *Vierteljahrshefte für Zeitgeschichte* 3 (1955): 227–39.
———. "Zeitgeschichte als Aufgabe." *Vierteljahrshefte für Zeitgeschichte* 1 (1953): 1–9.
Rousso, Henry. *The Vichy Syndrome: History and Memory in France since 1944.* Translated by Arthur Goldhammer. Cambridge, Mass.: Harvard University Press, 1991.
Rückerl, Adalbert. *NS-Verbrechen vor Gericht: Versuch einer Vergangenheitsbewältigung.* Heidelberg: C. F. Müller, 1982.
Rudolph, Hartmut. *Evangelische Kirche und Vertriebene, 1945 bis 1972.* Vol. 1. Göttingen: Vandenhoeck & Ruprecht, 1984.
Rüsen, Jörn. "Continuity, Innovation, and Self-Reflection in Late Historicism: Theodor Schieder (1908–1984)." In *Paths of Continuity: Central European Historiography from the 1930s to the 1950s*, edited by Hartmut Lehmann and James van Horn Melton, 353–88. Cambridge: Cambridge University Press, 1994.
Ryback, Timothy W. "Dateline Sudetenland: Hostages to History." *Foreign Policy*, no. 105 (1996): 162–78.
———. "The First Draft: Writing History for the General Public." In *A User's Guide to German Cultural Studies*, edited by Scott Denham, Irene Kacandes, and Jonathan Petropoulos, 367–76. Ann Arbor: University of Michigan Press, 1997.
Sagi, Nana. *German Reparations: A History of the Negotiations.* New York: St. Martin's Press, 1986.
Salzmann, Rainer. "Adenauers Moskaureise in sowjetischer Sicht." In *Konrad Adenauer und seine Zeit: Politik und Persönlichkeit des ersten Bundeskanzlers*, vol. 2: *Beiträge der Wissenschaft*, edited by Dieter Blumenwitz et al., 131–59. Stuttgart: Deutsche Verlags-Anstalt, 1976.
Sander, Helke, and Barbara Johr, eds. *BeFreier und Befreite: Krieg, Vergewaltigungen, Kinder.* Munich: Antje Kunstmann, 1992.
Sanders-Brahms, Helma. *Deutschland, bleiche Mutter: Film Erzählung.* Reinbek bei Hamburg: Rowohlt, 1980.
Santner, Eric L. *Stranded Objects: Mourning, Memory, and Film in Postwar Germany.* Ithaca, N.Y.: Cornell University Press, 1990.

Schelsky, Helmut. *Die skeptische Generation: Eine Soziologie der deutschen Jugend.* Frankfurt am Main: Ullstein, [1957] 1984.

———. *Wandlungen der deutschen Familie in der Gegenwart: Dartstellung und Deutung einer empirisch-soziologischen Tatbestandsaufnahme.* 4th ed. Stuttgart: Ferdinand Enke, 1960.

Schenck, E. G., and W. von Nathusius, eds. *Extreme Lebensverhältnisse und ihre Folgen: Handbuch der ärztlichen Erfahrungen aus der Gefangenschaft.* 8 vols. Schriftenreihe des ärztlich-wissenschaftlichen Beirates des Verbandes der Heimkehrer Deutschlands e.V. N.p., 1958–59.

Scheurig, Bodo. *Free Germany: The National Committee and the League of German Officers.* Translated by Herbert Arnold. Middletown, Conn.: Wesleyan University Press, 1969.

Schick, Christa. "Die Internierungslager." In *Von Stalingrad zur Währungsreform: Zur Sozialgeschichte des Umbruchs in Deutschland,* edited by Martin Broszat, Klaus-Dietmar Henke, and Hans Woller, 301–25. Munich: R. Oldenbourg, 1988.

Schieder, Theodor. "Die Vertreibung der Deutschen aus dem Osten als wissenschaftliches Problem." *Vierteljahrshefte für Zeitgeschichte* 8 (1960): 1–16.

Schieder, Wolfgang. "Sozialgeschichte zwischen Soziologie und Geschichte: Das wissenschaftliche Lebenswerk Werner Conzes." *Geschichte und Gesellschaft* 13 (1987): 244–66.

Schildt, Axel. "From Reconstruction to 'Leisure Society': Free Time, Recreational Behaviour, and the Discourse on Leisure Time in the West German Recovery Society of the 1950s." *Contemporary European History* 5 (1996): 191–222.

———. *Moderne Zeiten: Freizeit, Massenmedien und "Zeitgeist" in der Bundesrepublik der 50er Jahre.* Hamburg: Hans Christians, 1995.

Schildt, Axel, and Arnold Sywottek, "'Reconstruction' and 'Modernization': West German Social History during the 1950s." In *West Germany Under Construction: Politics, Society, and Culture in the Adenauer Era,* edited by Robert G. Moeller, 413–43. Ann Arbor: University of Michigan Press, 1997.

Schillinger, Reinhold. *Der Entscheidungsprozess beim Lastenausgleich, 1945–1952.* St. Katharinen: Scripta Mercaturae, 1985.

Schmacke, Norbert, and Hans-Georg Güse. *Zwangssterilisiert, verleugnet, vergessen: Zur Geschichte der nationalsozialistischen Rassenhygiene am Beispiel Bremen.* Bremen: Brockkamp, 1984.

Schmidt, Ute. "Hitler ist tot und Ulbricht lebt: Die CDU, der Nationalsozialismus und der Holocaust." In *Schwieriges Erbe: Der Umgang mit Nationalsozialismus und Antisemitismus in Österreich, der DDR und der Bundesrepublik Deutschland,* edited by Werner Bergmann, Rainer Erb, and Albert Lichtblau, 65–101. Frankfurt: Campus, 1995.

Schmidt, Wolf-Dietrich. "'Wir sind die Verfolgten geblieben': Zur Geschichte der Vereinigung der Verfolgten des Naziregimes (VVN) in Hamburg, 1945–1951." In *Das andere Hamburg: Freiheitliche Bestrebungen in der Hansestadt seit dem Spätmittelalter,* edited by Jörg Berlin, 329–56. Cologne: Pahl-Rugenstein, 1981.

Schoenberg, Hans W. *Germans from the East: A Study of their Migration, Re-*

settlement, and Subsequent Group History since 1945. The Hague: Martinus Nijhoff, 1970.

Schönwälder, Karen. *Historiker und Politik: Geschichtswissenschaft im Nationalsozialismus.* Frankfurt am Main: Campus, 1992.

Schornstheimer, Michael. "'Harmlose Idealisten und draufgängerische Soldaten': Militär und Krieg in den Illustriertenromanen der fünfziger Jahre." In *Vernichtungskrieg: Verbrechen der Wehrmacht, 1941–1944,* edited by Hannes Heer and Klaus Naumann, 634–50. Hamburg: Hamburger Edition, 1995.

———. *Die leuchtenden Augen der Frontsoldaten: Nationalsozialismus und Krieg in den Illustriertenromanen der fünfziger Jahre.* Berlin: Metropol, 1995.

Schröder, Hans Joachim. *Die gestohlenen Jahre: Erzählgeschichten und Geschichtserzählung im Interview—der Zweite Weltkrieg aus der Sicht ehemaliger Mannschaftssoldaten.* Tübingen: Max Niemeyer, 1992.

———. "Die Vergegenwärtigung des Zweiten Weltkriegs in biographischen Interviewerzählungen." *Militärgeschichtliche Mitteilungen* 49 (1991): 9–37.

Schröder, Hans-Jürgen. "Kanzler der Alliierten? Die Bedeutung der USA für die Aussenpolitik Adenauers." In *Adenauer und die deutsche Frage,* edited by Josef Foschepoth, 118–45. Göttingen: Vandenhoeck & Ruprecht, 1988.

Schroeder, Gregory Frederick. "The Long Road Home: German Evacuees of the Second World War, Postwar Victim Identities, and Social Policy in the Federal Republic." Ph.D. diss., Indiana University, 1997.

Schulte, Theo J. *The German Army and Nazi Policies in Occupied Russia.* Oxford: Berg, 1989.

Schulte-Sasse, Linda. *Entertaining the Third Reich: Illusions of Wholeness in Nazi Cinema.* Durham: Duke University Press, 1996.

Schulze, Rainer. "Growing Discontent: Relations between Native and Refugee Populations in a Rural District in Western Germany after the Second World War." In *West Germany Under Construction: Politics, Society, and Culture in the Adenauer Era,* edited by Robert G. Moeller, 53–72. Ann Arbor: University of Michigan Press, 1997.

Schulze, Winfried. "German Historiography from the 1930s to the 1950s." In *Paths of Continuity: Central European Historiography from the 1930s to the 1950s,* edited by Hartmut Lehmann and James van Horn Melton, 19–42. Cambridge: Cambridge University Press, 1994.

Schulze, Winfried, and Otto Gerhard Oexle, eds., with the assistance of Gerd Helm and Thomas Ott. *Deutsche Historiker im Nationalsozialismus.* Frankfurt am Main: Fischer Taschenbuch Verlag, 1999.

Schulze, Winfried, Gerd Helm, and Thomas Ott. "Deutsche Historiker im Nationalsozialismus: Beobachtungen und Überlegungen zu einer Debatte." In *Deutsche Historiker im Nationalsozialismus,* edited by Winfried Schulze and Otto Gerhard Oexle, with the assistance of Gerd Helm and Thomas Ott, 11–48. Frankfurt am Main: Fischer Taschenbuch Verlag, 1999.

Schulze-Vorberg, Max. "Die Moskaureise, 1955." In *Konrad Adenauer und seine Zeit: Politik und Persönlichkeit des ersten Bundeskanzlers,* vol. 1: *Beiträge von Weg- und Zeitgenossen,* edited by Dieter Blumenwitz et al., 651–64. Stuttgart: Deutsche Verlags-Anstalt, 1976.

Schwartz, Thomas Alan. *America's Germany: John J. McCloy and the Federal Republic of Germany.* Cambridge, Mass.: Harvard University Press, 1991.

———. "John J. McCloy and the Landsberg Cases." In *American Policy and the Reconstruction of West Germany, 1945–1955,* edited by Jeffry M. Diefendorf, Axel Frohn, and Hermann-Josef Rupieper, 433–54. New York: Cambridge University Press, 1993.

Schwarz, Hans-Peter. *Die Ära Adenauer: Gründerjahre der Republik, 1949–1957.* Stuttgart: Deutsche Verlags-Anstalt, 1981.

———. *Konrad Adenauer: A German Politician and Statesman in a Period of War, Revolution, and Reconstruction.* Vol. 2: *The Statesman: 1952–1967.* Providence, R.I.: Berghahn Books, 1997.

Schwarz, Michael. "Vertreibung und Vergangenheitspolitik: Ein Versuch über geteilte deutsche Nachkriegsidentitäten." *Deutschlandarchiv* 30 (1997): 177–95.

Schwarz, Walter. "Die Wiedergutmachung nationalsozialistischen Unrechts durch die Bundesrepublik Deutschland: Ein Überblick." In *Wiedergutmachung in der Bundesrepublik Deutschland,* edited by Ludolf Herbst and Constantin Goschler, 33–54. Munich: R. Oldenbourg, 1989.

Schwarz, Wolfgang. *Die Flucht und Vertreibung: Oberschlesien 1945/46.* Bad Nauheim: Podzun, 1965.

Seesslen, Georg. "Durch die Heimat und so weiter: Heimatfilme, Schlagerfilme und Ferienfilme der fünfziger Jahre." In *Zwischen Gestern und Morgen: Westdeutscher Nachkriegsfilm, 1946–1962,* edited by Hilmar Hoffmann and Walter Schobert, 136–63. Frankfurt am Main: Deutsches Filmmuseum, 1989.

Segev, Tom. *The Seventh Million: The Israelis and the Holocaust.* Translated by Haim Watzman. New York: Hill & Wang, 1994.

Seidl, Claus. *Der deutsche Film der fünfziger Jahre.* Munich: Wilhelm Heyne, 1987.

Die Sexualität des Heimkehrers: Vorträge gehalten auf dem (4.) Kongress der Deutschen Gesellschaft für Sexualforschung in Erlangen, 1956. Stuttgart: Ferdinand Enke, 1957.

Shafir, Schlomo. "Die SPD und die Wiedergutmachung gegenüber Israel." In *Wiedergutmachung in der Bundesrepublik,* edited by Ludolf Herbst and Constantin Goschler, 191–204. Munich: R. Oldenbourg Verlag, 1989.

Shavit, Zohar. "Aus Kindermund: Historisches Bewusstsein und nationaler Diskurs in Deutschland nach 1945." *Neue Sammlung* 36 (1996): 355–74.

Sherman, Daniel J. "Bodies and Names: The Emergence of Commemoration in Interwar France." *American Historical Review* 103 (1998): 443–66.

———. "Monuments, Mourning, and Masculinity in France after World War I." *Gender and History* 8 (1996): 82–107.

Siebel-Achenbach, Sebastian. *Lower Silesia from Nazi Germany to Communist Poland, 1942–49.* New York: St. Martin's Press, 1994.

Sigl, Klaus, Werner Schneider, and Ingo Tornow. *Jede Menge Kohle? Kunst und Kommerz auf dem deutschen Filmmarkt der Nachkriegszeit, Filmpreise und Kassenerfolge, 1949–1985.* Munich: Filmland Presse, 1986.

Smith, Arthur L. *Heimkehr aus dem Zweiten Weltkrieg: Die Entlassung der deutschen Kriegsgefangenen.* Stuttgart: Deutsche Verlags-Anstalt, 1985.

Sommer, Theo, ed. *Gehorsam bis zum Mord? Der verschwiegene Krieg der deutschen Wehrmacht—Fakten, Analysen, Debatte.* Gütersloh: Mohndruck, n.d.

Spitta, Arnold. "Entschädigung für Zigeuner? Geschichte eines Vorurteils." In *Wiedergutmachung in der Bundesrepublik Deutschland,* edited by Ludolf Herbst and Constantin Goschler, 385–401. Munich: R. Oldenbourg, 1989.

Stehle, Hansjakob. "Adenauer, Polen und die Deutsche Frage." In *Adenauer und die deutsche Frage,* edited by Josef Foschepoth, 80–98. Göttingen: Vandenhoeck & Ruprecht, 1988.

Steinbach, Peter. "Jenseits von Zeit und Raum: Kriegsgefangenschaft in der Frühgeschichte der Bundesrepublik Deutschland." *Universitas* 7 (1990): 637–49.

———. "Die sozialgeschichtliche Dimension der Kriegsheimkehr." In *Heimkehr 1948,* edited by Annette Kaminsky, 325–40. Munich: C. H. Beck, 1998.

———. "Zur Sozialgeschichte der deutschen Kriegsgefangenschaft in der Sowjetunion im zweiten Weltkrieg und in der Frühgeschichte der Bundesrepublik Deutschland: Ein Beitrag zum Problem der historischen Kontinuität." *Zeitgeschichte* 17 (1989): 1–18.

Steinbach, Peter, and Johannes Tuchel, eds. *Widerstand gegen den Nationalsozialismus.* Berlin: Akademie, 1994.

Steinert, Johannes-Dieter. *Flüchtlinge, Vertriebene und Aussiedler in Niedersachsen: Eine annotierte Bibliographie.* Osnabrück: H. Th. Wenner, 1986.

Steinert, Marlis G. *Hitler's War and the Germans: Public Mood and Attitude during the Second World War.* Edited and translated by Thomas E. J. de Witt. Athens: Ohio State University Press, 1977.

Steininger, Rolf. "Some Reflections on the Maschke Commission." In *Eisenhower and the German POWS: Facts against Falsehood,* edited by Günter Bischof and Stephen E. Ambrose, 170–80. Baton Rouge: Louisiana State University Press, 1992.

Steinweis, Alan E. "German Cultural Imperialism in Czechoslovakia and Poland, 1938–1945." *International History Review* 13 (1991): 466–80.

Stent, Angela. *From Embargo to Ostpolitik: The Political Economy of West German-Soviet Relations, 1955–1980.* Cambridge: Cambridge University Press, 1981.

Stern, Frank. "The Historic Triangle: Occupiers, Germans and Jews in Postwar Germany." In *West Germany Under Construction: Politics, Society, and Culture in the Adenauer Era,* edited by Robert G. Moeller, 199–229. Ann Arbor: University of Michigan Press, 1997.

———. "Philosemitism: The Whitewashing of the Yellow Badge in West Germany, 1945–1952." *Holocaust and Genocide Studies* 4 (1989): 463–77.

———. *The Whitewashing of the Yellow Badge: Antisemitism and Philosemitism in Postwar Germany.* Translated by William Templer. Oxford: Pergamon Press, 1992.

Streibel, Robert, ed. *Flucht und Vertreibung: Zwischen Aufrechnung und Verdrängung.* Vienna: Picus, 1994.

Streim, Alfred. "Saubere Wehrmacht? Die Verfolgung von Kriegs- und NS-Verbrechen in der Bundesrepublik und in der DDR." In *Vernichtungskrieg:*

Verbrechen der Wehrmacht, 1941–1944, edited by Hannes Heer and Klaus Naumann, 569–97. Hamburg: Hamburger Edition, 1995.

Streit, Christian. "The German Army and the Policies of Genocide." In *The Policies of Genocide: Jews and Soviet Prisoners of War in Nazi Germany,* edited by Gerhard Hirschfeld, 1–14. London: Allen & Unwin, 1986.

———. *Keine Kameraden: Die Wehrmacht und die sowjetischen Kriegsgefangenen, 1941–1945.* Stuttgart: Deutsche Verlags-Anstalt, 1978.

———. "Ostkrieg, Antibolschewismus und 'Endlösung.'" *Geschichte und Gesellschaft* 17 (1991): 242–55.

Struve, Walter. "The Wartime Economy: Foreign Workers, 'Half Jews,' and Other Prisoners in a German Town, 1939–1945." *German Studies Review* 16 (1993): 463–82.

Stürmer, Michael. "Kein Eigentum der Deutschen: Die deutsche Frage." In *Die Identität der Deutschen,* edited by Werner Weidenfeld, 83–101. Munich: Carl Hanser, 1983.

———. "Weder verdrängen noch bewältigen: Geschichte und Gegenwartsbewusstsein der Deutschen." *Schweizer Monatshefte* 66 (September 1986): 689–94.

Surminski, Arno. *Jokehnen: oder, Wie lange fährt man von Ostpreussen nach Deutschland?* Stuttgart: Werner Gebühr, 1974.

Szöllösi-Janze, Margit. "'Aussuchen und abschiessen': Der Heimatfilm der fünfziger Jahre als historische Quelle." *Geschichte in Wissenschaft und Unterricht* 44 (1993): 308–21.

Teschner, Manfred. "Entwicklung eines Interessenverbandes: Ein empirischer Beitrag zum Problem der Verselbständigung von Massenorganisationen." Ph.D. diss., Johann Wolfgang Goethe–Universität, 1961.

Thadden, Rudolf von. "Die Gebiete östlich der Oder-Neisse in den Übergangsjahren 1945–1949: Eine Vorstudie." In *Flüchtlinge und Vertriebene in der westdeutschen Nachkriegsgeschichte: Bilanzierung der Forschung und Perspektiven für die künftige Forschungsarbeit,* edited by Rainer Schulze, Doris von der Brelie-Lewien, and Helga Grebing, 117–25. Hildesheim: August Lax, 1987.

Ther, Philipp. *Deutsche und polnische Vertriebene: Gesellschaft und Vertriebenenpolitik in der SBZ/DDR und in Polen, 1945–1956.* Göttingen: Vandenhoeck & Ruprecht, 1998.

———. "The Integration of Expellees in Germany and Poland after World War II: A Historical Reassessment." *Slavic Review* 55 (1996): 789–805.

Theweleit, Klaus. *Male Fantasies.* 2 vols. Translated by Erica Carter, Stephen Conway, and Chris Turner. Minneapolis: University of Minnesota Press, 1987–89.

Thiel, Reinold E. "Acht Typen des Kriegsfilms." *Filmkritik,* no. 11 (1961): 514–19.

Thorwald, Jürgen. *Das Ende an der Elbe.* 2d printing. Stuttgart: Steingrüben, 1950.

———. *Es begann an der Weichsel.* 3d printing. Stuttgart: Steingrüben, 1950.

Thoss, Bruno. "Der Beitritt der Bundesrepublik zur WEU und NATO im Spannungsfeld von Blockbildung und Entspannung (1954–1956)." In *Die NATO-Option,* by Hans Ehlert, Christian Greiner, Georg Meyer, and Bruno Thoss, vol. 3 of *Anfänge westdeutscher Sicherheitspolitik, 1945–1956,* edited by the Militärgeschichtliches Forschungsamt, 1–234. Munich: R. Oldenbourg, 1993.

Tilkovszky, Loránd. "The Late Interwar Years and World War II." In *A History of Hungary,* edited by Peter F. Sugar, Péter Hanák, and Tibor Frank, 339–55. Bloomington: Indiana University Press, 1990.

Ueberschär, Gerd R., ed. *Der 20. Juli 1944: Bewertung und Rezeption des deutschen Widerstands gegen das NS-Regime.* Cologne: Bund-Verlag, 1994.

———, ed. *Das Nationalkomitee "Freies Deutschland" und der Bund Deutscher Offiziere.* Frankfurt am Main: Fischer Taschenbuch Verlag, 1995.

Uertz, Rudolf. *Christentum und Sozialismus in der frühen CDU: Grundlagen und Wirkungen der christlich-sozialen Ideen in der Union, 1945–1949.* Stuttgart: Deutsche Verlags-Anstalt, 1981.

Ullrich, Volker. "'Wir haben nichts gewusst': Ein deutsches Trauma." *1999: Zeitschrift für Sozialgeschichte des 20. und 21. Jahrhunderts* 6 (1991): 11–46.

Umbreit, Hans. *Deutsche Militärverwaltungen 1938/39: Die militärische Besetzung der Tschechoslowakei und Polens.* Stuttgart: Deutsche Verlags-Anstalt, 1977.

Unfug, Douglas A. "Comment: Hans Rothfels." In *Paths of Continuity: Central European Historiography from the 1930s to the 1950s,* edited by Hartmut Lehmann and James van Horn Melton, 137–54. Cambridge: Cambridge University Press, 1994.

Veit-Brause, Irmline. "Werner Conze (1910–1986): The Measure of History and the Historian's Measures." In *Paths of Continuity: Central European Historiography from the 1930s to the 1950s,* edited by Hartmut Lehmann and James van Horn Melton, 299–343. Cambridge: Cambridge University Press, 1994.

Vogel, Detlef. "German Intervention in the Balkans." In *Germany and the Second World War,* vol. 3: *The Mediterranean, South-east Europe, and North Africa, 1939–1941,* edited by the Militärgeschichtliches Forschungsamt, 449–555. Oxford: Clarendon Press, 1995.

Vogel, Rolf, ed. *Deutschlands Weg nach Israel: Eine Dokumentation mit einem Geleitwort von Konrad Adenauer.* Stuttgart: Seewald, 1967.

Wagenlehner, Günther, ed. *Stalins Willkürjustiz gegen die deutschen Kriegsgefangenen: Dokumentation und Analyse.* Bonn: Verlag der Heimkehrer, 1993.

Waldmann, Peter. "Die Eingliederung der ostdeutschen Vertriebenen in die westdeutsche Gesellschaft." In *Vorgeschichte der Bundesrepublik Deutschland: Zwischen Kapitulation und Grundgesetz,* edited by Josef Becker, Theo Stammen, and Peter Waldmann, 163–92. Munich: Wilhelm Fink, 1979.

Wambach, Manfred. *Verbändestaat und Parteienoligopol: Macht und Ohnmacht der Vertriebenenverbände.* Stuttgart: Ferdinand Enke, 1971.

Wasser, Bruno. *Himmlers Raumplanung im Osten: Der Generalplan Ost in Polen, 1940–1944.* Basel: Birkhäuser, 1993.

Weber, Jürgen, and Peter Steinbach, eds. *Vergangenheitsbewältigung durch Strafverfahren? NS-Prozesse in der Bundesrepublik Deutschland.* Munich: Olzog, 1984.

Wehler, Hans-Ulrich. *Entsorgung der Vergangenheit? Ein polemischer Essay zum "Historkerstreit."* Munich: C. H. Beck, 1988.

————. "Nachruf auf Theodor Schieder, 11. April 1908–8. Oktober 1984." *Geschichte und Gesellschaft* 11 (1985): 143–53.

————. *Nationalitätenpolitik in Jugoslawien: Die deutsche Minderheit, 1918–1978*. Göttingen: Vandenhoeck & Ruprecht, 1980.

————. "Nationalsozialismus und Historiker." In *Deutsche Historiker im Nationalsozialismus*, edited by Winfried Schulze and Otto Gerhard Oexle with the assistance of Gerd Helm and Thomas Ott, 306–39. Frankfurt am Main: Fischer Taschenbuch Verlag, 1999.

————, ed. *Sozialgeschichte Heute: Festschrift für Hans Rosenberg zum 70. Geburtstag*. Göttingen: Vandenhoeck & Ruprecht, 1974.

Weigelt, Klaus, ed. *Flucht und Vertreibung in der Nachkriegsliteratur: Formen ostdeutscher Kulturförderung*. Melle: Ernst Knoth, 1986.

Weinberg, Gerhard L. *A World at Arms: A Global History of World War II*. Cambridge: Cambridge University Press, 1994.

Weitz, Eric D. *Creating German Communism, 1890–1990: From Popular Protests to Socialist State*. Princeton: Princeton University Press, 1997.

Welch, David. *Propaganda and the German Cinema, 1933–1945*. Oxford: Clarendon Press, 1983.

Wengst, Udo. "Geschichtswissenschaft und 'Vergangenheitsbewältigung' in Deutschland nach 1945 und nach 1989/90." *Geschichte in Wissenschaft und Unterricht* 46 (1995): 189–205.

Werle, Gerhard, and Thomas Wandres. *Auschwitz vor Gericht: Völkermord und bundesdeutsche Strafjustiz*. Munich: C. H. Beck, 1995.

Westermann, Bärbel. *Nationale Identität im Spielfilm der fünfziger Jahre*. Frankfurt am Main: Peter Lang, 1990.

Wette, Wolfram. "Das Russlandbild in der NS-Propaganda: Ein Problemaufriss." In *Das Russlandbild im Dritten Reich*, edited by Hans-Erich Volkmann, 55–78. Cologne: Böhlau, 1994.

Wette, Wolfram, and Gerd R. Ueberschär. *Stalingrad: Mythos und Wirklichkeit einer Schlacht*. Frankfurt am Main: Fischer Taschenbuch Verlag, 1992.

Wettig, Gerhard. *Entmilitarisierung und Wiederbewaffnung in Deutschland, 1943–1955: Internationale Auseinandersetzung um die Rolle der Deutschen in Europa*. Munich: R. Oldenbourg, 1967.

Weymar, Paul. *Konrad Adenauer: Die autorisierte Biographie*. Munich: Kindler, 1955.

Wiegand, Lutz. "Kriegsfolgengesetzgebung in der Bundesrepublik Deutschland." *Archiv für Sozialgeschichte* 35 (1995): 71–90.

Wieland, Lothar. *Das Bundesministerium für Vertriebene, Flüchtlinge und Kriegsgeschädigte*. Frankfurt am Main: Athenäum, 1968.

Wiesen, S. Jonathan. "Overcoming Nazism: Big Business, Public Relations, and the Politics of Memory, 1945–50." *Central European History* 29 (1996): 201–26.

————. "Reconstruction and Recollection: West German Industry and the Challenge of the Nazi Past, 1945–1955." Ph.D. diss., Brown University, 1998.

Wilharm, Irmgard. "Krieg in deutschen Nachkriegsspielfilmen." In *Lernen aus dem Krieg? Deutsche Nachkriegszeiten 1918 und 1945*, edited by Gottfried Niedhart and Dieter Riesenberger, 281–99. Munich: C. H. Beck, 1992.

Wille, Manfred, Johannes Hoffmann, and Wolfgang Meinicke, eds. *Sie hatten alles verloren: Flüchtlinge und Vertriebene in der sowjetischen Besatzungszone Deutschlands*. Wiesbaden: Harrassowitz, 1993.

Wingfield, Nancy. *Minority Politics in a Multinational State: The German Social Democrats in Czechoslovakia, 1918–1938*. Boulder, Colo.: East European Monographs, 1989.

Wiskemann, Elizabeth. *Germany's Eastern Neighbours: Problems Relating to the Oder-Neisse Line and the Czech Frontier Regions*. London: Oxford University Press, 1956.

Witte, Karsten. "Of the Greatness of the Small People: The Rehabilitation of a Genre." *New German Critique*, no. 36 (1985): 7–8.

Wolffsohn, Michael. "Das deutsch-israelische Wiedergutmachungsabkommen von 1952 im internationalen Zusammenhang." *Vierteljahrshefte für Zeitgeschichte* 36 (1988): 691–731.

———. "Globalentschädigung für Israel und die Juden? Adenauer und die Opposition in der Bundesregierung." In *Widergutmachung in der Bundesrepublik Deutschland*, edited by Ludolf Herbst and Constantin Goschler, 161–90. Munich: R. Oldenbourg, 1989.

———. "Von der verordneten zur freiwilligen 'Vergangenheitsbewältigung'? Eine Skizze der bundesdeutschen Entwicklung 1955/1965 (zugleich eine Dokumentation über die Krisensitzung des Bundeskabinetts vom 4. und 5. März 1965 und die Böhm-Schäffer-Kontroverse 1957/1958)." *German Studies Review* 12 (1989): 111–37.

———. "Das Wiedergutmachungsabkommen mit Israel: Eine Untersuchung bundesdeutscher und ausländischer Umfragen." In *Westdeutschland, 1945–1955: Unterwerfung, Kontrolle, Integration*, edited by Ludolf Herbst, 203–18. Munich: R. Oldenbourg, 1986.

Wolfrum, Edgar. "Zwischen Geschichtsschreibung und Geschichtspolitik: Forschungen zu Flucht und Vertreibung nach dem Zweiten Weltkrieg." *Archiv für Sozialgeschichte* 36 (1996): 500–522.

Wollstein, Günter. "Andreas Hillgruber: Historiker der Grossmacht Deutsches Reich." *Militärgeschichtliche Mitteilungen* 46 (1989): 9–19.

Young, James E. *The Texture of Memory: Holocaust Memorials and Meaning*. New Haven: Yale University Press, 1993.

Youngblood, Denise J. "*Ivan's Childhood* (USSR, 1962) and *Come and See* (USSR, 1985): Post-Stalinist Cinema and the Myth of World War II." In *World War II, Film, and History*, edited by John Whiteclay Chambers II and David Culbert, 85–96. New York: Oxford University Press, 1996.

Zank, Wolfgang. *Wirtschaft und Arbeit in Ostdeutschland, 1945–1949: Probleme des Wiederaufbaus in der sowjetischen Besatzungszone Deutschlands*. Munich: R. Oldenbourg, 1987.

Zayas, Alfred M. de. *Nemesis at Potsdam: The Expulsion of the Germans from the East*. 3d ed. Lincoln: University of Nebraska Press, 1989.

———. *A Terrible Revenge: The Ethnic Cleansing of the East European Germans, 1944–1950*. New York: St. Martin's Press, 1994.

Zeidler, Manfred. *Kriegsende im Osten: Die Rote Armee und die Besetzung*

Deutschlands östlich von Oder und Neisse, 1944/45. Munich: R. Oldenbourg, 1996.

Zelizer, Barbie. *Remembering to Forget: Holocaust Memory through the Camera's Eye.* Chicago: University of Chicago Press, 1998.

Zipfel, Friedrich. "Schicksal und Vertreibung der Deutschen aus Ungarn, Rumänien und der Tschechoslowakei." *Jahrbuch für die Geschichte Mittel- und Ostdeutschlands* 7 (1958): 379–93.

———. "Vernichtung und Austreibung der Deutschen aus den Gebieten östlich der Oder-Neisse-Linie." *Jahrbuch für die Geschichte Mittel- und Ostdeutschlands* 3 (1954): 145–79.

Index

Adenauer, Konrad, 16, 47, 49, 55, 117, 142, 175, 183, 247n80; biography of, 93, 120, 242n16; cabinet of, 32, 35, 44; and compensation of victims, 22, 25–27, 31, 33, 76, 85; and economic miracle, 89–90; and parliamentary forum, 21–23, 25–27, 31, 33, 38, 44; paternal image of, 89, 93–95, 105, 120, 154; petitions addressed to, 93–96; and release of German POWs, 89, 90, 91, 94–96, 99, 102–3, 105, 119–20, 172; and reunification of Germany, 90–91, 92, 95; and trip to Moscow, 89–105, 150, 166, 172, fig. 20, fig. 21

Adorno, Theodor, 14–15, 16, 18, 149

Ahonen, Pertti, 18

Allies: bombing by, 5, 181; and border determination, 35–36; and collective guilt, 24–25, 43; and compensation schemes, 28, 43; and demilitarization, 24; and democratization, 24, 43; and denazification, 17, 24–25, 57; and German expellees, 12, 34, 35–36, 38, 43, 224n106, 231n22; and German POWs, 21, 37, 38; and German rearmament, 38; and German war crimes, 24–26, 39, 85, 153; and occupation of Germany, 6, 24, 28, 34, 43, 44, 46, 47, 49, 54, 67, 69–70, 90, 105, 107, 140, 197; and political organizations, 34, 47; and reeducation programs, 6, 24, 80, 85

Alten, Jürgen von, 258n14

Aly, Götz, 229n11

Anderson, Benedict, 5

Ännchen von Tharau, 123–24, 126, 140–43, fig. 30, fig. 31

Anti-Americanism, 184

Anti-Communism, 5, 6, 36, 43, 46, 173, 191; and German expellees, 43, 48, 61, 63, 70–71, 83, 86, 182; and German POWs, 48–49, 112, 113; and postwar German films, 126, 167

Anti-Semitism, 21, 26, 30, 31, 76, 81, 83, 175, 179, 189, 190, 273n77

Antifascism, 11, 18, 114, 161, 197

Applegate, Celia, 128

Armstrong, Louis "Satchmo," 108

Arzt von Stalingrad, Der, 14, 127, 149–55, 156, 179, fig. 36, fig. 37

Asocial victims, 29–30, 183

Atomic bomb, 1, 153

Auschwitz, 1, 11, 75, 80, 99, 101, 112, 167, 172, 176, 181, 182, 185, 190, 191

Austria, 275n98

Authoritarianism, 48

Bamberger, Peter, 163, 169

Bartok, Eva, 127, 151, 155, fig. 36

Basic Law (*Grundgesetz*), 5, 34, 44

Bauer, Josef M., 265n103

Bavaria, 134, 135, 139

Beer, Erica, 136

BeFreier und Befreite, 194, 266n2

Text: 10/13 Sabon
Display: Sabon
Composition: Integrated Composition Systems, Inc.
Printing and binding: Thomson-Shore, Inc.